By Antonio Escohotado

Reality and Substance (1986)

Philosophy and Methodology in the Sciences (1987)

The Spirit of Comedy (1991)

Whores and Wives (1993)

From Physis to Polis (1995)

The Question of Cannabis (1997)

Portrait of a Libertine (1998)

Chaos and Order (2000)

Learning About Drugs (2002)

Sixty Weeks in the Tropics (2003)

Elementary History of Drugs (2003)

Four Myths on Sex and Duty (2003)

The Enemies of Commerce (2008)

THE GENERAL HISTORY OF DRUGS

Volume Four Part Two

Antonio Escohotado

translated and edited by
G. W. Robinette

GRAFFITI MILITANTE PRESS
Valparaiso, Chile
2025

Graffiti Militante Press
Valparaiso, Chile

First English Edition

ISBN: 978-1-735-7878-2-4

Cover:

For Albert Hofmann and Tom Szasz, who with their friendship and advice helped to distill the essence of this chronicle.

Note. – This endeavor to bring it about, that our own likes and dislikes should meet with universal approval, is really ambition ...; wherefore we see that every one by nature desires ... that the rest of mankind should live according to his own individual disposition: when such a desire is equally present in all, every one stands in every one else's way, and in wishing to be loved or praised by all, all become mutually hateful.[1]

-- Benedict de Spinoza (1632 – 1677)

I owe gratitude also to Pablo Fernandez-Florez who was always distrustful of the project even though he ended up writing various portions and contributed valuable documentation for the rest; to Luis Gil, who guided me decisively through Greco-Latin antiquity, moreover remediating some inappropriate remarks in the proofs; to Ramon Sala, for making accessible to me many sources about the contemporary period; and to Monica Bacazar, my wife, who stoically supported the birth of the whole book, collaborating also in the typewritten transcription. With their economic assistance, the Center for Sociological Investigations first, and later the Ministry of Culture, permitted an undivided attention to the work in its initial and final stages.

---

1 Improvement of the Understanding, Ethics and Correspondence, tr. R. H. M. Elwes. London: L. Beling Tetens, 1901 [archive.org, hereinafter AO], Part III. Origin and Nature of the Emotions, Proposition XXXI, p. 152; *Schol. Hic conatus efficiendi ... odio invicen sunt* (Benedicti de Spinoza. Opera, Vol. I. Lipsiae: Typis et Sumtibus Bernh. Tauchnitz Jun., 1843 AO, Pars Tertia De Origine et Natura Affectum, p. 294).

Author's Preface

It has not been very common to unite theory and practice in the matter of drugs, and this explains perhaps some adventures that accompanied the composition of *La historia general de las drogas*. In 1988 the criminal court of Palma condemned me (being then a professor of Sociology) to two years and a day of prison, having found me guilty of drug trafficking. The six year punishment requested by the prosecutor was reduced by two-thirds, because for one judge of the court the offence was found to be *en grado de tentativa imposible* [literally, a crime impossible to commit]. Effectively, those who were offering to sell and those who were offering to buy (by means of three interposed users, one of whom was myself) were agents of the police or their pawns. Just one week after this judgment, the criminal court of Cordoba declared a verdict of pure entrapment upon similar facts, whereupon they proceeded to annul all the charges, an interpretation that in time would become the accepted jurisprudence in Spain.

Apprehensive over what might end up happening on an appeal to the Supreme Court in a litigation where a certain citizen was alleging to have been blackmailed by the authorities, while they in turn were accusing him of being an opulent drug dealer who hid his criminal empire behind the lectern of the scholar, I preferred to serve the sentence without delay. As a then magistrate of the Supreme Court made clear, the matter was poisoned by the fact of my being a spokesperson for reform on the issue, already well-known since 1983. Given the facts of the case, to absolve without conditions would incriminate in some manner the incriminator, and would open a path toward a demand for a scandalous reparation.

After some inquiries, I discovered that, thanks to its understanding Director, the jail at Cuenca would concede me the three things necessary to take advantage of such a stay: a light switch inside the cell, an ancient PC, and isolation. During that fully-paid (albeit humble) vacation, four-fifths of this work was written. Naturally, I had entered into that establishment with no small number of kilos of index cards and notes, gathered during many long years. I had only to structure them, polishing the final exposition.

It could be added that I did not lose much time, and for this same reason neither was I downhearted. However, the conditions for bibliographic consultation are not ideal in a penitentiary and before I could abandon it this book began to be published,[1] so that it was dogged from the beginning by innumerable imprecisions, more than those which trouble any really extensive work. Some of them were remediated in the third edition, thanks above all to the effort of the chemist and ethnobotanist Jonathan Ott who tirelessly inserted the many changes and additions necessary, thoroughly revising the system of references and transforming entire sections of the text.

With this new English edition, the degree of precision demanded in a scientific work has been perfected once more, completed by a researcher who has been able to confirm and amplify my work making use of various libraries and the internet. As a result, the edition that the reader now holds in his hands not only suffers from far fewer errors and oversights, but also hopes to fulfill even closer the goal of an academic standard with regards to the precision of its information. No doubt, in twenty years this history will need to be revised again as new data becomes available. I look forward to reading that book.

La Navata
February 2021

[1] Volumes I and II in the *Alianza* edition.

Translator's Preface

This will also be posthumously published. I miss our long, rambling midnight talks. The translation and research of Antonio's work is a graduate course encompassing history, sociology, psychology, literature, biology and chemistry among many other disciplines. To read him is to watch a great mind wrestle with an expansive subject. Though not many ever really learn from the past, for sure no one will ever learn if there is no past upon which to reflect. So far Escohotado has written the best history of drugs that exists.

This is the second part of the fourth volume, subtitled Volume Four, Part Two. The first part of the fourth volume, subtitled Volume Four, Part One, was published in 2024. I have issued these parts separately for the same reason that at my age I eat dessert first.

I implore you to read it in the original Spanish, just for his style if nothing else. This first English edition of the second half of the fourth volume has been annotated with many primary sources newly accessible online. These help illustrate the original themes with a deeper and more nuanced understanding of drugs and drug policy in the early to middle twentieth century. In a few instances the text has also been updated to reflect changes in fact and perspective over the last forty years.

E. H. Carr called history a dialogue between the present and the past. To paraphrase Dr. Johnson, when new facts emerge, I change my mind. What do you do? It's been a privilege to do my part to bring Escohotado's work to an English language audience. All errors are mine. Enjoy.

G. W. R.
Sydney, Australia
November 2025

P. S. This one is also for solitude.

Contents

Chapter 26. Latency **1827**
A. Creating the Pharmacracy 1830
B. The Drug Abuse Industrial Complex 1835
1. Draconian Laws 1843
a. The Postwar Social Climate 1845
b. The Postwar Legal Climate 1851
2. The Syndicate 1867
a. Chinese and French Connections 1870
b. Political Alliances 1878
3. The Therapeutic Estate 1883
a. The ABA/AMA Report 1883
b. Pharmacratic Ideology 1891
c. The Dope Fiend 1897
C. Radical Anti-Therapeutism 1907

Chapter 27. The Pharmacratic Peace **1923**
A. The Single Convention 1924
1. Use versus Abuse 1927
2. Creating a Monopoly 1931
B. Amphetamines 1940
1. Compared to Cocaine 1946
2. Toxicity 1949
3. In the Military and Sports 1951
4. In Medicine 1959
5. In Spain 1968
C. Barbiturates 1971
D. Semisynthetic and Synthetic Narcotics 1982
E. Tranquilizers and Anxiolytics 2001
1. The Major Tranquilizers 2003
2. The Minor Tranquilizers 2012
F. Nonbarbiturate Hypnotics 2026
G. The Addicted Society 2039

Chapter 28. The Pagan Plot (I) **2051**
A. Exploring the Unconscious 2057
1. The Trials of Walter 2069
2. The Essays of Aldous 2074
3. The Insight of Albert 2078
B. Experimenting with Consciousness 2085
1. Mescaline 2086
2. Psilocybin 2094
3. LSD 2104
4. *Amanita muscaria* 2113
5. Similitudes 2121
C. Arms for the Cold War 2135
1. Truth Drugs 2140
2. Behavior Modification 2144
3. Chemical Warfare 2149
D. Technique versus Chemistry 2153
E. The Pagan Plot Unfolds 2168
1. Pharmacological Caution 2168
2. Political Circumspection 2170
3. The Final Revolution 2173

Chapter 29. The Pagan Plot (II) **2191**
A. Clinica 2197
1. Psychotherapy 2199
2. Alcoholism 2210
3. Palliation 2215
B. Academia 2220
1. The Harvard Psilocybin Experiment 2227
2. The Concord Prison Experiment 2230
3. The Good Friday Experiment 2235
4. The New Sacrament 2240
5. Opposition 2246
6. Paradise Found 2251
7. Paradise Lost 2255
8. Leary's Theory 2262
9. Leary's *Zeitgeist* 2274
10. The Hunt for the Hierophant 2281
C. The Psychedelic Movement 2289
1. Hollywood 2292
2. Kesey 2295
3. Peddlers and Cooks 2319
D. The Acts of Accusation 2327
1. Therapeutic Inutility 2329
2. Miscegenation, Apostasy, Insanity, Addiction, Laziness 2337
3. Promiscuity 2342
4. Murder, Suicide, Madness, Teratogeny 2349
E. The Return of the Pagan 2362

Bibliography **2371**

Index **2419**

Illustrations

Figure 360. Huxley by Cecil Beaton xxiii

Chapter 26. Latency

Figure 361. Amerika 1825
Figure 362. Parke-Davis Pill Packers 1829
Figure 363. Ratcatcher 1831
Figure 364. Anslinger 1833
Figure 365. Huxley, on ESP 1840
Figure 366. Heroin Gear 1842
Figure 367. Rosenbergs 1844
Figure 368. McCarthy and Cohn 1846
Figure 369. Nixon, Pumpkin, Film 1846
Figure 370. Paul Thomas Mann 1850
Figure 371. Price Daniel 1855
Figure 372. Valachi 1860
Figure 373. Cairo Conference 1864
Figure 374. Tang Jiyao 1869
Figure 375. Huang Jinyong 1873
Figure 376. Due Yuesheng 1875
Figure 377. Three Bosses 1876
Figure 378. Johnson/Ngo Dinh Nhu 1882
Figure 379. Brooklyn Pot Bust 1890
Figure 380. William Douglas 1896
Figure 381. Burroughs 1898
Figure 382. Ginsberg, Carr, Burroughs 1900
Figure 383. Trocchi 1902
Figure 384. Durkheim 1906
Figure 385. The Menningers 1910
Figure 386. Szasz 1912
Figure 387. Crumb 1920

Chapter 27. The Pharmacratic Peace

Figure 388. Dr. Feelgood 1921
Figure 389. UN Conference 1961 1926
Figure 390. The INCB 1930
Figure 391. Coffee Council 1934

Figure 392.	International Tin Council	1936
Figure 393.	Cocoa Council	1938
Figure 394.	Nagai Nagayoshi	1939
Figure 395.	Ephedra	1940
Figure 396.	Ko Kui Chen	1941
Figure 397	Benzedrine Inhaler	1943
Figure 398.	Methedrine	1945
Figure 399.	Manco Capac	1947
Figure 400.	Pervitin	1952
Figure 401.	Hitler Awards Doctor	1953
Figure 402.	Tom Simpson	1958
Figure 403.	Beauvoir and Sartre	1963
Figure 404.	JFK	1964
Figure 405.	Obestat	1967
Figure 406.	Centramina	1969
Figure 407.	Elixir Amytal	1971
Figure 408.	Marilyn	1979
Figure 409.	Barbital	1981
Figure 410.	Demerol	1983
Figure 411.	Methajade	1986
Figure 412.	Paracodeine	1997
Figure 413.	Rauwolfia	2002
Figure 414.	Reserpine	2004
Figure 415.	Chlorpromazine	2007
Figure 416.	Meprobamate	2012
Figure 417.	Equilite Plus	2018
Figure 418.	Valium	2021
Figure 419.	Persedon	2027
Figure 420.	Thalidomide	2030
Figure 421.	Dr. Widukind Lenz	2037
Figure 422.	Joel Fort	2038
Figure 423.	Daniel Craig	2047
	Chapter 28. The Pagan Plot (I)	
Figure 424.	Vom Mutterkorn	2049
Figure 425.	Mitchell	2056

Figure 426. Ellis 2058
Figure 427. Heffter 2059
Figure 428. Artaud 2061
Figure 429. Schultes 2063
Figure 430. Alles 2065
Figure 431. Hofmann 2066
Figure 432. Graves 2068
Figure 433. Benjamin 2070
Figure 434. Huxley and Friends 2075
Figure 435. Hofmann and Sons 2077
Figure 436. Delysid 2084
Figure 437. Michaux 2085
Figure 438. Osmond 2088
Figure 439. Hubbard 2091
Figure 440. Wassons 2095
Figure 441. María Sabina 2097
Figure 442. Journey 2102
Figure 443. Ginsberg 2106
Figure 444. *Amanita* 2112
Figure 445. *Misérable* 2119
Figure 446. *Protokoll X* 2120
Figure 447. Huxley 2127
Figure 448. Hofmann/Jünger 2128
Figure 449. Nin 2130
Figure 450. Memo 2139
Figure 451. CIA/LSD 2148
Figure 452. Key 2154
Figure 453. Huxley, 1958 2164
Figure 454. Huxley, California 2174

Chapter 28. The Pagan Plot (II)

Figure 455. Casady and Leary on the bus 2189
Figure 456. Powick 2196
Figure 457. Cohen 2205
Figure 458. Weyburn 2209
Figure 459. Hoffer 2212

Figure 460.	Leary	2219
Figure 461.	Hallucinations	2226
Figure 462.	Concord	2229
Figure 463.	Marsh Chapel	2233
Figure 464.	Pahnke	2234
Figure 465.	Hollingshead	2239
Figure 466.	Kerouac/Ginsberg	2245
Figure 467.	Catalina	2250
Figure 468.	Weil	2254
Figure 469.	Leary, Metzner, Millbrook	2259
Figure 470.	Lorenz	2261
Figure 471.	Marcuse	2267
Figure 472.	March	2272
Figure 473.	Woodstock	2273
Figure 474.	Brothers	2279
Figure 475.	Leary/Cleaver	2280
Figure 476.	Meyer	2288
Figure 477.	Grant/Loren	2291
Figure 478.	Kesey	2294
Figure 479.	Nicholson	2297
Figure 480.	Furthur	2301
Figure 481.	Grateful	2307
Figure 482.	Test	2308
Figure 483.	Griffin	2315
Figure 484.	Stanley/Garcia	2318
Figure 485.	Toribio	2326
Figure 486.	RFK	2331
Figure 487.	Commune	2336
Figure 488.	Shattering	2341
Figure 489.	MacDonald	2348
Figure 490.	Peppers	2361
Figure 491.	Beatles	2366
Figure 492.	Flower	2370

Introduction

The second half of Volume Four covers the early to middle twentieth century. Chapter 26 reviews the formal attempts at the creation of a pharmacracy, the passage of Draconian laws, the post-WWII conformism, the linking of drugs with communism, the outlawing of maintenance doses for narcotic addicts, the subsequent development of a black market to fill the demand, the influence of the Mafia in the drug trade, the Chinese and French connections, the international alliances that serve the trade, the involvement of state security agencies for political and economic reasons, the creation of a therapeutic estate, and the invention of the dope fiend, with special attention to the writings of Burroughs, Trocchi, Ginsberg, Carr, Durkheim, Szasz, and Becker.

Chapter 27 discusses the destruction of the pharmacratic peace with the creation of an international pharmaceutical monopoly called the 1961 Single Convention, comparisons with other failed international monopolistic treaties on coffee, tin, sugar, and cocoa, the development of amphetamines and their chronic use in sports and the militaries of countries at war with one another, their widespread use among the literati and political elites, the marketing of barbiturates and their connection to accidental euthanasia, the sales of codeine, semisynthetic and synthetic narcotics like pethidine, methadone, ketobemidone, dextromoramide, normethadone, ethylmorphine, and paracodeine, the increase in the use of the major tranquilizers and anxiolytics like chlorpromazine, the minor tranquilizers meprobamate, diazepam, and chlordiazepoxide, and the nonbarbiturate hypnotics pyrithyldione, glutethimide, and thalidomide, while simultaneously governments and businesses fund increasing sales of caffeine, alcohol and nicotine.

Chapter 28 explores the unconscious as Mitchell and Ellis eat peyote buttons, Heffter isolates mescaline, Benjamin and friends experiment with hashish, opium and mescaline, Huxley needs a new drug, Artaud dances with the Tarahumaras, Schultes studies ayahuasca, Alles experiments with MDA, Hofmann rides a bike, Graves eats mushrooms, Michaux, Paz and Jünger write of their experiences with mescaline, Osmond brings Huxley his new drug, Hubbard bootlegs whiskey, the Wassons go to Mexico, Hofmann synthesizes psilocybin, the Greeks get high, Janiger turns on Cary Grant, the Wassons study amanita, Nin and Watts try LSD, Burroughs prefers heroin, the CIA wants a truth drug, and Dalí finds a key.

Chapter 29 describes the unfolding of this pagan plot as LSD is used in psychotherapy, alcoholism, and palliation, Leary, Dass and Metzner study psilocybin and LSD at Harvard, Leary finds and loses paradise, Leary flees to Algeria, Switzerland, and Afghanistan, Hollywood loves drugs, Kesey takes a bus ride, the Grateful Dead play at the acid tests, Owsley and many others fabricate and distribute LSD to the masses, the authorities accuse the drug on the one hand of being of no utility whatsoever and on the other hand of being responsible for miscegenation, apostasy, insanity, addiction, laziness, promiscuity, murder, suicide, madness and teratogeny, while a younger generation returns to the land espousing ecology, sexual liberation, pacifism, humanism and the counterculture, the DEA is invented, the Beatles are banned, and the echoes of this era reverberate around the world to this day.

The Insurgents

Figure 360. Portrait of Aldous Huxley (1894 – 1963), by Cecil Beaton (1904 – 1980). Vintage bromide print on white card mount, 1936. National Portrait Gallery, London UK [npg.org, hereinafter NPG].

R. Crumb
AMERIKA
Esso
OPEN 24·7
Cornélius

Figure 361. Amerika. 2004 adaptation of Robert Crumb cartoon by French publisher Cornélius [researchgate.net, hereinafter RGN].

26
Latency

D[uke]. Thou art a silly empty dog, says the d___, and if there is such a place as a hell, though I believe nothing of it, it is a place for fools, such as thou art. Gr[aceless]. I wonder, then, what heaven the great wits go to, such as my lord duke? I don't care to go there, let it be where it will; they are a plaguy tiresome kind of people, there's no bearing them, they'll make a hell wherever they come.[1]

-- Daniel Defoe (1660 – 1731)

A. Creating the Pharmacracy

B. The Drug Abuse Industrial Complex

- **1. Draconian Laws**
  - **a. The Postwar Social Climate**
  - **b. The Postwar Legal Climate**
- **2. The Syndicate**
  - **a. Chinese and French Connections**
  - **b. Political Alliances**
- **3. The Therapeutic Estate**
  - **a. The ABA/AMA Report**
  - **b. Pharmacratic Ideology**
  - **c. The Dope Fiend**

C. Radical Anti-Therapeutism

---

[1] The Political History of the Devil, in one volume. Oxford, UK: Printed for D. A. Talboys, for Thomas Tegg, 1840 (reprint of 1726 edition) [annas-archive.org, hereinafter AA], Part I, Chapter II Of the word 'devil,' as it is a proper name to the Devil, and any or all his host, angels, &c, p. 18.

Except for those countries producing opium and coca (which international legislation will considerably affect) and except for the United States (which had been carrying on the crusade for twenty years), the other nations signing the Geneva drug conventions only supposed that they were taking preventive measures. In other words any actual problem was more conspicuous for its absence than its presence. The anti-drug initiatives were inscribed within a fundamentally humanitarian policy, indiscernible from efforts to found hospitals, teach literacy, raise living standards, and analogous goals. With this philanthropic aspect motivating it, the entire program appeared to be a scientific project, its proponents preoccupied with health concerns, which were beginning to absorb an increasingly larger volume of state activity in economically advanced countries.

Knowing in some detail the genesis of Northamerican prohibitionism (including the universal history preceding it) causes an objective observer to doubt that the specific measures adopted could be defined as anything arising necessarily out of philanthropy or science. But what is not in doubt is that for the man in the street and for those political entities not yet beset with any real drug problem, this prohibitionist policy was based on public health and scientific progress. To oppose it was equivalent to embracing convictions both retrograde and cruel. Only a part of the American therapeutic estate would be in any position to say otherwise.

Figure 362. "Female employees packaging ampules and pills." Parke-Davis Manufacturing Plant, Detroit, MI. Encyclopedia of Detroit [Detroithistorical.org, hereinafter DHO].

A. Creating the Pharmacracy

Objectively, these prohibitionist initiatives were becoming chronic. The original goal of snuffing out a transient epidemic had now led to a self-sustaining mechanism of intervention. Yet, until the beginning of the 1960s (as religious fundamentalism slowly cedes ground to existentialism) there will be no statistically significant signs of disobedience.

According to a lecture by the philosopher, essayist and author Fernando Fernández-Savater Martin (b. 1947), a famine devastated Europe in the times of Louis XIV (1638 – 1715), and the monarch (arguably a man of foresight and organization) created an official corps of vermin hunters to combat it. They struggled the best they could against hares, rabbits, weasels, foxes, birds of prey and other enemies of field and barn. Other nations also confronted the famine with royal offices. In mid-nineteenth century England, for example, one Jack Black was appointed "V. R. rat and mole destroyer to Her Majesty."[2] But the hunger passed, and with it its consequences. Within a few years the situation appeared to have been resolved all over Europe and the peasants breathed a sigh of relief. For France, however, the future was still indistinct and uncertain. The vermin were under control, though the threat remained. Fortunately, the king's corps of vermin hunters also remained to prevent a greater evil.

---

[2] Mayhew, Henry. London Labour and the London Poor; Cyclopaedia of the Condition and Earnings of Those that *Will* Work, Those that *Cannot* Work, and Those that *Will Not* Work, Volume III. London: Griffin, Bohn, and Company, 1861 AO, p. 11.

Figure 363. "Jack Black, Her Majesty's Ratcatcher."
Mayhew, 1861, The Destroyers of Vermin, p. 11.

In contrast with what occurred with alcohol, the poorly defined legislation on so-called narcotics consolidated at least three spheres of pharmacratic[3] power. Each was defined by its own dynamic but converging expansion. These correspond to the political, criminal and therapeutic estates.

Politically, the signers of the Geneva accords had committed themselves to establish local anti-drug brigades. These groups around 1940 had only some hundreds of inspectors in the entire world, while two decades later (though the rebellion had still not exploded) they were comprised of thousands of national and international functionaries determinedly defending their ideology in periodicals and conferences. Though inevitably exposed to grave temptation, they espoused an *esprit de corps* best evidenced by Harry Jacob Anslinger (1892 – 1975) whose aim was to overcome drug addiction militarily, locking up the culprits and seizing their drugs: "As an indication of the Justice Department's level of frustration, the problem of combating drug use has been viewed in military terms."[4]

A second group could be termed worldwide organized crime, with important centers in the United States, the Mediterranean and China. This group had as its natural enemies the so-called protectors. Thanks to them it could construct an empire of illegal trafficking with monopolistic advantages, even collaborating with the political authority when convenient.

---

[3] See Szasz, Thomas. Ceremonial Chemistry: The Ritual Persecution of Drugs, Addicts, and Pushers. Garden City, NY: Anchor Press/Doubleday, 1974 AA, III. Pharmacracy: Medicine as Social Control, p. 124 et seq.

[4] McWilliams, John C. The Protectors: Harry J. Anslinger and the Federal Bureau of Narcotics, 1930-1962. Newark, NJ: University of Delaware Press, 1990 AA, Introduction, p. 18.

Figure 364. "Harry Jacob Anslinger (1892 – 1975)."
McWilliams, 1990, Cover Photograph.

A third group (more dedicated to prevention than repression or illicit commerce) was made up of a mix of therapists, psychologists and psychiatrists, legal scholars and social science researchers to whom was entrusted treatment, surveys, analysis and advice. In 1973, for example, with complete sincerity the chairman of the National Commission on Marihuana and Drug Abuse described the result of the last half-century of prohibitionist measures as the creation of a sprawling, overfunded, underanalyzed and unevaluated drug abuse industrial complex:

> The last four years have seen a dramatic upsurge in the amount of government resources allocated to combatting the drug problem. At all levels of government, new agencies have been created and old agencies have developed new specialties. In fiscal year 1969, the federal government spent $66.4 million for all phases of its drug 'abuse' program, including law enforcement, treatment and rehabilitation, education, training, research, and evaluation. By fiscal year 1973, total funding had reached $791.3 million, an increase of 1092% which is still heading upwards. ... Yet, as federal spending approaches the $1 billion dollar mark, establishing an entirely new 'drug abuse industrial complex,' no one has systematically analyzed either the problem to be solved or evaluated the solutions to be employed [quotation marks original].[5]

---

[5] Schafer, Raymond P., Chairman. drug use in america: problem in perspective, Second Report of the National Commission on Marihuana and Drug Abuse. Washington, DC: US Government Printing Office, 1973 AA, chapter four toward a coherent social policy, III Defining the Government's Role, General Guidelines, p. 280.

B. The Drug Abuse Industrial Complex

Flanked by these three groups, as we have seen,[6] the users of illicit drugs underwent a clear evolution in demography. The pharmaceutical vagueness in the concept of stupefacient offered a wide range of legal psychoactive substances, some with a narcotic power superior to the opiates and others that could be considered potent forms of cocaine. Given the circumstances, few preferred to be seen as perverse addicts when they could pass for users of respectable medicines.

It is useful to compare for example pre-war and post-war patterns in admissions to the Lexington, Kentucky and Fort Worth, Texas narcotic clinics:

> An analysis of the admissions to the two hospitals shows two main patterns. The 'southern' pattern, a survival from 1915, is found in Alabama, Georgia, Kentucky. Addicts tend to be 90 per cent white, aged about 43, and usually using the old morphine mixtures: pergoric, Dilaudid, and sometimes morphine itself. The modern pattern of imported heroin use is found in New York, Puerto Rico, the District of Columbia and Chicago. Two thirds of those from the first three States are Negro or Puerto Rican, and their average age is about 27. It is also possible to compare Lexington's population now with that in 1937, when the first study of the hospital's intake was made. In 1937 the southern type was more common and outweighed admissions from New York and Illinois. During the interruption of world communications during the Second World War heroin was very difficult to come by and addiction rates fell. After the war it rose again to a peak of 1,823 cases in 1950, and is now slowly falling [quotation marks original].[7]

---

[6] For a more extensive discussion, see GHDV4P1, Chapter 24, pp. 1687 et seq.

[7] Laurie, Peter. Drugs: Medical, Psychological and Social Facts. Baltimore, MD: Penguin Books, 1967 AA, Chapter Two, Archetypal Heroin, *American addiction*, p. 30.

Clearly, the geographic, racial and ethnic composition of the patient population at the two hospitals had changed between 1937 and 1962:

> In 1937, the highest rates of admission were from the southern states. Thus, what has occurred since 1937 has been a substantial increase in the number of patients from northern metropolitan centers. ... The racial and ethnic composition of the hospital population has altered markedly during this twenty-five year period. In 1937, 88.4 percent of the male patients were white, 8.9 percent Negro, 1.2 percent Mexican and, together, Chinese, Japanese, and Indian were 1.5 percent. In 1962, 51.0 percent of the male patients were white, 30.4 percent Negro, 12.2 percent Puerto Rican, 4.9 percent Mexican, and others 1.5 percent. There has, then, been a notable increase in the number of addicts from the minority groups in American society.[8]

The numbers do not reflect the population as they are based on persons belonging to criminal circles; there could be a similar number of opiate addicts among medical practitioners.[9]

As for other drugs, in 1962 there was little prior use of cocaine among the patients at the two federal clinics: "Of the 3301 addict patients discharged from the Lexington and Fort Worth Hospitals in 1962 ... [t]here were no first drug diagnoses of cocaine ...."[10] Habitual users of amphetamines were not eligible for treatment at the two institutions.[11] Only 8 of the patients (0.2 percent) had a first diagnosis of cannabis.[12]

---

[8] Ball, John C. "Two Patterns of Narcotic Drug Addiction in the United States," *Journal of Criminal Law and Criminology*, Volume 56, Issue 2, June 1965 AA, Demographic Changes in the Pattern of Opiate Addiction, pp. 208-209.

[9] See Laurie, 1967, pp. 30-31.

[10] Ball, 1965, p. 206; "There were, however, six second drug diagnoses of cocaine use and one of peyote use" (fn 19, p. 206).

[11] Ball, 1965, p. 205, and see footnote 16.

[12] Ball, 1965, Table 1 First Drug Diagnosis of 3301 Addict Patients at Lexington and

Cocaine use also declined overseas. If in 1925 there were large numbers of cocaine users in Paris, by 1937 the amphetamines had been thoroughly commercialized and many switched to a legal alternative. The same thing happened in other European cities traditionally affected by the drug (Vienna, Milan, Rome, Berlin, Munich) and in the United States, where the threat of cocaine seems to have evaporated. As for marijuana, it had never been consumed by a significant number of persons in Northamerica or Europe, and still wasn't.

It would have been an especially opportune moment for international authorities to congratulate themselves on the effectiveness of their drug policies. Prohibition had achieved just what had been intended, since those opposed to the white pharmacological diet were ethnic minorities, groups marginalized by their poverty and thought of as human detritus. Up until 1937 the white southern, over forty, affluent addict of iatrogenic origin predominated in the US; from then on the so-called modern type proliferates, a minority or marginalized individual with an average age of 25 and living in the poorest neighborhoods of Chicago, New York and Washington.[13] Only the heads of the police brigades continued to state that drugs were still a grave problem.

Fort Worth Hospitals – 1962, p. 205.

[13] The District of Columbia ranked number one in per capita consumption of 5.67 gallons of alcohol in 1986, surpassing that of Nevada in 1977 (Sullivan, Louis W., Secretary of Health and Human Services. Seventh Special Report to the U.S. Congress on Alcohol and Health. Rockville, MD: Public Health Service, 1990 AA, Chapter 2 Epidemiology, Table 1. Apparent per capital alcohol consumption for the fifty states and the District of Columbia, 1977 and 1986, with decile rankings for 1986, p. 17).

Three criteria were needed to maintain this pharmacratic peace: a) the status quo had to be maintained unchanged, with a wide range of alternative legal drugs; b) there had to be no progress in the organization of the black market by groups like the Mafia, which could take advantage of more severe laws to increase their profit margin even if it meant using minors as dealers; and, c) that the miserable status of the addict should not become an esthetic and literary myth, with paradoxically indirect benefits. But none of these could be fulfilled.

Within the drug abuse industrial complex, it was inevitable that the repressive sector would demand ever more draconian laws (denouncing the very existence and seeking to restrict the availability of narcotics and synthetic stimulants), the criminal sector would harvest the fruits of this political self-mutilation by organizing into a global syndicate (infiltrating itself into the highest political circles), while the decisive factor in this transition may well have been the attacks by the therapeutic sector made up of psychologists, psychiatrists and sociologists, rejecting not the premise of repressing the voluntary consumption of certain drugs, but only the attempt to solve the problem with punitive measures alone. The combined actions of all three interested parties dress the stage for the most singular moral drama of modern times.

A war arises between the so-called Moral Majority and small groups obstinately devoted to consuming heroin, between vampirish witch-finders greedy for blood and individuals approximating ever closer the ideal of the Christian martyr, desperately imploring the pardon of the Father. Little by little this conflict will become a specialized cinematic performance representing socially and individually the value of one's very existence in a consumer society. Some admit the postponement of their pleasures to be achieved through labor, and others want everything cheap and right now, impatient with and apathetic to any such struggle, resorting to a soothing vice to suffer their lives. Over time this passion play will reduce the dealer to the cliché of the dope fiend and the user to an involuntary victim, that is, someone who is so-called sick:

> The media have tended to reinforce this outlook by depicting the international heroin traffic as a medieval morality play: the traffickers are portrayed as the basest criminals, continually on the run from the minions of law and order; and American diplomats and law enforcement personnel are depicted as modern-day knights-errant staunchly committed to the total, immediate eradication of heroin trafficking.[14]

In the 1930s the still, small voice raised against this absurdist theatre is that of the English writer and philosopher Aldous Leonard Huxley (1894 – 1963). In a 1931 essay inspired by Lewin's "unreadable" *Phantastica* Huxley explores addiction, prohibition and the obvious solution to both:

> All existing drugs are treacherous and harmful. The heaven into which they usher their victims soon turns into a hell of sickness and moral degradation. They kill, first the soul, then, in a few years, the body. What is the remedy? 'Prohibition,' answer all contemporary governments in chorus. But the results of prohibition are not encouraging. Men and women feel such an urgent need to take occasional holidays from reality, that they will do almost anything to procure the means of escape. The only justification for prohibition would be success; but it is not and, in the nature of things, cannot be successful. The way to prevent people from drinking too much alcohol, or becoming addicts to morphine or cocaine, is to give them an efficient but wholesome substitute for these delicious and (in the present imperfect world) necessary poisons. The man who invents such a substance will be counted among the greatest benefactors of suffering humanity [quotation marks original].[15]

---

[14] McCoy, Alfred W. The Politics of Heroin in Southeast Asia. NY: Harper & Row, Publishers, 1973 AA Introduction: The Consequences of Complicity, Heroin: The Logistics of Heroin, p. 14.

[15] Horowitz, Michael and Cynthia Palmer, editors. Moksha: Aldous Huxley's Classic Writings on Psychedelics and the Visionary Experience. Rochester, VT: Park Street

Figure 365. "Aldous Huxley." Huxley, Aldous. "A Case for ESP, PK and PSI," *Life Magazine*, Volume 36, No. 2, 11 Jan 1954 [books.google.com, hereinafter BGC], p. 97.

Press, 1999 AA, Chapter 1 1931 A Treatise on Drugs, pp. 4-5, published in *The Chicago Herald and Examiner*, October 10, 1931, reprinted under the title "Drugs" in Nash's *Pall Mall Magazine* (March, 1932), p. 54.

By contrast, in the non-literary world governments continued to pretend to help their citizens by blocking their access to lenitives for their suffering, without admitting that the realistic solution to these evils were better lenitives, euphoric vehicles suited to a species already the owners of technology capable of transforming the face of the planet. Humans not only want to move mountains, reclaim land from the sea, or be seduced by various propagandas, but also to possess equally powerful resources to combat the lack of both peace and motivation. If societies threatened by a monstrously increasing population density are going to survive without descending into pure horror, it will only be by multiplying the interior space of the individual. Acceptable as a laboratory goal, this will only be reconsidered a quarter century later when the passive resistance to the pharmacracy becomes active.

With Brave New World (1932) Huxley then invents just such a panacea he calls soma, "Christianity without tears, morality in a bottle."[16] For the time being Huxley prefers mockery, as when the Controller explains to the Savage why the citizens of his new utopia will never need to write nor understand *Othello*:

> The world's stable now. People are happy; they get what they want, and they never want what they can't get. They're well off; they're safe; they're never ill; they're not afraid of death; they're blissfully ignorant of passion and old age; they're plagued with no mothers or fathers; they've got no wives, or children, or lovers to feel strongly about; they're so conditioned that they practically can't help behaving as they ought to behave. And if anything should go wrong, there's *soma* [italics original].[17]

---

[16] Horowitz, 1999 AA, Introduction by Alexander T. Shulgin, p. xvi.

[17] Huxley, Aldous. Brave New World *and* Brave New World Revisited. NY: Harper & Brothers, Publishers, 1960 AA, Brave New World, Chapter Sixteen, pp. 263-264.

Nothing appears at the time (and still has not appeared) that merits being called by the name, soma.

Things were unfolding in a completely different direction, however. It might even be said that the driving force for this change was a subculture of writers and musicians, who advertised the harsh conditions of the life of an opiate addict as a kind of authenticity and courage. This is the peculiar mythology of the junkie, which will receive a decisive impetus in the novels of the American William Seward Burroughs (1914 – 1997) and the Scotsman Alexander Whitelaw Robertson Trocchi (1925 – 1984), whom we will come to soon.

From a chronological viewpoint, it would be inexact to believe that these new addicts predate significant changes in American legislation, organized delinquency or modern therapeutism. Until the end of the 1950s one cannot observe a rapid increase in the number of American heroin addicts, and by then the repressors, trafficantes and investigators will have new instruments to fight their respective battles. It is a good moment, consequently, to scrupulously examine the dates of each event so as to not establish unfounded causal connections.

Figure 366. "Heroin Addict's Equipment." Piel, Gerard. "Narcotics: War has brought illicit traffic to all-time low but U.S. Treasury fears rising post-war addiction," *Life*, Volume 15, No. 3, 1943 AO, p. 91.

1. Draconian Laws

The Federal Bureau of Narcotics (FBN) was warning as early as 1943 that at the end of the First World War many soldiers had returned addicted and that the same thing could only happen again:

> Yet officials of the Bureau of Narcotics and officials of the League of Nations now in Washington are deeply concerned about the future. They foresee the very real danger of a postwar epidemic of drug addiction. They have cogent reasons for so thinking. One is that addiction has usually increased alarmingly after major wars in the past. In Europe, after the last war, drug-taking became not only common-place but fashionable.[18]

In any case, they argued it was better not to relax the controls over drugs because the war against the Germans and Japanese could only have demoralized former prisoners and returning troops. A second reason was that "when the war ends, enormous quantities of narcotics may be available to illicit merchants. ... The Reich's great stocks of medicinal drugs ... might easily be scattered and sold off."[19] Though the FBN admitted that Greeks, Egyptians, Chinese and Italians all smuggled drugs, in the midst of World War Two the Japanese were especially singled out: "Japan is the worst sort of criminal when it comes to soaking its conquered peoples in opium."[20]

---

[18] Piel, "Narcotics," *Life*, p. 83.

[19] Piel, 1943, p. 83.

[20] Piel, 1943, p. 92.

Figure 367. "Julius and Ethel Rosenberg, separated by heavy wire screen as they leave US Court House after being found guilty by jury." B&W film copy, negative, 1951 by Roger Higgins. *New York World-Telegram & Sun* Newspaper Photograph Collection. Library of Congress Prints and Photographs Division [loc.gov, hereinafter LG].

a. The Postwar Social Climate

Americanism experienced its apogee in the years following the Second World War, a revival of the jingoist sentiment in the years just prior to the First World War. The intellectuals were of course the prime suspects. On scant evidence [only corroborated after the fall of the Soviet Union] Julius (1918 – 1953) and Ethel (1915 – 1953) Rosenberg were tried and electrocuted for espionage during the Korean War (1950 – 1953). With the US in a new state of national effervescence, the ringmaster of inquisitions is the demagogic junior Senator from Wisconsin, Joseph Raymond McCarthy (D. WI, 1908 – 1957), who after several years of nearly omnipotent power was censored by a vote of no confidence in the upper house in 1954. His opposite number in the lower chamber was Richard Milhouse Nixon (R. CA, 1913 – 1994), a member of the House Un-American Activities Committee (HUAC) and former attorney for the mob boss Meyer Lansky (Maier Suchowljansky, 1902 – 1983):

> Lansky's devotion to Nixon ... went way back: they'd become friends in Havana in the 1940s, where the mob boss gave Nixon free hotel accommodations. Meyer was also the first major criminal figure ... to start green-lighting tainted underworld cash in quid pro quo deals with the rookie California politician ....[21]

Both McCarthy and Nixon denounced an ideological invasion and in both cases the solution was not just to institute new punishments but also to let special police units fight the battle with impunity, without interference from outside agencies. Symptoms of loyalty to America were being a team player, passive adjustment to regulations, military style discipline, and social conformity as guided by the media.

---

[21] Fulsom, Don. The Mafia's President: Nixon and the Mob. NY: St. Martin's Press, 2017 AA, Chapter Two The Nixon-Mafia Relationship, p. 12.

Figure 368. "Senator Joseph McCarthy chats with his attorney Roy Cohn during Senate Subcommittee Hearings." B&W film copy negative, 1954. Library of Congress Prints and Photographs Division, LG.

Figure 369. "Nixon examines film found in a pumpkin." From "Ten things you need to know about Nixon the Congressman," [Nixonfoundation.org, hereinafter NFO].

On the other side, in the midst of economic splendor and the wave of patriotic sentiment, not only defenders of those persecuted for anti-Americanism appear, but also voices of a more general dissidence who view the American Dream as something halfway between a fraud and a nightmare. It was the era of maximum faith in personality tests as impartial arbiters of knowledge, but also the moment when the tendentiousness of their underlying criteria becomes apparent in the kinds of human beings who did well on them. Students, employees and managers were only considered ideal employees when their characters exhibited a mixture of innate boredom, simplicity and authoritarianism; real culture, the taste for solitude, a critical sense and similar traits closed rather than opened the path to scholarships, jobs and promotions. What was normal and sane then would later be called unidimensionality.

One of the first sociological treatises to become a bestseller was The Lonely Crowd (1950), whose lead author, the American sociologist David Reisman (1909 – 2002) timidly advances the theory that alienation and conformity are basic characteristics of American consumerist society, distinguishing between the inner- and outer-directed individual:

> My major thesis in these opening chapters is that: the conformity of earlier generations of Americans of the type I term 'inner-directed' was mainly assured by their internalization of adult authority. The middle-class urban American of today, the 'other- directed,' is, by contrast, in a characterological sense more the product of his peers – that is, in sociological terms, his 'peer-groups,' the other kids at school or in the block. In adult life he continues to respond to these peers, not only with overt conformity, as do people in all times and places, but also in a deeper sense, in the very quality of his feeling [quotation marks original].[22]

---

[22] David Reisman, in collaboration with Reuel Denney and Nathan Glazer. The Lonely Crowd: A Study of the Changing American Character. New Haven, CT:

It's sometimes suggested that the former category displays an individualism based upon firmness of character and resistance to frustration while the latter seeks meaning in the bland recitation of slogans, but this would be unwarranted, says the author:

> I should like to warn the reader lest his judgment be prejudiced by the term 'inner-directed,' which apart from the definition, sounds like a more autonomous and therefore better type than 'other-directed.' This inference would not be warranted; more should not be read into the terms than is intended [quotation marks original].[23]

At a moment when statistics indicated there were more clerks and employees than agricultural and industrial workers in the United States, the American sociologist and Columbia professor C. Wright Mills (1916 – 1962) brought out his study of the emerging middle classes, White Collar (1951) whose opening lines record this new phenomenon:

> The white-collar people slipped quietly into modern society. Whatever history they have had is a history without events; whatever common interests they have do not lead to unity; whatever future they have will not be of their own making. If they aspire at all it is to a middle course, at a time when no middle course is available, and hence to an illusory course in an imaginary society.[24]

The same period also sees the publication of Fahrenheit 451 (1953) by the American science fiction writer Ray Bradbury (1920 – 2012), decrying government censorship: "There is more than one way

---

Yale University Press, 1955 (Sixth Printing) AA, Preface, p. v.

[23] Reisman, 1955, p. vi.

[24] Mills, C. Wright. White Collar: The American Middle Classes. London: Oxford University Press, 1969 AO, Introduction, p. ix.

to burn a book. And the world is full of people running about with lit matches."[25]

A few years later, the American urbanist and analyst William H. Whyte (1917 – 1999) published The Organization Man (1956), describing those who are

> not the workers, nor are they the white-collar people in the usual, clerk sense of the word. These people only work for The Organization. The ones I am talking about *belong* to it as well. They are the ones of our middle class who have left home, spiritually as well as physically, to take the vows of organization life, and it is they who are the mind and soul of our great self-perpetuating institutions [capitalization and italics original].[26]

All these books enjoy a success both noteworthy and unforeseen, a symptom of the alarm felt before the progress of irrational forces in society, ever more sophisticated and implacable.

This dissatisfaction appears in a phenomenon of a generalized and widespread rejection of social norms by the rebel without a cause and the angry youth who see nonconformity as an alternative ethic and aesthetic to the attitude embodied in national heroes like Senator McCarthy and Anslinger. Marginalization becomes a deliberate choice, just as informality in habits, tastes and dress is counterposed to institutionally recognized customs. Toward the end of the same decade, Norman Kingsley Mailer (Nachem Malech Mailer, 1923 – 2007) publishes an essay contrasting rebellion and conformity that helps to circulate the term, hipster:

---

25 Bradbury, Ray. Fahrenheit 451. NY: Ballantine Books, 1979 AA, Author's Afterword, p. 148.

26 Whyte, William H. The Organization Man. Harmondsworth, Middlesex, UK: Penguin Books, Ltd., 1963 AA, *Part One* The Ideology of Organization Man, Chapter 1 *Introduction*, p. 8.

One is Hip or one is Square (the alternative which each new generation coming into American life is beginning to feel), one is a rebel or one conforms, one is a frontiersman in the Wild West of American night life, or else a Square cell, trapped in the totalitarian tissues of American society, doomed willy-nilly to conform if one is to succeed.[27]

Figure 370. "Paul Thomas Mann (1875 – 1955)." B&W film negative, 1937, Carl Van Vechten (1800 – 1964). Library of Congress Prints and Photographs Division, LG.

[27] Mailer, Norman. "The White Negro: Superficial Reflections on the Hipster," *Dissent*, Volume IV, Number 3, Summer 1957 AA, Section II, p. 278.

b. The Postwar Legal Climate

Before the supposed threats from China and the Soviet Union, in a by now routine post-war purification ritual President Harry S. Truman (1884 – 1972) signed Executive Order 9835 in 1947 establishing a loyalty program mandating full investigations for both applicants and current employees of the federal government. Besides sabotage and treason, disloyalty included "(m)embership in, affiliation with or sympathetic association with any foreign or domestic organization, association, movement, group or combination of persons, designated by the Attorney General as totalitarian, fascist, communist, or subversive."[28]

Pushback arrived from (among many other intellectuals and entertainers) the novelist and recipient of the 1929 Nobel Prize for Literature Paul Thomas Mann (1875 – 1955), a naturalized American, who did not hesitate to warn the listeners of a radio broadcast that same year that this political trend had only just recently led to fascism and war:

> As an American citizen of German birth, I finally testified that I am painfully familiar with certain political trends. Spiritual intolerance, political inquisitions and declining legal security, and all this in the name of an alleged state of emergency, that's how it started in Germany. What followed was fascism and what followed fascism was war.[29]

---

[28] Truman, Harry S. Executive Order 9835 – Prescribing Procedures for the Administration of an Employees Loyalty Program in the Executive Branch of the Government. The American Presidency Project, University of Santa Barbara, 21 March 1947 [presidency.usb.edu, hereinafter PUE], part V. Standards, section f, p. 5.

[29] "ABC: Hollywood Fights Back," broadcast 2 November 1947, transcript [Youtube, hereinafter YT], speech begins at 24:16 and ends at 24:51.

In November 1951 Congress passed the *Bogg's Act* (a revision of the *Narcotic Drugs Import and Export Act*) which imposed a mandatory minimum sentence of two year's incarceration for a first drug offense with no parole for subsequent offenses:

> Whoever fraudulently or knowingly imports or brings any narcotic drug into the United States or any territory under its control or jurisdiction, contrary to law, or receives, conceals, buys, sells, or in any manner facilitates the transportation, concealment, or sale of any such narcotic drug after being imported or brought in, knowing the same to have been imported contrary to law, or conspires to commit any of such acts in violation of the laws of the United States, shall be fined not more than $2,000 and imprisoned not less than two or more than five years. ... Upon conviction for a second or subsequent offense, the imposition or execution of sentence shall not be suspended and probation shall not be granted.[30]

If the government's interpretation of the *Harrison Act* had deprived the medical estate of discretion over the use of certain drugs, the *Bogg's Act* suppressed judicial discretion. In the background were insinuations from the FBN to Congress that judges were excessively lenient with dope fiends. Anslinger insisted that his department be allowed to wage war without external interference, since the academic training of physicians and magistrates often blinded them to the simplicity of the subject.

Taking into account that the crime of trafficking was a non-violent act with a presumed victim, the *Bogg's Act* permitted imprisonment without parole without any determination as to the real effect of his action on any specific person. Even in Roman law such

---

[30] United States Statutes at Large containing the Laws and Concurrent Resolutions Enacted during the Eighty-Second Congress of the United States of America, 1951, Volume 65. Washington, DC: Government Printing Office, 1952 [govinfo.gov, hereinafter GIG], Public Law 255, Chapter 666, p. 767.

conduct was a typical case of an impossible crime (like killing a corpse), where there is only intention and not the circumstances and means to carry it to fruition. The impossible crime of selling illicit drugs to someone who from the beginning intends to destroy it (the anti-drug police) is equated to the real crime of effectively introducing into the market a venomous agent, or to specifically harming the health of specific individuals. As in inquisitional cases, the intent is enough. It was enough even in those cases where the intent was compromised by the influence of a complex plan to provoke it (entrapments practiced assiduously on physicians and pharmacists), and not able, for this reason, to be considered spontaneous.

As for substantive guarantees, the system of symbolic incrimination erases the difference between the effective result of an action and the possible result, between consummated and hypothetical evil. It was now irrelevant whether the product sold was pure or adulterated, whether the buyer was induced or not to purchase, whether or not the buyer contracted a habit as a result of the sale, whether or not he was the victim of a toxic substitute and so forth. For this reason, the essential judicial differences between consummated, frustrated and attempted crimes as well as those between author, accomplice and accessory were eliminated. Further, the burden of proof was reversed:

> Whenever on trial for a violation of this subdivision the defendant is shown to have or to have had possession of the narcotic drug, such possession shall be deemed sufficient evidence to authorize conviction unless the defendant explains the possession to the satisfaction of the jury.[31]

---

[31] United States Statutes, 1952, p. 768.

As with political crimes, and as in the crime of *lese majeste* centuries earlier, it was unnecessary to present a real victim for this offense. Lacking another, the person accused of illegal possession serves as the victim. On the other hand, all of these irregularities (in contrast with the procedures for robbery, assassination, rape, blackmail and so forth) were indispensable for the police. The immense majority of such so-called crimes are never reported, and in order to encounter the guilty the forces of order literally have to provoke it, mounting various sting operations, a point made by the Chief of Police of Austin, Texas a few years later in testimony before the Daniel Subcommittee:

Chief Thorp: ... I know that an officer cannot, at least is not supposed to violate a law in order to enforce a law, but this law we have, called entrapment, I am sure it has a place. But we intend and I do as long as I am head of the police department, to gig them and trap them and then trap them just as long as I am here and let the burden fall upon them and not upon us, until some judge tells me I am wrong. We are fighting fire and we have got to fight it with fire. I am speaking of pushers and peddlers.
Senator Daniel: And when you used the word 'entrapment' you mean the use of undercover men or other people?
Chief Thorp: Yes, sir.
Senator Daniel: To catch the pushers and peddlers in their sales?
Chief Thorp: That's right; yes, sir.
Senator Daniel: And you have been using that, and you think it is a method that you should continue to use?
Chief Thorp: Yes, sir. I will have to if I expect to accomplish anything [quotation marks original].[32]

---

[32] Daniel, Price, Chairman. Illicit Narcotics Traffic, Hearings before the Subcommittee on Improvements in the Federal Criminal Code of the Committee of the Judiciary, United States Senate, Eighty-Fourth Congress, First Session, Part 7. Washington, DC: US Government Printing Office, 1956 [books.googleuser content.com, hereinafter BGU], Testimony of R. D. Thorp, Chief of Police, Austin Police Department, pp. 2386-7.

Figure 371. "Price Daniel [right] is sworn into office, Austin, Texas." B&W film negative, 4x5, Douglas Neal, photographer, 1948. Austin History Center, Austin Public Library [texashistory.unt.edu, hereinafter THU].

As expected, the new law not only affected the judiciary but the legal profession generally. Without delay, the American Bar Association (ABA) solicited Congress for a revision of the statute, believing that it was misguided and violated fundamental judicial principles. The Upper House accepted their proposal and assigned it to a Subcommittee on Improvements in the Federal Criminal Code of the Committee on the Judiciary to evaluate the problem, slowly. But their leisureliness did not prevent a surprising result for the judges and lawyers.

Senator Marion Price Daniel (D. TX, 1910 – 1988) and his subcommittee colleagues considered the judicial complaints unfounded and sided with the FBN. No longer at issue were drugs of puerile and degenerate races, those of the black and Puerto Rican ghettoes in the Northeast. No longer was Japan trying to enslave the republic. Permissiveness was now a Chinese and Russian conspiracy to demoralize America. A Texas congressman who had "offered the first resolution calling for a nationwide investigation of the narcotics traffic" stated on the record that subversion through drug addiction was without any doubt a goal of the Chinese communists:

There is another factor of even greater importance. ... This factor is the use of narcotics as a 'cold war' weapon by international communism. The major point that I wish to urge upon this committee is consideration of the narcotics traffic as an instrument of communism. This instrument fell into the hands of the bolshevik leaders when they took over the opium-producing sections of China. It would have been too much to expect the Communists to ignore the possibilities of the drug trade. They have long since abandoned any moral scruples which conflict with their designs for world conquest. In narcotics, they found a double-edged weapon to help them achieve their goal [quotation marks original].[33]

Anslinger's FBN was now using the cold war to denounce not a Japanese but a communist plot to clandestinely export opiates into the United States:

The fact that our country is a drug target of Communist China has been attested by Harry J. Anslinger, United States representative to the U. N. Commission on Narcotic Drugs. He has repeatedly laid before that body documented cases of Communist efforts to bring large supplies into our country through the west coast.[34]

---

[33] Daniel, 1956, Wednesday, October 12, 1955, Statement of Hon. Homer Thornberry, p. 2359.

[34] Daniel, 1956, Thornberry, p. 2360.

The subcommittee's conclusions birthed the *Narcotics Control Act*, unanimously approved in 1956. This norm (the most severe up to then that had ever been promulgated on drugs at the federal level) elevated the mandatory minimum punishment from two to five year's imprisonment for a first offense:

> (c) Whoever fraudulently or knowingly imports or brings any narcotic drug into the United States or any territory under its control or jurisdiction, contrary to law, or receives, conceals, buys, sells, or in any manner facilitates the transportation, concealment, or sale of any such narcotic drug after being imported or brought in, knowing the same to have been imported or brought into the United States contrary to law, or conspires to commit any of such acts in violation of the laws of the United States, shall be imprisoned not less than five or more than twenty years and, in addition, may be fined not more than $20,000.[35]

Moreover, the same law empowered a jury to impose the death sentence on anyone over the age of eighteen who sold heroin to anyone under the age of eighteen:

> (i) Notwithstanding any other provision of law, whoever, having attained the age of eighteen years, knowingly sells, gives away, furnishes, or dispenses, facilitates the sale, giving, furnishing, or dispensing, or conspires to sell, give away, furnish, or dispense, any heroin unlawfully imported or otherwise brought into the United States, to any person who has not attained the age of eighteen years, may be fined not more than $20,000, and shall be imprisoned for life, or for not less than ten years, except that the offender shall suffer death if the jury in its discretion shall so direct.[36]

---

[35] United States Statutes at Large, Volume 70. Washington, DC: Government Printing Office, 1956 GIG, Public Law 728, Chapter 629, Section 105, Importation, Etc., of Narcotic Drugs, p. 570.

[36] United States Statutes at Large, Volume 70, 1956, Section 107 Sale of Heroin to Juveniles – Penalties, p. 571.

A minor acting as a police informant who tricked an adult vendor into selling heroin, could send him to the electric chair or the gas chamber without the necessity of proving any concrete harm to the minor or any third party: "Throughout the 1950s, the Boggs Act was amended to allow a life sentence or death penalty for those who committed a third offense."[37] The judges were deprived of the right to fit the punishment to the crime in any particular case, and the police powers of federal government were raised to the maximum.

Not all the testimony however went according to script. Senator Daniel tried to elicit from a token self-confessed addict that heroin was a living death, but instead received the following testimonial to physician prescribed maintenance doses:

> Mr. Turner: Well, the big trouble about an addict, what I found I am speaking of my experience it's not. I've worked and I have got that drug and used it in moderate amounts and it didn't interfere with my work because I could buy it in a manner, get it from a doctor, getting the prescription filled in a drugstore, it didn't interfere with my work. In fact, I put on weight. It didn't have any bearing on my health.[38]

Mr. Turner also praised the English system and pointed out that profit was driving the traffic but the Senators could not conceive of allowing physicians to supply maintenance doses to addicts.[39]

---

[37] Khadraoui, Norah. "Comparing the Anti-Drug Abuse Act of 1986 to the Boggs Act of 1951 and the Narcotic Control Act of 1956 in Levels of Severity," *The Young Researcher*, Volume 3, Issue 1, 2019 [Royal St. George's College, theyoungresearcher.com, hereinafter YR], p. 117, citing Henry S. Wallace, "Mandatory Minimums and the Betrayal of Sentencing Reform: A Legislative Dr. Jekyll and Mr. Hyde," *Journal of Correctional Philosophy and Practice* 57, no. 3 (1993): 9.

[38] Daniel, 1956, Testimony of Perry Milton Turner, p. 2373.

[39] Daniel, 1956, pp. 2376, 2380.

To the objections from the ABA, Anslinger replied that these should have been made to the *Harrison Act*, of which the *Narcotic Control Act* was only a development. Accompanied by the habitual reproach of old-fashioned liberalism, the ABA responded that they could not equate a tax law (though interpreted abusively by the executive branch) with a substantive penal statute, and that in a civilized country one could not trust the application of any law exclusively to the police. Even before the law was passed, a team of lawyers and sociologists worked with another team of physicians to counteract the FBN, with a report they thought might sway the judiciary.

Though we will speak of it soon, beforehand it is useful to highlight that the 1956 law produced some curious effects. Satisfied with a significant price subsidy, the black market took advantage of the new law. It increased adulteration and used minors to sell drugs on the street, avoiding with disconcerting flexibility the obstacles raised by the language of the new law concerning sales by adults to minors.

The same effects would occur after Nixon's anti-drug initiatives in the late 1960s and early 1970s:

> As expected, the new drug laws did not work. New sources of supply and organizers evolved, more drugs were used – often of greater riskiness and/or lower purity, profits and police corruption increased, and the media and politicians continued their cover-up and profiteering. ... As was predicted by drug experts outside of government, illegal drugs remained readily and sometimes flagrantly available, prices increased, purity decreased, arrests and convictions stayed about the same as did prison sentences for drug felonies (12 percent of those arrested received them). More young people under sixteen were introduced to drug trafficking since they would be excluded from jail sentences.[40]

---

[40] Fort, Joel. The Addicted Society: Pleasure-Seeking and Punishment Revisited. NY: Grove Press, Inc., 1981 AA, Chapter 4 The Criminalization of the User and the

Figure 372. "Mafioso Joseph Valachi testifying before the McClellan Committee." B&W film negative, Warren K. Leffler, 1963. *US News and World Report* Collection, Library of Congress Prints and Photographs Division, LG.

Within months of the law coming into effect, in 1957 a famous reunion of the Cosa Nostra took place outside the rural hamlet of Apalachin, New York (the knowledge of which we have thanks to the mob informant Joseph Michael Valachi (1904 – 1971) of the Genovese family) in order to discuss both internal succession and narcotics:

> The first order of business was to have the ruling council anoint [Vito] Genovese as a Family boss. ... Finally, on the agenda, was what to do about the Bureau of Narcotics. There was some sentiment for murdering known agents. But the prevailing mood was to outlaw drug traffic for all Families, with death the penalty for disobedience; while realistically it would have much the same effect on some elements in the Cosa Nostra as Prohibition had for the nation, it was considered worth trying as a deterrent.[41]

Neglect of the Seller, as Performed by Politicians and Narcs, pp. 78-79.

[41] Maas, Peter. The Valachi Papers. NY: G. P. Putnam's Sons, 1968 AA, Chapter 11, pp. 251-252.

This wasn't the first time such a self-imposed ban on the narcotics business had been ignored by the mob:

The Cosa Nostra and traffic in drugs, especially heroin, are almost synonymous. But like everything else about the Cosa Nostra, even this has not always been quite what it seemed. In 1948 Frank Costello, while still acting boss of the Luciano Family, ordered its membership to stay out of dope. According to Valachi, the canny Costello had two reasons for the edict. One was his realization that there were rackets and rackets; bootlegging and gambling, for instance, enjoyed wide public acceptance or, at worst, indifference, while heroin not only was giving organized crime a relative black eye, but also was spurring law enforcement efforts against it in other areas. Much more important, however, was the dogged harassment of the Bureau of Narcotics.[42]

Some families ignored the ban while others left it up to the individual mobster to take advantage of easy money:

Costello's stand produced a varying response in the Cosa Nostra. The Lucchese Family, heavily involved in narcotics, simply ignored it. Others, like the Stefano Magaddino Family in Buffalo, gave it lip service, but privately continued to bring in heroin. ... In the Accardo Family ... the command to get out of narcotics triggered a serious breakdown in Cosa Nostra discipline. The temptation for quick profits was too much, and individual members, particularly those short on cash, persisted in handling heroin secretly. And while Vito Genovese, when he finally displaced Costello, went along with the narcotics ban, it turned out that he had a double standard; if he was given a cut of the take off the top, he always managed to look the other way.[43]

---

[42] Maas, 1968, p. 236.

[43] Maas, 1968, p. 237.

Hundreds of kilos of heroin from Europe in the 1950s were now being imported through Havana, Cuba, a city which had become a capital of organized crime in Latin America.[44] Until then heroin had been arriving almost undisturbed from the Mediterranean and Asia, in a quantity calculated by the Mafia clans as being in synchrony with the progressive hardening of the law. Though the Cosa Nostra "controls much of the importation of heroin, it has increasingly left the wholesale market in this country to the Negro and Puerto Rican underworld."[45] From then on, the contemporary junkie has a green card, and customs agents report a sustained increase in the quantities of drugs apprehended.

In Lexington and Fort Worth the number of addicts being treated in 1956 amounted to a thousand individuals of both sexes, with another thousand in Chicago, New York and Washington. Yet, in 1960 the US reported to the United Nations Commission on Narcotic Drugs: "There were 44,906 addicts in the United States ...."[46] In the 1960s the special adjutant to the Attorney General, Myles Joseph Ambrose (1926 – 2014), estimated that there were nearly 60,000 addicts in the US:

In the fifties and the early sixties I used to have an expression that the public isn't going to really care about drug enforcement, drug use, until heroin left Harlem and went to Scarsdale. And that's what happened. It went to Scarsdale. We used to estimate in the late fifties and the early sixties that there were probably 60,000 heroin

---

[44] *centenas de quilos de heroína a partir da Europa, via Havana, cidade que se convertera na capital do crime organizado na América Latin* (Olmo, Rosa del. A Face Oculta da Droga, tr. Teresa Ottoni. Rio de Janeiro, Brazil: Editora Revan, 1990 AA, I. Na década de cinqüenta, p. 31).

[45] Maas, 1968, p. 278.

[46] Lindesmith, Alfred R. The Addict and the Law. Bloomington, IN: Indiana University Press, 1965 AA, p. 100.

addicts in the United States. That figure was subject to some question, but certainly had some validity. In the late sixties you probably had 70,000 or 60,000 heroin addicts in three blocks in some areas of the United States .... The interesting statistic at that point in '69 and '70 – we were losing more people in the United States from drug overdoses per week that we were losing in Vietnam. That was a figure that used to scare me ....[47]

The jump was so abrupt that it suggested a self-interested manipulation of the figures, as had happened in the 1920s. Indeed, a careful researcher concluded the numbers were ultimately unreliable:

The conclusions which emerge from this discussion are: that the number of addicts in the United States in 1914 is unknown and cannot be reliably estimated; that it is even more hazardous to estimate the extent of the problem today; and that federal narcotics officials have, over a long period of years, underreported and underestimated the problem.[48]

However, the political profit in making such statements was nil, and the change in attitude in the courts suggests that, effectively, the population of dope fiends had skyrocketed in a few short years. It had been growing steadily since the *Boggs Act* of 1951, even though the largest increase was only experienced after the *Narcotic Control Act* of 1956. Now conditions were ripe for not only a chronic infection but a progressively worsening one.

Nothing was said about American patronage of Corsican and Chinese drug smugglers (the latter directed by the political and military dictator Chiang Kai-shek (1887 – 1975), since displaced to Taiwan) using the Turkish-Marseilles and Kuomintang-Thailand routes, respectively and whose principal customers were Northamericans.

---

[47] "Interview with Myles J. Ambrose," *Frontline*, WGBH [pbs.org, hereinafter PBS].

[48] Lindesmith, 1965, p. 122.

Figure 373. "Chiang Kai-shek [left], Franklin D. Roosevelt and Winston Churchill." Cairo, Egypt, 1943. National Archives and Records Administration, FDR Library, Hyde Park, NY.

Chiang was in this epoch the symbol of an allied hero of democracy, who would soon reconquer the lost continent:

The KMT leader, Chiang Kai-Shek, on Taiwan, had a mammoth lobbying and propaganda operation that over-whelmed the U.S. Congress and press. ... The most powerful American press voice during the Chinese Revolution and its immediate aftermath was Henry Luce, head of Time Inc. ... Luce, a staunch Christian moralist, and his wife, Clare Boothe Luce, were close personal friends of Chiang and Madame Chiang. ... During the Truman and Eisenhower presidencies ... Chiang was not an ally of convenience, but a sacred cause. ... [T]he U.S. commander, General Douglas MacArthur ... insisted on taking the war to China in a coordinated effort with Chiang to help the KMT reconquer the mainland.[49]

[49] Kwitny, Jonathan. The Crimes of Patriots: A True Tale of Dope, Dirty Money,

As for the accusations made to the Daniel Subcommittee, nothing has ever been proven to date. This does not discount the fact that China as well as the former Soviet Union have exported part of the heroin consumed in western markets, not so much as a form of subversion but to obtain needed currency and to blackmail the relatives of high officials. Since the Cold War (and even prior) ethics in international affairs have always been so neglected that anything is possible (even probable) and nothing is ever conclusively proven, because in the worst case scenario, when the privileges of a state are not enough to achieve without interference what at the individual level would be risky, diplomatic compromises can cover up the most shocking operation.[50] It is evident that if country A decides to prohibit

---

and the CIA. NY: Simon and Schuster Inc., 1987, pp. 48-49.

50 An informal survey of heroin traffickers incarcerated in Spain led me to see that more than half of them obtained or had obtained their product from Syrians, some attached to their European embassies, and also from Lebanese, whose country suffers a significant Syrian presence. The Soviet Union, which already had a medium sized commerce in opium in the 1920s, added much new productive potential when it annexed territories traditionally controlled by Persia and Bulgaria, as both areas have cultivated poppies for millennia. Working within the realm of pure hypothesis, the Soviets could have transformed a small portion of their crude opium into morphine and codeine for its hospitals and pharmacies, exporting the rest (with adequate protection) to Beirut and Damascus, where it could be converted into refined (at least to some extent) heroin. An additional advantage of the system would be to avoid the presence of large quantities on Soviet territory, especially in the form of its alkaloids. This could explain, moreover, that the authorities have never really captured massive shipments of heroin (although the sum of what has been seized oscillates between three and five tons annually over the decade of the 1980s). The only exceptions were a Soviet cargo ship in Rotterdam in which was discovered 220 kilos of heroin (Reuters, Rotterdam, 18 August 1986, 18:00 EDT: "*Un buque sovietico traslado el mayor alijo de heroina hallado en Europa*," *El Pais Internacional* [elpais.com, hereinafter EP]), and a large container truck detained upon suspicion by Berlin

in its territory something produced in country B with which it maintains a cold war relationship, the former is clearly promoting an export policy in the latter. With regards to China, the unheard of grievance, blackmail and manipulation suffered in its history at the hands of western powers (not only during the epoch of opium prohibition but also afterward) would more than justify any reprisal.

Even so, it seems probable that they had not embarked upon such an enterprise, perhaps for fear for their own population. On the contrary one can find only isolated and indirect evidence. Thus, although it was not absolutely clear that the Soviet Union and China were organizing subversion via addictive drugs, and although it was clear, in contrast, that the CIA was supporting either directly or indirectly the exporting centers of Marseilles and Chiang Mai, the intention of Anslinger and the FBN was to confront the so-called communist threat through the system of substantially elevating the penalties for traffickers and users of illegal drugs in the United States.

---

customs, which the Soviet authorities denied permission to inspect and which finally was allowed to enter, no doubt in exchange for concessions. Both news reports (the latter amply publicized on television) ceased to be so within twenty-four hours. They could be simple hoaxes, or the result of a busy jaded news cycle, but one must take into account the advantages for the Soviet Union to traffic through other countries.

2. The Syndicate

The history of the syndicate in the United States is one of fierce rivalries. The principal Northamerican gangs only managed to achieve an accord with the imminence of the Twenty-First Amendment, which would repeal the *Volstead Act*. In 1934, the year alcohol was re-legalized, a syndicate in peace and harmony had distributed by common agreement both their territories and businesses. But some families were already working heroin as an alternative, though they were conscious that it would take years to establish a monopoly remotely comparable in profits to what they had previously obtained over wines and liquors.

If in this shadow government the Minister of the Interior is the Sicilian Charles "Lucky" Luciano (Salvatore Lucania, 1897 – 1962), the Minister of Finance is his longtime associate the Jewish Meyer Lansky, as well as Luciano's former lieutenant Vito Genovese (1897 – 1969). It was Luciano who expanded mob business into prostitution and heroin:

> With the end of prohibition in sight, Luciano made the decision to take the Mafia into the lucrative prostitution and heroin rackets. This decision was determined more by financial considerations than anything else. ... Heroin was an attractive substitute because its relatively recent prohibition had left a large market that could be exploited and expanded easily. Although heroin addicts in no way compared with drinkers in numbers, heroin profits could be just as substantial ....[51]

Meyer Lansky, in particular, made a major European tour in 1949-1950 to establish Marseilles as a heroin processing center. His purpose was to establish refineries for Turkish opium in the south of France. The Corsicans already controlled the underworld in Marseilles

[51] McCoy, 1973, Chapter 1 Sicily: Home of the Mafia, The Mafia in America, p. 18.

and Toulon, were already involved in relatively vulgar businesses like prostitution and blackmail, and they welcomed Lansky's proposal:

> Lansky played a key role in organizing Luciano's heroin syndicate: he supervised smuggling operations, negotiated with Corsican heroin manufacturers, and managed the collection and concealment of the enormous profits. ... [His] 1949-1950 European tour was instrumental in promoting Marseille's heroin industry. ... Lansky traveled through France, where he met with high-ranking Corsican syndicate leaders on the Riviera and in Paris ... concerning the international heroin traffic.[52]

By 1958 Genovese was in prison for heroin trafficking where he died in 1969. A year later Lansky retired and "turned over much of the major decision making to his subordinates. Thus, by "death and default, the responsibility logically fell to [the head of operations in Florida and Cuba] Santo Trafficante, Jr. [1914 – 1987],"[53] who, in "an attempt to secure new sources of heroin for Mafia distributors inside the United States,"[54] visited Saigon in 1968 and is believed to have contacted Corsican syndicate leaders there."[55] But before continuing it is useful to consider the history of the heroin traffic from Marseilles and the Far East.

---

[52] McCoy, 1973, pp. 25, 28.

[53] McCoy, 1973, p. 55.

[54] McCoy, 1973, p. 212.

[55] McCoy, 1973, p. 216.

Figure 374. "Tang Jiyao (1883 – 1927)." Unknown provenance.

a. Chinese and French Connections

The Ten Year Accord, reluctantly signed onto by the Chinese imperial government at the Shanghai Conference (1909), required the suppression of all poppy cultivation by 1920. As the government feared, the announcement was enough to vigorously stimulate secret societies; this and the weak, newly arrived Republican regime produced a plethora of feudal lords in the southern provinces. Specifically in Yunnan province (bordering Myanmar and Laos), the British and French supported the military governor, warlord and general Tang Jiyao (1883 – 1927), later succeeded by Long Yun (1927 – 1945). The policy of the warlords was to encourage poppy plantations as much as possible through severe labor tributes and taxes on the peasantry:

> By 1922, the only concrete result of the opium regulations was the rise in the drug's price and the subsequent introduction of morphine and heroin onto the market. ... The reports were uniformly the same; opium was enjoying a resurgence everywhere. ... All reports pointed to local warlords as the culprits. Warlords used creative methods to reintroduce and tax opium. Most generals followed the examples set in the European colonies. They created monopolies, imposed land taxes on poppy fields, and issued licensing fees. General Tang Jiyao of Yunnan ... instituted such a measure in his province, which soon became a major producer once again.[56]

The existing large Chinese populations in Southeast Asia were supplied from the Golden Triangle, a mountainous and agriculturally poor area where the prohibition had provoked intensive sowing of

---

[56] Meyer, Kathryn and Terry Parssinen. Webs of Smoke: Smuggler, Warlords, Spies, and the History of the International Drug Trade. Lanham, MD: Rowman & Littlefield Publishers, Inc., 1998 AA, Chapter Six Warlords 1916 – 1937, The Warlords, p. 144.

opium poppies. This area, bordering on the north the Yunnan plateau, ethnically Meo and Yeo, is ancestrally the home of poppy cultivation:

> Yunnan is an area that lends itself to the illegal traffic. It is remote from the centers of authority and blessed with a rugged, mountainous landscape beloved of poppy growers. It is an area of diverse ethnic groups located on China's southern border. From 1912 on Yunnan smugglers began to adapt to the new market. They developed routes to get their product to urban centers. ... The drug could also be smuggled into French Indochina to the south where it would be transshipped by sea from Haiphong to Hong Kong or Shanghai.[57]

During the turbulent period of the civil war between the nationalist Chiang Kai-shek and the revolutionary communist Mao Zedong (1893 – 1976) who founded the People's Republic of China, the history of opium is far from clear. It appears that the Shanghai Massacre of communist party members in 1927 was organized by opium traffickers who saw in communism a danger for their own interests:

> To appease the Western powers, the League of Nations, and the anti-opium activists within their own party, the Nationalists covered their opium policies with the rhetoric of suppression, a ploy that had been used elsewhere by the warlords, by Japan, and by European nations in their own colonies. ... Instead, in the name of suppression, Guomindang officials, led by Chiang Kai-shek's brother-in-law, T. V. Soong, in 1932 developed a thinly disguised monopoly that came to full form by May 1935. The government, needing funds to fight Communists and other opponents, gradually centralized the opium trade. ... The local market temporarily collapsed and the price of opium dropped when the Chinese Communists came through the area on their historic Long March.[58]

---

[57] Meyer, 1998, Chapter Two Merchants 1906 – 1919, Events in Yunnan Province, p. 54.

[58] Meyer, 1998, Chapter Six, Opium and the Nationalists, p. 155.

Chiang Kai-shek established a state monopoly on the drug until forced to nominally renounce the scheme under pressure from western allies. To appease them, in Shanghai he subleased control of the drug trade to one of the two largest secret societies:

These Shanghai criminal organizations were dominated by two secret society groups called the Green and Red Circles or Gangs. Secret societies, whether political, social or criminal, were traditionally an important force in Chinese society whenever central authority broke down. During the nineteenth century the Red and Green Gangs had drawn their membership from people involved in transporting grain and smuggling salt along the Grand Canal, China's primary north-south inland waterway. ... Shanghai had been an important Chinese center for the opium traffic since the 1840s, when Britain's victory in the Opium War opened the port to foreign trade and the establishment of foreign-controlled areas or concessions, which by the 1930s included almost a third of the city's 3.5 million people. The city's tradition of involvement in opium and other vices that tend to accompany the Western presence in Asia was tailor-made for the Green and Red Gangs. Both evolved into criminal organizations whose role in the narcotics trade and in the anti-Communist movement suggests parallels with the roles of the Sicilian Mafia and Corsican syndicate groups in Europe. ... Prior to 1918 Shanghai's opium traffic was based in the British concession, under the control of Chinese from the Swatow area of Kwangtung province. In 1918 the British concession cracked down on opium, depriving the Swatow group of its base and opening the traffic to takeover by the Green Gang operating from the French concession.[59]

The leader of the Green Gang (who doubled as a police officer[60]) was Huang Jinrong (Pockmarked Huang, 1868 – 1953), connected with the French Concession as well as exports to the United States:

---

[59] Adams, Leonard P. "Appendix China: The Historical Setting of Asia's Profitable Plague, The Tarnished Crusades," in McCoy, 1973 AA, p. 371.

[60] Lintner, Bertil. Blood Brothers: The Criminal Underworld of Asia. NY: Palgrave MacMillan, 2003 AA, Chapter One Whore of the East, p. 23.

Figure 375. "Huang Jinyong (1868 – 1953)." Unknown provenance.

> The French Concession harboured a roaring opium trade, the highest-ranking Chinese officer in the gendarmerie having a bigger stake in it than anyone. He was Huang Jinrong, running with the hare and hunting with the hounds. The French had cynically recognised the world of Shanghai for what it was, a jungle of bums, adventurers, opportunists and swindlers, where one culture had to dictate to another with neither side remotely understanding the other. To the French there were worse sins to a police force than having as its Chinese head a man who, by virtue of his influence in the underworld, kept the level of crime from brimming over.[61]

Inextricably linked with Huang Jinrong was Du Yuesheng (1888 – 1951), who ended opium hijacking by rival gangs and eliminated the communist threat in Shanghai:

> One of Du's most celebrated coups was to make gangland safe for opium. Because of the warring factions in the underworld, a consignment of opium suffered high risks of being hijacked by a rival gang at nearly every point in its passage from the ship to the warehouse. With immense skill and assurance, Du seized on a profit-sharing plan of operation which ended the banditry once and for all, and achieved a lasting peace in the underworld. A life of increasing political importance followed. By setting Green Gang toughs upon the communists in the 1927 uprising, he helped Chiang Kai-shek secure Shanghai for the Kuomintang. He was a supremely gifted arbitrator, and could be counted on by the Chinese, French and British alike to step in whenever there was a whiff of trouble in the air. There was no communist that could not be put out of action, no strike that could not be controlled. He became a dedicated nationalist, his sympathies reaching perhaps their clearest expression in the Sino-Japanese war ....[62]

Du Yuesheng became one of the

---

[61] Pan Ling. In Search of Old Shanghai. Hongkong: Joint Publishing Co., 1983 AA, p. 97.

[62] Pan Ling, 1983, pp. 97-98.

Figure 376. "Due Yuesheng (1888 – 1951)." Unknown provenance.

'Big Three' among the Shanghai gangsters, working with Pockmarked Huang and Chang Hsiao-lin [Zhang Xiaolin (1877 – 1940)]. This unholy triumvirate controlled the city's underworld in early 1927, when Chiang's Northern Expedition forces approached. ... In appreciation for their services and their delivered and anticipated performance as intermediaries between Chiang and the foreign community, the Big Three were appointed as 'honorary advisers' to the Nationalist government [quotation marks original].[63]

Figure 377. "The Three Bosses of Shanghai [L-R]: Zhang Xiaolin (1877 – 1940), Huang Jinyong (1868 – 1953) and Due Yuesheng (1888 – 1951)." Unknown provenance.

[63] Adams, in McCoy, 1973, pp. 372, 373.

To be fair, the largest volume of opium traffic occurred with the Japanese invasion of 1931, as Japan had for years been the principal client at the stifling Calcutta export market between 1920 and 1930, making acquisitions of enormous magnitude, many tons of which were destined for the production of morphine:

> At first, most of the morphine entering China came from Europe and the United States via Japan. While their government strictly controlled the drug at home, Japanese nationals began to sell morphine in China and then to manufacture it there. And by 1920, according to one estimate, enough was arriving annually via Japan alone to give every person in China four doses.[64]

After the creation of the puppet state of Manchuria, the Japanese high command followed the policy of inundating this and its other occupied territories with opium, morphine and heroin. The purpose, according to one author, was to endanger the

> morale and efficiency, not to mention the health of the native [Chinese] population ... just as, a century and more ago, Indian opium threatened and then demoralized large sections of the Chinese population. ... For the Japanese have been carrying on ... a 'new form of chemical warfare' .... Japan has undertaken an invasion of the country by drugs, which is just as deadly as bombardment in its devastation. The ghastly effect of this invasion by drugs is visible wherever the Japanese Army has been ... [in] a systematic effort to undermine the Chinese population by making new addicts and encouraging old consumers of opium [quotation marks original].[65]

Thus, prior to 1939, both to China and the United States two separate supply lines of opiates had been established and were functioning well until yoked by World War Two.

---

64 Adams, in McCoy, 1973, p. 366.

65 Goldsmith, Margaret. The Trail of Opium: The Eleventh Plague. London: Robert Hale Limited, 1939, Chapters 16, 17, pp. 226-227, 239-240.

b. Political Alliances

Now however the situation became quite delicate. Luciano had ended up being condemned to life imprisonment for pimping. It was then that fate, in the form of a world war, took a turn in his favor.

Luciano attended daily to a number of visitors in his jail cell, assisted by his attorney Moses Polakoff (1896 – 1993), formerly a high functionary in the police department and later that of the Attorney General. Through Polakoff, the US Secret Service became interested in the collaboration of the syndicate in the coming invasion of Sicily:

> American officials made a bargain with leaders of the Mafia to get criminal gangs to help in the invasion of Sicily. Mobsters were sprung from prison in exchange for their rallying the Mafia's covert army in Sicily and providing the ultimate in translator/guide services for U.S. military leaders. Lucky Luciano and Vito Genovese, mayber the two most powerful men in U.S. crime, both heavily into the dope business, were loosed on the world by such deals.[66]

The collaboration with the US government produced a commutation of his sentence and a deportation to Sicily for Luciano, where he went right back into business:

> Luciano was able to build an awesome international narcotics syndicate soon after his arrival in Italy. ... After resurrecting the narcotics traffic, Luciano's first problem was securing a reliable supply of heroin. ... Thanks to his contacts in the Middle East, Luciano ... protected raw opium from Turkey's Anatolian plateau into Lebanon, its processing into morphine base, and its final export to the laboratories in Sicily and Marseille.[67]

---

[66] Kwitny, 1987, Chapter Three The Golden Triangle, p. 44.

[67] McCoy, 1973, Luciano Organizes the Postwar Heroin Trade, pp. 24-25.

After his death in 1962 the body was later returned to the US.[68]

Genovese was extradited back to the US for murder and died in prison. Polakoff retired from syndicate business, but not before recommending a lawyer to the all-powerful Lansky, a curious successor, the young congressman Nixon who would go on to excel in other endeavors before ascending to the Presidency of the United States in 1969. Naturally, the end of the war reestablished both the French and the Asian connections with the syndicate.

But this was not the end of the mutual aid between the political and criminal estates. Postwar, the forerunner of the Central Intelligence Agency (CIA) known as the Office of Strategic Services (OSS) made two decisions that strengthened their connections to the syndicate. The first was to support the Corsican gangsters' control of the docks in the south of France, apparently out of fear that socialist trade unions would support a communist strike:

> [I]n the late 1940s, the OSS/CIA became alarmed that the socialist leaders of the dock unions in southern France might side with Communist political movements. There was fear that strikes might redound against the Christian Democratic governments the United States was supporting. To forestall this threat, the United States conducted a vast covert operation to put control of the dock unions in the hands of Corsican gangsters, and take them out of the hands of the socialist unions. The operation was funded by contributions that the State Department helped wheedle out of large American corporations, and it was aided further by the international division of the AFL-CIO. It concentrated particularly on the prime French port of Marseille. It worked. But besides chasing socialists out of power, the gangsters arranged the port's affairs for their own illicit business.[69]

---

[68] The inscription on his tomb at Section 3, Row C, Grave 10, Section 003 in New York's Saint John Cemetery and Mausoleum reads: *Il Nostro Caro Fratello Salvatore Lucania, Nato L'11 Novembre 1898, Morto Il 26 Gennaio 1962* [Findagrave.com, hereinafter FG].

[69] Kwitny, 1987, pp. 44-45.

The maneuver succeeded and the Guerini brothers, Antoine (1902 – 1967) and Barthélemy (Mémé, 1908 – 1982) became the undisputed power in Marseilles.

The second was to supply and protect defeated Chinese Kuomintang (KMT) anti-communist troops taking refuge in the Golden Triangle when the Chinese civil war ended. Claiming that these groups could obstruct Mao and even reconquer the country, the CIA mounted in 1949 two cargo airlines (the Civil Air Transport, based in Taiwan, and the Sea Supply Corporation, based out of Bangkok) when

> the remnants of Chiang Kai-shek's crumbling western armies were chased out of China's Yunnan Province by the Communist Revolution. Thousands of these defeated soldiers from Chiang's Kuomintang, or KMT, government, melted into the jungles of neighboring Burma. Burma didn't want the KMT soldiers any more than their native country did. But when Burma threatened to chase the cornered KMT out, the U.S. Government decided the KMT were needed, to harass and possibly even reconquer China .... So the CIA began supplying the KMT through two front companies: Civil Air Transport, headquartered in Taiwan, and Sea Supply Corporation, headquartered in Bangkok. Only a few people with top security clearance knew that both companies were covertly owned by the U.S. Government.[70]

Like the Corsican gangsters in Marseilles, the KMT helped transform the Golden Triangle into one of the largest single opium exporting regions for the American market and the world: "By the end of the 1950s, Burma, Laos, and Thailand together had become a massive producer, and the source of more than half the world's present illicit supply of 1,250 to 1,400 tons annually. Moreover, with this increase in output the region of the Far East and Southeast Asia

[70] Kwitny, 1987, pp. 45-46.

quickly became self-sufficient in opium."[71] In the opinion of the American Professor of History at the University of Wisconsin-Madison Alfred W. McCoy (b. 1945), who conducted an exhaustive investigation (not without many attempts by the Agency to halt his research and publication), from the very beginning the CIA knew the Kuomintang were collecting opium taxes on the Meo and marketing the substance through Thailand. To be exact, its principal contact for these ends was General Phao Sriyanond (1910 – 1960), the director general of the Thai Police, the CIA's man in Thailand because he was "Thailand's most ardent anti-Communist."[72] Neither is this all because in 1954 when the US decided to inherit the deteriorating French position in Vietnam, the CIA again cooperated decisively in a connection between Saigon and the Golden Triangle providing logistical support for a corrupt local oligarchy of a dozen Corsican gangsters who greased the skids for a systematic export of heroin on the part of Ngo Dinh Nhu (1910 – 1963), brother of President Ngo Dinh Diem (1901 – 1963), the American installed puppet:[73]

When Ngo Dinh Nhu, brother and chief adviser of South Vietnam's late president, Ngo Dinh Diem, decided to revive the opium traffic to finance his repression of mounting armed insurgency and political dissent, he used Vietnamese intelligence agents operating in Laos and Indochina's Corsican underworld as his contacts. From 1958 to 1960 Nhu relied mainly on small Corsican charter airlines for transport, but in 1961-1962 he also used the First Transport Group (which was then flying intelligence missions into Laos for the CIA and was under the control of Nguyen Cao Ky) to ship raw opium to Saigon.[74]

---

[71] McCoy, 1973, Chapter 4 Cold War Opium Boom, p. 145, quoting U.S. Bureau of Narcotics and Dangerous Drugs, "The World Opium Situation," p. 29.

[72] McCoy, 1973, p. 139.

[73] Kwitny, 1987, p. 50.

[74] McCoy, 1973, p. 153.

All this occurs before a large increase in the number of heroin addicts is detected in the United States.

Figure 378. "Vice President Lyndon Johnson greets Ngo Dinh Nhu." Gia Long Palace, Saigon, 12 May 1961. USIA, LBJ Library.

3. The Therapeutic Estate

The liberal reaction to the draconian laws was not long in coming. The AMA and the ABA convened a joint committee in 1955. They published their conclusions four years later. The FBN attacked the report while dope fiends began to proliferate.

a. The ABA/AMA Report

The Interim *and* Final Reports of the Joint Committee of the American Bar Association and the American Medical Association on Narcotic Drugs (1958 – 1959) was later edited in the form of a book, Drug Addiction: Crime or Disease (1961) with a cautious and modest prologue by University of Indiana professor of sociology Alfred Ray Lindesmith (1905 – 1991). This document considered the drug policies followed until then counterproductive, denouncing the clichés in vogue as unsustainable prejudices, insisting on the investigation of cures or treatments in place of punishment for addiction, and lamenting the unjust and unconstitutional legislation lacking the formal and substantive requirements for any statute in a country governed by the rule of law:

> Its principal conclusions are two: that present methods of dealing with narcotic addiction and narcotic addicts raise questions which are urgently in need of study; and that the legal and medical professions, equally concerned, can most fruitfully pursue the subject in close cooperation through their respective associations. ... It does not attempt to provide solutions, but does reflect a degree of dissatisfaction within the legal and medical professions concerning current policies which tend to emphasize repression and prohibition to the exclusion of other possible methods of dealing with addicts and the drug traffic. ... Though drug peddling is acknowledged to be a vicious and predatory crime, a grave question remains whether severe jail and prison sentences are the most rational way of dealing with narcotic addicts. And the

unusual statutory basis of present drug-law enforcement, substantial federal domination in a local police-power field established by means of an excise measure enforced by a federal fiscal agency, invites critical scrutiny. ... There must be a new determination of the limits of good medical practice in the treatment of drug addiction, and an objective inquiry into the question whether existing enforcement policies, practices and attitudes, as well as existing laws, have unduly or improperly interfered with good medical practice in this area.[75]

It was the most serious attack suffered up to then by the prohibitionists, not only due to the prestige and political clout of the intervening organizations, but also because heroes like McCarthy and Anslinger had managed to exasperate the cultured sectors of American society. This reaction became crystallized in the so-called New Left movement, which wished to recover the original principles of the American republic, harmonizing them with ideas from European socialist thought.

The principal thesis of these reports was that the crusade against drugs was a pseudomedical and pseudolegal enterprise, which instead of solving the problems of marginalization had produced them. The American sociologist and one of the so-called founding fathers of modern sociology Robert King Merton (Meyer Robert Schkolnick, 1910 – 2003) had just finished publishing his Social Structure and Social Theory (1949), one of the definitive books of the era, in which among others he develops the concept of the self-fulfilling prophecy:

---

[75] King, Rufus, Chairman, Joint Committee of the American Bar Association and the American Medical Association on Narcotic Drugs. Drug Addiction: Crime or Disease? Interim *and* Final Reports. Bloomington, IN: Indiana University Press, 1971 AA, Final Report of the Joint Committee of the American Bar Association and the American Medical Association on Narcotic Drugs, pp. 160, 161, 163, 164.

> [P]ublic definitions of a situation (prophecies or predictions) become an integral part of the situation and thus affect subsequent developments. This is peculiar to human affairs. It is not found in the world of nature. Predictions of the return of Halley's comet do not influence its orbit.[76]

The ABA/AMA reports served to amplify this concept, presenting the results of the pharmacological crusade as the consequences of circular reasoning, where a certain image of reality is imposed upon it, and then is presented as an independent effect of the imposition. This is also known as the Thomas Theorem, after the American sociologist William Isaac Thomas (1863 – 1947): "If men define situations as real, they are real in their consequences."[77] The phenomenon of the self-fulfilling prophecy with regards to drug criminalization is based on the fact that (even given adequate means of coercion)

> the policy of criminalizing certain drugs constitutes a self-referential system, a system that reproduces itself both ideologically and materially. By ideological reproduction is understood here the general mechanism by which each actor or group of actors within the system finds confirmation in their own image of the reality of the attitude of the other actors. This mechanism can be symbolized as a circle: it deals with, in effect, a circular process in which each actor depends upon the others, in such a way that this dependence makes any modification of their own image of reality or their attitude difficult or improbable [tr. gwr].[78]

---

[76] Merton, Robert K. Social Theory and Social Structure: Toward the Codification of Theory and Research. Glencoe, IL: The Free Press, 1949 AA, Part II, Chapter VII The Self-Fulfilling Prophecy, p. 181.

[77] Merton, 1949, p. 179.

[78] *la política de criminalización ... difícil o improbable una modificación de la propia imagen de la realidad y de su actitud* (Baratta, Alessandro. "*Introducción a la Criminología de la Droga,*" tr. Mauricio Martinez, *Comunidad y droga*, 3, 1988 AA, 1. La Política Actual de Criminalización de las Drogas como Sistema Cerrado y Autoreproductivo, p. 329).

Indistinguishable from the crusades against heresy and witchcraft, the pharmacological crusade creates and maintains the problem it pretends to want to solve, ignoring the intimate correlation existing between so-called drug abuse and the fact of declaring certain drugs abusable and illegal. According to the ABA/AMA reports, no prohibition can suppress the consumption of a particular drug, as summarily demonstrated in the experiences of both China and America. The only thing it had achieved was to modify the structure of the consuming population; in consequence, one could not attribute to any given substance the fact that its users were adolescents, criminals or undesirables, because this would be to take an effect for a cause. Such a thing depended on the existing repressive policy, not the reverse.

The Interim Report included two appendices. The first appendix critiqued the current repressive legislation, describing the inoperability of existing US laws filling the prisons:

> no matter how severe law enforcement may be, the drug traffic cannot be eliminated under present prohibitory repressive statutes. ... Strict law enforcement and severe penalties are therefore not the easy answers to problems of drug addiction. We must look elsewhere for a rational drug control program for this country. ... Mere possession of a narcotic drug which the addict must have to ward off withdrawal distress is a violation of the narcotic laws. Thus, every drug addict is subject to arrest by the police, and as we have seen, the arrests of addicts and of narcotic law violators have gone up by leaps and bounds. Addicts guilty of no other crime than illegal possession of narcotics are filling the jails, prisons and penitentiaries of the country.[79]

---

[79] Ploscowe, Morris. "Appendix A: Some Basic Problems in Drug Addiction and Suggestions for Research," in Drug Addiction: Crime or Disease? Interim *and* Final Reports of the American Bar Association and the American Medical Association on Narcotic Drugs. Bloomington, IN: Indiana University Press, 1971, pp. 21, 22, 64.

It also criticized the current policy in the US where "the physician has largely been deprived of an appropriate role in the treatment of drug addicts."[80] Despite an exception in the *Harrison Act*,

> in favor of physicians many doctors were subjected to criminal prosecution because of the charge that their treatment of and prescription for drug addicts was not legitimate 'professional practice' within the meaning of the Act. Targets of the initial prosecution were doctors who had many addict patients for whom they prescribed large amounts of drugs. Such doctors were charged with the illegal sale of narcotics in violation of the Act [quotation marks original].[81]

Judicial precedents "enabled the Narcotics Bureau to prosecute many physicians, and unquestionably resulted in most doctors leaving the narcotic addict severely alone."[82]

Nor did institutionalization in narcotics' clinics work: "The statistics on relapse to addiction after attempted cures at narcotics hospitals like Lexington, Fort Worth or Riverside tell the stark story of the basic failure of the hospital centered approach in dealing with problems of drug addiction."[83]

Confirming the proposal of the New York State Medical Society "for the legalization of the distribution of narcotics to addicts,"[84] this appendix supported the existence of maintenance clinics, noting that other "physicians and medical societies have favored the establishment of narcotic clinics, where drugs could be legally dispensed to addicts" and that cures should be attempted

---

80 Ploscowe, 1971, IX. Methods of Treatment of Drug Addiction, 1. The Doctor and the Drug Addict, p. 69.

81 Ploscowe, 1971, p. 70.

82 Ploscowe, 1971, p. 73.

83 Ploscowe, 1971, p. 88.

84 King, 1971, Interim Report, Background, p. 5.

"through voluntary hospitalization, if possible," avoiding "forcible confinement."[85]

The second appendix praised the English method of treating addicts as much for its practical results as for its fundamental theory:

> England (and the U. K. countries which follow her pattern) has no significant drug-addiction problem, no organized illicit trafficking, and no drug-law enforcement activities that could be regarded as comparable to those which preoccupy our own authorities. The key to this difference appears to be that the British medical profession is in full and virtually unchallenged control of the distribution of drugs, and this includes distribution, by prescription or administration, to addicts when necessary. The police function is to aid and protect medical control, rather than to substitute for it.[86]

In 1960 British addicts could acquire morphine or heroin free of charge from a number of physicians working in the National Health Service, or from other doctors as well. According to the law then in effect in Britain, an addict under the care of a physician was a person in treatment, even though he might have returned to using the drug:

> The controlling fact is that the medical profession accepts and treats addicts as patients so that virtually none are driven to support a black market; the prime corollary is that if all curative efforts fail the incurable addict may still be provided for on a medically-supervised regime; and the remarkable consequence is that the number of persons in the incurable or extended-regime category – out of Britain's population of over fifty millions – remains year after year in the range between three and four hundred. At the end of 1956 the figure was 333.[87]

---

[85] Ploscowe, 1971, XI. The Suggested Clinics for Legal Narcotics Distribution, p. 93.
[86] King, Rufus. "Appendix B: An Appraisal of International, British and Selected European Narcotic Drug Laws, Regulations and Policies," Drug Addiction, 1971, Great Britain, p. 127.
[87] King, 1971, pp. 127-128.

Further, the purity and low cost of the product prevented deaths from adulteration and serious crime.

At the end of the 1950s a number of specific investigations were initiated to try to answer whether or not the opiates produce paradisiacal mental states from the outset, with immediate changes in metabolism requiring new doses either organically and/or psychologically. Although the results still lacked something definitive and concrete, it was soon clear that these studies would contravene the FBN's cliché of euphoria causing addiction.

Indeed, healthy subjects experienced displeasure or nothing when given repeated doses of heroin. Only three hospitalized patients experienced euphoria, with few wishing to repeat the experience:

> The majority of normal subjects, young men ranging in age from twenty-one to twenty-seven, in controlled studies of response to drugs, reported displeasure or experienced no effects on their moods from initial injection of heroin or morphine. Pleasure was experienced by only the minority of nonaddicts; the typical response was indifference or actual dislike. Those subjects who received second injections of morphine or heroin had essentially the same reactions as they did to their first. There is no evidence that repeating the experience enhances the acceptability or liking of these drugs. ... Hospitalized men and women, ranging in age from forty-five to eighty-seven, chronically ill with malignant disease or neurological disorder, described their responses to the injections of drugs. Only one-third felt happy (or 'happier') after injections of heroin or morphine. Since the same proportion felt happy (or 'happier') after the injection of a placebo, there is no evidence that the opiates are inherently euphoriant even for individuals suffering from pain or the distress of chronic illness. Indeed, the use of morphine for relief of pain is rarely followed by euphoria; only three of 150 postoperative patients ... had genuine euphoria following morphine, although a larger minority felt 'pleased' for relief of their pain [quotation marks original].[88]

---

[88] Chien, Isidor et al. The ROAD to H: Narcotics, Delinquency, and Social Policy. NY: Basic Books, *Inc. Publishers*, 1964 AA, Chapter XIV *Some Matters of Perspective* (II),

Thus, the current legislation was not only opposed to the opinions of doctors and lawyers (as well as the consciences of judges and mayors) but also to all the social science disciplines grouped together, a serious adversary indeed. Noticing the faltering zeal of the state, associations of parents also challenged the tiresome war on drugs. These associations soon had as many members as the Anti-Saloon League, and then many more. It is significant that this confederation initially saw social science as an enemy to be fought but that with the course of time it became a boss to be manipulated.[89]

Figure 379. "Pot Bust, Brooklyn, 1938." *NY Daily News*, 28 Aug 2019.

Individual Responses to Drugs, pp. 347-348.

[89] *de un enemigo al que combatir a un jefe al que es preciso manipular* (Comas Arnau, Domingo. "*La Medida de la Incidencia, Prevalencia y Problemas Causados por Drogas Ilegales*," REIS 1986 [dialnet.uniroja.es, hereinafter DUE], p. 59).

b. Pharmacratic Ideology

The response from the FBN was predictable. The editors of the ABA/AMA report were accused of conniving with traffickers, irresponsibility and a lack of patriotism. Anslinger's FBN made dire predictions about the future of a country confused by pointy-headed liberals. Now the agency would not only have to struggle against a plague of dope fiends, but against their defenders in the medical, legal and judicial estates, more attentive to leftist intellectual utopias than the principles of the American Dream.

Prior to and indeed motivating the publication of the ABA/AMA reports,

> a comprehensive attack upon it was published in 1959 by the federal Bureau of Narcotics. The sale of this pamphlet was discontinued after an attack upon the Supreme Court which it contained was given unfavorable newspaper publicity, but by this time the document had already been widely circulated to libraries and law enforcement officials throughout the country.[90]

But from the second half of the decade of the 1950s it began to be empirically indefensible that the cause of an addiction was solely due to a particular illegal substance (heroin, morphine, opium and so forth). As in cases of alcoholism, contracting a habit was not at all independent of a person's psychopathology:

---

[90] Lindesmith, Alfred R. "Introduction" in Drug Addiction, 1971, pp. x-xi; see also Comments on Narcotic Drugs: Interim Report of the Joint Committee of the American Bar Association and the American Medical Association on Narcotic Drugs by Advisory Committee to the Federal Bureau of Narcotics, US, Treasury Department, Bureau of Narcotics. Washington, DC: Government Printing Office, 1959.

> Personality classifications have been made on large groups of addicts. ... Among the addicts studied at Lexington and in city and state prisons there is a preponderance of psychopaths, whereas they make up only a small percentage of the patients examined in private institutions. ... But the majority of patients come under the classification of constitutional psychopathic inferior, character disorder or psychoneurosis. Some workers in the field of drug addiction believe that all addicts might well be classified as sub-clinical schizophrenics. Their severe obsessional preoccupation with drugs and the destructiveness of their pursuits in an otherwise normal personality are so bizarre as to be strongly suggestive of schizophrenia. In support of this theory, it may be pointed out that patients whose behavior is so negligibly guided by reality reveal the disordered thinking characteristic of that condition. This is further confirmed by observation in a number of post-addicts of psychosis which disappears with the administration of morphine.[91]

Already in 1957 the disagreement between the psychoanalytic and pharmacological approaches to addiction had been correctly observed:

> This disagreement is perhaps based on the psychoanalyst's use of metaphor and observation, as opposed to the pharmacologist's precise language and research design. The psychoanalyst looks for large patterns, while the pharmacologist is more likely to look for measurable effects. These two approaches actually complement each other, since the addict is a person with certain personality characteristics who happens to have selected this way of coping with his problems for a variety of reasons, of which he is usually unaware. Not the least of these reasons is his access to a social group in which drug use was both practiced and valued.[92]

Further, a person prone to becoming dependent upon opiates was plagued with unpleasant sensations, and one of his more obvious

---

[91] Nyswander, Marie. *The Drug Addict as a Patient*. NY: Grune & Stratton, 1956 AA, Chapter IV. Psychology, The Addict's Personality, Psychiatric Diagnosis, p. 62.

[92] Winnick, Charles. "Narcotic Addiction and its Treatment," *Law and Contemporary Problems*, Volume 22, Winter 1957, p. 22.

characteristic mental states was the attempt to overcome anxiety with short term solutions. That someone could use an opiate in order to overcome a crisis, and then abandon it, is unthinkable for the prohibitionist. Yet this has always been the principal therapeutic use of opium and its derivatives from the beginning of time, and such cases were not the exception but the rule before illegalization.

Thought impossible, not until the 1960s would there be a questionnaire which (with a satisfactory guarantee of secrecy) asked the subject to mark two distinct boxes, one if he had ever administered heroin, and another if he had administered it in the last week. No one had ever asked such a thing before, because officially only junkies in the ceremonial sense can exist as users of opiates. However, the result (which we will discuss in the next chapter) was sixteen to one for the unthinkable. In other words, in spite of the manner in which both the social stigma and the conditions necessary to access these drugs had converted their consumption into a symbol of pure satanism, the cases of voluntary abandonment (not as a consequence of institutional so-called treatment) were far superior to those in which an irresistible magnetism was alleged from the first dose.

In spite of his vociferous protests, Anslinger anticipated that the courts would soon declare some disagreeable novelty, and under the circumstances the best option was to take advantage of the unconditional support of Congress and the Executive. If these anti-prohibitionist ideals were ever adopted, he argued, the need for more control would skyrocket. To avoid demoralization in his Bureau, and panic in the country, it was necessary to drastically increase his budget.

His reasoning was accepted without dissent, and in the early 1960s the number of agents in the FBN grew from three hundred to three thousand, rising before the end of the decade to ten thousand. This increase in personnel and what it would result in were the ultimate legacy of the man known as the so-called Prohibition Czar for his ability to influence both national and international events. A year later, upon his retirement, he restricted his efforts to presiding over the American delegation to international organizations dedicated to the criminalization of drugs, using his free time to write his memoirs.

In reality, he was encouraged to resign by a new mentality in Congress, once a hotbed of prohibitionism. The everyday user of opiates was not some diabolical being who was attempting to devour children (as was said of the witches in the middle ages), hooking them for the sake of it, or a communist infiltrating elementary schools, but someone who precisely because of these clichés justified himself before his family, friends and the larger society in the midst of his own existential anguish:

> This latent anguish bedevils the addict and produces, at bottom, a cynical attitude toward his life. To become completely interchangeable and replaceable, like peat in a bog, and really to have no personal justification that will stand up to inquiry even by himself, in the long run means he must fall short when judged by what might be called existential standards, the standards of the good and valid life. The way seems open only to hopeless nihilism or else to a resolute decision to be responsible to oneself. It is one of the ironies of drug addiction that a man is compelled, even against his will, to feed his habit, and then to rationalize this as a form of responsibility. But even this feeling of pride in maintaining one's habit yields to a deeper feeling of being indispensable only in a limited way, of being a creature to oneself or at least to a fraction of oneself. In sum, the addict experiences the anguish of being incomplete.[93]

The user of opiates felt like a powerless victim before police persecution. Reduced to essentials, he simply dramatized a cry for

---

[93] Fiddle, Seymour. Portraits from a Shooting Gallery: Life Styles from the Drug Addict World. NY: Harper and Row, Publishers, 1967 AA, Chapter Two Notes on the Heroin Addict and His Culture, A Life of Contingency: A Dispensable Being, pp. 37-38.

help, the desire for death and the lack of courage to take the decisive step.

At this moment there was no other choice for the FBN but to risk an even more public war with the judicial, medical and scientific estates or to make certain concessions, in other words, to grant said estates certain powers while making sure not to lose those of their own. This point of view is enshrined in the preamble to the Single Convention of 1961 which recognizes that the medical use of drugs continues to be indispensable for mitigating pain and that their availability must be guaranteed: "that the medical use of narcotic drugs continues to be indispensable for the relief of pain and suffering and that adequate provision must be made to ensure the availability of narcotic drugs for such purposes ...."[94] After the US signed the treaty, the FBN had no choice but to devolve part of their prerogatives to the medical estate, in exchange for proceeding without popular scandal. In return the FBN would dedicate itself (finally) to proceeding against the large traffickers, without molesting the work of physicians and pharmacists through entrapment.

In addition to this general renovation, a year later the United States Supreme Court rendered a majority opinion (with one abstention and two dissents) that a law punishing addiction was cruel and unusual, reasoning that addicts were not criminal monsters but simply people who were sick. Associate Justice William Orville Douglas (1898 – 1980) wrote in one of the two concurring opinions: "I do not see how under our system being an addict can be punished as a crime. If addicts can be punished for their addiction, then the

---

[94] Single Convention on Narcotic Drugs, 1961, as amended by the 1972 Protocol amending the Single Convention on Narcotic Drugs, 1961 [United Nations, unodc.org, hereinafter UN], Preamble, p. 1.

insane can also be punished for their insanity. Each has a disease and each must be treated as a sick person."[95]

Thus, after various decades of legal uncertainty, the Supreme Court finally equated the status of the habitual user of illegal drugs with that of the habitual alcohol drinker under the Dry Law. From 1914 certain drugs had been prosecuted as the ancients had persecuted impurity, judging any person involved to be contaminated. Now it was considered inevitable to distinguish traffickers from users.

Figure 380. "William Orville Douglas (1898 – 1980)." B&W film negative, Harris & Ewing, 1930. Library of Congress Prints and Photographs Division, LG.

[95] *Robinson v. California*, 370 U.S. 660 (1962), at 674 [justicia.com, hereinafter JU].

c. The Dope Fiend

While before 1920 perhaps ninety-nine percent of people who did not assiduously use opiates or cocaine believed in dope fiends (being for this reason a typical case of passive belief), from the middle of the 1950s there is hardly any consumer of these drugs who does not wrap himself in the flag and creed of the dope fiend (swallowing whole an active belief in the cliché). Representing a complete inversion with respect to the typical heroin user at the beginning of the century (who only maintained his vice in secret and used the drug to better fulfill his domestic and work obligations), the manifesto of this guild (logically anterior to the diffusion of this attitude) can be found in the work of Burroughs:

> The question is frequently asked: Why does a man become a drug addict? The answer is that he usually does not intend to become an addict. You don't wake up one morning and decide to be a drug addict. It takes at least three months' shooting twice a day to get any habit at all. And you don't really know what junk sickness is until you have had several habits. It took me almost six months to get my first habit, and then the withdrawal symptoms were mild. I think it no exaggeration to say it takes about a year and several hundred injections to make an addict. The questions, of course, could be asked: Why did you ever try narcotics? Why did you continue using it long enough to become an addict? You become a narcotics addict because you do not have strong motivations in any other direction. Junk wins by default. I tried it as a matter of curiosity. I drifted along taking shots when I could score. I ended up hooked. Most addicts I have talked to report a similar experience. They did not start using drugs for any reason they can remember. They just drifted along until they got hooked. If you have never been addicted, you can have no clear idea what it means to need junk with the addict's special need. You don't decide to be an addict. One morning you wake up sick and you're an addict.[96]

---

[96] Burroughs, William S. Junky. London: Penguin Books Ltd., 1977 AA, Prologue, p. xv.

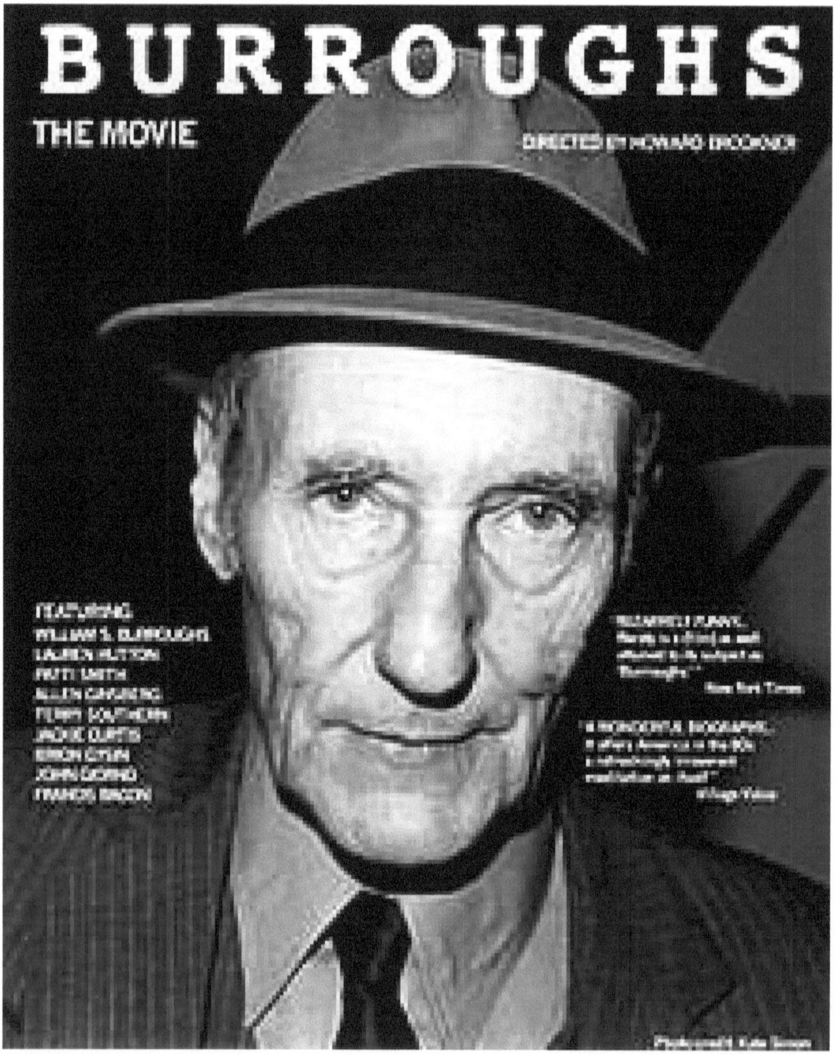

Figure 381. "Burroughs." Movie Poster, 1983 [imdb.org, hereinafter IMDB].

A self-described "intellectual dilettante" journalist investigating adolescent heroin users in England in the 1960s was struck by their desire for publicity:

> It has been remarked that the most striking characteristic of the new adolescent addicts is their desire for publicity. The inquirer, thinking that it is going to be difficult to meet drug users, is immediately overwhelmed by them showing off their spiritual sores like medieval beggars; willing to discuss their most intimate affairs at exhaustive, and soon tedious, length. It is clearly no use being drug dependent in London unless one is seen to be so.[97]

One addict saw in his addiction a release from a deadening middle-class existence:

> 'Man, wouldn't I love to lead a decent life – all us junkies would. But man! Don't you see? I'm a junkie, I'm hooked, I can't get away, I can't wash/earn a living/get up/make the breakfast/pay income tax. I need my shots. Oh monkey, get off my back, man.'[98]

A convincing and nuanced analysis of the mythology of addiction highlights the secondary benefits derived from adopting the same image constructed by prohibitionist ideologues. The junkie not only buys into a very precious social good such as irresponsibility, but also a specific kind of time management (injecting his dosis many times a day), as well as a form of dress and speech, within a group of equals to whom he can relate. The world of the contemporary addict is reduced to its essentials which Burroughs describes as the *Algebra of Need*:

---

[97] Laurie, 1967, Chapter 4 Attitudes to Opiates, *The British Addict's Life*, p. 51.

[98] Laurie, 1967, p. 48.

Figure 382. "Allen Ginsberg, Lucien Carr and William S. Burroughs." Foto Universidad de Arizona. Cedillo, Jaime. "*William S. Burroughs, el más sangriento de la generación 'beat,'*" *El Cultural*, 1 agosto 2022 [El Español.com, hereinafter EE].

The face of 'evil' is always the face of total need. A dope fiend is a man in total need of dope. Beyond a certain frequency need knows absolutely no limit or control. In the words of total need: 'Wouldn't you?' Yes you would. You would lie, cheat, inform on your friends, steal, do anything to satisfy total need. Because you would be in a state of total sickness, total possession, and not in a position to act in any other way. Dope fiends are sick people who cannot act other than they do [quotation marks original].[99]

---

[99] Burroughs, William S. Naked Lunch. London: Harper Collins *Publishers*, 1993 AA, Introduction *deposition: testimony concerning a sickness*, p. 8.

CH. 26 LATENCY

Existence is simplified to only two things: walking the streets in search of the drug, and then administering it with all due ceremony:

> The knowledgeable addict – in this case a writer – pursues a different system. He entertains his visitors with the ritual of the fix; boils up a pill of heroin in a medicine bottle – tension, will the glass break in the flame? Then he wraps a mysterious, spittle-wetted strip of paper round the nose of an eye-dropper, produces a hypodermic needle and shoves it over the paper. Then he sucks up the dissolved heroin into the dropper and balances it precariously on the edge of the table. Another cliff-hanging situation: will it fall? But the intrepid Scotsman coolly removes his belt – more tension, the trousers – then winds it round his left bicep. Pulling it tight with his teeth, he massages up a vein in the crook of his elbow, and then with great delicacy slides the needle into the swollen vessel. Here he explains the advantage of the dropper – the pressure of the thumb and forefinger in expelling the liquid balance each other and act across the axis of the needle, so it neither goes in nor comes out. The pressure needed to work an ordinary syringe tends to drive the needle through the vein and into the elbow joint where the heroin does little good, and invariably causes pain. That all the drug cannot be squeezed out of the eye-dropper is also turned to advantage: the belt is released and the arm allowed to fall; pulsing, the dropper fills with blood. He squeezes this back, lets it fill, squeezes and whips the needle out letting a little spurt of blood run down his arm. He dries this 'splash,' conversing casually of other matters [quotation marks original].[100]

The fact that the junkie does not know the interviewer, who is only received as someone interested in knowing things about the underground, spares him from other parts of the common ritual. For example, imperious pleas to help tighten the tourniquet along with sincere laments for not being able to find a vein. The ceremony normally includes a complex series of acts that often ends with the frustration of having left out some of the product (where it burns and does not alleviate), or with the triumph of getting others to participate

[100] Laurie, 1967, pp. 52-53.

in various phases of it, holding one apparatus or another, witnessing the details of a routine operation, which for this reason feels like so much more. This ritual celebration has been maintained practically unchanged from the end of the 1950s, as an initiation rite for those inclined to join the brotherhood of dope fiends, and has not ceased to pique the curiosity of every kind of tourist.

Figure 383. "Alexander Trocchi (1925 – 1984)." Photograph by Marvin Lichtner, 1967, *Time* & *Life* Pictures. Munson, Sam. "The Outsiders' Insider," NY Times, 7 Sep 2008 [nytimes.com, hereinafter NYT].

Some additional facts illustrate the importance of the mythic/ritual aspect of the junkie lifestyle. For example, addicts prefer to buy eighths of a gram (at a much higher price, with inferior quality and with the tiresomeness of going out four times a day in search of product) rather than acquire quantities that would allow them autonomy for weeks or months, certainly much cheaper and more pure; the unspoken motive behind this strange habit is the use of time, or if you prefer, the fact of having one's time full, because the junkie described by Burroughs or Trocchi never feels more himself than when he is in search of a fix. In the same way, he prefers to use heroin of a lesser quality than the best, if it means he has to use the latter in some manner other than intravenously, even though his pretension is to need the drug and nothing but the drug.

The attraction of this mythologized ritual can even be seen in the purely allegorical, the multitude of cases of faked addiction:

> One of Narcotics Anonymous' ... first customers was a pale eighteen-year-old from Leeds who had stupefied himself on barbiturates, but insisted he was a real junkie. He carried, to prove the point, a gigantic chromium-plated veterinary syringe for injecting high-class cows. He had never used it, nor would dare to.[101]

> [An American jazz musician] was admitted to hospital a second time with hepatitis. Since he used junkie slang in his speech, it was suspected that he might be an addict .... This character admitted shamefully that he had tried heroin twice and hadn't enjoyed it either time; he begged his doctors not to tell his wife or family since he would lose the status of being hooked. His need for psychic dependence on a drug – any drug – was so great that they could get him to abide by the regimen for hepatitis only by convincing him this too was being hooked and added to his strength and character.[102]

---

[101] Laurie, 1967, p. 48.

[102] Laurie, 1967, Chapter 4 Attitudes to Opiates, pp. 48-49, quoting Zinberg, N. E. and Lewis, D. C. *New England Journal of Medicine*, 270, 1964, pp. 989, 1045.

A journalist of twenty-five years who became a junkie described the essence of his role, saying, "'As long as you eat and sleep, you're ahead of the game. Anything else in this life is a bonus.'"[103] Thou shalt have no other god before me is the credo of the prohibited church, and the most interesting part of the previous testimony is that the speaker only temporarily was caught up in the algebra of need. In his own words: "The thing about H – it makes it unnecessary to worry about the things you have been worrying about. So you stop worrying, but the very fact you're not worrying means you don't have to worry. So after a bit I didn't need H, and I gave it up."[104]

Burroughs also records his awakening from addiction using the apomorphine cure:

> I awoke from The Sickness at the age of forty-five, calm and sane, and in reasonably good health except for a weakened liver and the look of borrowed flesh common to all who survive The Sickness. ... The Sickness is drug addiction and I was an addict for fifteen years. ... The vaccine that can relegate the junk virus to a land-locked past is in existence. This vaccine is the Apomorphine Treatment .... I saw the apomorphine treatment really work. Eight days later I left the nursing home eating and sleeping normally. I remained completely off junk for two full years – a twelve year record. I did relapse for some months as a result of pain and illness. Another apomorphine cure has kept me off junk through this writing [capitalization original].[105]

In the guild of addicts there is no shortage of those with singular eloquence, like Trocchi, for whom the essence of the habit was not to take or not take something but to keep himself occupied so as to distract from the "desert at the centre of his being."[106] Both he

---

[103] Laurie, 1967, p. 53.

[104] Laurie, 1967, p. 46.

[105] Burroughs, 1993, pp. 7, 9, 11.

[106] Trocchi, Alexander. Cain's Book. London: John Calder, 1992 AA p. 78.

and Burroughs observed the prevailing system with a caustic wit, with more truth than humor, describing a profit driven global conspiracy:

> Drugs are the ultimate merchandise, Burroughs has written, and he sees addiction as part of the global conspiracy by the presiding powers of our world – the media conglomerates, the vast political and commercial bureaucracies, and a profit-driven medical science – which are determined to reduce us to the total dependency of addicts, while teasing us with the mirage of transgressive sex.[107]

Trocchi points out that scapegoating young drug users as juvenile delinquents is not only a necessary consequence of the criminalization of the drug but also that it supports the entire drug abuse industrial complex:

> It's a nice tangible cause for juvenile delinquency. And it lets most people out because they're alcoholics. There's an available pool of wasted-looking bastards to stand trial as corrupters of their children. It provides the police with something to do, and as junkies and potheads are relatively easy to apprehend because they have to take so many chances to get hold of their drugs, a heroic police can make spectacular arrests, lawyers can do a brisk business, judges can make speeches, the big peddlars can make fortunes, the tabloids can sell millions of copies. John Citizen can sit back and watch evil get its just deserts.[108]

---

[107] Ballard, J. G. "Introduction by J. G. Ballard," in Burroughs, 1993, unpaged.

[108] Trocchi, 1992, p. 77.

Figure 384. "Émile Durkheim (1858 – 1917)." Pictorial Press, Ltd./Alamy, Encyclopedia Britannica.

C. Radical Anti-Therapeutism

Curiously, Trocchi's opinion coincides with the thesis of French sociologist David Émile Durkheim (1858 – 1917), one of the founders of that discipline, when analyzing the generic function of criminal punishment. Dead before the pharmacological crusade had gathered any traction, to the question, if a draconian law (even with light punishment) would produce delinquency, Durkheim would have answered without hesitation in the affirmative. But to the follow-up question, why then promulgate such laws, he would have responded with robust positivism:

> We can thus say without paradox that punishment is above all designed to act upon upright people, for, since it serves to heal the wounds made upon collective sentiments, it can fill this role only where these sentiments exist, and commensurately with their vivacity.[109]

For this reason moral defiance is always both criminal and necessary:

> Imagine a society of saints, an exemplary and perfect cloister. Crimes properly defined would be unknown there .... For this reason the perfectly honest man judges the least moral defiance with a severity which the crowd reserves for truly harmful acts. ... Thus, crime is necessary [tr. gwr] ....[110]

---

[109] Durkheim, Emile. The Division of Labor in Society, tr. George Simpson. Glencoe, IL: The Free Press, 1933 AA, Book One Chapter Two Mechanical Solidarity through Likeness, pp. 108-109; *On peut donc dire sans paradoxe ... ils sont vivants* (Durkheim, Émile. *De la Division du Travail Social: Étude sur L'organisation des Sociétés Supérieures*. Paris: Ancienne Librarie Germer Baillière et Cie, 1893 AO, Livre I, Chapitre II, p. 116).

[110] *Imaginez une société de saints ... Le crime est donc nécessaire* (Durkheim, Émile. *Les Règles de la Méthode Sociologique*, Septiéme Édition. Paris: Librairie Félix Alcan, 1919 AO, Chapitre III Règles Relatives a la Distinction du Normal et du Pathologique, Section

It would be, then, gravely myopic to think that this type of precept is intended to dissuade certain persons from using certain drugs. This is only its apparent purpose. The real aim is for honest men to feel at once both fear (before the prospect of stigma) and pleasure (seeing deviance punished). As the goal is to reaffirm the attitudes of a particular group; this is not a law for dope fiends but only *autos-da-fe* for so many others. As a result it does not matter that the precept produces extensive disrespect for the law, nor a criminalization of entire sectors, because all this is necessary and is in large measure what is sought: "Even though the law's repression does not greatly frighten away potential consumers from drugs, it does greatly help to strengthen one's own beliefs [tr. gwr]."[111]

But potential accused began to multiply by two or three times every year, and the true motive for this increase was not fit for public consumption. To be precise, it was a valid argument not for the numerical majority but for the Moral Majority, who adhered to the repression as a means of avoiding (while creating) the marginalized. If in order not to feel temptation or wounded feelings, a certain nucleus needs to stigmatize growing sectors of society, other sectors could well dissent (as was the case with various professional corporations), and do so more and more stentorically.

A radical minority suspected that this so-called progress in depenalizing drug use might lead only to a dangerous substitution, akin to replacing Elliot Ness and Anslinger as overseer with that of Portuguese neurosurgeon António Caetano de Abreu Egas Moniz

---

III, pp. 85, 87).

[111] *aunque la represión penal no atemorice gran cosa a los potenciales consumidores de «droga», ayuda mucho al robustecimiento de las propias creencias* (Castillo, Jose Castillo. "*La Funcion Social del Castigo: El Caso de la Prohibicion Legal del Consumo de «Droga»*," *REIS* 34/86, p. 14).

(1874 – 1955), the 1949 Nobel Prize winner for the invention of the leucotomy (lobotomy). The radicals maintained that the use of drugs was a private and extralegal matter for adults like the rest of one's diet, laws on this subject comparable to those criminalizing the Sabbath, heresy and books. Therefore, the policy to follow would be to gradually dismantle the stereotypes that had been disseminated by the press, the government and medical corporations, with the aim of soothing the growing social conflict that had arisen as a result. Of course, the consumers of drugs who asked for social assistance or hospital treatment would be treated with the best available care.

The radicals alleged that the result of this proposed changeover from the criminal to the therapeutic would be more hypocritical than the regime established for alcohol under the *Volstead Act*. The imbibers of alcohol did not need to be institutionally rehabilitated, suffering only high prices, adulteration and contact with criminal suppliers; along with these inconveniences, the users of opiates, cocaine and cannabis were declared to be sick, just like those suffering peptic ulcer or pneumonia, except that their illness was considered epidemic and would be treated with quarantine. The alcoholic was a vicious person, but the addict and even the simple sporadic user of these other drugs were not suffering from a vice, but a specific clinical entity, so-called drug abuse, until then unknown in any textbooks on pathology. It did not show up there for the same reason that neither did articles on insolence, gluttony, obscenity and other character traits. If an addict was not free to govern himself without outside help, then consciously or unconsciously what followed was the ancient proposal of one of the signers of the US Constitution and founders of psychiatry, Benjamin Rush (1745 – 1813), to treat human beings as if they were all mad: "The majority of mankind are *madmen at large* [italics original]."[112]

Figure 385. "Dr. and Mrs. Karl Menninger." Second Annual Tallgrass Prarie Conference, 1974, Patricia D. Duncan, photographer. Still Picture Record Section, National Archives at College Park, MD.

[112] Rush, Benjamin. Letters of Benjamin Rush, Volume II: 1793 – 1813, ed. L. H. Butterfield. Princeton, NJ: Princeton University Press, 1951 AO, VI. Last Years of a Republican Physician, 1809 – 1813, To John Adams, Philadelphia, 20 July 1811, p. 1090; for more see GHDV3P2, Chapter 18 The Anti-Liberal Reaction, p. 1217.

The president of the American Pharmaceutical Association (APhA) at this time, psychiatrist Karl Menninger (1893 – 1980), expressed with edifying conviction the necessity of ending with the punishment of drug users, substituting for it the firm resolution of kindly treatment. The thesis of his aptly titled bestseller, The Crime of Punishment (1966), was that a sophisticated paternalism must replace the barbarous methods of the past:

> Do I believe there is effective treatment for offenders, and that they *can* be changed? *Most certainly and definitely I do.* ... The willfulness and the viciousness of offenders are part of the thing for which they have to be treated. These must not thwart the therapeutic attitude. It is simply not true that most of them are 'fully aware' of what they are doing, nor is it true that they want no help from anyone, although some of them say so [italics and quotation marks original].[113]

Some disagreed, writing with ample critical apparatus and caustic style. The physician and psychiatrist Thomas Szasz (1920 – 2012) had already published The Myth of Mental Illness (1961), a theme that he would return to years later with The Manufacture of Madness (1970), in which he dissects the ideology he baptized as therapeutism: "[I]n the so-called free West, where 'therapeutism' has achieved a power unchecked by any effective countervailing force, Medicine has succeeded in becoming one of the greatest sources of suffering [capitalization and quotation marks original]."[114] To Szasz, the offer of Menninger and his defenders was only a thin veneer of humanist varnish under which lay, unmodified, a more ancient

---

113 Menninger, Karl. The Crime of Punishment. NY: The Viking Press, 1968 AA, Chapter 10 Love Against Hate, pp. 257, 261-262.

114 Szasz, Thomas. The Theology of Medicine: The Political-Theological Foundations of Medical Ethics. NY: Harper & Row, Publishers, 1977 AA, Introduction, p. xvi.

barbarism: the business of manipulating the lives of other people, added to the ambition of fusing medicine and the state.

Figure 386. "Dr. Thomas Szasz (1920 – 2012)." Carey, Benedict. "Dr. Thomas Szasz, Psychiatrist Who Led Movement Against His Field, Dies at 92," *NY Times*, 11 Sep 2012.

CH. 26 LATENCY

The first comfortable supposition of therapeutism, Szasz argues, is that the so-called sick drug addict wishes to be cured:

> Religious and medical propaganda to the contrary notwithstanding, I hold some simple truths to be self-evident. One of these truths is that just as the dead do not rise from the grave, so drugs do not commit crimes. The dead remain dead. Drugs are inert chemicals that have no effect on human beings who choose not to use them. No one has to smoke cigarettes, and no one has to shoot heroin. People smoke cigarettes because they want to, and they shoot heroin because they want to.[115]

The second is that prior to compulsory treatment his intellectual faculties as an adult member of the human race are overshadowed by the artificial paradise of the drug:

> The drug abuser is a person lacking adequate internal controls over his drug use; hence, he requires – for his own protection as well as for the protection of society – external restraints upon it. This, then, justifies the prohibition of 'dangerous drugs,' the incarceration and involuntary treatment of 'addicts,' the eradication of 'pushers' – and much else besides [quotation marks original].[116]

Well then, what happens if the subject will not renounce explicitly this desire, and is someone like Freud, for example, who used narcotics on a regular basis? Accepting the premises of Menninger, there are only two alternatives: to consider him a delinquent (and punish him for a thought crime like apologizing for the drug), or to consider him not simply ill but dementedly ill, before proceeding to use the traditional psychiatric remedies such as insulin, electroshock, the

---

[115] Szasz, Thomas. "The Protocols of the Learned Experts on Heroin," *The Libertarian Review*, Volume 10 No. 7, July 1981 AO, p. 14.

[116] Szasz, Ceremonial Chemistry, 1974 AA, Part III Pharmacracy: Medicine as Social Control, Chapter 12 The Control of Conduct: Authority versus Autonomy, p. 179.

straightjacket, solitary confinement, lobotomy, malariatherapy and so forth. However, the individual remains the same, this example highlighting simply the phariseeism asked of him if he does not wish to see his mind embalmed. The essential continues to be denied, that the so-called drug addict is simply someone who uses certain drugs, in the beginning appearing to be a devil, now presenting as someone sick, both cases justifying a subjugation of his will.

Forced religious conversion, Szasz foresaw, would be succeeded by a forced change of personality through psychotherapy, leaving untouched the central barbarity of omitting one's right to personal responsibility, an inexcusable corollary to liberty. With the presumption that our fellow humans are not fully conscious of what they are doing, a wide range of deviations (not only self-medication, but also eccentric sexuality, suicidal tendency and many other disequilibria of personality) are also converted into illnesses requiring forced treatment.

Thus, psychiatry offers to fulfill in the contemporary state the same functions performed by the clerical establishment in the theocratic state. And the well-meaning humanitarian forgets that to receive so-called treatment for such disequilibria may very well take a lifetime, since for these kinds of things there is no more effective therapy than good faith and a free and spontaneous will to change. In reality, several weeks of involuntary clinical treatment are enough to torture any patient, ruining his mental equilibrium with the company he is forced to keep and his physical equilibrium with the arsenal of psychiatric resources. Moreover, no kind of label arouses in society as much suspicion and hostility as that of criminal other than that of criminal undergoing psychiatric treatment, with the aggravating factor of enjoying only the minimum of the ordinary guarantees of law:

> The clients of the therapeutic state increasingly recognize it as a two-edged sword. They fear that the label of treatment engenders in the public as much suspicion and hostility toward the one who is being treated as does the criminal label; they fear that in the name of therapy society seeks to impose controls over people and behavior that should be free of societal intervention; and they fear, finally, that the therapeutic state possesses tools of human control that far exceed in their threat to individual liberty the sanctions possessed by the criminal model.[117]

The British scholar and theologian Clive Staples Lewis (1898 – 1963) called such involuntary cures nothing more than tyranny:

> Of all tyrannies a tyranny sincerely exercised for the good of its victims may be the most oppressive. ... To be 'cured' against one's will and cured of states which we may not regard as disease is to be put on a level with those who have not yet reached the age of reason or those who never will: to be classed with infants, imbeciles, and domestic animals [quotation marks original].[118]

In short, the radicals wielded the argument of Jefferson on introducing the amendment on religious liberty. The laws are concerned with injuries to others, not to ourselves: "The legitimate powers of government extend to fuch acts only as are injurious to others."[119]

No one criticizes an addict for asking help in overcoming a vice. But it is a vice, a weakness of the will like cowardice or parasitism, not an infectious disease like syphilis or pneumonia. The problem begins when instead of looking to a therapist for help, the

---

[117] Kitrie, Nicholas N. The Right to Be Different: Deviance and Enforced Therapy. Baltimore, MD: The Johns Hopkins Press, 1971 AA, Preface: The Dynamics of the Therapeutic State, The Vision of the Apprehensive Patient, p. xvii.

[118] Lewis, Clive Staples. "The Humanitarian Theory of Punishment," *Res Judicatae*, Volume 6, 1953 [heinonline, hereinafter HO], p. 228.

[119] Jefferson, Thomas. Notes on the State of Virginia. London: John Stockdale, 1788 AO, Query XVII THE different religions received into that ftate? p. 265; see also the 1853 edition at tile.loc.gov.

subject is forced into so-called rehabilitation, success the more improbable the less it is voluntarily sought. One thing is to not abandon someone who seeks help, and another completely distinct thing to pretend to give it by force. The price of the latter is simply ineffectivity, the scandalous proportion of failures that characterize every variant of rehabilitation imposed coercively.

The point of view of sociology as science (in the sense of not admitting as an explanation of social facts anything other than previous social facts) achieves its highest expression in the work of American sociologist Howard S. Becker (1928 – 2023), who begins with an analysis of cannabis consumers in the United States which he then expands into a general theory of deviance, also known also as the interactionist approach.[120] Making use of concepts like labeling, he writes that deviance is simply that which is so labeled as such, that deviance, like beauty, is in the eye of the beholder:

> I mean, rather, that *social groups create deviance by making the rules whose infraction constitutes deviance*, and by applying those rules to particular people and labeling them as outsiders. From this point of view, deviance is *not* a quality of the act the person commits, but rather a consequence of the application by others of rules and sanctions to an 'offender.' The deviant is one to whom that label has successfully been applied; deviant behavior is behavior that people so label [italics, quotation marks original].[121]

This necessarily requires interpretation to distinguish one viewpoint from another:

---

[120] See also Rubington, Earl and Martin S. Weinberg. Deviance: The Interactionist Perspective; Text and Readings in the Sociology of Deviance. London: The Macmillan Company, 1968 AA.

[121] Becker, Howard S. Outsiders: Studies in the Sociology of Deviance. NY: The Free Press, 1963 AA, Chapter 1 Outsiders, Deviance and the Responses of Others, p. 9.

[W]e cannot construct a description of a situation or process that in some way fuses the perceptions and interpretations made by both parties involved in a process of deviance. ... If we study drug addicts, they will surely tell us and we will be bound to report that they believe the outsiders who judge them are wrong and inspired by low motives. If we point to those aspects of the addict's experiences which seem to him to confirm his beliefs, we will seem to be making an apology for the addict. On the other hand, if we view the phenomenon of addiction from the point of view of enforcement officials, they will tell ns and we will be bound to report that they believe addicts are criminal types, have disturbed personalities, have no morals, and cannot be trusted.[122]

Becker suggests that not only the consumer of illicit drugs, but also other deviances were precisely the consequences of teachings imparted by those who pretend to repress the deviation. For this reason, the so-called contemporary drug addict is chiefly a phenomenon of societal learning, and any attempt to understand it without this premise is condemned to failure and methodological incoherence. Opposing the traditional sociological scheme based on deviance as something inherent in the deviant who influenced others by communicating disintegrating elements, Becker emphasized that individuals interiorize patterns and values previously imposed by dominant groups:

In so far as the delinquent can define himself as lacking responsibility for his deviant actions, the disapproval of self or others is sharply reduced in effectiveness as a restraining influence. ... By learning to view himself as more acted upon than acting, the delinquent prepares the way for deviance from the dominant normative system without the necessity of a frontal assault on the norms themselves.[123]

---

[122] Becker, 1963, Chapter 9 The Study of Deviance: Problems and Sympathies, pp. 173-174.

[123] Becker, 1963, Chapter 2 Kinds of Deviance: A Sequential Model, Deviant Careers, p. 28.

It is the label, interpreted, which converts diffuse tendencies into defined channels of behavior.

But if the interactionist perspective lends a technical means of analyzing self-fulfilling prophecies, approximately in the same years as Becker was elaborating his theory of the outsiders, another American sociologist and jurist, Edwin M. Schur (b. 1930), extended the consequences of the radical viewpoint to the idea of victimless crimes, a concept that

> refers essentially to the willing exchange, among adults, of strongly demanded but legally proscribed goods and services. ... Crimes without victims involve attempts to legislate morality for its own sake; the two conceptions very largely relate to the same thing. From the sociological standpoint, however, reference to the victimless nature of the offense may have certain advantages. It reveals the basis for saying that certain laws are indeed designed merely to legislate morality.[124]

As noticed earlier, in his famous essay on political liberty from the middle of the nineteenth century, the philosopher and clerk of the East India Company John Stuart Mill (1806 – 1873) wrote that no one can legitimately be compelled to do or not do something because in the opinion of others it would be prudent or even correct:

> That the only purpose for which power can be rightfully exercised over any member of a civilized community, against his will, is to prevent harm to others. His own good, either physical or moral, is not a sufficient warrant. He cannot rightfully be compelled to do or forbear because it will be better for him to do so, because it will make him happier, because, in the opinions of others, to do so would be wise, or even right.[125]

---

[124] Schur, Edwin M. Crimes Without Victims: Deviant Behavior and Public Policy; Abortion, Homosexuality, Drug Addiction. Englewood Cliffs, NJ: Prentice-Hall, Inc., 1965 AA, Crimes without Victims, The Concept, p. 169.

[125] Mill, John Stuart. On Liberty, Third Edition. London: Longman, Green,

With this principle as his north star, Schur made the connection on several levels between law and morality, proposing that it violates the nature of law to recognize as a crime something that can not cause physical or patrimonial damage to another, denounced by this other or by his relatives:

> Where there is direct offense by one person against another person or his property, the victim and the victimizer are easily identified. On the other hand, in a crime against the state or a crime against morals, the victim becomes more elusive. ... In the examples considered here, the 'harm' seen in the proscribed transaction seems primarily to be harm to the participating individuals themselves (apart from any alleged harm to general morals) [quotation marks original].[126]

To use certain drugs is only one among many other activities without a *corpus delicti* which have been converted into crimes, as has occurred in various times and places with homosexuality, prostitution, euthanasia, unauthorized gambling, pornography and so forth. These are in fact nothing more than voluntary exchanges among adults of solicited goods and services.

Consequently, it could be said that in the first half of the 1960s a critical discourse against prohibition was completely constructed, as much on the political level as on the judicial, sociological and psychiatric. In essence, it consists of three interrelated arguments: a) the phenomenon of drug addiction receives a stereotypical definition, which generates the distortion; b) the state has no right to protect an adult from himself; and, c) the illegalization of a certain drug is not only ineffective but counterproductive in terms of avoiding abuses in its administration.

Longman, Roberts & Green, 1864 AO, Chapter I. Introductory, p. 22; see also GHDV3P1, Chapter 15 Liberalism and Its Repercussions, pp. 990-991.

[126] Schur, 1965, p. 170.

On the other hand, to the interests and values that counsel maintaining the current system can be added therapeutism, a still virgin possibility that promises to give work to a practically infinite range of experts. The pharmacracy only can be constructed when to the repressors and the illicit trafficking organizations this third sector is added, whose moderate reformism will gradually absorb an increasing amount of funds destined to combat so-called drug abuse. But before describing what happens in the second half of the 1960s it's useful to examine the drugs consumed from the *Harrison Act* to the Single Convention of 1961. Only in this way can the polemic between repressors, delinquents, therapists and radicals be understood, no less than the actual pharmacological situation.

Figure 387. "Help Build a Better America." Poster by Robert Crumb. "Special Report: G2 in Crumbland," *The Guardian*, Monday 7 Mar 2005 [guardian.co.uk, hereinafter GC].

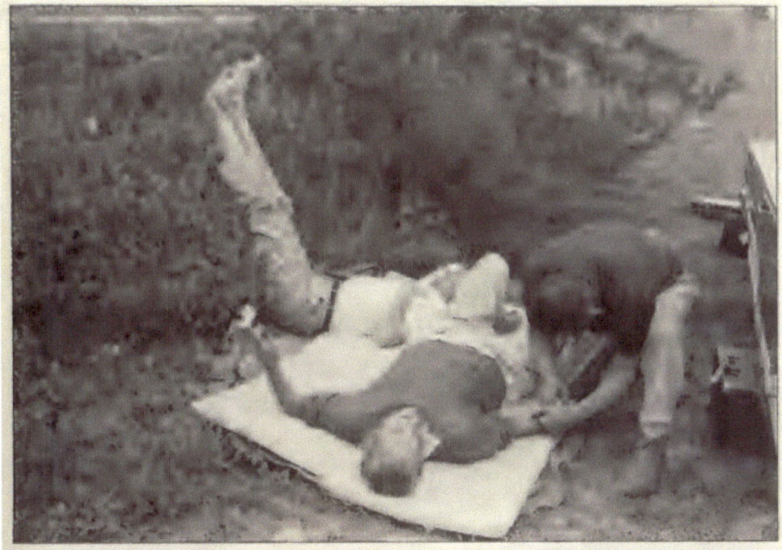

Max injecting Prince Stash Radziwill. Chuck Spalding is waiting for his injection. © Mark Shaw/mptvimages.com

Figure 388. Dr. Feelgood injects Prince Radziwill. Lertzman, Richard A. and William J. Birnes. Dr. Feelgood: The Shocking Story of the Doctor Who May Have Changed History By Treating and Drugging JFK, Marilyn, Elvis, and Other Prominent Figures. NY: MJF Books, 2013 AA, between pages 103 and 105.

27
The Pharmacratic Peace

Though we have ceased to assume the infallibility of our theological beliefs and so ceased to enact them, we have not ceased to enact hosts of other beliefs of an equally doubtful kind. Though we no longer coerce men for their spiritual good, we still think ourselves called upon to coerce them for their material good: not seeing that the one is as useless and as unwarrantable as the other.[1]

-- Herbert Spencer (1820 – 1903)

A. The Single Convention
- **1. Use versus Abuse**
- **2. Creating a Monopoly**

B. Amphetamines
- **1. Compared to Cocaine**
- **2. Toxicity**
- **3. In the Military and Sports**
- **4. In Medicine**
- **5. In Spain**

C. Barbiturates

D. Semisynthetic and Synthetic Narcotics

E. Tranquilizers and Anxiolytics
- **1. The Major Tranquilizers**
- **2. The Minor Tranquilizers**

F. Nonbarbiturate Hypnotics

G. The Addicted Society

---

[1] The Man Versus The State, With Six Essays on Government, Society and Freedom. Indianapolis, IN: Liberty *Classics*, 1981 [oll.libertyfund.org, hereinafter OLF], Over-Legislation (1853), II, pp. 267-268 [*spiritual good* and *material good* are italicized in the original].

The solution was to enshrine the conflict between repressors and therapeutists into law. This compromise is exemplified by the Single Convention on Narcotic Drugs, 1961. It was signed by the representatives of a record 73 countries (Ceylon sent an observer).[2]

A. The Single Convention

The first words of the Preamble call attention to the nobility of purpose on all sides: "*The Parties*, *Concerned* with the health and welfare of mankind [italics original] ...."[3] Similar language will be maintained in the Preamble to the Convention on Psychotropic Substances, 1971: "*The Parties*, *Being Concerned* with the health and welfare of mankind [italics original] ...."[4] It will reappear substantially altered in the Preamble to the United Nations Convention Against Illicit Traffic in Narcotic Drugs and Psychotropic Substances, 1988: "*The Parties to this Convention*, *Deeply Concerned* by the magnitude of and rising trend in the illicit production of, demand for and traffic in narcotic drugs and psychotropic substances, which pose a serious threat to the health and welfare of human beings and adversely affect the economic, cultural and political foundations of society [italics original] ...."[5] In little over a quarter century, a concern becomes a state of being that then deepens. How much of this unctuous deepening of concern over the so-called health and welfare of mankind was the result of the treaties themselves is itself worthy of investigation.

---

[2] Single Convention on Narcotic Drugs, 1961, as Amended by the 1972 Protocol Amending the Single Convention on Narcotic Drugs, 1961. United Nations [unodc.org, hereinafter UN], second through fifth pages.

[3] Single Convention, 1961 UN, Preamble, p. 1.

[4] Convention on Psychotropic Substances, 1971 UN, Preamble, p. 1.

[5] United Nations Convention Against Illicit Traffic in Narcotic Drugs and Psychotropic Substances, 1988 UN, Preamble, p. 1.

Taken as a whole, the Single Convention is the very model of repressive therapeutism (a clear product of the reigning tranquility) which had begun to recommend itself as being a compromise between the strict and the civilized. Repressors received the strong language of punishment and imprisonment in the Article 36 (1) (a) Penal Provisions:

1. a) Subject to its constitutional limitations, each Party shall adopt such measures as will ensure that cultivation, production, manufacture, extraction, preparation, possession, offering, offering for sale, distribution, purchase, sale, delivery on any terms whatsoever, brokerage, dispatch, dispatch in transit, transport, importation and exportation of drugs contrary to the provisions of this Convention, and any other action which in the opinion of such Party may be contrary to the provisions of this Convention, shall be punishable offences when committed intentionally, and that serious offences shall be liable to adequate punishment particularly by imprisonment or other penalties of deprivation of liberty.[6]

This was followed immediately by a nod to the therapists and their so-called modern alternatives to the scourge of drug abuse:

b) Notwithstanding the preceding subparagraph, when abusers of drugs have committed such offences, the Parties may provide, either as an alternative to conviction or punishment or in addition to conviction or punishment, that such abusers shall undergo measures of treatment, education, after-care, rehabilitation and social reintegration in conformity with paragraph 1 of article 38.[7]

The parties shall punish but may provide involuntary treatment as an alternative.

---

[6] Single Convention, 1961 UN, Article 36 (1) (a), p. 18.

[7] Single Convention, 1961 UN, Article 36 (1) (b), p. 18.

This so-called treatment required broad cooperation with experts not necessarily drawn from law enforcement, as seen in the first two sections of Article 38 Measures Against the Abuse of Drugs:

1. The Parties shall give special attention to and take all practicable measures for the prevention of abuse of drugs and for the early identification, treatment, education, after-care, rehabilitation and social reintegration of the persons involved and shall co-ordinate their efforts to these ends.
2. The Parties shall as far as possible promote the training of personnel in the treatment, after-care, rehabilitation and social reintegration of abusers of drugs.[8]

As always the Northamericans would face the largest problems, due now to the appearance of the so-called opiate junkie.

Figure 389. View of the Conference Room on January 24, 1961 at the United Nations in New York. United Nations Photo, UN.

[8] Single Convention, 1961 UN, Article 38, p. 19.

1. Use versus Abuse

Neither use nor abuse however was defined anywhere in the Article 1 definitions.[9] The Preamble recognized medical use as indispensable for the relief of pain and suffering but did not further define it.[10] What really distinguished use from abuse [*consumo indebido*, in Spanish, meaning undue, improper, or unnecessary consumption] was only legal authorization: "The Parties shall not permit the possession of drugs except under legal authority."[11] A drug was deemed to have been consumed when it had been "supplied to any person or enterprise for retail distribution, medical use or scientific research."[12]

Though the Preamble noted addiction was a serious evil, and abuse needed coordinated and universal action, addiction was not defined in the Article 1 definitions, either.[13] Indeed, a person could take a particular drug once, in a prudent dose without incurring undesirable side effects and be guilty of abuse, while another person could inebriate himself on it chronically, even dying of an overdose and only be guilty of use. Traditional use, sometimes called non-medical, quasi-medical or recreational, could only be abuse.

Licit cultivation, manufacture and trade required a license:

---

[9] Single Convention, 1961 UN, Article 1 Definitions, pp. 1-2.

[10] Single Convention, 1961 UN, Preamble UN, p. 1.

[11] Single Convention, 1961 UN, Article 33 Possession of Drugs, p. 17.

[12] Single Convention, 1961 UN, Article 1 Definitions (2), p. 2.

[13] Single Convention, 1961 UN, Preamble UN, p. 1, Article 1 Definitions, pp. 1-2.

b) Only cultivators licensed by the Agency shall be authorized to engage in such cultivation. ...
c) Require that licensed manufacturers of drugs obtain periodical permits specifying the kinds and amounts of drugs which they shall be entitled to manufacture. ...
ii) Control under licence the establishments and premises in which such trade or distribution may take place.[14]

Illicit trafficking was simply commerce "contrary to the provisions of this Convention."[15]

However, while the treaty was presented as a progressive document, it reserved a specific stipulation that any Party would always be able to adopt even harsher measures if desired:

Notwithstanding anything contained in this Convention, a Party shall not be, or be deemed to be, precluded from adopting measures of control more strict or severe than those provided by this Convention and in particular from requiring that preparations in Schedule III or drugs in Schedule II be subject to all or such of the measures of control applicable to drugs in Schedule I as in its opinion is necessary or desirable for the protection of the public health or welfare.[16]

A drug was defined only as a substance on a list: "'Drug' means any of the substances in Schedules I and II, whether natural or synthetic [quotation marks original]."[17] Lacking any other criterion, the Single Convention simply inaugurates a system of lists of drugs organized in four Schedules. As of 5 March 1990, Schedule I

---

[14] Single Convention, 1961 UN, Article 23 National Opium Agencies (2) (b), p. 12, Article 29 Manufacture (2) (c), p. 14, Article 30 Trade and Distribution (1) (b) (ii), p. 15.

[15] Single Convention, 1961 UN, Article 1 Definitions (1) (l), p. 2.

[16] Single Convention, 1961 UN, Article 39 Application of Stricter National Control Measures Than Those Required Under This Convention, p. 20.

[17] Single Convention, 1961 UN, Article 1 Definitions (l) (j), p. 1.

contained over a hundred different drugs including cannabis, coca, fentanyl, heroin, methadone, morphine, opium and a number of semi-synthetic and synthetic opiates.[18] Schedule II as of the same date contained ten more including codeine.[19] Schedule III contained preparations of some of the same drugs in the first two schedules mixed with other ingredients not exceeding certain concentrations, such as codeine

> containing not more than 100 milligrams of the drug per dosage unit and with a concentration of not more than 2.5 per cent in undivided preparations ... Cocaine containing not more than 0.1 per cent of cocaine calculated as cocaine base and preparations of opium or morphine containing not more than 0.2 per cent of morphine calculated as anhydrous morphine base ....[20]

Schedule IV contained seventeen other drugs including cannabis, heroin and certain synthetic opiates.[21]

Schedule I drugs were limited "exclusively to medical and scientific purposes"[22] and required estimates, statistical returns, licenses for manufacture, trade, import and export, medical prescriptions for dispensation, inspections of records, and could be seized and confiscated. Schedule II drugs were "subject to the same measures of control as drugs in Schedule I"[23] except that dispensing did not require

---

[18] Single Convention, 1961 UN, List of Drugs Included in Schedule I, unpaged, first, second and third pages following page 25.

[19] Single Convention, 1961 UN, List of Drugs Included in Schedule II, unpaged, fourth page following page 25.

[20] Single Convention, 1961 UN, List of Preparations Included in Schedule III (1) (4), unpaged, fifth page following page 25.

[21] Single Convention, 1961 UN, List of Drugs Included in Schedule IV, unpaged, sixth page following page 25.

[22] Single Convention, 1961 UN, Article 2 Substances Under Control (1), p. 2.

[23] Single Convention, 1961 UN, Article 2 (2), p. 2.

prescriptions nor did the retail trade have to list the exact weight or percentage of the drug on the label. Preparations in Schedule III were "subject to the same measures of control as preparations containing drugs in Schedule II"[24] except for estimates, import and export certificates, and consignment regulations. Schedule IV drugs were also included in Schedule I and in addition states could "adopt any special measures of control which in its opinion are necessary having regard to the particularly dangerous properties of a drug so included"[25] as well as other prohibitions.

Figure 390. The International Narcotics Control Board, 4 Nov 2021 UNIS/NAR/1448 [incb.org, hereinafter INCB].

[24] Single Convention, 1961 UN, Article 2 (4), p. 2.

[25] Single Convention, 1961 UN, Article 2 (5) (a) (b), p. 3.

2. Creating a Monopoly

The treaty also established the executive organs and bureaucratic mechanisms necessary for the enforcement of an international monopoly on the so-called narcotic drugs. Article 5 entrusted the operation of the treaty to the "Commission on Narcotic Drugs of the Economic and Social Council [hereinafter, the Commission], and to the International Narcotics Control Board [hereinafter, the Board]."[26] The thirteen member Board would be made up of "(t)hree members with medical, pharmacological or pharmaceutical experience ... and ... (t)en members from a list of persons nominated by the Members of the United Nations and by Parties which are not Members of the United Nations."[27] The repressors need never be placed in the minority, or even on an equal footing in the operation of this monopoly.

The function of the Board was to

> limit the cultivation, production, manufacture and use of drugs to an adequate amount required for medical and scientific purposes, to ensure their availability for such purposes and to prevent illicit cultivation, production and manufacture of, and illicit trafficking in and use of, drugs.[28]

For this it needed to be able to estimate what was an adequate amount for each signatory nation, requiring each signatory nation to submit annual estimates of quantities of drugs needed, area under cultivation, quantities of drugs (both natural and synthetic) produced and numbers of manufacturing establishments:

---

[26] Single Convention, 1961 UN, Article 5 The International Control Organs, p. 4.

[27] Single Convention, 1961 UN, Article 9 Composition and Functions of the Board (1) (a) (b), p. 5.

[28] Single Convention, 1961 UN, Article 9 (4), p. 5.

The Parties shall furnish to the Board each year ... estimates ... of the following matters:

a) Quantities of drugs to be consumed for medical and scientific purposes;

b) Quantities of drugs to be utilized for the manufacture of other drugs ...;

e) The area (in hectares) and the geographical location of land to be used for the cultivation of the opium poppy;

f) Approximate quantity of opium to be produced;

g) The number of industrial establishments which will manufacture synthetic drugs; and

h) The quantities of synthetic drugs to be manufactured by each of the establishments referred to in the preceding subparagraph.[29]

The Board further required statistical reports from each country of what had actually been produced, how it had been used, how much had been consumed, the imports, exports, seizures, stocks and area under cultivation for the previous year:

The Parties shall furnish to the Board ... statistical returns ... in respect of the following matters:

a) Production or manufacture of drugs;

b) Utilization of drugs for the manufacture of other drugs ... and utilization of poppy straw for the manufacture of drugs;

c) Consumption of drugs;

d) Imports and exports of drugs and poppy straw;

e) Seizures of drugs and disposal thereof;

f) Stocks of drugs as at 31 December of the year to which the returns relate; and

g) Ascertainable area of cultivation of the opium poppy.[30]

With this information the Board could establish limits [quotas] on manufacture and importation for each participating country:

---

[29] Single Convention, 1961 UN, Article 19 Estimates of Drug Requirements (1), p. 9.

[30] Single Convention, 1961 UN, Article 20 Statistical Returns to be Furnished to the Board (1), p. 10.

> 1. The total of the quantities of each drug manufactured and imported by any country or territory in any one year shall not exceed the sum of the following:
> a) The quantity consumed, within the limit of the relevant estimate, for medical and scientific purposes;
> b) The quantity used, within the limit of the relevant estimate, for the manufacture of other drugs, of preparations in Schedule III, and of substances not covered by this Convention;
> c) The quantity exported;
> d) The quantity added to the stock for the purpose of bringing that stock up to the level specified in the relevant estimate; and
> e) The quantity acquired within the limit of the relevant estimate for special purposes.[31]

The treaty also specifically limited a country's production of opium to the estimates provided, and empowered the Board to deduct any excess from next year's production:

> 1. The production of opium by any country or territory shall be organized and controlled in such manner as to ensure that, as far as possible, the quantity produced in any one year shall not exceed the estimate of opium to be produced ....
> 2. If the Board finds ... that a Party ... has not limited opium ... to licit purposes in accordance with relevant estimates and that a significant amount of opium ... has been introduced into the illicit traffic, it may ... decide to deduct ... an amount from the quantity to be produced ... for the next year ....[32]

Finally, the treaty also limited the production of opium for international trade to the estimates provided by the Board:

---

31 Single Convention, 1961 UN, Article 21 Limitation of Manufacture and Exportation, p. 11.

32 Single Convention, 1961 UN, Article 21 bis Limitation of Production of Opium, p. 11.

1. a) If any Party intends to initiate the production of opium or to increase existing production, it shall take account of the prevailing world need for opium in accordance with the estimates thereof published by the Board so that the production of opium by such Party does not result in overproduction of opium in the world.
b) A Party shall not permit the production of opium or increase the existing production thereof if in its opinion such production or increased production in its territory may result in illicit traffic in opium.[33]

Figure 391. Tom Fabrozzi, Chair of the International Coffee Council, 2024 [ICO.org, hereinafter, ICO].

---

[33] Single Convention, 1961 UN, Article 24 Limitation on Production of Opium for International Trade, p. 12.

But these executive organs and bureaucratic mechanisms are also the hallmarks of the international monopolies on other commodities. The First International Coffee Agreement also created an "International Coffee Organization ... to administer the provisions of the Agreement and to supervise its operation ... [with an] "International Coffee Council, its Executive Board, its Executive Director, and its staff."[34] It also uses production estimates: "At least 30 days before the beginning of each coffee year the Council shall adopt by a two-thirds majority vote an estimate of total world imports for the following coffee year ...."[35] As well, it can require "regular statistical reports on coffee production, exports and imports, distribution, consumption, stocks and taxation ...."[36] Its purpose is to limit the production of coffee using quotas: "the importing Members undertake ... to cooperate with the producing Members in their plans for limiting the production of coffee;"[37] "The Council may establish an International Coffee Fund. The Fund shall be used to further the objective of limiting the production of coffee ...;"[38] "In the light of these estimates the Council shall forthwith fix annual export quotas ...."[39] As with the Single Convention, a country that exceeds its quota can have that excess deducted in the future:

---

[34] First International Coffee Agreement, 1962. United Nations Treaty Series, No. 6791, 1963 [treaties.un.org, hereinafter TUO], Chapter IV, Article 7 (1) (3) Establishment, Seat and Structure of the International Coffee Organization, pp. 180, 182.

[35] First, 1963 TUO, Chapter VII, Article 30 (1) Fixing of Annual Export Quotas, p. 200.

[36] First, 1963 TUO, Chapter XVI, Article 58 (2) Information, pp. 228, 230.

[37] First, 1963 TUO, Chapter XI, Article 50 Co-operation of Importing Members, p. 224.

[38] First, 1963 TUO, Chapter XV, Article 57 International Coffee Fund, p. 228.

[39] First, 1963 TUO, Chapter VII, Article 30 (2) Fixing of Annual Export Quotas, p.

Exporting Members subject to quotas shall adopt the measures required to ensure full compliance with all provisions of the Agreement relating to quotas. ... Exporting Members shall not exceed the annual and quarterly export quotas allocated to them. ... If an exporting Member exceeds its quota for any quarter, the Council shall deduct from one or more of its future quotas a total amount equal to that excess.[40]

Figure 392. The International Tin Association launches new industry platform, 8 Feb 2018 [internationaltin.org, hereinafter ITO].

200.

[40] First, 1963 TUO, Chapter VII, Article 36 (1) (2) (3) Compliance with Export Quotas, p. 204.

Similarly, the Fifth International Tin Agreement (1975) created an "International Tin Council"[41] which estimates "the probable production and consumption of tin"[42] and can "request participating countries to furnish available data concerning tin production, the production costs of tin, the level of tin production, tin consumption, international trade in and stocks of tin ...."[43] The Council sets production limits: "The limitation of exports under this Agreement in each control period shall depend on the decision of the Council ...."[44]

The International Sugar Agreement (1958) operates under the aegis of an "International Sugar Council"[45] which "shall make an estimate of the net import requirements ... during such year for sugar"[46] while the members "undertake to make available and supply all such statistics and information as are necessary ...."[47] It also uses limits and quotas: "The Government of each ... exporting country agrees that exports ... will not exceed ... the export quotas established for it under the provisions of this Agreement."[48]

---

41 Fifth International Tin Agreement (with annexes). Concluded at Geneva on 21 June 1975, Volume 1014, No. 14851. United Nations Treaty Series 1976 TUO, Article 3 (a), The Council, p. 47.

42 Fifth, 1976 TUO, Chapter IV Powers and Functions, Article 9 Statistics and Studies, p. 48.

43 Fifth, 1976 TUO, Chapter IV, Article 7 (c), p. 48.

44 Fifth, 1976 TUO, Chapter XIV, Article 32 (c) Determination of Export Control, p. 63.

45 International Sugar Agreement of 1958, No. 5534. United Nations Treaty Series 1961 TUO, Chapter XIII Administration, Article 27 (1), p. 178.

46 International, 1961 TUO, Chapter VII Regulation of Exports, Article 18 (1), p. 162.

47 International, 1961 TUO, Chapter XIII, Article 28 (5), p. 180.

48 International, 1961 TUO, Chapter V, Article 8 (1), p. 148.

The International Cocoa Agreement (1975) establishes an "International Cocoa Organization"[49] which shall "adopt an estimate of the world net import demand for cocoa"[50] and publish "statistical information on world production, sales, prices, exports and imports, consumption and stocks of cocoa ...."[51] Exports are limited by an International Cocoa Council which "shall forthwith determine annual export quotas ...."[52]

Figure 393. Opening a new Africa-based headquarters in Abidjan, Côte d'Ivoire [confectioneryproduction.com, hereinafter CP].

[49] International Cocoa Agreement, 1975, Volume 1023, No. 15033. United Nations Treaty Series 1976 TUO, Chapter IV Organization and Administration, Article 5 (1), p. 259.

[50] International, 1976 TUO, Chapter VII Price, Quotas, Buffer Stock and Diversion to Non-Traditional Uses, Article 31 (1) Annual Export Quotas, p. 268.

[51] International, 1976 TUO, Chapter XIII Information and Studies, Article 57 Information (1) (a), p. 281.

[52] International, 1976 TUO, Chapter VII, Article 31 (1) Annual export quotas, p. 268.

All of these attempts at international monopolies on other commodities have also failed, though for different reasons:

> The tin agreement did collapse, but for sugar and cocoa adverse market conditions and lack of general support made stabilization impractical. Control of the coffee market ceased largely because of disagreements both between and within the producing countries on the division of the benefits resulting from higher prices.[53]

It is important to clarify that the natural opiates, cannabis and coca have been used since time immemorial, and the rest of the hundred or so psychoactive substances listed in the treaty schedules had been freely used for many decades (some for a half century or more) as the traditional therapeutic panaceas of their day. But before considering the history of the restricted drugs, it's useful to review the history of other drugs, some of them conspicuous by their absence (at least initially) from the Single Convention of 30 March 1961. This will serve to calibrate to what extent the admittedly undefined concept of drug or narcotic drug is based upon its pharmacology.

Figure 394. Nagai Nagayoshi. Matsuyama University Library Archives, 1917 [prabook.com, hereinafter PB].

[53] Gilbert, Christopher L. "International Commodity Agreements: An Obituary," *World Development*, Volume 24, No. 1, 1996, Summary, p. 1.

B. Amphetamines

In 1885 the Japanese pharmacist Nagai Nagayoshi (1844 – 1929) isolated the alkaloid ephedrine from *Ma Huang* (*Ephedra vulgaris*),[54] a plant listed in the *Shen Nung Pen Tshao Ching* (by tradition dated to circa 2800 BC) for treating wind stroke, headache, warm malaria, "cold damage and resolving the muscles [as an antispasmodic]. ... Ephedra never fails to open and free the interstices to drive out the evil through sweating."[55]

Figure 395. *Éphedra: définitions, proprietés et prix* [Ooreka.com, hereinafter OO].

[54] Lock, Margaret M. East Asian Medicine in Urban Japan. Berkeley, CA: University of California Press, 1980 AA, Part One, Chapter 4 History of East Asian Medicine in Japan, p. 65.

[55] Chang, Hsin-pao. Commissioner Lin and the Opium War. New York: W.W. Norton and Co., Inc., 1964 AA, p. 51; see further GHDV1, Chapter III Profane Ebriety, D. China, 2. Cannabis, p. 140 and 4. Other Drugs, p. 144.

In 1924 the pioneering Chinese pharmacologist Ko Kuei Chen (1898 – 1988) "was the first to reveal the pharmacological action of ephedrine and apply it in clinical treatment."[56] In 1923 Chen "reisolated ephedrine from ma huang by the ammonia-chloroform method. ... The outstanding effects of ephedrine are due to stimulation of the sympathetic nervous system and are qualitatively identical with those of epinephrine."[57]

Figure 396. Ko Kuei Chen. B&W Negative, Encyclopedia of Indianapolis [iuidigital.contentdm.odc.org, hereinafter IUI].

[56] Liu, Huan et al. "Ko Kuei Chen: a pioneer of modern pharmacological research in China," *Protein & Cell*, 14, 2023 NIH, Recollection, p. 316.

[57] Chen K. K. and Schmidt, Carl F. "The action and clinical use of ephedrine: an alkaloid isolated from the Chinese drug Ma Huang," *Journal of the American Medical Association*, Volume 87, No. 11, 11 September 1926 AO, p. 836.

Amphetamine was originally developed as a cheaper synthetic substitute for ephedrine:

> Although racemic α-methylphenethylamine (amphetamine) was discovered by Barger and Dale in 1910, it was not until 1927 that this molecule was first synthesised by the chemist, G. A. Alles, whilst he was searching for a less costly and more easily synthesised substitute for ephedrine.[58]

Amphetamine exists in two forms:

> the dextro- (or *d*-) and levo- (or *l*-) isomers .... Smith, Kline and French synthesised both isomers, and in 1937 commenced marketing of *d*-amphetamine, which was the more potent of the two isomers, under the trade name of Dexedrine® [italics original].[59]

Benzedrine (levamphetamine) had earlier been introduced "onto the market in 1935 as a treatment for narcolepsy (for which it is still used today), mild depression, post-encephalitic Parkinsonism and a raft of other disorders"[60] not long after the end of Prohibition.

In the 1930s, hospitalized patients suffering from anxiety, depression, hysteria, schizophrenia, obsessional neurosis and epilepsy were given twenty milligrams of Benzedrine and then retested on the Cattell intelligence test. The average score of the control group "remained the same, but both groups given benzedrine showed an increase in score of over 8 per cent., representing a rise in the intelligence quotient of approximately 7 points."[61] However,

---

[58] Heal, David J. et al. "Amphetamine, past and present – a pharmacological and clinical perspective," *Journal of Psychopharmacology*, 27(6) 2013 NIH, p. 479.

[59] Heal, 2013, p. 479.

[60] Heal, 2013, p. 479.

[61] Sargent, William and J. M. Blackburn. "The Effect of Benzedrine on Intelligence Scores," *The Lancet* 12 December 1936 AO, p. 1386; Freud reported similar effects

psychologists quickly established that improvements on intelligence tests were more subjective than real; any gains in performance ... stemmed mainly from amphetamine's ability to increase confidence and initiative rather than actual improvement in mental capacity.[62]

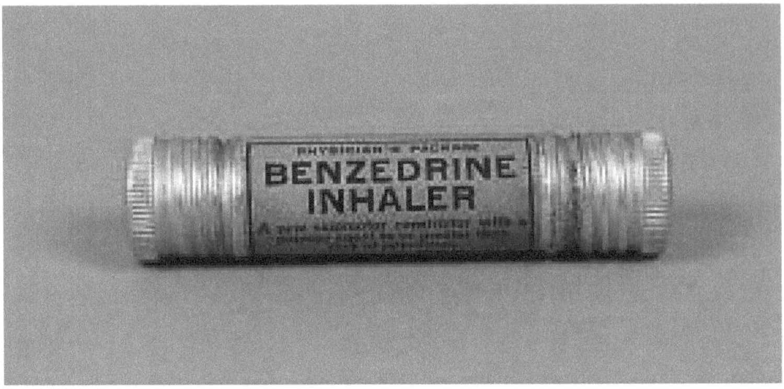

Figure 397. Benzedrine inhaler, physician's sample, c. 1933. National Museum of American History [Americanhistory.si.edu, hereinafter NMAH].

Inhalers began to appear in the pharmacies recommended for rhinitis, coryza [catarrhal inflammation of the mucus membranes], common colds, allergies and all kinds of nasal congestion. Benzedrine and Dexedrine thus enter the market as substitutes for Privine [nophazoline, a decongestant and vasoconstrictor] and other nasal drops, just as heroin [a potent cough suppressant] forty years earlier found promise for treating tuberculosis.

Methamphetamine (Pervitin) was also introduced in 1937:

---

from the use of cocaine.

[62] Rasmussen, Nicolas. "Medical Science and the Military: The Allies' Use of Amphetamine during WWII," *Journal of Interdisciplinary History*, XLII:2, Autumn 2011 [jstor.org, hereinafter JO], p. 208.

> The German chemist Friedrich Hauschild ... managed to synthesize methamphetamine, a close cousin of amphetamine, while working for Temmler-Werke, a Berlin-based pharmaceutical company. Temmler-Werke began selling methamphetamine under the brand name Pervitin in the winter of 1937. ... The tablets were wildly popular and could be purchased without a prescription in pharmacies. One could even buy boxed chocolates spiked with methamphetamine.[63]

First reports extolled the widespread ability of amphetamines to "reduce stress and improve concentration and intellectual performance by academics, students and medical professionals."[64] By 1962 amphetamines had become popular in England with "middle-aged obese housewives, and the commonest reasons for the use of the drugs were obesity, depression, tiredness and anxiety."[65] The craftiness of the laboratories did not stem from ignoring the fact that they were selling the most active stimulants ever discovered. Only their pharmacratic principles prohibited them from openly advertising the euphoric effects of the new drugs.

The influence of extra-pharmacological factors in determining whether or not a particular substance is classified as a useful medicine or a dangerous drug can clearly be seen in the case of these stimulants. In this, the policy of the United States merits a brief commentary. Even in the middle of the 1960s, the Federal Bureau of Narcotics along with the other national drug agencies around the world were united doctrinally in stating nonsense like amphetamines do not produce tolerance nor any tendency to increase the dose.[66]

---

[63] Andreas, Peter. Killer High: A History of War in Six Drugs. NY: Oxford University Press, 2020 AA, p. 193/349.

[64] Heal, 2013, p. 479.

[65] Connell, P. H. "Amphetamine Dependence," *Proc. R. Soc. Med.* Volume 61, February 1968 NIH, p. 178.

[66] As late as 1968 the chief of the Spanish *Brigada Central de Estupefacientes* maintained

Only when Harry Jacob Anslinger (1892 – 1975) is no longer the head of the agency do the amphetamines come under the sway of repressive legislation, and even then the US does not support the initiative to place these drugs under international control. Commercially, this can be understood as they are synthetic products, exported to underdeveloped countries rather than imported from them, providing healthy royalties for their American manufacturers. In addition, their users come from across the professional spectrum, not connected with the poor or marginalized, avoiding the stigmatization of social or racial prejudice.

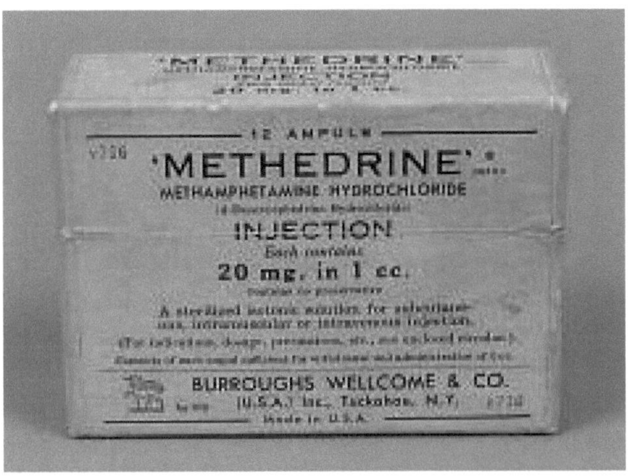

Figure 398. Methedrine, methamphetamine hydrochloride injection. Burroughs Wellcome and Company NMAH.

---

this (Mato Reboredo, Jose Maria. Curso monográfico sobre drogas nocivas. Madrid: Altamira Rotopress, 1969, p. 30).

1. Compared to Cocaine

The divine brother of the Sun,[67] the first Inca [King] Manco Capac gave coca leaves to his people to help them struggle to live under harsh environmental conditions:

The things offered to the Sun were of divers ſorts: the chief and principal Sacrifice was that of Lambs; but beſides, they offered all ſorts of cattel ... all ſorts of Grane, the Herb *Cuca* ...; all which they burnt in the place of Incenſe, rendring thanks and acknowledgments to the Sun, for having ſuſtained and nouriſhed all thoſe things for the uſe and ſupport of Mankind. ... All theſe Laws in Government, and Rites in Religion, they pretend for the greater authority of them to have received from their firſt *Inca, Manco Capac* .... Amongſt many other Virtues of the *Cuca*, they ſay it corroborates the Gums, and fortifies the Teeth, and that it gives ſtrength and vigour to any perſon that labours and toils, onely by carrying it in his mouth.[68]

---

[67] De la Vega, Garcilasso. The Royal Commentaries of Peru, in Two Parts, tr. Sir Paul Rycaut. London: Printed for *Miles Fleſher*, for *Jacob Tonſon*, 1688 AO, Book I, Chap. IX. *The Actions of the firſt* Indian *King, called* Manco Capac, p. 14; *Nueſtro Inca ſe llamo Mãco Capac, y nueſtra Coya Mama ... hermanos, hijos del Sol y de la Luna nueſtros padres* (De la Vega, Garcilaſſo. *Primera Parte de los Commentarios Reales*. Lisboa: En la officina de Pedro Crasbeeck, 1609 AO, Primer Libro, Cap. XVII Lo que reduxo el primer Inco Manco Capac, p. 16).

[68] De la Vega, 1688 AO, Book II, Chap. IV. *Of the things ſacrificed to the Sun; and that the Prieſts, Rites, Ceremonies and Laws were all taught and delivered by the firſt Inca*, pp. 31-32; Book VIII, Chap. XV. *Of the pretious Leaf called* Cuca, *and of* Tobacco, p. 326; *Los ſacrificios que los Incas ... haſta la yerua Cuca ... para ſuſtento de los hombres* (De la Vega, 1609 AO, Libro ſegundo, Cap. VIII. Las coſas que ſacrificicauan al Sol, p. 34); *ſiēpre lo atribuyeron al primer Inca Manco Capac, diziendo q[ue] el las auia ordenado todas* (De la Vega, 1609 AO, Libro ſegundo, Cap. IX. Los ſacerdotes, ritos, y ceremonias, y ſus leyes atribuyen al primer Inca, p. 35); *Entre otras virtudes de la Cuca ... la trae en la boca* (De la Vega, 1609 AO, Libro otauo, Cap. XV. De la preciado hoja llamado Cuca, y del Tabaco, p. 212).

Figure 399. Manco Capac. *Historia del Perú* [historiaperuana.pe /biografia/manco-capac, hereinafter HP].

The amphetamines act on the human body much like cocaine. Indeed, it has been experimentally verified that experienced users cannot initially distinguish intravenous injections of cocaine from amphetamine:

> Investigators in the Faculty of Medicine at the University of Chicago found that their subjects could not distinguish the immediate effects of an intravenous injection of cocaine from that of amphetamine, though after some time it was evident they were able to distinguish between the two drugs [tr. gwr].[69]

Only with experience could they distinguish between the two.

The advantage of cocaine over the amphetamines (besides its lower toxicity) is that the consumption of the former hardly causes morbidity, tolerance and withdrawal symptoms:

> Two national commissions on drug abuse reported that amphetamine, but not cocaine, caused substantial morbidity. ... The usual response of the nervous system to persistent, drug-induced neurochemical perturbation is compensatory adaptation in the perturbed systems, which takes the form, behaviorally, of tolerance and drug withdrawal. It had been assumed that such neuroadaptation did not occur in cocaine abuse because no gross physiologic abnormalities appear during withdrawal. The perception that cocaine was only psychologically addicting, and thus less dangerous, contributed to the rapid spread of cocaine dependence.[70]

---

[69] *Investigadores en la Facultad ... las diferencias entre estas drogas* (Van Dyke, Craig and Robert Byck. "*Cocaína*," *Investigacion y Ciencia, Edición en español de Scientific American*, Número 68, Mayo 1982 AA, p. 100).

[70] Gawin, Frank H., et al. "Cocaine and other stimulants: Actions, Abuse and Treatment (Medical Progress)," *The New England Journal of Medicine*, Volume 318, No. 18, May 1988, reprinted in Nadelmann, Ethan A., director. Stimulants: Cocaine and Amphetamine. NY: Open Society Institute, 1995 AA, pp. 17, 22.

Cocaine is also metabolized quickly, while amphetamine is metabolized slowly: "It has been suggested that the accumulation of metabolites may contribute to generation of psychotic symptoms and to general amphetamine neurotoxicity."[71]

Everything that can be said positively or negatively of cocaine can be said, amplified, of the coarser amphetamine. On the favorable side, one would have to include the induction of wakefulness and alertness, a sensation of clarity and mental strength, an upbeat mood and resistance to every kind of fatigue: "In a mild way, amphetamine is a 'superman' drug. Although the only clinical sign of having taken it is its presence in the urine, it objectively increases the capacity for simple physical and mental tasks ... [quotation marks original]."[72]

2. Toxicity

On the unfavorable side are the bodily and mental costs. Submitted to autopsy, the cadavers of adolescents addicted to what will come to be known as speed reveal a visceral deterioration usually only found in seventy year olds:

> Chronic users of methamphetamine have multiple abnormalities in brain chemistry, function, and structure, particularly in the striatum of the basal ganglia, the brain region with the highest dopamine concentrations. ... Autopsy data, which have demonstrated deficits in dopamine, the dopamine transporter, and tyrosine hydroxylase, can be interpreted as consistent with dopaminergic damage ....[73]

Toxic psychosis can occur with high doses of amphetamines:

---

71 Berman, 2009, p. 18.

72 Laurie, 1967, Chapter Six Thrusters, pp. 70-71.

73 Berman, Steven M., et al. "Potential Adverse Effects of Amphetamine Treatment on Brain and Behavior: A Review," *Mol Psychiatry*, 14 (2), February 2009 NIH, p. 14.

High doses of amphetamines can produce psychotic behavior indistinguishable from schizophrenia in asymptomatic schizophrenics and in some healthy human subjects. ... In one study of healthy volunteers, repeated administration of 5 – 10 mg of oral dextroamphetamine produced paranoid delusions in all subjects at cumulative dosages between 55 and 75 mg.[74]

Chronic use produces insomnia, loss of appetite and aggressive excitability:

Adverse effects listed in drug labels of prescription amphetamines include disturbances of mood and behavior in addition to cardiac and gastrointestinal effects. ... The most common drug-related effects are loss of appetite, insomnia, emotional lability, nervousness and fever.[75]

To these inconveniences one can add an extraordinary induced tolerance:

After chronic exposure to amphetamines, animals exhibit either tolerance (an attenuated response) or sensitization (an augmented response) during subsequent drug administration, indicating that adaptations in the neurobiological substrates of these behaviors. ... Abuse of amphetamine is associated with tolerance and psychological dependence and is difficult to treat. Withdrawal generally produces fatigue, depression and social disability.[76]

An assiduous consumer can take many times the dose capable of provoking an attack of furious madness in a neophyte, with broader consequences no less serious because the relative mental control even under these enormous doses will not avoid a correlative organic, especially neurological deterioration.

---

[74] Berman, 2009, Amphetamine Psychosis, p. 17.

[75] Berman, 2009, CNS Side Effects, p. 5.

[76] Berman, 2009, pp. 7, 10.

3. In the Military and Sports

Though these effects were well known, the major powers in the Second World War gave their troops Benzedrine to ignore fatigue, keep alert and avoid depression. The seamen that supplied the warring sides were the first guinea pigs to test the substance, followed shortly afterwards by German paratroopers on maneuvers: "The first non-medical use was in ships' survival packs during the Spanish Civil War; at about the same time it was issued to German paratroops for routine operational use. Both sides had it during the Second World War."[77] Militarily, the result was considered satisfactory by all.

As would be expected, we lack exact knowledge of the quantities used by the different armies in the conflict. The German military pioneered its use early in the combat. "*Blitzkrieg* was guided by methamphetamine. If not to say that *Blitzkrieg* was founded on methamphetamine."[78] Some say that Adolf Hitler (Alois Schicklgruber, 1889 – 1945) gave personal orders to suspend the use of Pervitin in some theaters of battle, as it caused more havoc than the opposing side:

> Amid growing worries about the addictive potential and negative side effects of overusing the drug, the German military began to cut back on allocations of methamphetamine by the end of 1940. Consumption declined sharply in 1941 and 1942, when the medical establishment formally acknowledged that amphetamines were addictive. ... Nevertheless, the drug continued to be dispensed on both the western and eastern fronts. Temmler-Werke, the maker of the drug, remained as profitable as ever, despite rising awareness of its side effects.[79]

---

[77] Laurie, Peter. Drugs: Medical, Psychological and Social Facts. Baltimore, MD: Penguin Books, 1967 AA, Chapter 6 Thrusters, p. 70

[78] Andreas, 2020 AA, p. 196/349, quoting Peter Steinkamp.

[79] Andreas, 2020 AA, p. 204/349.

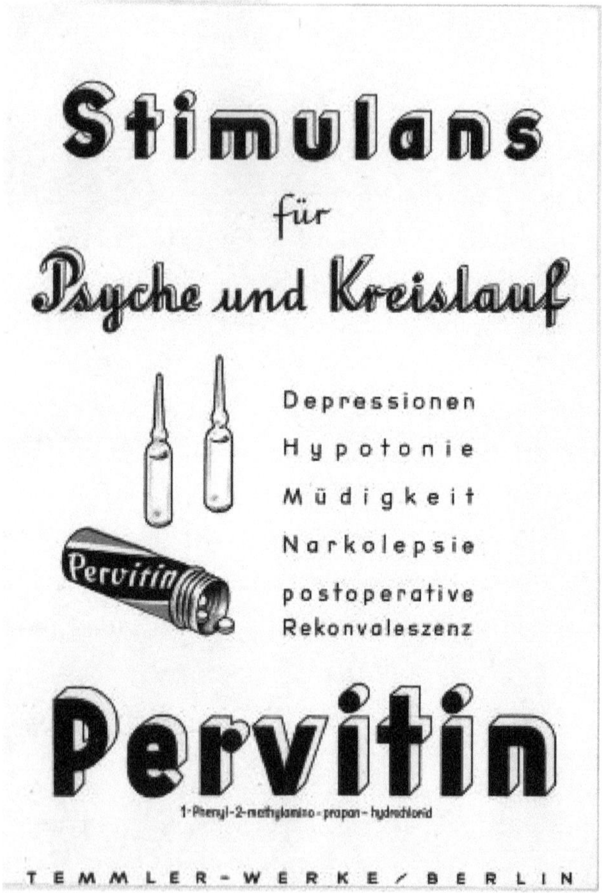

Figure 400. Advertisement for Pervitin. Ohler, Norman. Blitzed: *Drugs in Nazi Germany*, tr. Shaun Whiteside. NY: Penguin Books, 2016 AA, Chapter 1 Methamphetamine, the *Volksdroge* (1922 – 1938), p. 32/208.

Hitler was also an addict:

While he avoided tobacco, alcohol, and caffeine, he was routinely injected with various painkillers and hormones, as well as mood and mindaltering substances. Hitler's personal physician, Dr. Theodor Morell, who kept a detailed diary of his experience, gave the leader regular injections of a mixture of cocaine, amphetamines, synthetic morphine, glucose, testosterone, and corticosteroids, among other substances.[80]

Figure 401. Adolf Hitler awards the Merit Knight Cross to his private doctor, Theodor Morell, in 1944. Cooke, Rachel. "High Hitler: how Nazi drug abuse steered the course of history," *The Observer*, 25 Sep 2016 [theguardian.com, hereinafter TG].

[80] Andreas, 2020 AA, p. 206/349.

On the Allied side of the conflict, according to official figures from the Ministry of Supply the British army distributed some seventy million pills during the war, especially to aviators but also to their troops in North Africa:

> Seventy-two million tablets were issued to British forces to be used tactically to keep troops in the line when they, and the other side too, would normally have been too exhausted to fight. Amphetamines were to be 'withheld until the men were markedly fatigued physically or mentally, in circumstances calling for a special effort.' The maximum military doses were 10 mg. in twelve hours, or 30 mg. in a week – roughly the ordinary teenager's weekend dose, but one fourth of the maximum clinical dose recommended, say, for Benzedrine [quotation marks original].[81]

In the spring of 1944, the US Army Air Surgeon compared the value of a single tablet of benzedrine to that of a B-17: "Rather, the use of benzedrine fortification in such an emergency becomes a great boon; one pill may be worth a Flying Fortress when the man who is flying it can no longer stay awake."[82]

The US, German, British, Japanese and German militaries all

> supplied Benzedrine to servicemen during the war, mainly as 5-mg tablets, for routine use in aviation, as a general medical supply, and in emergency kits. ... [T]here were rules limiting the drug's use. However, these were not well observed. For instance, in a 1945 army survey of fighter pilots, of the 15% (13 of 85) who regularly used amphetamine in combat, the majority 'made their own rules' and took Benzedrine whenever they 'felt like it' rather than as directed [quotation marks original].[83]

---

[81] Laurie, 1967, p. 70, citing *Medindex*, 1966, *2*.

[82] Grant, David N. W. "Benzedrine Alert," *The Air Surgeon's Bulletin*, Volume One, No. 2, February 1944 BGU, p. 20.

[83] Rasmussen, Nicolas. "America's First Amphetamine Epidemic 1929–1971: A

Japanese pilots, especially the kamikaze, flew literally embalmed in methamphetamine:

> Kamikaze pilots in particular took large doses of methamphetamine via injection before their suicide missions. They were also given pep pills stamped with the crest of the emperor. These consisted of methamphetamine mixed with green tea powder and were called *Totsugeki-Jo* or *Tokkou-Jo*, known otherwise as 'storming tablets' [italics and quotation marks original].[84]

Japan continued to increase production to barely conceivable levels though the war was lost. After signing the peace treaty, the warehouse stocks disappeared, and in 1950 the country had at least half a million delirious addicts and many, many more not quite as suicidal. One investigator commented several years later: "Nevertheless, we may safely say that the number of addicts – estimated to be about 500,000-550,000 in 1955 – has greatly decreased."[85]

After favoring its use during the glorious imperial sacrifice, the post-war government was now obliged to apprehend an average of 30,000 people a year for offenses in connection with amphetamines between 1951 and 1955.[86] Amphetamine maniacs turned to crime, thousands were hospitalized each year with a diagnosis of schizophrenia and an undetermined number contracted permanent

---

Quantitative and Qualitative Retrospective With Implications for the Present," *American Journal of Public Health*, Vol 98, No. 6, June 2008 NIH, p. 975.

[84] Andreas, 2020 AA, p. 209/349.

[85] Morimoto, Kiyoshi. "The Problem of the Abuse of Amphetamines in Japan," *Bulletin on Narcotics*, United Nations Office of Drugs and Crime, 1 January 1957 UN, unpaged, following the tables in F, last paragraph.

[86] Morimoto, 1957, 3. Control of Amphetamines, Table 2 Number of cases and persons apprehended for offences in connexion with amphetamines, unpaged, fourth from start.

cerebral lesions. The majority of users were said to inject the product. In 1956 the largest majority of users were younger than thirty, corresponding to those who were young and adolescent during the war.[87]

Yet when Japanese researchers petitioned the Expert Committee of the World Health Organization in the early 1950s to classify amphetamines as being at least as dangerous as cocaine and perhaps even more so than heroin, their monographs were received politely and filed away without further action as a local problem:

> The [Expert] Committee took note of the memorandum presented by Dr T. Masaki on the amphetamine problem in Japan, and had its attention drawn to the occurrence of abuse of amphetamine and amphetamine-like substances in other areas to an extent which constitutes a hazard to public health. The Committee noted that stern measures are already being taken by one of the governments concerned to meet the situation, and that suggestions have been made for local measures for improvement in other areas. The Committee proposed, as it had done previously, to keep close watch on the situation, but was of the opinion that abuse of amphetamine continued to be a local problem and not one for international action.[88]

---

[87] Morimoto, 1957, 6. Present State of the Problem, Table B Users of Amphetamines by Age, unpaged. Never had so many taken cocaine in Germany as during the Weimar Republic after the end of the First World War. Both this and the Japanese case with amphetamine after the Second World War presents certain analogies with China and opium after the nineteenth century First and Second Opium Wars. In China the drug was an analgesic, while in Japan and Germany it was a stimulant, but in all these cases the legal status of the drugs was altered only after serious internal and external conflicts. It could be said that societies are so-called invaded by drugs (show less restraint in their traditional consumption) when basic social and economic factors change their way of life, not the reverse as is often maintained.

[88] Unknown author. "World Health Organization: Expert Committee on Drugs liable to Produce Addiction – Sixth Report," *Bulletin on Narcotics*, Volume VIII, No. 1, January-March 1956 UN, p. 39; see also Morimoto, 1957.

Along with their warlike uses amphetamines are some of the first drugs to be used in peacetime (excepting dueling), specifically in doping. One widely known case was that of English cyclist Tom Simpson (1937 – 1967), would-be champion of the Tour de France, who died while trying to scale Mont Ventoux with the help of Tonedron: "The amphetamine found on Simpson when he died, Tonedron, was one of the more expensive varieties – 'the Rolls-Royce of amphetamines,' ... compared to the basic and far cheaper Benzedrine [quotation marks original]."[89] The same drug was found in his system and was said to be a contributory factor in his collapse:

> When Tom Simpson died on Mont Ventoux whilst competing in the 1967 Tour de France traces of drugs from the amphetamine group were found in his body. Similar drugs were allegedly found in his clothing. ... Because of this, notwithstanding that the official cause of his death, arrived at after investigation by the French authorities, was heart failure due to dehydration and heat exhaustion ... it was said that the drugs could have been a contributory factor.[90]

Brandy may have been another.[91] What is not in dispute is that the pioneers of doping in sports had been the principal contenders in the Second World War.

---

[89] Fotheringham, William. Put Me Back on My Bike: *In Search of Tom Simpson*. London: Yellow Jersey Press, 2002 AA, Chapter 7 'If it takes ten to kill you, I'll take nine,' p. 143.

[90] Sidwells, Chris. Mr. Tom: The True Story of Tom Simpson. Norwich, UK: Mousehold Press, 2000 AA, Preface, p. 1.

[91] Fotheringham, 2002, Chapter 2 'You Don't Have to be Mad to Go Up the Ventoux, But You're Mad if You Go Back,' p. 32.

Figure 402. Tom Simpson, 1959. Elton-Waters, Jack. "Tom Simpson 1937 – 1967: A Life in Pictures," *Cycling Weekly*, 31 July 2017 [cyclingweekly.com, hereinafter CW].

4. In Medicine

Clinically, the amphetamines were originally designed to be used as antidepressants and to increase productivity, "prolong wakefulness, increase focus and feelings of energy as well as decrease fatigue. They can produce euphoria, induce anorexia, and be used to treat narcolepsy and attention deficit/hyperactivity disorder (ADHD)."[92] But from the beginning there were indications, later confirmed, that the administration of high doses can produce irreversible neural lesions while ten years of intravenous administration causes paranoid psychosis in many cases:

> Observations strongly suggest a relationship between the intake of amphetamines and the development of acute psychosis. First, early studies demonstrated that amphetamines could trigger acute psychosis in healthy subjects. ... Secondly, psychosis has been viewed as an adverse event, although rare, in children with ADHD who have been treated with amphetamine .... Thirdly, drug-induced psychosis has been reported in 8–46% of regular users of amphetamines ....[93]

The pharmacies sold hundreds of different brands in different countries, also discovering potent substitutes like phenmetrazine (Preludin). Soon the sales figures for Europe and America suggested daily consumption in the millions.

In the United States, even before the war had ended, a pair of experiments made on disturbed children indicated that during "the period of benzedrine medication, sociability, co-operation, attention,

---

[92] Bramness, Jørgen G. et al. "Amphetamine-induced psychosis – a separate diagnostic entity or primary psychosis triggered in the vulnerable?" *BMC Psychiatry*, Issue 12, 2012 [biomedcentral.com, hereinafter BMC], p. 221 (1 of 7).

[93] Bramness, 2012, p. 222 (2 of 7).

and alertness all seemed to be improved."[94] One of the foremost psychologists of the era, the German born British Hans Jurgen Eysenck (1916 – 1997), after personal investigation, postulated that these amines increase introversion and diminish nervous inhibition:

> The individual, although subjected during a long period of time to the conditioning processes of society, fails to condition because of certain defects in his central nervous system. With the use of the drug, the properties of his central nervous system are modified to make him more receptive to conditioning and, for the period of drug administration, he is effectively in the position of an introvert.[95]

For this reason they were consumed by housewives and young people, groups proverbially given to boredom and a lack of motivation.

In certain English cities like Newcastle upon Tyne the largest number (85%) of inveterate users were anxious, dieting housewives:

> The amount of amphetamines prescribed by two general hospitals in Newcastle to both inpatients and outpatients ... showed an average equivalent to 200,000 5mg tablets, 53% of which were dispensed as Drinamyl. ... Of the survey population ... 90 (14.5%) were men, 530 (85.5%) women. The largest group was middle-aged obese housewives, and the commonest reasons for the use of the drugs were obesity, depression, tiredness and anxiety.[96]

Although amphetamines do not belong to the group of stupefacients (nor were they yet included in any international regulation), locally restrictive measures created excessive use and

---

[94] Eysenck, H. J. Crime and Personality. Great Britain: Routledge & Kegan Paul Ltd, 1964 AA, p. 175, citing D. D. Lindsley and C. E. Henry, *Psychosomatic Medicine*, 1942, 4, p. 140.

[95] Eysenck, 1964 AA, p. 178.

[96] Connell, P. H. "Amphetamine Dependence," *Proceedings of the Royal Society of Medicine*, Volume 61, February 1968 NIH, p. 178.

deaths by overdose, and cases of transitory or permanent mental disturbance within an important black market, created by an initial perception of misuse:

> Many of the drugs currently abused were once not only on open sale, but often promoted as beneficial substances by the food and pharmaceutical industries. A pattern developed whereby initial misuse of pharmaceutical products such as morphine, cocaine and amphetamine led to increasing legal restrictions and the consequent rise of an illicit industry.[97]

In Sweden, for example, which also pioneers this restrictive policy, the result has certain similarities to that of post-war Japan. After its streets and press in the 1950s were filled with advertisements to the effect that two pills were better than a month's vacation, by 1970 the authorities discovered that some ten to twelve thousand mostly young people were injecting the drugs, out of a population roughly equal to that of New York City:

> There are now between 10,000 and 12,000 addicts, about 6,000 of them in Stockholm, the rest principally in Goteborg and the Malmo Lund area. Thus Sweden, with a population approximating that of New York City, has about 10 per cent of New York's problem, now estimated at 100,000 addicts. ... But Swedish addicts remain pretty much committed to mainlining Preludin, which is legally sold in the United States as a weight reducing capsule, and Ritalin, legally prescribed in the United States as an antidepressant. ... Both drugs have been removed from Sweden's pharmacopoeia and their use is illegal. ... Sweden's addicts, like their counterparts in New York, are resorting to crime ....[98]

---

[97] King, Leslie A. The Misuse of Drugs Act: A Guide for Forensic Scientists. Cambridge, UK: The Royal Society of Chemistry, 2003, p. 1.

[98] Severo, Richard. "Mainlining Amphetamines Rising Problem in Sweden," *The New York Times*, 10 April 1970 [nytimes.com, hereinafter NYT], p. 37.

The most commonly used version in Germany, Czechoslovakia, Poland, France, Belgium and England is phenmetrazine sold as an anorexic for weight loss.

Meanwhile, a large number of Americans obtained their amphetamines from respectable pharmacies, as psychiatrists and other physicians continued to liberally prescribe them. To be exact, the annual Northamerican production for internal use achieved in 1962

> an estimated 80000 kg of amphetamine salts, corresponding to consumption of 43 standard 10-mg doses per person per year on a total-population basis. ... Through the rest of the 1960s, FDA estimates of amphetamine production would grow little beyond 8 billion 10-mg doses ....[99]

One could say that the amphetamines were bound to provoke ambivalence in the parents of teens:

> [A]mphetamine seems very quickly to have become a deeply rooted part of mass culture. The study of adolescent delinquents in a remand home found that the girls' mothers would bring them pills on visiting days .... Public horror over use of the drug by teenagers; public complacency over its necessity in thousands of homes: these are two sides, one might say, of the same tablet.[100]

In fact, they could be both devastating and excellent at the same time, a pure *pharmakon*, whose ultimate benefit or harm would always depend on set and setting.

Neither would the amphetamines lack those who would sing their praises (as earlier had the most assiduous users of opium, cocaine, cannabis or wine). These include the acclaimed existentialist writer Jean-Paul Sartre (1905 – 1980), essayist and memoirist Simone de

---

[99] Rasmussen, 2008, p. 977.

[100] Laurie, 1967, Chapter Six Thrusters, p. 81.

Beauvoir (1908 – 1996), as well as Wanda Kosakiewicz (1917 – 1989), one of their many lovers:

> Beauvoir struggled with despair. What was she doing there? Would she ever again experience passion? She took corydrane, an amphetamine mixed with aspirin, in order to be able to work on her new novel .... Wanda developed paranoia. She thought everyone was plotting against her, and her hatred grew violent. Her mental state was not helped by drugs. For the past decade she had been rivaling Sartre with her intake of amphetamines and barbiturates.[101]

Figure 403. Simone de Beauvoir and Jean-Paul Sartre in Beijing. Xinhua News Agency, 1 October, 1955 [delo.si, hereinafter DS].

[101] Rowley, Hazel. Tête-à-Tête: *The Tumultuous Lives and Loves of* Simone de Beauvoir *and* Jean-Paul Sartre. NY: Harper Perennial, 2005 AA, pp. 204, 300.

Figure 404. John F. Kennedy. Lertzman, et al, 2013, cover photo.

The thirty-fifth President of the United States John Fitzgerald Kennedy (1917 – 1963) and his wife Jaqueline Lee Kennedy Onassis, née Bouvier (Jackie, 1929 – 1994) took amphetamine injections by way of Dr. Max Jacobson (Dr. Feelgood, 1900 – 1979). The New York physician traveled with them during their meeting with the First Secretary of the Communist Party Nikita Sergeyevich Khrushchev (1894 – 1971) in Vienna:

> The most famous of the doctor's patients were President and Mrs. Kennedy. Dr. Jacobson frequently visited the White House and often traveled with the Kennedys. In 1961, for example, he went with the President to Vienna for the summit meeting with Khrushchev and, Dr. Jacobson said in an interview, gave the President injections there.[102]

A decade later the Governor of New York, Nelson Aldrich Rockefeller (Rocky, 1908 – 1979) dithered over whether to impose the death penalty or life imprisonment for street peddlers of the same substance, after a wave of indignation from some Negro leaders:

> Reverend George McMurray ... wanted convicted drug dealers to spend the rest of their lives behind bars. ... The debate leading up to passage of the laws in 1973 was fierce, exposing rifts within the community. Some black lawmakers dismissed Gov. Nelson Rockefeller's black allies as 'palace pets.' Others, like Brooklyn's Vander L. Beatty, one of the top black legislators at the time, said the Rockefeller laws didn't go far enough. He wanted the death penalty [quotation marks original].[103]

---

[102] Rensberger, Boyce et al. "Amphetamines Used by a Physician to Lift Moods of Famous Patients," *The New York Times*, 4 December 1972 NYT, p. 3/19.

[103] NCPR News Reporters. "Why did black leaders support America's drug war for so long," NCPR, 19August 2013 [northcountrypublicradio.org, hereinafter NCPR], unpaged.

In the US (after some years of light use on the weekends), with rigorous illegalization punished by life imprisonment for traffickers there now appears the so-called speed junkie, a young demented paranoid with a life expectancy very inferior to that of the opiate junkie.

Executives, older men and adolescents predominated in some areas. The last group, who began taking them as a fad in London and San Francisco in the 1960s, excited scandal and curious polemics. In those years, when a liberalization of sexual mores was just beginning, teens often got together at someone's house on the weekends, using amphetamines as their vehicle of ebriety in place of alcohol. They tended to be moderate in their doses, according to one well-known English journalist who published various articles defending the custom as an improvement with respect to previous habits of drunken pub crawls:

> They [the teenagers] are looking for, and getting, stimulation and intoxication. They want greater awareness, not escape. And the confidence and articulacy that the drugs of the amphetamine group give them is quite different from the drunken rowdiness of previous generations on a night out.[104]

However, the alarm created by this teenage drug use caused a number of restrictive measures. By the middle of the 1960s, the first national restrictions appear, among which for its severity the British *Drugs (Prevention of Misuse) Act* of 1964 stands out, focused specifically on amphetamines and the combination of amphetamines and barbiturates:

---

[104] Wilson, Andrew. "Mixing the Medicine: The Unintended Consequence of Amphetamine Control on the Northern Soul Scene," February 2009 [researchgate.net, hereinafter RG], quoting Anne Sharpley (1928 – 1989), "My Pep Pill Soho Trip," *London Evening Standard*, 3 February 1964.

> This [Act] contained a statement intended to cover a range of synthetic stimulants. ... While this did indeed encompass compounds such as phentermine, methylphenidate and diethylpropion, it soon became clear that a refined interpretation of the generic statement unwittingly included dozens of drugs that were not stimulants. In fact, it could be argued that some barbiturates were also covered.[105]

Compounds combining barbiturates and amphetamines had been appearing since 1950, the one largely ameliorating the insufferable side effects of the other. With these combinations physicians could diagnose and treat in a matter of minutes mild depression, unexplainable indolence, or an appetite leading to obesity.

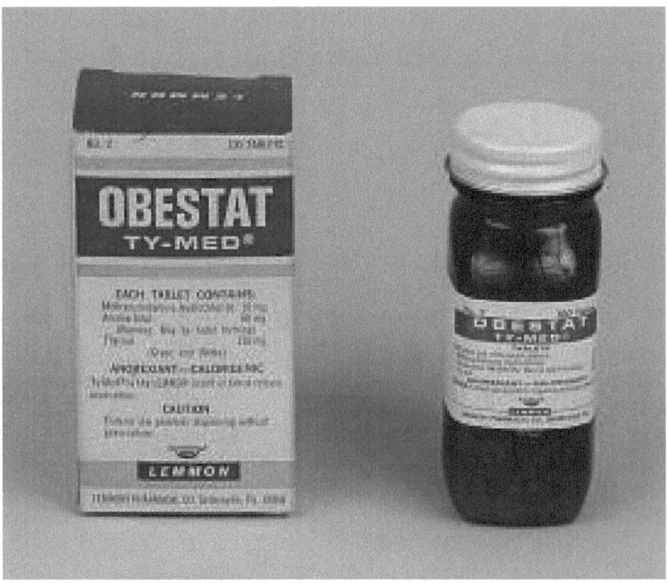

Figure 405. Obestat TY-MED, 100 (methamphetamine hydrochloride, amobarbital, thryoid), 1960s NMAH.

[105] King, 2003, Chapter 1 Introduction, p. 2.

5. In Spain

One country that took no such repressive measures was Spain, to whose pharmacies customers repaired from all over Europe buying cartons of boxes of amphetamines, barbiturates and other tranquilizers or hypnotics; indeed, these products were referred to not only by their consumers but in international forums as the so-called Spanish drugs. While other Western countries were experiencing reactions to local prohibitions, after decades of massive diffusion and the sale of amphetamines as innocuous remedies Spain renovated its pharmaceutical industry with the extra benefits that came from being a country unhindered by such repressive policies. In 1955 a correspondent from the Spanish press based in Paris commented on the rapid oscillation in the consumption of the most popular amphetamine: in June (the date of exams) some hundred thousand packages were sold while in August barely a tenth of that. A considerable number of students used them to study, often on the advice of the family doctor and with the blessings of their parents. In 1969 even when they were already controlled, albeit laxly, and their therapeutic prestige had notably declined, a study of 517 Spanish students found that sixty-six percent had taken or were taking amphetamines and that half had taken them multiple times.[106] A separate study of those detained between 1972 and 1977 revealed an average of twenty-five percent had taken amphetamines.[107] The Ministry of Culture study reported similar results (22.2%).[108]

---

[106] Calcedo-Ordonez, A. "*Uso, abuso y dependencia de los psicoestimulantes*," *Rev. de Psiq. y Psicol. Med.* 516, 1970.

[107] Mato Reboredo, Jose Maria. "*Droga y Criminalidad en España*," Conferencia Universidad Madrid, mayo, 1979 [minerva.usc.es, hereinafter MUE], p. 88.

[108] Mato Reboredo, 1979, p. 89.

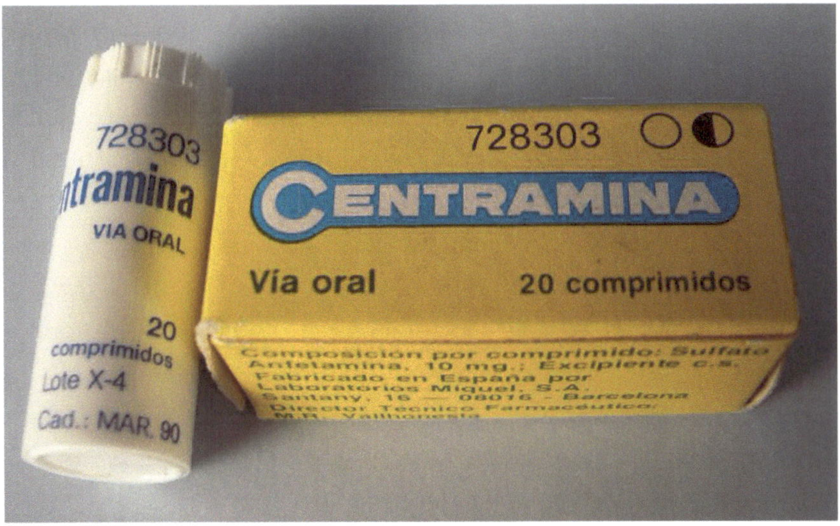

Figure 406. *Centramina* (amphetamine sulphate), 10 mg. Laboratorios Miguel S. A. Santany, Barcelona [ub.edu, hereinafter UB].

These figures were almost as high in relative terms as those of Japan and Sweden, yet the vast majority of use was moderate and occasional. Besides exams, pharmacy sales increased during certain celebrations, like that of San Fermin [a week long bullfight and drunken carouse]. Even so, the Pamplona pharmacists were clear that the consumption abruptly ceased with the end of the festival. It is indisputable that armies of speed junkies have never been seen in Spain, nor widespread injection of these drugs. And neither can this lack of problems be blamed on the backwardness of the country, as if they would have to arrive sooner or later, because in the 1980s after the amphetamine fever had passed and it was no longer so easy to obtain them without a prescription, the country continued without any signs of conflict.

Of course, the reason was that amphetamines had not actually disappeared from the pharmacies. Although many students, housewives and laborers now resorted to very strong coffees to replace a *Centramina* or *Bustaid* pill, in 1979 Spanish pharmacies sold more than six million boxes (some 130 million pills), and something very similar occurred in 1980.[109] This quantity would have sustained a hundred thousand needle freaks.

Yet nothing similar happened before or since, indicating what occurs when a very active drug receives no stigma, can be found pure and cheap in the pharmacies and is not the object of a promotional campaign by the manufacturers. In order to understand this phenomenon, it seems a good moment to comment as well on the permissiveness of the elders toward the consumption of the adolescents, avoiding the glamour of the forbidden during the proverbial epoch of teenage rebellion. One could say that the large majority of Spanish adults were familiar with these drugs, and that only a tiny minority abused them for personal problems. As a result, the black market was practically nonexistent, in clear contrast with less permissive countries.

Amphetamine, levamphetamine, dexamphetamine, and methamphetamine cannot be found in the Single Convention of 30 March 1961; amphetamine, dexamphetamine and methamphetamine are listed in Schedule II of the 21 February 1971 Convention on Psychotropic Substances; none are listed in the revised Single Convention as at 18 May 2016; and, all four are listed in Schedule II of the revised Convention on Psychotropic Substances as at 13 November 2016.[110]

---

[109] Aguar, Octavio. *Drogas y farmacos de abuso*. Madrid: Consejo General de Colegios Oficiales de Farmaceuticos, 1982, pp. 54-55.

[110] United Nations. Chapter VI. Narcotic Drugs and Psychotropic Substances. Title 15: Single Convention on Narcotic Drugs, 1961. New York: 30 March 1961 UN, Schedules, pp. 239-244; United Nations. Chapter VI. Narcotic Drugs and Psychotropic Substances. Title 6.16 Convention on Psychotropic Substances.

C. Barbiturates

The early history and general effects of the barbiturates were mentioned previously in some detail.[111] To recap: in 1863, Baeyer discovers malonylurea which he names barbituric acid, after Saint Barbara; in 1903 Fischer and Mering find a new hypnotic, barbital; in 1919, Hörlein introduces phenobarbital (Luminal); in 1923, Shonle synthesizes amylobarbitone (Amytal) and pentobarbitone (Nembutal); in 1932 I. G. Farbenindustrie AG introduces an ultra-short-acting barbiturate, hexobarbitone (Evipan); another, thiopentone (Pentothal), arrives in 1934; methohexitone (Brietal) emerges in 1957.[112]

But no one sings of barbiturates, because no one sings of stupefaction itself. Taking the concept literally, a stupefacient is something that stuns or stupefies. Few drugs will be more stupefying than the barbiturates until the 1950s with the discoveries of the so-called neuroleptics or major tranquilizers, drugs capable of honorably disputing the title.

Nevertheless, stupefaction turns out to be useful, especially if there are no opiates, even more so if alcohol is prohibited as occurred in the United States in the 1920s and early 1930s when the barbiturates

---

Vienna, Austria: 21 February 1971 UN, unpaged; United Nations. The International Drug Control Conventions, Schedules of the Single Convention on Narcotic Drugs of 1961 as amended by the 1972 Protocol, as at 18 May 2016. New York: ST/CND/1/Add.1/Rev.2, 2016 UN, pp. 1-8; United Nations. The International Drug Control Conventions, Schedules of the Convention on Psychotropic Substances of 1971, as at 13 November 2016. New York: ST/CND/1/Add.2/Rev.2, 2016 UN, List of Substances in Schedule II, p. 3.

111 See GHDV3P1, Chapter 15 Liberalism and its Repercussions, B. Other Major Narcotics, 4. The First Barbiturates, pp. 1051 et seq.

112 Cozanitis, Dimitri A. "One hundred years of barbiturates and their saint," *Journal of the Royal Society of Medicine*, Volume 97, December 2004 NIH, pp. 594-596.

first began to spread throughout the country: "Between the 1920s and the mid-1950s, practically the only drugs used as sedatives and hypnotics were barbiturates."[113] As with large quantities of alcohol or amphetamines, barbiturates are drugs that induce extraversion and disinhibition, appreciated chiefly by introverts who have difficulty crossing the barrier between interior thought and exterior action. Their ostensible effect is a mixture of inebriation and dreaminess, accompanied by the pleasure of stifling a harassing conscience and the satisfaction of unconditionally abandoning timidity.

The fact that they were not considered narcotics meant they were substituted for the opiates and even alcohol in specific long term therapies, which then was accompanied by the risk of addiction: "[I]f the daily dose exceeds 500 mg. continuously, physical dependence may occur, and if the dose is more than 800 to 900 mg. daily for at least 60 days, the patient will likely develop delirium and convulsions if the drug is suddenly withdrawn."[114]

Given that, the dangers are obvious, even more so if the pills are advertised as non-narcotic hypnotics, a product of modern synthetic chemistry, without the inconveniences of stupefaction. Attracted by the hype (and driven by insomnia), a large number of people began to keep a bottle on their bedside tables; of this group a smaller number began to use them every night, and an even smaller number began to explore the effects of even larger daily doses. Only the latter would experience a dependence more intense and harmful than heroin.

---

[113] López-Muñoz, Francisco et al. "The history of barbiturates a century after their introduction," *Neuropsychiatric Disease and Treatment*, I (4), 2005 NIH, p. 331.

[114] Devenyi, Paul and Mary Wilson. "Barbiturate abuse and addiction and their relationship to alcohol and alcoholism," *C. M. A. Journal*, Volume 104, 6 February 1971 NIH, p. 216.

Though it is "difficult to estimate the extent of dependence on, or misuse of, barbiturates ... it is likely that the figure for the United Kingdom might be of the order of 150-250 per 100,000 population."[115] "Regular use without dependence" is estimated at 800-1200 per 100,000.[116] In sum, perhaps "2 per cent of the population might be taking barbiturates regularly in small amounts."[117] In fact, it was not unusual for UK hospital staff to be initially unaware that admittees were suffering from an addiction to barbiturates:

> Not infrequently the true state of affairs is not even recognized in hospital when the patient, as often occurs, gives a misleading history, and then a state of true addiction comes to light by the supervention of physical withdrawal symptoms. Thus a middle-aged man recently admitted in an abusive and violent state developed in quick succession three grand mal seizures three days after admission. It later came out that this man had been taking 12 gr. of sodium amytal daily over the past six months in order to 'steady the nerves' .... Another patient, a middle-aged female of an hysterical type, was frequently admitted to hospital after an overdosage or in a state of chronic barbiturate intoxication. On an earlier occasion she was said to have had two epileptiform convulsions two days after admission and an acute psychotic episode with auditory hallucinations on the fifth day. Her state of depression, confusion, irritability and slight unsteadiness usually cleared up fairly rapidly in hospital [quotation marks original] ....[118]

---

115 Bewley, Thomas. "Recent changes in the pattern of drug abuse in the United Kingdom," *Bulletin on Narcotics*, 01/01/1966 UN, unpaged, follows Figure 10.

116 Bewley, 1966, unpaged, see Table 3 Estimate of incidence of drug misuse in the United Kingdom (1966).

117 Bewley, 1966, unpaged, follows Figure 10.

118 Glatt, M. M. "The abuse of barbiturates in the United Kingdom," *Bulletin on Narcotics*, 01/01/1962 UN, IV. Barbiturate habituation, addiction and chronic intoxication, unpaged.

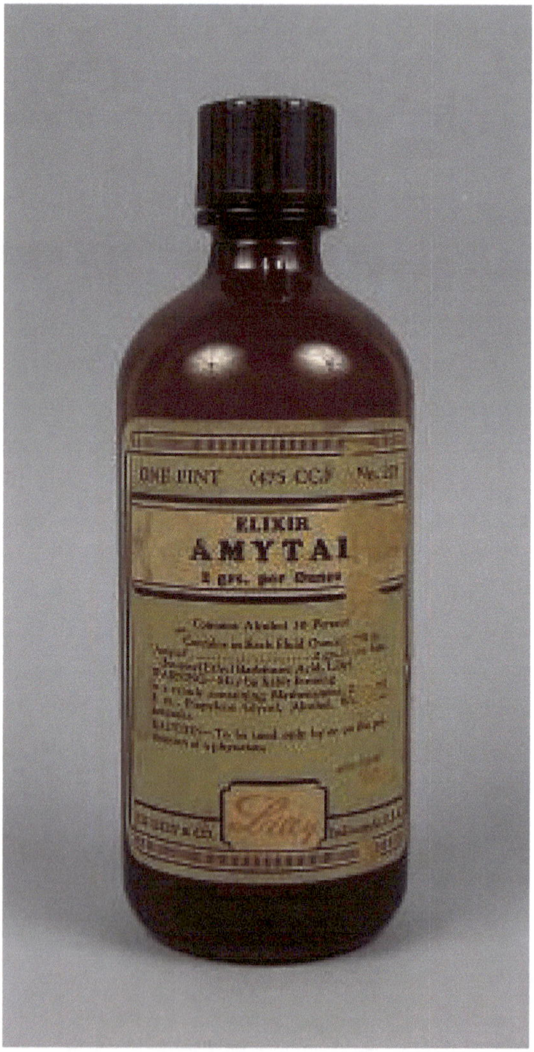

Figure 407. Elixir Amytal (Eli Lilly and Company), 2 grs., post 1938 NMAH.

Around the same time, other European countries experienced similar problems in their psych wards and drug clinics: "The experience of psychiatric clinical wards in Norway suggests that 75% of the drug addicts are using barbiturates."[119] At the Bispebjerg Intoxication Centre in Copenhagen, Denmark, in 1958 some 72% of the so-called narcotic poisonings were from barbiturates:[120] "Intoxication from barbiturates in Scandinavia after World War II was enormous .... Annual barbiturate deaths at that time numbered 'somewhat over 400' in Denmark although 'not fully 100' in Sweden [quotation marks original]."[121]

The United States in 1960 manufactured 852,000 pounds of these drugs, 977,000 in 1966.[122] (It's pertinent to remember that the first voices of alarm in the United States over the problem of narcotics were connected to the discovery that the country in the year 1902 was importing some 250 metric tons (548,674 pounds) of medicinal opium annually.[123]) In 1962 President Kennedy hosted a two-day White House Conference on Narcotics and Drug Abuse. There was general agreement that "the field now is characterized by misinformation and

---

119 Kåss, Erik, et al. "Barbiturate intoxication and addiction as a public health problem in Oslo," *Bulletin on Narcotics*, Volume XI, No. 3, July-September, 1959 UN, Summary, p. 27.

120 Trubuhovich, R. V. "Pioneering early Intensive Care Medicine by the 'Scandinavian Method' of treatment for severe acute barbiturate poisoning." *Anaesthesiology Intensive Care*, History Supplement 2015 [journals.sagepub.com, hereinafter SA], p. 31.

121 Trubuhovich, 2015, p. 29.

122 Statistical Abstract of the United States, Part 2, 1971 [census.gov, hereinafter CG], Selected Medicinal Chemicals – Production and Sales: 1945 *to* 1969, p. 75.

123 See GHDV3P2, Chapter 20 The Effect of *Laissez Faire*, B. The Impact of Freedom on Consumption, p. 1412.

inadequate information."[124] Indeed, the participants could not even agree on the number of addicts in the entire country, which ranged from a high of 100,000 by the Mayor of New York City to 45,391 by the Federal Bureau of Narcotics (compared to 500 in the entire United Kingdom), "far fewer than the number of alcoholics ...."[125] No estimate of the number of barbiturate addicts was provided by any of the participants. Indeed, "the words 'Drug Abuse' were added to the Conference title" only because in March of that same year President Kennedy had without irony "pointed out that 'an extensive underground traffic exists in habit-forming barbiturates (sedatives) and amphetamines (stimulants)' [quotation marks original]."[126]

With the illegalization of the opiates, not only the respectable, socially integrated user prior to the 1930s, but the entire range of street addicts began injecting barbiturates either sporadically or chronically, often without their knowledge:

> It is fairly common to find chronic barbiturate use in heroin addicts. About a third of all addicts admitted to [the US Public Health Hospital at] Lexington [Kentucky], most of whom use heroin, also use barbiturates. ... Occasionally mystified patients at Lexington find that they are not really heroin addicts at all; their suppliers have them fooled – and hooked on an alien drug of low status.[127]

In the 1950s and 1960s the black market was as opaque as it would become in the 1980s. According to legendary literary junkie Alexander Trocchi (1925 – 1984),

---

124 Proceedings White House Conference on Narcotics and Drug Abuse. Washington, DC: U.S. Government Printing Office, 1962 [googlebooks.com, hereinafter GB], Introduction, Background, p. xviii.

125 Proceedings, 1962, pp. 16, 88, 111, 132.

126 Proceedings, 1962, pp. xvi, xvii.

127 Laurie, 1967, p. 65.

my mind always came back as I looked down at the little heap of whitish powder to wonder what an analyst would find there. The horse is cut with all manner of adulterous powders, until, at the average user's end, there remains 3% heroin. You can usually count on 3%. But there are times when codeine or even a barbiturate is substituted for the real thing ... so long as they stun you, they calculate. And so you look to cop again, at once, and so it goes on.[128]

In spite of everything, the barbiturates received good press, and before the flood of suicides, cases of dependence and accidental overdoses, the official experts maintained that it was only harmful when abused. One British investigator related that "a senior police officer at Scotland Yard, who is directly responsible for drug control in the Metropolitan area, told me that barbiturates were in no sense addictive and that they presented no problem."[129] The legislative counsel for the Pharmaceutical Manufacturers Association reminded the attendees of the 1962 White House Conference that these drugs were useful unless abused:

It must be remembered that barbiturates and stimulant drugs are highly beneficial and have many important uses. They can only be dispensed on prescription of a licensed practitioner. When used under medical supervision they are safe and effective. But when abused they may present problems in public health, involving antisocial behavior.[130]

These opinions naturally irritated less politicized pharmacologists, because a similar position was applicable to every psychoactive drug, many submitted to a diametrically opposed legal regime.

At Lexington it was already known from the 1940s that no dependence was more destructive to the personality than barbiturates:

---

[128] Trocchi, Cain's Book, 1992, p. 216.

[129] Laurie, 1967, p. 61.

[130] Proceedings, 1962, The Pharmaceutical Manufacturer's Viewpoint, p. 46.

"Furthermore, the use of sedative drugs prolongs emotional dependence on drug therapy and one may succeed in transferring the addiction to barbiturates which is a far more damaging and serious matter than is addiction to morphine."[131] Specifically, it was known that the same patients

> who have been seen at Lexington under the influence of both opiates and hypnotics, who are said to be sensible, restrained, skilled at their jobs and to show reduced sexuality on opiates, are obstinate, aggressive, apt to masturbate in public, and full of Irish excuses for their stumbling gait and confused speech when they are on barbiturates.[132]

Also well known was the catastrophic character of barbiturate withdrawal, more prolonged than heroin and with greater risk of death, in the convulsive phase as well as the posterior psychotic phase. With rapid withdrawal "some addicts may die, and this makes withdrawal from barbiturates more dangerous than withdrawal from opiates."[133] The user was then faced with the risk of death or continuing a vice that would inexorably destroy his social life and his body.

The capacity for euthanasia was discovered by the general public, though this never figured in the prospectus without being surrounded by elaborate euphemisms. As a final inconvenience, these drugs were responsible for a rising number of so-called accidental overdose deaths annually in Northamerica. Though some ingested them when very drunk, and some simply took them, forgot, and then took them again, others deliberately overdosed. The latter appeared to have happened with the actress and model Norma Jeane Mortenson

---

131 Vogel, Victor H. and Harris Isbell. "Medical Aspects of Addiction to Analgesic Drugs," *Bulletin on Narcotics*, Volume II, No. 4, October 1950 AO, p. 38.

132 Laurie, 1967, Chapter Five Sleepers, p. 63.

133 Devenyi, 1971, p. 216.

(Marilyn Monroe, 1926 – 1962), whose death was "caused by a self-administered overdose of sedative drugs [nembutol, chloral hydrate] and that the mode of death was probable suicide."[134]

Figure 408. Marilyn. Nelson, Elyda. "for the first time! the true life story of Marilyn Monroe," *Modern Screen*, Volume 46, No. 1, December 1952 AO, p. 51.

---

[134] Curphey, Theodore J. "Statement by Theodore J. Curphey, M.D., Chief Medical Examiner-Coroner, County of Los Angeles, 17 August 1962," Marilyn Monroe Autopsy Report, 5 August 1962 [autopsyfiles.org, hereinafter AF], unpaged 9/18.

But until meprobamate (Miltown, Equanil) and the benzodiazepines appear in 1955 and 1960 respectively, there is no other legal recourse for certain functional disorders and insomnia, and combinations of barbiturates and amphetamines were liberally prescribed, often with minimal patient examinations.[135] The half century long reign of the barbiturates only managed to addict two or three million Westerners forced to walk the miserable path opened before them. The vast majority of users kept the same bottle of Lilly's quinalbarbitone (Seconal) or Merck's barbital (Veronal)[136] on their nightstands for long periods of time, resorting to them only occasionally.

Except in cases of deliberate deceit, few consciously chose an immoderate use of barbiturates and amphetamines during this period of relative pharmacratic peace. This echoes those few who three or four decades earlier had abused the opiates and cocaine. Like the amphetamines, the barbiturates never came to symbolize social or ethnic minorities and the lack of social stigma shielded them from the allure of the forbidden.

Barbital (Veronal), phenobarbital (Luminal), amylobarbitone (Amytal), pentobarbitone (Nembutal), hexobarbitone (Evipan), thiopentone (Pentothal), methohexitone (Brietal), and quinalbarbitone (Seconal) cannot be found in the Single Convention of 30 March 1961; Amobarbital, cyclobarbital, pentobarbital and secobarbital are listed in

---

135 This I can attest to personally in the case of my father, who received a barbiturate preparation for a digestive complaint (probably psychosomatic), and without knowing he was taking an addictive drug he became intensely dependent to the end of his days. Indeed, we only found out years later that the preparation was basically amylobarbitone (Amytal). Nevertheless, it is worth noting that this convenient, cheap, pure and easily accessible therapeutic nerve tonic did less damage that it could have done.

136 Cozanitis, 2004, pp. 594, 596.

Schedule III and barbital, methylphenobarbital and phenobarbital are listed in Schedule IV of the 21 February 1971 Convention on Psychotropic Substances; none are listed in the revised Single Convention as at 18 May 2016; secobarbital is listed in Schedule II, amobarbital, cyclobarbital and pentobarbital are listed in Schedule III, while allobarbital, barbital, phenobarbital, and secbutabarbital are listed in Schedule IV of the revised Convention on Psychotropic Substances as at 13 November 2016.[137]

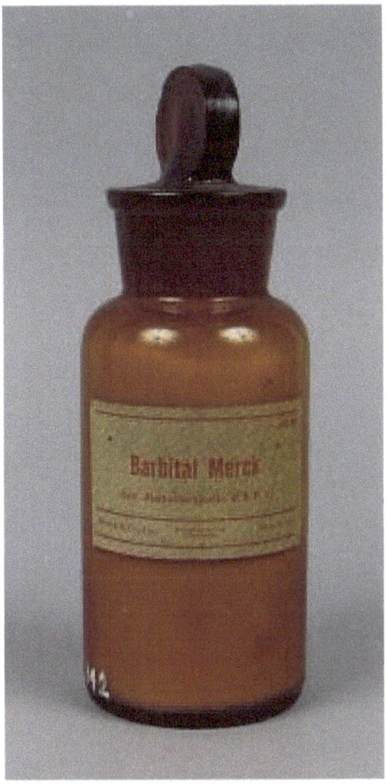

Figure 409. Barbital (Merck and Company), NMAH.

137 United Nations, 30 March 1961, Schedules, pp. 239-244; United Nations, 21 February 1971 UN, unpaged; United Nations, 18 May 2016, pp. 1-8; United Nations, 13 November 2016, List of Substances in Schedule II, List of Substamces in Schedule III, List of Substances in Schedule IV, pp. 4, 5, 6, 8.

D. Semisynthetic and Synthetic Narcotics

Even today, there is no non-addictive analgesic, defined as one not producing an abstinence syndrome upon withdrawal, proportional to the degree of intoxication achieved before the interruption of its administration: "[T]he most widely used definition of addiction ... states that addiction is a condition brought about by the repeated administration of a drug such that its use becomes necessary and cessation of it causes mental and physical disturbances."[138] Neither has anyone discovered any analgesic that is instantly addictive (or even rapidly so). It always takes at least a number of weeks (at least four) of assiduous use with high doses to begin to feed a dependency, while the clinical result of deprivation in such cases is relatively mild.

This can be observed in the natural, as well as in the semisynthethic and synthetic opiates. The latter term is reserved for those manufactured largely from coal tar and crude oil (important in the dye industry) which appeared both a little before and a little after the Second World War. They were pioneered by a number of laboratories in Germany which arguably did not wish to be dependent upon imports of opium, though this is also disputed: "There has been no hard evidence to support the often-repeated assertion ... of a specific German attempt, directed by Hitler, to replace opium supplies that had been cut off by the war."[139]

---

[138] Vogel and Isbell, Ocober 1950, p. 38.

[139] Preston, Andrew and Gerald Bennett. "The history of methadone and methadone prescribing," in Methadone Matters: Evolving Community Methadone Treatment of Opiate Addiction, eds. Gillian Tober and John Strang. Boca Raton, FL: CRC Press, 2003 AA, Chapter 2 The German origins of methadone, p. 13.

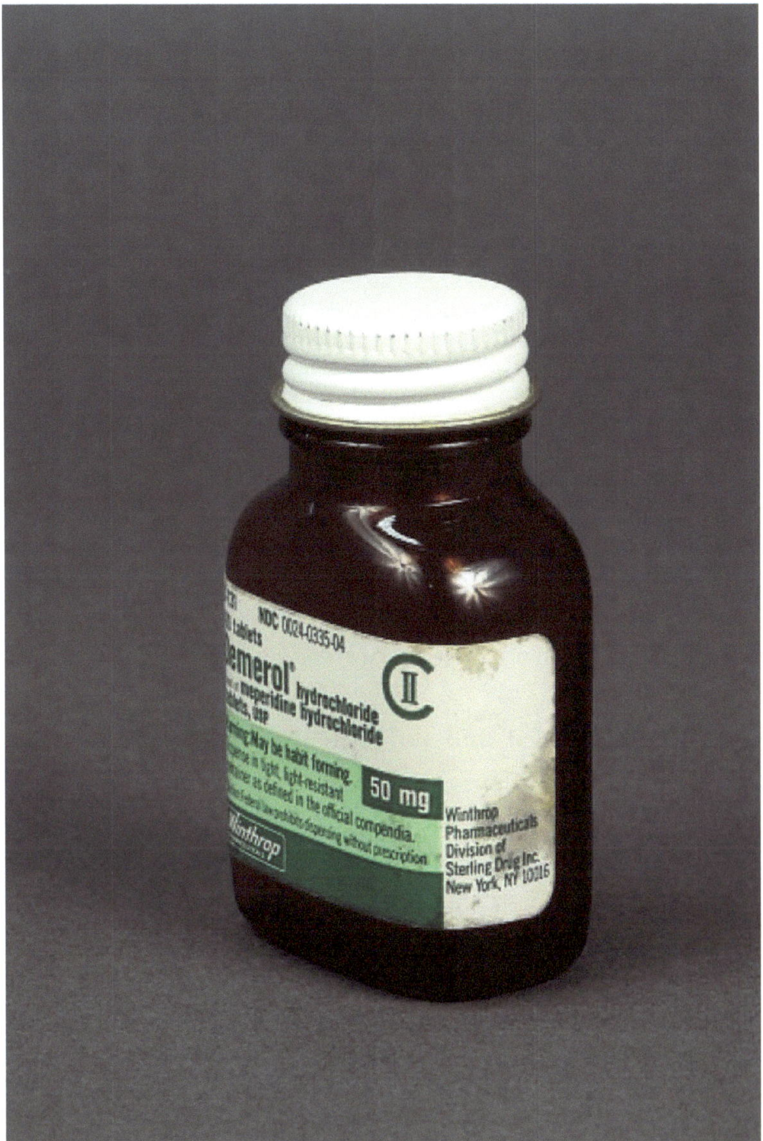

Figure 410. Demerol (Winthrop Pharmaceuticals), ca. 1990 NMAH.

Pethidine (Dolantin, Demerol)

With respect to the synthetic opiates, pethidine or meperidine[140] was created in 1939 and commercialized under the trade names Dolantin in Germany and later Demerol in the United States, respectively:

> [D]uring the course of the methodical search for effective opiate-like drugs ... the pharmaceutical company I. G. Farbenindustrie pursued a research programme at Hoechst-Am-Main in Germany to develop effective analgesics that did not have the dependence potential of diamorphine [heroin]. Eisleb and Schaumann ... in 1939 ... had patented an effective opioid analgesic drug ... called Dolantin .... This drug is known as pethidine and it is still widely used today for pain relief. As with diamorphine before, and buprenorphine since, the early hopes of having discovered a new non-addictive analgesic were mistaken. However, the powerful analgesic action of pethidine was much needed by the Germans during the Second World War, and it was rapidly brought into commercial production. At the height of the conflict, in 1944, it was being manufactured at the rate of 1600 kg per year.[141]

It was introduced into the legal market as a promising new analgesic preparation lacking both opiates and barbiturates. However, from 1940 in pharmaceutical circles, it was known that when substituted for morphine it could provoke an abstinence syndrome.[142] In dispute was "whether meperidine would produce addiction when

---

140 1-methyl-4-phenylpiperidine-4-carboxylic acid ethyl ester (Unknown author. "Development of Synthetic Narcotic Drugs," *Bulletin on Narcotics*, 01/01/1956 UN, p. 11).

141 Preston and Bennett, 2003, p. 13.

142 Rasor, Robert W. and H. James Crecraft. "Addiction to Meperidine (Demerol) Hydrochloride," *The Journal of the American Medical Association*, Volume 157, No. 8, 19 February 1955 AO, p. 654, citing von Brucke, S. "*Ueber Dolantinabusus und einen Fall von Dolantindelir*," *Wiener klinische Wochenschrift* 53: 854 (Oct. 18) 1940.

used in the ordinary practice of medicine. Some investigators ... minimized the addiction liability of the drug."[143]

The drug had no public stigma, but between 1950 and 1953 "[d]uring a 39 month period 457 meperidine addicts were admitted"[144] to the U. S. Public Health Service Hospital at Lexington, Kentucky. Most of the primary [original addiction only to meperidine] admissions were voluntary: "A higher percentage (91%) of the primary meperidine addicts admitted to the hospital were voluntary patients as compared to the addicts in general admitted to the hospital (84% voluntary)."[145] They were incapable of confronting alone an iatrogenic habit in the vast majority of the cases: "An outstanding finding was the high percentage (80%) of all meperidine addicts who gave chronic discomfort arising from some medical or psychiatric condition as being responsible for their addiction."[146]

Consumption had been increasing. According to one report, since

> meperidine became available in 1944, there has been a substantial increase in the production and consumption of the drug. In 1946, 7,710 lb. (3,470 kg.) were produced and 6,318 lb. (2,844 kg.) were consumed, while in 1952, 15,688 lb. (7,060 kg.) were produced and 17,697 lb. (7,965 kg.) were consumed.[147]

According to another, in the middle 1950s pethidine

---

143 Rasor and Crecraft, 1955, p. 654.

144 Rasor and Crecraft, 1955, p. 655.

145 Rasor and Crecraft, 1955, p. 655.

146 Rasor and Crecraft, 1955, p. 656.

147 Rasor and Crecraft, 1955, p. 655.

consumption has been increasing from year to year, rising from 10.3 tons in 1952 to 13.5 tons in 1956. The increase was, however, most marked in 1955. Pethidine is consumed practically throughout the entire world, but the 9 tons consumed in the United States in 1956 represented two-thirds of world consumption in that year. After some decline in 1953 the production of pethidine increased in the two following years and then remained stationary (15 tons). During the whole period from 1952 to 1956 – with the exception of 1953 – production exceeded consumption and the surplus was put into stocks. At the end of 1956 these were equal to about one year's consumption.[148]

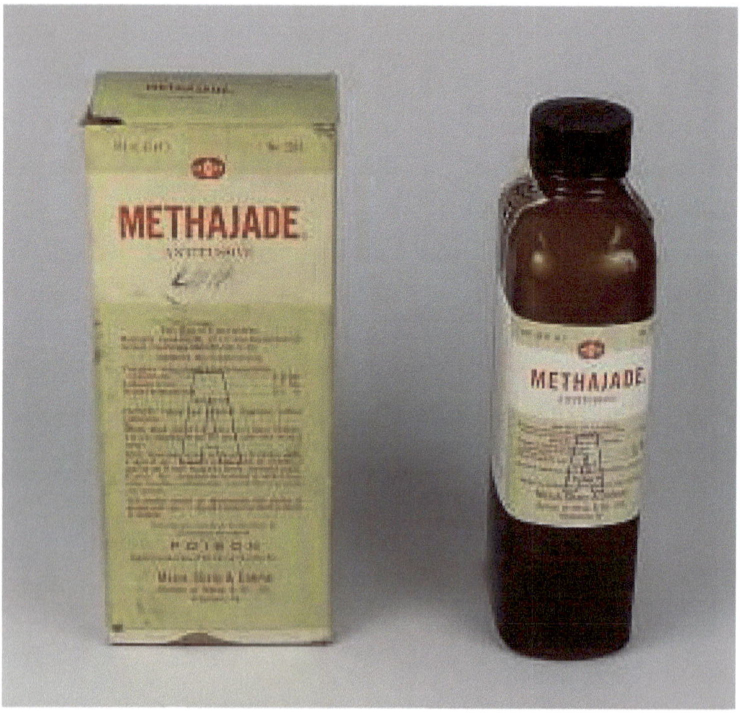

Figure 411. Methajade Antitussive (Merck, Sharpe and Dohme), methadone hydrochloride, 10 mg. per 30 cc, NMAH.

---

[148] Report of the Permanent Central Opium Board. "Legal Trade in Narcotics," *Bulletin on Narcotics*, 01/01/1958 UN, p. 5/7.

Methadone (Polamidon, Methajade, Physeptone)

As a result of their success with pethidine, scientists at I. G. Farbenindustrie also synthesized methadone just before the Second World War:

> Max Bockmühl and Gustav Ehrhart ... were working on compounds with a similar structure to Dolantin. They were hoping to find hypnotic substances that were water-soluble, effective drugs to slow the gastrointestinal tract to make surgery easier ... and effective analgesics that were structurally dissimilar to morphine in the hope that they would be non-addictive and escape the strict controls on opiates. ... During 1937 and the spring and summer of 1938, Bockmühl and Ehrhart's systematic manipulation of the compounds resulted in the creation of another new substance which they labeled ... 'Polamidon.' A patent application was filed on 11 September 1941 [quotation marks original].[149]

After animal testing, it was handed over to the German military in 1942 although the German army ended up renouncing the new drug, considering it too toxic:

> However, there was no attempt to get the new drug into commercial production .... One explanation for this was ... that they had discounted its use because of the side effects [as] the doses used in the experiments had been too high, causing nausea and overdose [quotation marks original].[150]

With the end of the Second World War, the formula was obtained by Northamerican chemists as (similarly to what occurred with heroin after the end of the First World War) all German

---

149 Preston and Bennett, 2003, p. 13.

150 Preston and Bennett, 2003, p. 14.

products, patents and trade names, including those for Polamidon, were requisitioned by the Allies as spoils of war. ... The formulae of all the analgesics developed by I. G. Farbenindustrie before and during the war were distributed around the world by the Allies. Because they were then freely available to many companies, drugs such as methadone have many different trade names around the world.[151]

In the second half of the 1940s it was introduced on a large scale into medical practice as an analgesic and cough remedy:

There were many early studies, all of which found methadone to be an effective analgesic. ... The earliest accounts of methadone use in the UK include a study of its use as an obstetric analgesic at University College, London .... This study, however, was terminated because of respiratory depression in the newborn babies. Early advertisements claimed that Physeptone (Wellcome's trade name for methadone) carried 'little risk of addiction' and the consensus was that it was a better analgesic than morphine. It is therefore likely that the first people who became dependent on it had either been treated for pain or treated by doctors who thought it to be less dependence-forming than other opiates. Although a weaker ... form is still used for treatment of chronic cough (usually those caused by malignant tumour), it is not generally used as an analgesic in the UK. In those countries where methadone is widely used as an analgesic, it has been chosen because of the less strict regulatory framework around the prescribing of methadone compared with diamorphine [heroin], which has a superior analgesic effect and fewer problems with accumulation of the drug in the system, rather than because of any greater efficacy of methadone [quotation marks original].[152]

---

[151] Preston and Bennett, 2003, p. 14; one of the first trade names, Dolophine, incorrectly said to have been derived from Adolph, was in fact the creation of Eli Lilly post war, from the Latin for pain, dolor, with an ending alluding to morphine (p. 14).

[152] Preston and Bennett, 2003, Early use of methadone in general medical practice, p. 15.

Almost immediately investigators at Lexington found that high levels of methadone produced both tolerance and euphoria with the addictive power of heroin:

They gave volunteers up to 200 mg 4 times daily, and found rapidly developing tolerance and euphoria. They had to reduce levels with patients on these high doses because of, among other things: 'signs of toxicity ... inflammation of the skin ... deep narcosis and ... a general clinical appearance of illness.' ... They concluded that methadone had high addiction potential: 'We believe that unless the manufacture and use of methadon [methadone] are controlled, addiction to it will become a serious health problem' [quotation marks original].[153]

However, an important finding at Lexington was that methadone could be substituted for morphine, especially during withdrawal. Compared to morphine, the withdrawal from methadone was less intense as the

syndrome of abstinence from methadon developed slowly as compared with morphine ... reached maximum intensity more slowly ... subsided more slowly and was not so intense as abstinence from morphine. ... A great majority of the patients stated that the abstinence from methadon was much less intense than that from morphine. Most of them expressed the opinion that they would prefer to go through abstinence from methadon than from morphine. ... Methadon completely alleviated the morphine abstinence syndrome in man. ... Methadon prevented the appearance of signs of physical dependence in 12 men who had been proved to be addicted to morphine.[154]

---

[153] Preston and Bennett, 2003, Early use of methadone in general medical practice, pp. 14-15.

[154] Isbell, Harris, et al. "Tolerance and Addiction Liability of 6-dimethylamino-4-4-diphenyl-heptanone-3 (methadon)," *The Journal of the American Medical Association*, Volume 135, Number 14, 6 December 1947 AO, pp. 892, 894.

This led to the establishment of methadone maintenance programs in the early 1960s in New York, which were so successful they caused a reevaluation of traditional theories of addiction which had been based on the addict's sociopathic personality:

> The dramatic improvements in social status of patients on this program have exceeded expectations. The study started with the hope that heroin-seeking behavior would be stopped by a narcotic blockade (and this has proven to be true), but it certainly was not expected that we would be able to retain more than 90% of the patients and that almost three fourths would be socially productive and living as normal citizens in the community after only six months of treatment. ... The unexpected response of these patients to a simple medical program forced us to reexamine some assumptions that we brought to the study. ... The rapid disappearance of theft and antisocial behavior in patients on the methadone maintenance program strongly supports the hypothesis that the crimes that they had previously committed as addicts were a consequence of drug hunger, not the expression of some more basic psychopathology. The so-called sociopathic personality is no longer evident in our patients.[155]

The consumption of methadone increased steadily in the middle 1950s and "in 1954 reached the figure of 570 kg, the highest ever recorded. Since then it has been falling, to 539 kg in 1955 and 450 kg in 1956."[156]

---

[155] Dole, Vincent P. and Marie E. Nyswander. "Heroin Addiction – A Metabolic Disease," *Archives of Internal Medicine*, Volume 120, July 1967 [doraweiner.com, hereinafter DW], pp. 20-21.

[156] Report of the PCOB, "Legal Trade," 1958, p. 5/7.

Ketobemidone

Ketobemidone[157] was for some time the most powerful of the synthetic narcotics, still used for severe pain: "It has been reported to have an analgesic activity as strong as that of morphine."[158] It produces a rapid physical dependence and an abstinence syndrome more serious than barbiturates: "The first clinical experiments on former addicts gave the impression that it was a particularly dangerous drug ...."[159]

As a result, "production was not initiated in the U.S.A. Ketobemidone is, however, being produced in two countries – Switzerland and Denmark. The world consumption of this drug totaled 64 kg in 1954, and the estimated requirement for 1956 is a little over 72 kg."[160] In 1956 "eight countries (five in 1952) consumed 1 kg or more of ketobemidone: the Federal Republic of Germany (21 kg), Denmark (19 kg), Sweden (10 kg), Italy (4 kg), Norway (4 kg), Switzerland (4 kg), Belgium (2 kg) and Finland (2 kg)."[161] Two years earlier, the Economic and Social Council had urged governments to "prohibit the manufacture, import and export of this drug, its salts, preparations and preparations of its salts."[162] The country most affected appears to have been Denmark.

---

157 4-(3-hydroxyphenyl)-l-methyl-4-piperidyl-ethyl-ketone, 1-methyl-4-metahydroxy phenyl-4-propionyl-piperidine (Unknown author, "Development," 1956, p. 11).

158 Unknown author, "Development," 1956, p. 4/6.

159 Unknown author, "Development," 1956, p. 4/6.

160 Unknown author, "Development," 1956, p. 4/6.

161 Report of the PCOB, "Legal Trade," 1958, p. 5/7.

162 Unknown author, "Development," 1956, p. 4/6.

Dextromoramide (Palfium)

Dextromoramide was synthesized in 1955 by a research team working under the direction of Dr. Paul Adrian Jan Janssen (1926 – 2003) and approved for human use in 1957:[163]

> [L]aunched in Europe, but never in the United States, [it] was not so important for its commercial success but, rather, because it was significantly more potent than morphine and for awhile was the most potent opioid available in the world for clinical use.[164]

The Italian writer and filmmaker of uncertain political allegiance (republican, nationalist, fascist, and communist) Kurt Erich Suckert (Curzio Malaparte, 1898 – 1958), who for so much of his life had abstained from coffee, tobacco and above all alcohol[165] is supposed to have written that his agony had been relieved by the drug as he was dying of cancer.[166] Indeed, a double blind trial of dextromoramide, methadone and pethidine for severe pain in 1964 showed "dextromoramide does show marginal advantages over the other two agents. The average duration of pain relief was slightly

---

[163] Stanley, Theodore H. et al. "A Tribute to Dr. Paul A. J. Janssen: Entrepreneur Extraordinaire, Innovative Scientist, and Significant Contributor to Anesthesiology," *Anesthesia & Analgesia*, Volume 106, No. 2, February 2008, Table 2. A List of the Most Important Drugs Produced by Dr. Paul Janssen, p. 458.

[164] Stanley, 2008, p. 454.

[165] *vivere in completa astinenza di caffè, tabacco e soprattutto alcol* (Serra, Mauricio. *Malaparte: Vite e leggende*, tr. Alberto Folin. Venezia: Marsilio Editori, 2012 AA, Introduzione Volti e maschere di un esteta armato, unpaged, citing a letter to Howard B. Bishop of 15 April 1947, in Malaparte, VII, pp. 558-559).

[166] Flood, Richard. "Curzio Malaparte: Casa Malaparte, 1938," *Artforum Newsletters*, Volume 35, No. 10, Summer 1997 [artforum.com, hereinafter ART], unpaged.

higher, the incidence of side-effects lower and there were no cases in which respiratory depression was a feature."[167]

Initially, some investigators based on rat studies "concluded that there was practically no habituation to dextromoramide," a clinical study found "the same doses of dextromoramide can be given almost indefinitely," a separate clinical study "was unable to observe the occurrence of a dependence phenomenon," and a surgeon concluded "that administration of this substance does not entail withdrawal phenomena, which goes to confirm the absence of habituation after prolonged treatment."[168]

However, by the middle of the 1960s cases of iatrogenic addiction were being reported in the *British Medical Journal*: a patient with severe back pain "reached the stage of taking 50 Palfium tablets per week,"[169] two heavy drinkers who had been prescribed the drug (using 40 tablets and 70 tablets a day, respectively) were referred to hospital in the early 1960s for dextromoramide addiction,[170] and a post-operative patient took 4,400 tablets in less than a year.[171] Researchers at Lexington

---

[167] Matts, S. G. Flavell, et al. "Double Blind Trial of Dextromoramide, Methadone and Pethidine in the Treatment of Severe Pain," *Postgraduate Medical Journal*, Volume 40, February 1964 NIH, Discussion, p. 105.

[168] La Barre, Jean. "The pharmacological properties and therapeutic use of dextromoramide," *Bulletin on Narcotics*, Issue 4, 01/01/1959 UN, 5. Research on the addiction-producing properties of dextromoramide, pp. 6/15, 8/15.

[169] Thompson, Brian A. M. "Addiction to Dextromoramide," *British Medical Jouanal*, 31 October 1964 NIH, Correspondence, p. 1136.

[170] Seymour-Shove, R. "Dependence on Dextromoramide," *British Medical Journal*, 14 January 1967 NIH, Case Reports, p. 89.

[171] Cormack, Jack. "Dependence on Dextromoramide," *British Medical Journal*, 11 February 1967, p. 362.

demonstrated the elimination of the abstinence syndrome by dextromoramide in addicts with a stabilized consumption of 200 to 340 mg of morphine per day. Their conclusions lead them to believe that dextromoramide has addiction-producing properties at least equivalent to those of morphine.[172]

In 1958 the Permanent Central Committee on Opium recognized the drug "as being more dangerous than morphine."[173]

Normethadone (Ticardia)

Something very similar to what happened with Palfium (at around the same time) occurred with normethadone, defended before the Permanent Central Opium Board by its principal producer, Germany, as a non-addictive substance, which then ended up being as addictive as its brother synthetics:

This narcotic drug was brought under control in November 1954, but production statistics are only complete from 1956. In that year 1,571 kg were manufactured in the Federal Republic of Germany, 20 kg in Italy and 5 kg in Finland. Consumption figures are incomplete because the Federal Republic of Germany, which must be the largest consumer of this drug, has not brought it under the national control applying to narcotic drugs and has so far only declared its 1956 production. Five countries declared consumption of normethadone in 1956: Belgium (13 kg), Australia (4 kg), the Netherlands (2 kg), Switzerland (2 kg) and Finland (1 kg). Brazil, which imports the drug, has not yet declared its consumption.[174]

The Permanent Central Opium Board regarded it

---

[172] La Barre, 1959, p. 8/15.

[173] Permanent Central Opium Board. Report to the Economic and Social Council on the Work of the Board in 1958, Document E/OB/14. Geneva, CH: United Nations Publications, November 1958 UN, V. Shortcomings in National Control, p. 16.

[174] Report of the PCOB, "Legal trade," 1958, p. 5/7.

as being no less dangerous than morphine .... The Federal Republic of Germany is the chief manufacturer. Not being a party to the 1948 Protocol, this country was not bound to bring the drug under national control, nor has it yet felt moved to do so. Accordingly the manufacturer of the drug has been at liberty to export it ... without the authority of import certificates issued by the governments of the importing countries. Learning that Ticardia was in fact being widely distributed, the Board wrote in 1957 to the Government of the Federal Republic of Germany and was informed that 1,571 kg. of normethadone had been manufactured, and 329 kg. exported, in 1956. ... According to the information supplied for 1956 by the Federal Republic of Germany, normethadone or Ticardia was exported that year to no less than 56 countries and non-metropolitan territories.[175]

Ethylmorphine (Tussipax, Cosylan)

Developed by Merck in 1884, the semisynthetic ethylmorphine,[176] also known as codethyline or dionine, is marketed as an antitussive syrup sold as Tussipax (codeine and ethylmorphine) in France by Laboratoires Bailleul and as Cosylan by Parke-Davis in Norway. Patient information in France suggests it has the possibility of "abuse, dependence, abstinence syndrome in the case of prolonged use."[177] Researchers in Norway write that it "has an analgesic effect, and some potential for abuse" and "is metabolised to morphine in humans ...."[178]

---

[175] Permanent, E/OB/14, 1958, p. 16.

[176] The 3-ethoxy congener of morphine (Aasmundstad, Tor A., et al. "Biotransformation and pharmacokinetics of ethylmorphine after a single dose," *British Journal of Clinical Pharmacology*, Volume 39, 1995 [bpspubs.onlinelibrary.wiley.com, hereinafter BPS], p. 612).

[177] *Abus, dépendance, syndrome de sevrage en cas d'utilisation prolongée* (Tussipax, sirop – Notice patient [base-donnees-publique.medicaments.gouv.fr, hereinafter BDF], unpaged).

[178] Aasmundstad, 1995, p. 612.

In the early 1950s,

the production of ethylmorphine has varied little, the minimum being in 1953 (5.1 tons) and the maximum in 1955 (5.9 tons). Consumption increased, rising from 4.8 tons in 1952 to 5.9 tons in 1956. The increase was most marked in France: from 0.8 ton in 1952 to 1.9 ton in 1956.[179]

Paracodeine

After ethylmorphine, the most widely used of the semisynthetics was for some time paracodeine, also known as dihydrocodeine, especially in Germany. According to the Commandant of the interrogation center at Mondorf-les-Bains, Luxembourg, when Reichsmarshall Hermann Wilhelm Goering (1893 – 1946) arrived in 1945 he was carrying a suitcase filled with twenty thousand tablets of this drug, of which he was taking forty daily:

> After he had been taken upstairs, there was a knock at my door. A sentinel appeared carrying one of Goering's fine leather cases. 'I felt you should see this, sir.' He opened it to reveal the biggest collection of pills I had ever seen in my life. Goering was called back. They were Paracodin pills. He needed them 'for his heart.' There were approximately twenty thousand in the case and he was in the habit of swallowing forty a day – twenty in the morning and twenty at night [quotation marks original].[180]

World production of dihydrocodeine rose from 592 kilos in 1953 to 1,481 kilos in 1956.[181]

---

[179] Report of the PCOB, "Legal Trade," 1958, p. 4/7

[180] Andrus, Burton C. I Was the Nuremberg Jailer. NY: Tower Publications, Inc., 1969 AA, 3. The guests arrive, p. 24.

[181] Report of the PCOB, "Legal Trade," 1958, see Table World Production (kilogrammes), p. 4/7.

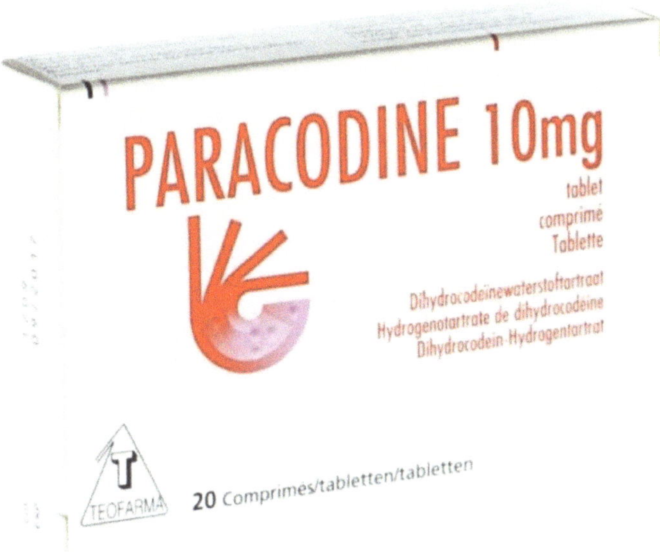

Figure 412. Paracodeine (Merck: Teofarma), 10 mg. [apotheekvanderhaegen.be, hereinafter AV].

Codeine

This natural opiate has already been considered at some length.[182] To reiterate, French chemist Pierre-Jean Robiquet (1780 – 1840) isolated it from opium, naming it codeine [*kōdeia*, poppy head]: "This substance, to which I have given the name of codeine, is insoluble in alkali solutions; it combines well with acids and forms true salts; the nitrate in particular crystallizes easily [tr. gwr]."[183]

---

182 See GHDV3P1, Chapter 15 Liberalism and its Repercussions, A. Pharmacological Progress, 4. Codeine, pp. 1028 et seq.

183 *Cette matière, à laquelle j'ai donné le nom de codéine, est insoluble dans les solutionsalcalines; elle se combine bien avec les acides et forme de véritables sels; le nitrate surtout cristallise avec la plus*

Though addictions have been reported in the early twentieth century, in 1932 the British pharmacopoeia quoted Sir W. Willcox as saying that codeine "is not really dangerous as an addiction drug ... [and was] wisely excluded"[184] from the Dangerous Drugs Act of 1932. The International Narcotics Control Board reported that some 360,863 kg. (795,000 lbs.) of codeine had been manufactured in 2013 (compared to 522,557 kg. of morphine).[185] The World Health Organization has placed codeine on its List of Essential Medicines.[186]

Comparing the strength of one narcotic to another can be tricky as efficacy can be difficult to establish. In rat and mice studies done before 1960, "[n]early all authors find methadone more active than morphine, morphine more active than pethidine, and pethidine more active than codeine ...."[187] However, these animal studies may have limited applicability to subjective pain in human subjects:

---

grande facilité (Robiquet, Pierre-Jean. "*NOUVELLES Observations sur les principaux Produits de l'Opium*," *Annales de chimie et de physique*, ed. Gay-Lussac and Arago, Tome LI. Paris: Chez Crochard, 1832 [gallica.bnf.fr, hereinafter BNF], Chap. IV, p. 264).

184 Martindale, W. Harrison, rev. The Extra Pharmacopœia of Martindale and Westcott, Twentieth Edition, Vol. I. London: H. K. Lewis & Co., Ltd., 1932 AO, Codeina, p. 355.

185 International Narcotics Control Board. Narcotic Drugs: Estimated World Requirements for 2015, Statistics for 2013, Document E/INCB/2014/2. NY: United Nations, 2015 INCB, Part four. Statistical information on narcotic drugs, Table IX. Manufacture of the principal narcotic drugs, 2009-2013 (continued), p. 170.

186 Web Annex A. World Health Organization Model List of Essential Medicines – 23rd List, 2023. In: The selection and use of essential medicines 2023: Executive summary of the report of the 24th WHO Expert Committee on the Selection and Use of Essential Medicines, 24 – 28 April 2023. Geneva: World Health Organization, 2023 (WHO/MHP/HPS/EML/2023.02), 2. Medicines for Pain and Palliative Care, 2.2. Opioid analgesics, p. 2.

187 Janssen, Paul A. J. Synthetic Analgesics, Part I, Diphenylpropylamines. NY: Pergamon Press, 1960 AA, Chapter II The 'Analgesic' Activity of Methadone,

In view of the fact that pain is, by definition, a subjective sensation of mankind, it can, strictly speaking, only be studied in humans. What we are able to study in animals is not pain itself, but the behaviour of the animal following a stimulus which provokes pain in man ....[188]

[D]ata from opioids in animal studies cannot be uncritically translated to man. First of all animal studies are mainly based on motor reflexes or behavioural responses and such data can only partly be interpolated to human pain, which is a net result of complex sensory, affective and cognitive processing. Second, there are major differences between the effects of drugs across species (and even strains), and this limits generalization of findings.[189]

A systematic review of fifty-six studies in human subjects with parallel randomized controlled trials also observed "[n]o significant differences in pain relief ... between morphine and oxycodone, methadone and oxymorphone, but this was the expected outcome as doses normally are selected to be equianalgesic."[190] Further, individual responses swamped the data, especially with regards to cancer patients:

Despite there being no significant evidence on a population level of major differences between morphine and other strong opioids in terms of efficacy or tolerability, there is growing recognition of marked variation between individual patients in response to individual opioids for cancer pain. Not all patients respond well to each strong opioid. For example, up to 30% of cancer patients on morphine

---

Morphine, Pethidine and Codeine in Animals, p. 7; see in particular Table III – 'Analgesic' Potency Ratios of Methadone, Morphine, Pethidine and Codeine as Determined by S. C. Injection in Mice and Rats in Forty-Six Different Experimental Conditions, p. 12

188 Janssen, 1960, Chapter I 'Analgesic' Activity in Man and in Animals, p. 5.

189 Drewes, Asbjørn M., et al. "Differences Between Opioids: pharmacological, experimental, clinical and economical perspectives," *British Journal of Clinical Pharmacology*, Volume 75, Issue 1, 3 May 2012 NIH, Experimental Pain Studies, p. 64.

190 Drewes, 2012, Systematic Reviews, p. 67.

> fail to achieve adequate analgesia, despite escalating dose and/or experience intolerable or dose-limiting side effects. ... A similar pattern of response variability is seen with other strong opioids. Clinical experience and a number of studies have demonstrated variability in terms of the level of analgesia achieved, the side effects experienced and the daily dose of opioid required.[191]

Only five synthetics (pethidine, methadone, ketobemidone, dextromoramide and normethadone) and two semisynthetics (ethylmorphine and paracodeine) as well as one natural opiate (codeine) have been mentioned from the list of more than seventy in the schedules of the Single Convention of 1961. Pethidine, methadone, ketobemidone, dextromoramide, normethadone and paracodeine are listed in Schedule I, ethylmorphine and codeine in Schedule II, preparations of codeine and ethylmorphine in Schedule III, and ketobemidone in Schedule IV. Codeine is the only major opiate found naturally in opium (in small amounts, two to three percent) given favorable status, listed only in Schedules II and its preparations in Schedule III. For comparison cannabis and heroin are listed in Schedules I and IV.[192] All these drugs have a similar history: first they are launched onto the market as remedies free of the problems observed in existing drugs, then their addictivity appears and lastly they are submitted to prohibition.

---

[191] Drewes, 2012, Individual Difference in Response, p. 68.

[192] United Nations Conference for the Adoption of a Single Convention on Narcotic Drugs, Final Act, Volume I, Chapter VI. Narcotic Drugs and Psychotropic Substances, Title 15, 30 March 1961 UN, Schedules, pp. 239-244.

E. Tranquilizers and Anxiolytics

But neither barbiturates nor amphetamines are the best selling legal psychotropics in the Western world from the 1950s to the 1970s. Instead, it is substances of a completely different type that experience a vigorous commercial expansion during this period. These are worth a brief mention to complete the picture of the prevailing conditions during this era of pharmacratic peace.

The pharmacological revolution of the 1950s was based primarily on muscle relaxants and sedatives but used as soporifics. These drugs are sold for the stress and anxiety of modern life. They don't create a current of dreaminess like the opiates, nor foment attention or reflection like the amphetamines or analogous stimulants, but rather are employed to place the user in a state of dreamy indifference to the inner and outer worlds.

By design their pharmacology attempts to be the perfect specimen of the honestly evasive drug, capable of extricating the user from an afflicted or nervous state without carrying her to any other dimension of consciousness. Instead, they are pure lenitives, cushions against psychic intensity, which for a time turn the world a uniform grey though they are sold for their ability to turn it rosy. Instead of producing the emotional analgesia of opium (which induces the active play of fantasy and imagination), these muscle relaxants induce a kind of intellectual analgesia characterized by esthetic and logical indifference.

As for their side effects, they are like less toxic barbiturates. High doses stun the user and cause difficulties in muscle coordination and speech amid a general stupor. Long term use can damage sexual function. They dissipate slowly, so that withdrawal can occur even one or two weeks after taking them.

Perhaps because they constitute evasion itself (with no other purpose except to lessen the impact of existence), the authorities tend not to consider them drugs and therapists do not bother to question their use. The peculiar potential for social conformity with these drugs resides in a fundamentally passive drunkenness. If other drugs (like the entheogens) posit alternatives to societal beliefs and customs, the tranquilizers and anxiolytics operate inversely, diminishing the rhythm of ideation and reaction so that the patient simply is not too preoccupied with anything, as long as she has a sufficient concentration of the drug in her bloodstream.

Their trade names (more than a thousand) express the true offer they make to the user. Examples include Atarax (hydroxine, an antihistamine used against anxiety and insomnia), Dominal (prothipendyl, an anxiolytic), Decontractyl (a muscle relaxant containing mephenesin), Placidyl (ethclorvynol, a sedative and hypnotic), Quietal (chlorpromazine), Dogmatil (sulpiride, an anti-psychotic), Pertranquil (meprobamate) and many others. The substances in this group will enjoy an unequaled prestige in those countries dedicated to the crusade against stupefacients.

Figure 413. Rauwolfia Serpentine, NMAH.

1. The Major Tranquilizers

The so-called neuroleptics (etymologically, nerve affecting, from *leptikos*, seizing) or major tranquilizers have an ancient botanic analog in *Rauwolfia serpentina* (Sanskrit: Sarpagandha, Chandrika; English: Indian Snakeroot), "a historical plant which has been found in the literature ... as early as 1000-800 B.C."[193] It is described in the Indian *Materia Medica* as a climbing shrub found in the tropical Himalyas that is "indigenous to India, Bangladesh and other regions of Asia."[194] The root has been used to treat poisonous snakebite[195] as well as

> hypertension, sleeplessness, mental agitation, and gastrointestinal illnesses such as diarrhoea, dysentery, and cholera, trauma, anxiety, schizophrenia, sedative induced sleeplessness, epilepsy, and insanity. ... In the modern era, Sarpagandha is used as an effective Antihypertensive and it is the world's first hypertensive drug.[196]

Several crystalline alkaloids have been isolated from its roots: Ajmaline, Ajmalimine, Ajmalicine, Serpentine, Serpentinine,[197] Rescinnamidine, Yohimbine, Reserpine and others.[198]

---

193 Perera, W.M.D.S., et al. "Neuro-therapeutic effect of *Rauvolfia serpentina (Sarpagandha/Ekaweriya)*; A review," *Journal of Advances in Experimental Therapeutics and Neurotherapeutics*, Volume 1, Issue 2, June 2023 NIH, Introduction, p. 7.

194 Perera, 2023, p. 9.

195 Nadkarni, K. M. Dr. K. M. Nadkarni's Indian Materia Medica, Volume One, third revised edition by A. K. Nadkarni. Bombay: Popular Prakashan Private Limited, 1976 AO, 2099 Rauwolfia Serpentina, Benth, p. 1053.

196 Perera, 2023, p. 7.

197 Nadkarni, 1976, 2099 Rauwolfia Serpentina, Benth, pp. 1050-1051.

198 Perera, 2023, p. 9.

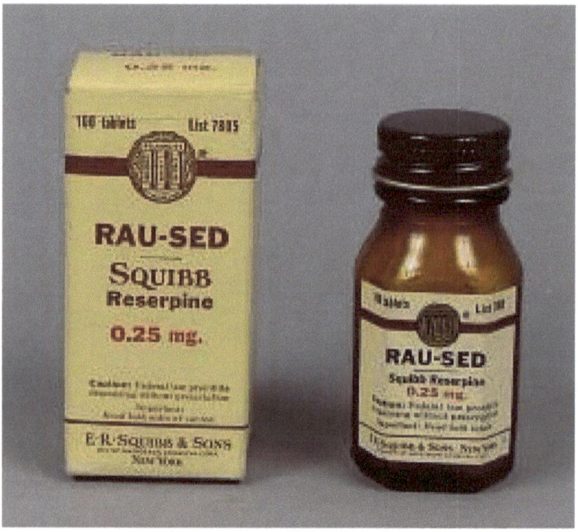

Figure 414. Rau-Sed Reserpine (E. R. Squibb & Sons), .25 mg., ca. 1956 NMAH.

Reserpine is considered its principal alkaloid and "became commercially available in Western medicine in 1952 after [the plant had been] ... used for centuries in Indian medicine for a variety of illnesses, including schizophrenia."[199] The alkaloid mainly acts as a "natural tranquillizer effective in the management of hypertension, cardiovascular diseases and neurological diseases."[200] [In contrast, Ajmalicine has antihypertensive properties and restores cerebral blood flow while Yohimbine "increases blood flow to the penis."[201]]

---

[199] Strawbridge, Rebecca et al. "The effects of reserpine on depression: A systematic review," *Journal of Psychopharmacology*, Volume 37, No. 3, 2023 NIH, p. 248, citing López-Muñoz F, Bhatara VS, Alamo C, et al. (2004) [Historical approach to reserpine discovery and its introduction in psychiatry]. *Actas Espanolas De Psiquiatria* 32: 387–395.

[200] Perera, 2023, p. 9.

[201] Perera, 2023, p. 9.

The use of reserpine "fell dramatically following reports of depression after treatment. ... The first reports of depression in humans, as a potential consequence of reserpine, emerged in the early 1950s."[202] Psychiatric complications included "sadness, fatigue and suicidal ideation in five patients with hypertension treated with large doses of reserpine. These were not observed in patients taking other antihypertensives, and symptoms ceased after reserpine discontinuation."[203] As a result its popularity as a treatment for schizophrenia was short-lived, although there is still "long-standing controversy surrounding the notion that reserpine causes depression."[204]

Chlorpromazine (Largactil, Thorazine) "was synthesized on December 11, 1951 ... in the laboratories of Rhône-Poulenc ... and released for clinical investigation in May 1952 as a possible potentiator of general anesthesia."[205] The investigating chemist proposed the name and noticed its very special pharmacodynamic properties.[206] A surgeon and physiologist in the French army, Henri Laborit (1914 – 1995) was one of the first to experiment with chlorpromazine (CPZ). Laborit is said to have noticed

---

202 Strawbridge, 2023, p. 248.

203 Strawbridge, 2023, p. 248.

204 Strawbridge, 2023, p. 258.

205 Ban, Thomas A. "Fifty years chlorpromazine: a historical perspective," *Neuropsychiatric Disease and Treatment*, Volume 3, No. 4, 2007 NIH, From synthesis to introduction, p. 495.

206 *propriétés pharmacodynamiques très particulières* (Charpentier, Paul et al. "*Recherches sur les diméthylaminopropyl-N phénothiazines substituées*," Comptes Rendus Hebdomadaires des Séances de l'Académie des Sciences, Tome Deux-Cent-Trente-Cinquième, Juillet – Décembre 1952 BNF, Séance du 7 Juillet 1952, p. 60).

not any loss of consciousness, not any change in the patient's mentality but a slight tendency to sleep and above all 'disinterest' for all that goes on around him. ... What he had noticed was an affective numbing similar, as was later suggested, to a 'chemical lobotomy' [quotation marks original].[207]

He is said to have employed the drug

as an adjunct to surgical anesthetics ('anesthetic cocktail,' 'lytic cocktail') because of its body temperature lowering effect. He found that CPZ, in the dosage of 50 to 100 mg given intravenously, produced disinterest without loss of consciousness and with only a slight tendency to sleep [quotation marks original].[208]

In 1954, of the 27 chronically overactive psychotic patients at a British mental hospital given chlorpromazine, seven patients definitely improved and eleven others slightly improved, but the same study also demonstrated antipsychotics do not cure schizophrenia:[209]

[I]n no case was the content of the psychosis changed. The schizophrenic and paraphrenic patients continued to be subject to delusions and hallucinations, though they appeared to be less disturbed by them. ... Few of these chronic psychotic patients showed improvement which enabled them to become more useful members of the mental hospital society. Others became less difficult nursing problems. ... The relief afforded by chlorpromazine thus appears to be principally symptomatic.[210]

---

207 Owens, David Cunningham and Eve C. Johnstone. "The development of antipsychotic drugs," *Brain and Neuroscience Advances*, Volume 2, 2018 NIH, The 1970s and 1980s: impact, theories and growing alarm, p. 2.

208 Ban, 2007, p. 496, citing Laborit H, Huguenard P, Alluaume R. 1952. Un noveau stabilisateur végétatif (le 4560 RP). *La Presse Médicale*, 60: 206–8.

209 Owens, et al, 2018, p. 2.

210 Elkes J. and Charmian Elkes. "Effect of Chlorpromazine on the Behaviour of Chronically Overactive Psychotic Patients," *British Medical Journal*, Volume 29, No. 4887, Saturday 4 September 1954 AA, p. 562.

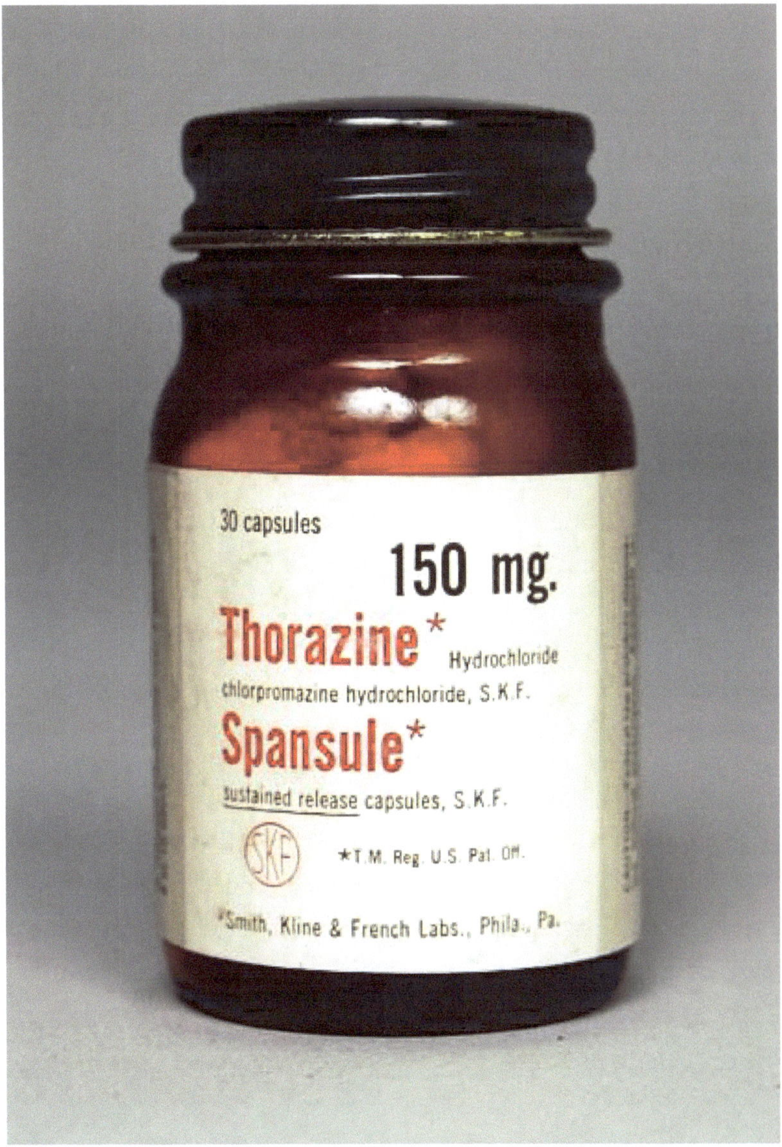

Figure 415. Chlorpromazine hydrochloride (Thorazine), Smith, Kline and French, 150 mg. NMAH.

Common side effects of chlorpromazine include severe diabetes, weight gain, and increased lipids, frequent orthostatic hypotension, tardive dyskinesia, anticholinergic effects and sedation, with occasional acute Parkinsonism, akathisia, and hyperprolactinemia.[211] Orthostatic hypotension "can lead to dizziness, syncope, falls, and worsening of angina,"[212] tardive dyskinesia is characterized by

> involuntary ... movements of the lower face, extremities and/or trunk muscles. Most commonly, these present as grimacing, lip-smacking/puckering, tongue movements, and excessive blinking. Most distressingly, symptoms persist long after the offending medication is discontinued, and may be permanent in some cases.[213]

Parkinsonism includes "a number of drug-induced symptoms resembling Parkinson's disease, such as bradykinesia, rigidity and tremor."[214] Anticholinergic side effects include

> decreased salivation leading to dry mouth, decreased intestinal mobility leading to constipation, inhibition of visual accommodation leading to blurred vision, increased pupil size, and tachycardia. These effects may lead to medical complications such as dental caries, ileus, and angina or myocardial infarction.[215]

Akathisia refers to "a feeling of restlessness and tension that usually (but not always) compels the sufferer to near-constant motion, inducing dysphoria and even suicidality."[216] Hyperprolactinemia is an

---

[211] Stroup, T. Scott and Neil Gray. "Management of common adverse effects of antipsychotic medications," *World Psychiatry*, Volume 17, Issue 3, October 2018 NIH, Table 1. Side effect profiles of selected antipsychotic drugs, p. 342.

[212] Stroup and Gray, 2018, p. 348.

[213] Stroup and Gray, 2018, p. 345.

[214] Stroup and Gray, 2018, p. 343.

[215] Stroup and Gray, 2018, p. 350.

[216] Stroup and Gray, 2018, p. 343.

increase in "the release of prolactin, which can lead to a number of acute side effects: sexual dysfunction, anovulation, inappropriate lactation (galactorrhea), and gynecomastia."[217]

Profound and long lasting disturbances in sexuality and affectivity are possible and some investigators have reasons to fear that the degradation of erotic desire is irreversible. It should be recalled that the working of the neuroleptics have been compared to a chemical castration and that the extent and reversibility of this effect have not been fully investigated.[218] In contrast, CPZ increases the oral appetite; it's as if the libido retreats from the genitals to the mouth. Other phenothiazines with similar effects include **thioridizine** (Meleril), a first generation antipsychotic used to treat schizophrenia and psychosis, **trifluoperazine** (Eskazine, Stelazine) and a long list of many, many more.

The surprising effect of the major tranquilizers is that they encase in an invisible straight jacket those who consume them, producing a state of emotional petrification (siderism, or star worship).[219] This characteristic has made them the pride of contemporary institutional psychiatry, because it permits ambulatory

---

217 Stroup and Gray, 2018, p. 347.

218 *Es sei daran erinnert ... kaum Untersuchungen vorliegen* (Brauchitsch, Hans V. "*Endokrinologisehe Aspekte des Wirkungsmechanismus nenroplegiseher Medikamente*," *Psychopharmacologia*, Volume 2, 1961 AO, 3. Sonstige Befunde a) Geschlechtshormone, p. 12).

219 "Therefore, the adoration of the stars was one of the most ancient religions" (Mohsan Fání. The Dabistán, or School of Manners, tr. David Shea and Anthony Troyer, Volume I. Paris: Printed for the Oriental Translation Fund of Great Britain and Ireland, 1843 AO, Preliminary Discourse: Part II. Synopsis of the Dynasties, Religions, Sects, and Philosophic Opinions, Treated of in the Dabistan, § I. – The First Religion – the Dynasties of Mahabad, Abad Azar, Shai Abad, Shai Giliv, Shai Mahbul, and Yasan, p. lxvi).

treatment of the mentally ill, reducing the number of inmates in asylums. In England, psychiatric bed numbers "have fallen markedly, from a high of 150,000 in the 1950s to <30,000 currently. ... Traditionally, most were occupied by long-stay patients with schizophrenia, and while a number of factors contributed to the shift to community care, the role of antipsychotics was crucial."[220]

In the 1960s, their reputation led the late President Kennedy to mention them in a Special Message to Congress, proposing that the mentally ill be treated rapidly and effectively in their communities, and returned to a useful place in society: "But tranquilizers and new therapeutic methods now permit mental illness to be treated successfully in a very high proportion of cases within relatively short periods of time – weeks or months, rather than years."[221]

As of 2023 their use is widespread because

> [a]ntipsychotics remain the drug class with the most robust evidence of effectiveness in psychotic disorders such as schizophrenia. ... They are also widely used in a range of other mental disorders, including in severe depression and bipolar disorder, and as off-licence treatments for symptom management in personality disorder, dementia, and some anxiety disorders. Altogether, nearly 800,000 individuals are prescribed these medications in England ... and prevalence is estimated at 1.7% in the US ... with increasing rates in children and adolescents.[222]

---

220 Owens and Johnstone, 2018, p. 2.

221 Kennedy, John F. "Special Message to the Congress on Mental Illness and Mental Retardation," The American Presidency Project 5 February 1963 [presidency.ucsb.edu, hereinafter PUC], Comprehensive Community Mental Health Centers, unpaged.

222 Chow, Rachel T. S., et al. "An umbrella review of adverse effects associated with antipsychotic medications: the need for complementary study designs," *Neuroscience and Behavioral Reviews*, Volume 155, 2023 NIH, Introduction, p. 1.

In reality, these are addictive drugs, which taken in large enough quantities over a prolonged period of time provoke intense withdrawal syndromes. Sadly, the addiction is unaccompanied by euphoria. While the chemically lobotomized appear phlegmatic and robotic, a basic feeling of sadness stays with them until the end of treatment, when the body manages to liberate itself from the intoxication. In this, the therapeutic efficacy depends upon the euphoria produced by the suspension of the dose.

What in the organism resists the effects of the drug is evidently what the ancients would have called the soul or spirit, which will not admit without disgust the displacement of the essence of the libido to the stomach and throat. These drugs make a reality of the pharmacratic dream of addictive drugs that are tolerated but shameful. In other words, they are admissible drugs on the moral level for the prohibitionist conscience.

Certainly, there has been much progress in neurological chemistry. The pharmacopoeia disposes of substances to treat violent schizophrenia by provoking a catatonic schizophrenia, understanding by this both a physical paralysis and an emotional disintegration proportionate to the dose. It is now unnecessary to lock certain types of people in insane asylums; it is enough to ensure they take their prescribed drugs at the prescribed time.

Chlorpromazine, thioridizine and trifluoperazine are not found in the Single Convention of 30 March 1961, nor in the Convention on Psychotropic Substances of 21 February 1971, nor in the revision of the Single Convention as amended by the 1972 Protocol as at 18 May 2016, nor in the revisions of the Convention on Psychotropic Substances of 1971, as at 13 November 2016. [223]

---

[223] UN, 30 March 1961, Schedules, pp. 239-244; UN, 1971, Lists of Substances in the Schedules, unpaged; UN, 18 May 2016, pp. 1-8; UN, 13 November 2016, pp. 1-9.

2. The Minor Tranquilizers

By the middle of the 1960s, the production figures for the barbiturates and amphetamines were "largely supplanted by the 'minor tranquilizers' of recent decades: first meprobamate (Miltown, Equanil) and now diazepam (Valium) and chlordiazepoxide (Librium) [quotation marks original]."[224]

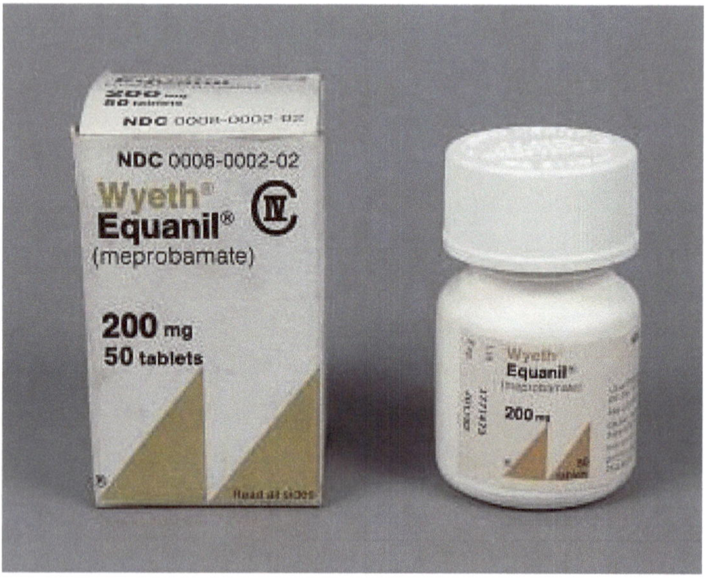

Figure 416. Meprobamate (Equanil), 200 mg.,
Wyeth Laboratories, ca. 1955 NMAH.

---

[224] Fort, Joel. The Addicted Society: Pleasure-Seeking and Punishment Revisited. NY: Grove Press, Inc., 1981 AA, Chapter 2 The What and How of Drugs from Alcohol and Heroin to Marijuana and Valium, Hypnosedatives (sleeping pills), Tranquilizers, and Antidepressants, p. 29.

Meprobamate (Miltown, Equanil) was first synthesized by Ludwig and Piech in 1951.[225] Frank M. Berger (1913 – 2008), who tested it the following year, reportedly described it "as an interneuronal blocking agent with pronounced muscle-relaxing properties"[226] while "[s]maller doses had general sedative and muscle-relaxant effects"[227] which also could moderate anxiety and tension. The effect was called ataraxia (perfect peace of mind, or moral tranquility) by the manufacturers, and in the US it was launched onto the market as a happiness pill, while in Europe it was spoken of as an innocuous remedy for the treatment of neurosis. Indeed, a clinical trial in 1956 of "83 alcoholics, 3 drug addicts, 3 patients with nervous tension and tremors, and 4 psychoneurotics" concluded it was safe and non-addictive:

> A safe, not habit-forming relaxant, meprobamate (Equanil) is useful for relief of anxiety, tension and depression, particularly after episodes of acute alcoholism. The results of this study indicate that Equanil is more satisfactory for relaxation of the alcoholic patient than the barbiturates.[228]

Although "the low toxicity of the drug, even when taken in large doses"[229] was emphasized, further clinical experience convinced

---

[225] Turvey, S. E. C. "Meprobamate (Equanil) for Relief of Anxiety and Nervous Tension from Various Causes," *The Canadian Medical Association Journal*, Volume 74, Number 11, 1 June 1956 NIH, p. 863, citing Ludwig, B. J. and Piech, E. C. *J. Am. Chem. Soc.*, **73**: 5779, 1951.

[226] Turvey, 1956, p. 863, citing Berger, F. M.. *J. Pharmacol. & Exper. Therap.*, **104**: 468, 1952.

[227] West, E. D. and A. Fernandes da Fonseca. "Controlled trial of meprobamate," *British Medical Journal*, 24 November 1956 NIH, p. 1207, citing Berger, F. M. (1954). *J. Pharmacol.*, **112**, 413.

[228] Turvey, 1956, Summary and Conclusions, p. 865.

[229] Shane, Aubrey M. and Solomon Hirsch. "Three Cases of Meprobamate

one of the first investigators (who had issued a preliminary report that meprobamate was not habit forming only four months earlier) that "a few patients do form a harmful habit for this drug."[230] He discovered that some of his patients had developed a physical dependency and others a psychologic dependency, while still others had engaged in excessive self-medication, manifesting "all the signs of intoxication, including euphoria, dysarthric speech, and generalized incoordination."[231] In an addendum he reported that nine patients "took increasing amounts of meprobamate to obtain the same effects. Apparently, a few patients do have a build-up of tolerance to this drug."[232]

That same year (1956) three cases of overdose were reported featuring "coma, marked muscle relaxation with absent reflexes, a dangerous fall in blood pressure in two of the cases, and quick recovery without sequelae. The reactions suggest that a greater dosage might well cause death."[233] A year later two other investigators reported addiction with withdrawal symptoms which included major convulsions, a seizure, postwithdrawal anxiety, and an episode of a gran mal seizure, adding that the "type of addiction caused by meprobamate resembles that caused by chronic intoxication with excessive amounts of barbiturates and alcohol."[234] There are more

---

Poisoning," *The Canadian Medical Association Journal*, Volume 74, Number 11, 1 June 1956 NIH, p. 909, citing Selling, L. S. *J. A. M. A.*, **157**: 1594, 1955 and Borrus, J. C. *J. A. M. A.*, **157**: 1596, 1955.

230 Lemere, Frederick. "Habit-forming Properties of Meprobamate (Miltown, Equanil)," *A. M. A. Archives of Neurology and Psychiatry*, **76**, August 1956 NIH, p. 205.

231 Lemere, August 1956, p. 205.

232 Lemere, August 1956, p. 206.

233 Shane and Hirsch, 1956, p. 909.

234 Essig, Carl F. and John D. Ainslie. "Addiction to Meprobamate (Miltown, Equanil)," *Journal of the American Medical Association*, 20 July 1957 NIH,

communications along the same lines in 1958 and 1959.[235] A case of primary (no previous) addiction is reported in 1963.[236] Investigators in Norway in 1964 found slightly more than a quarter of addicts admitted to a state clinic were addicted to meprobamate, some taking as much as 30 grams a day, with acute withdrawal symptoms:

> Among the psychopharmaceuticals, meprobamate seems to lead increasingly to dependence and addiction. Eleven of the forty patients were addicted to meprobamate. This drug is very widely used in milder forms of nervousness, and physicians have only recently become aware of the danger of dependence arising from its use. Several of our meprobamate addicts have taken as much as twenty to thirty grammes of this drug daily. The withdrawal of meprobamate is frequently accompanied by symptoms of acute distress, such as anxiety, sweating, fibrillary twitching, cramps, difficulty in breathing, nausea, vomiting, a tendency to diarrhoea, hallucinations with anxiety symptoms, dehydration and the like.[237]

Between 1958 and 1965 the first meprobamate addicts even began to show up in a drug addiction outpatient clinic in Calcutta: "There were five cases each of addiction to barbiturates and new psychotropic drugs like meprobamate and the amphetamines."[238] In

---

Correspondence, p. 1382.

[235] Little, J. Crawford. "A Case of Primary Addiction to Meprobamate," *British Medical Journal*, 28 September 1963 NIH, p. 794, citing Lemere, F. (1956). *Arch. Neurol. Psychiat.*, **76**, 205; Haizlip, T. M., and Ewing, J. A. (1958). *New Engl. J. Med.*, **258**, 1181; Mohr, R. C., and Mead, B. T. (1958). *New Engl. J. Med.*, **259**, 865; and Glatt, M. M. (1959). *Brit. med. J.*, **1**, 587.

[236] Little, 1963, p. 794.

[237] Teigen, Armfinn. "The Norwegian State Clinic for the Treatment of Addicts," *Bulletin on Narcotics*, 01/01/1964 UN, The drugs most frequently abused in Norway, p. 2/12.

[238] Chopra, M. D. G. S. and Chopra, M. D. Paramjeet Singh. "Studies on 300 Indian drug addicts with special reference to psychosociological aspects, etiology and treatment," *Bulletin on Narcotics*, 01/01/1965 UN, II. Statistical Data, (i) Drugs of

contrast, "225 persons (75 per cent) were addicted to opium."[239] Among a certain few, these petroleum derivatives were evidently as attractive as Kashmiri hashish was to a certain few in the US.

By the early 1960s consumption in Britain and the US was already widespread:

In view of the widespread adverse reports, it is surprising to learn that in 1961 meprobamate, with 870,000 prescriptions, accounted for 15% of all tranquillizer prescriptions on the N.H.S. in England and Wales. In the United States the consumption of the drug has been phenomenal.[240]

The popularity of meprobamate did not last when reports of tolerance, dependence, abuse and overdose began to surface:

Despite high clinical expectations and the enormous success of meprobamate in terms of sales, it was relatively short-lived commercially, as it was withdrawn from the North American markets in the mid-1960s, when problems of tolerance, abuse, lethal overdoses and dependence became apparent, which reminded many clinicians of the problems previously observed with the barbiturates.[241]

Chlordiazepoxide (Librium) accidentally achieved a comparable and even greater market than meprobamate. The Polish scientist Leo Henryk Sternbach (1908 – 2005), working for Hoffman-La Roche first in Basel, Switzerland and later Nutley, New Jersey, had previously studied azo dyes in Krakow:[242] "'My search led me to the

---

Addiction, p. 3/11.

239 Chopra and Chopra, 1965, p. 3/11.

240 Little, 1963, p. 794, citing *Lancet*, 1962, **2**, 1176.

241 López-Muñoz, Francisco, et al. "The discovery of chlordiazepoxide and the clinical introduction of the benzodiazepines: Half a century of anxiolytic drugs," *Journal of Anxiety Disorders*, **25,** 2011 NIH, p. 555.

242 Mendelson, Wallace B. "Benzodiazepines: The Accidental Tranquilizers,"

so-called benzheptoxdiazines, compounds with which I had become familiar in the 1930s, in connection with my studies related to dye chemistry' [quotation marks original]."[243] A colleague noticed an untested compound "stored on the researchers' disorganized workbench during a lab cleanup."[244] Animal studies showed it

> exhibited strong muscle relaxant and sedative effects in rats, along with powerful anticonvulsant properties and muscle relaxation in unanesthetized cats. ... Before conducting tests on humans, a preclinical study of the medication was also carried out on lions, panthers, leopards, and tigers from the San Diego and Boston zoos. The effect was described as 'taming' [quotation marks original].[245]

A popular advertisement "released by the company shows a 40-pound lynx with a ferocious expression in one frame, and in the next docilely sniffing a flower."[246]

The new compound had similar effects to meprobamate, but "was superior to meprobamate in many trials in terms of anxiolytic activity and as a central muscle relaxant ...."[247] Trials in outpatient and hospitalized psychiatric patients showed "chlordiazepoxide was an effective anxiolytic drug, with very few adverse effects, and with little effect on the state of awareness and intellectual activity."[248] The FDA

Psychology Today, 2 June 2020 (psychologytoday.com, hereinafter PT), p. 2/12.

[243] Junkes, Larissa et al. "Leo Sternbach and the benzodiazepines 60 years on: A revolutionary treatment for anxiety disorders," *Pharmacological Research* **207**, 2024 NIH, p. 2.

[244] Junkes, 2024, p. 2.

[245] Junkes, 2024, pp. 2, 3.

[246] Mendelson, 2020, p. 3/12.

[247] López-Muñoz, 2011, p. 556.

[248] López-Muñoz, 2011, p. 557.

approved the new drug "on 24 February 1960. Its trade name, Librium®, is now a key part of the history of pharmacology."[249]

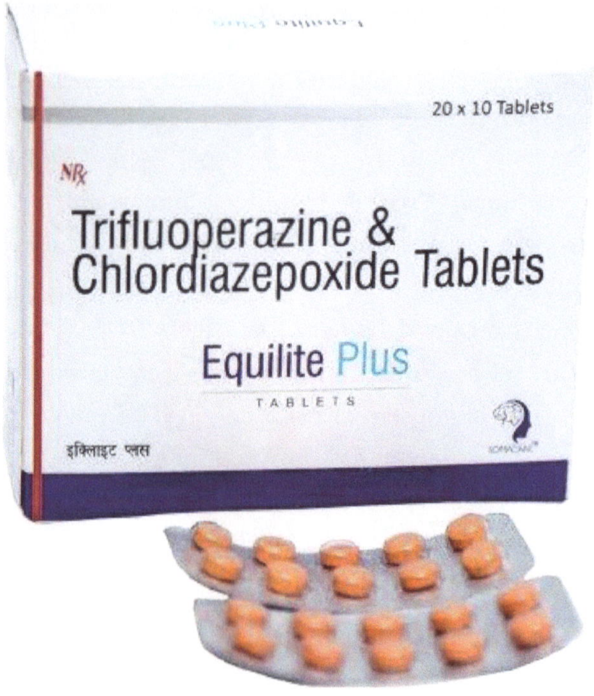

Figure 417. Equilite Plus (chlordiazepoxide and trifluoperazine) [indiamart.com, hereinafter IM].

[249] López-Muñoz, 2011, p. 557.

Two years later, a trial of 210 patients seen in general practice complaining of nervousness, tenseness and hyper-irritability found 204 (97%) "improved on Librium."[250] The new benzodiazepine was considered

> a revolution in the psychiatric treatment of anxiety disorders and convulsive disorders, due to its rapid onset of action, efficacy, and safety, with notable improvements compared to barbiturates, which caused significant respiratory depression.[251]

It began to be prescribed for everything from "panic disorders, phobias, seizures, low back pain, insomnia, and the management of alcohol and barbiturate withdrawal ...."[252] Indeed, the earliest communications were almost uniformly positive:

> investigators in a number of medical specialties, including internal medicine, cited impressive results obtained from use of methaminodiazepoxide [chlordiazepoxide] in a variety of conditions and a freedom from side effects at therapeutic dosage levels. ... In human tolerance studies of the drug under controlled conditions, there was no evidence of cardiovascular disturbances .... Evidence of habituation or postmedication depression has not been observed.[253]

However, in a by now notorious evolution, very soon its addictive nature became evident. A year after its introduction, "[t]hirty-six hospitalized psychiatric patients were treated with 100 to

---

[250] Reiser, P., et al. "The Use of Librium in General Practice," *Journal of the National Medical Association*, Volume 54, No. 2, March 1962 NIH, p. 247.

[251] Junkes, 2024, p. 3.

[252] Junkes, 2024, p. 3.

[253] Harris, Titus H. "Methaminodiazepoxide," *Journal of the American Medical Association*, 12 March 1960 [sci-hub.st, hereinafter SH], Preliminary Communications, pp. 1162-1163.

600 mg of chlordiazepoxide daily for one to seven months (most more than three months)" at the Veterans Hospital in Palo Alto, California.[254] Upon withdrawal some patients had seizures:

> Ten of 11 patients abruptly switched to placebos after several months of high daily doses (300-600 mg, 8-20 times the usual therapeutic range) of chlordiazepoxide experienced new symptoms and signs soon after. Depression, aggravation of psychoses, agitation, insomnia, loss of appetite, and nausea appeared between two and eight days following abrupt withdrawal. Two patients had seizures at seven and eight days. A third patient, not in the withdrawal study, had a seizure twelve days after discontinuation of a 300 mg daily dose.[255]

Specifically,

> the following symptoms and signs of withdrawal were observed: depression (6 subjects), seizures (2), twitching (1), insomnia (2), loss of appetite (4), agitation (3), and a worsening of their psychosis. Some of these signs appeared by the second day and persisted through the ninth day of withdrawal.[256]

As well, a woman who took 20 mg. five times a day, frequently doubling the evening dose for four years developed abdominal cramps, sweating and a crawling sensation under the skin when the drug was discontinued, suggesting "a true addiction to chlordiazepoxide,

---

[254] Hollister, Leo E., Francis P. Motzenbecker and Roger O. Degan. "Withdrawal reactions from chlordiazepoxide (Librium)," *Psychopharmacologia*, **2**: 63-68, 1961 [benzo.org.uk, hereinafter BOU], Preliminary Study, p. 1/5.

[255] Hollister, 1961, Summary, p. 4/5.

[256] Martin, William R. and L. F. McNicholas. "Benzodiazepine Studies in Rodents," in Benzodiazepines: A Review of Research Results, 1980, eds. Szara, Stephen I. and Jacqueline P. Ludford. Rockville, MD: National Institute on Drug Abuse, 1980, p. 39, citing Hollister, L.E., Motzenbecker, F.P., and Degan, R.O. "Withdrawal reactions from chlordiazepoxide (Librium)," *Psychopharmacologia*, **2**: 1961.

requiring ever-increasing dosage and having true withdrawal symptoms on discontinuation of the drug."[257]

Side effects from therapeutic use include drowsiness, impaired muscle control (ataxia), confusion, dizziness, skin problems, edema, minor menstrual irregularities, nausea, constipation, movement disorders, decreased desire for sexual activity (decreased libido), blood disorders, jaundice and liver dysfunction.[258] Nevertheless, the same researcher who produced the first withdrawal symptoms in 1961 by using 8 to 20 times the usual therapeutic dose wrote twenty years later that compared to meprobamate "the withdrawal syndrome from chlordiazepoxide ... [is] both milder and more attenuated."[259] This echoed his earlier conclusion: "Symptoms from withdrawal of chlordiazepoxide were slower to develop and less acute than those following withdrawal of barbiturates or meprobamate."[260]

Valium (diazepam) appears three years later and will become hegemonic in the world market. Once again, Leo Sternbach of Hoffman-La Roche led the research. Sold under various brand names, this is a benzodiazepine like Librium only more active but with a shorter half-life:

> Diazepam – a medication that was the most prescribed in America between 1969 and 1982, with over 2.3 billion doses sold in its peak year in 1978 – was developed right after [chlordiazepoxide], aiming for a more potent compound with a shorter half-life.

---

257 Slater, J. "Suspected Dependence on Chlordiazepoxide Hydrochloride (Librium)," *Canadian Medical Association Journal*, Volume 95, 27 August 1966 NIH, Letters to the Journal, p. 416.

258 Ogbru, Omudhome. "[C]hlordiazepoxide (Librium)," MedicineNet [medicinenet.com, hereinafter MN], p. 2/6

259 Hollister, Leo E. "Dependence on Benzodiazepines," in Benzodiazepines, 1980, p. 74.

260 Hollister, 1961, Withdrawal Study, p. 2/5.

Synthesized in 1959 and introduced in the United States in late 1963 ... Valium® ... was named from the Latin word *valere*, which means 'to be healthy' [italics and quotation marks original].[261]

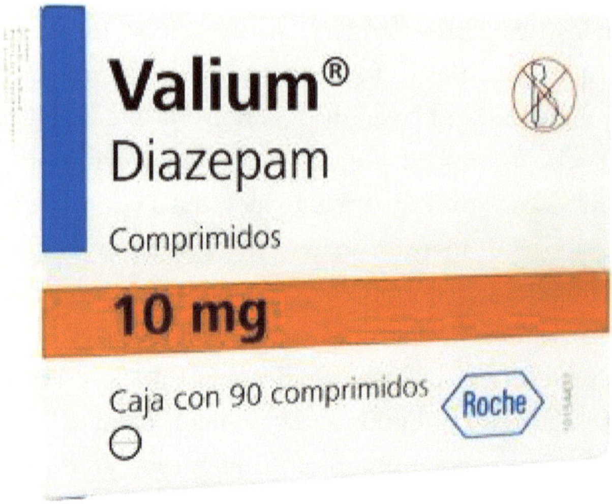

Figure 418. Valium (diazepam), 10 mg., Roche [superwalmart.com.mx, hereinafter WMX].

As it begins its ascent, in 1964 the Council on Drugs of the AMA warns of convulsions after abrupt withdrawal:

The most common adverse effects of diazepam are drowsiness, dizziness, fatigue, and ataxia .... Other untoward reactions ... are nausea, blurred vision, diplopia, hypotension, headache, impairment of memory, slurred speech, tremor, skin rash, incontinence and constipation .... Like other central nervous system depressants ... diazepam has been associated with the occurrence of withdrawal symptoms (including convulsions) in some patients when its administration was abruptly discontinued after prolonged use of large doses.[262]

---

[261] Junkes, 2024, p. 1.

[262] Council on Drugs. "Evaluation of a Tranquilizing Agent Diazepam (Valium),"

By 1970 "the benzodiazepines succeed in displacing the sales of barbiturates ...."[263] For the decade beginning in 1965

> these drugs became the most widely prescribed in the world, and became known in the non-scientific press as 'happy pills.' [D]iazepam was the most prescribed medical treatment and chlordiazepoxide was in third place. ... [I]n the USA at least, there was what can only be described as a passion for these anxiolytic agents, which were consumed on a regular basis by 10–20% of adults in the Western countries. ... Between 1973 and 1975, the annual number of benzodiazepine prescriptions exceeded 80 million [quotation marks original].[264]

The pushback was not long in coming. The UK Monopolies Commission published a report in 1973

> which showed the high cost to the government of mass consumption of diazepam and chlordiazepoxide. The British Government asked Hoffman–LaRoche to repay part of the costs generated by this problem. Despite the legal action taken by the company against the British Government, it had to pay almost four million pounds to the National Health Service. Similar actions began in various other European countries.[265]

The annual cost to the UK's National Health Service was

> approximately £8 million. ... The Commission ... reached the clear conclusion that United Kingdom prices for some years have been manifestly too high and that the Roche group has accordingly obtained from the sale of the drugs in this country profits far in excess of what is justifiable.[266]

Journal of the American Medical Association, Volume 189, No. 5, 3 August 1964 AA, p. 371.

263 Junkes, 2024, p. 3.

264 López-Muñoz, 2011, 5. The clinical introduction of the benzodiazepines: the rise, fall and rationalisation, p. 558.

265 López-Muñoz, 2011, p. 558.

266 The Earl of Limerick. "Tranquilizers: Monopolies Commission Report," *House of*

The pharmaceutical giant Hoffman-La Roche refused to disclose its sales:

The Roche parent company based in Switzerland refused to give the Monopolies Commission information on its world-wide sales and research costs, so that the [C]ommission's figure for the profits from the sale of the two drugs in the United Kingdom of £25 million over seven years is its own estimate.[267]

In the United States,

the increase in consumption of benzodiazepines ... was so marked in the early 1970s that the North American media launched a campaign to discredit these drugs, which they contemptuously labeled 'tranquillizing agents' and 'addictive drugs' [quotation marks original].[268]

The concern reached the US Senate where hearings were held. The chair of the Subcommittee on Health, Senator Edward Moore Kennedy (1932 – 2009) decried the increase in prescriptions:

Valium and Librium – these have almost become household words in the United States; 44.6 million prescriptions were filled or refilled for Valium alone in 1978, making it by far the largest selling drug in this country. ... The tranquilizing of America has become very big business. Millions of dollars are spent each year to convince physicians to use tranquilizers for a wide variety of things .... Our message to the American people is clear: If you require a daily dose of Valium to get through each day, you are hooked and you should seek help.[269]

Lords Debate, Volume 341, cc 786-91, 12 April 1973 Hansard [api.parliament.uk, hereinafter HAN], p. 1/3.

267 Unknown author. "Profits from Drugs," *British Medical Journal*, 21 April 1973 NIH, p. 132.

268 López-Muñoz, 2011, p. 558.

269 Kennedy, Edward M. "First session on examination on the use and misuse of valium, librium, and other minor tranquilizers, September 10, 1979," Use and Misuse

These hearings "resulted in a predictable aftereffect: a flood of testimonials in the media about adverse reactions and dependence, and congressional inquiries to various agencies."[270]

In 1984 the benzodiazepines were declared to be controlled substances as they "had the capacity to create a state of dependence and depression of the central nervous system which leads to distortions in motor function, behavior and personality."[271] As a consequence, "restrictions were implemented in the 1980s, leading to diazepam being removed from the market in 2002, and subsequently reintroduced shortly afterwards."[272]

The minor tranquilizers meprobamate, chlordiazepoxide and diazepam cannot be found in the Single Convention of 30 March 1961.[273] Meprobamate is the fifth substance listed in Schedule IV of the 1971 Psychotropic Convention.[274] As of 13 November 2016, all three are listed in Schedule IV of the Convention on Psychotropic Substances of 1971.[275]

---

of Benzodiazepines: Hearing before the Subcommittee on Health and Scientific Research of the Committee on Labor and Human Resources, United States Senate, Ninety-Sixth Congress. Washington, DC: US Government Printing Office, 1980 BGU, p. 1.

270 Szara, Stephen I. "Introduction," Benzodiazepines, 1980, pp. 1-2.

271 López-Muñoz, 2011, pp. 558-559.

272 Junkes, 2024, p. 3.

273 UN, 30 March 1961, Schedules, pp. 239-244.

274 UN, 1971, List of Substances in Schedule IV, unpaged.

275 UN, 13 November 2016, List of substances in Schedule IV, pp. 6, 7.

F. Nonbarbiturate Hypnotics

These drugs were investigated in search of a non-addictive analgesic and soporific, like the synthetic and semisynthetic opiates, and the already mentioned tranquilizers. It might be added that the result was not much different either. With marked obstinacy this ignores a biochemically inexact but logically coherent maxim, in that the molecule that creates the habit and the molecule that kills the pain are probably identical:

> Any opiate that relieves pain is habit forming, and the more effectively it relieves pain the more habit forming it is. The habit forming molecule and the pain killing molecule of morphine are probably identical, and the process by which morphine relieves pain is the same process that leads to tolerance and addiction. Non habit forming morphine appears to be a latter day Philosopher's Stone.[276]

Or, in other words, what provokes the habit is the euphoria itself, the happiness that arises from the experience of no longer being in pain:

> Most human beings become familiarized with narcotics thanks to their anesthetic properties. The feeling of happiness, the euphoria connected with their use, leads to addiction. The fact that depressive subjects succumb with particular pleasure to morphine is explained by the fact that they experience existence as such as pain.[277]

---

[276] Burroughs, William S. "Letter from a Master Addict to Dangerous Drugs," *The British Journal of Addiction*, Volume 53, No. 2, 1956 AA, p. 120.

[277] Jünger, Ernst. Approaches: Drugs and Ecstatic Intoxication, unknown translator. Unknown place of publication: Unknown publisher, 1970 AO, Chapter 1 Skulls and Reefs, Section 27, unpaged; *Die meisten Menschen ... schmerzhaft empfunden wird* (Annäherungen: Drogen und Rausch. Stuttgart, DE: Ernst Klett Verlag, 1970 AA, Section 27, p. 46).

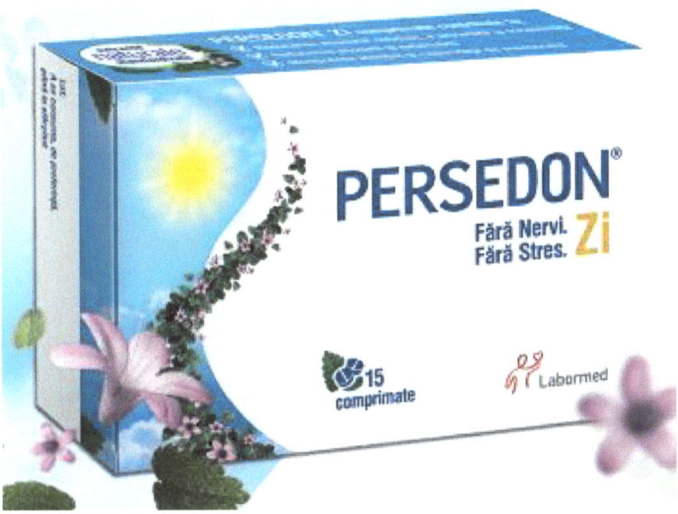

Figure 419. Persedon Zi (pyrithyldione), 500 mg., S.C. Sandoz S.R.L. [prospecte.net, hereinafter PN].

Pyrithyldione (Persedon, Pyridione, Presidon) is among the oldest of these drugs, discovered at the beginning of the Second World War: "The pharmacologic properties of the drug were first reported in 1940 by Koppanyi et al., who discussed the actions and toxic effects of 3,3-diethyl-2,4-dioxotetrahydropyridine, which they refer to as 'Pyridione' [quotation marks original]."[278] The drug was advertised as "a sedative hypnotic predictable in its effect, rapid in onset, with negligible side effects, little tendency to habit formation, slight properties of tolerance and completely nontoxic and safe."[279]

---

[278] Covner, Albert H. and Seymour L. Halpern. "Fatal Agranulocytosis Following Therapy with 'Presidon' (3,3-diethyl-2,4-dioxotetrahydropyridine), a New Sedative Hypnotic Agent," *The New England Journal of Medicine*, Volume 242, No. 2, 12 January 1950 NIH, Discussion, p. 50.

[279] Covner and Halpern, 1950, p. 49.

However, in 1950 a 64-year-old woman complaining of nervous exhaustion was given Presidon for severe insomnia. She was then admitted to hospital and died from a "case of fatal agranulocytosis [an extreme form of neutropenia, the presence of too few infection-fighting neutrophils in the blood][280] ... [indicating] that this sedative hypnotic may not be the safe drug it is believed to be."[281]

In Spain, the data on

> agranulocytosis and pyrithyldione were presented to the National Commission of Pharmacovigilance when eight cases of pyrithyldione-induced agranulocytosis had been identified. The Commission unanimously recommended withdrawal of pyrithyldione from the market, based on ... its association with a high risk of agranulocytosis. However, the Ministry of Health took more than 2 years after that to withdraw the drug, and six additional cases occurred ....[282]

Glutethimide (Doriden), an anticonvulsant nonbarbiturate compound, was launched with great fanfare in 1955 as another innocuous alternative to the barbiturate sedatives: "It was found to have approximately the same hypnotic activity as pentobarbital in the dosages recommended ...."[283] In 1968 some 582,000 prescriptions for the drug were written in the UK alone.[284] One outpatient study in

---

[280] Stroup and Gray, 2018, p. 349.

[281] Covner and Halpern, 1950, p. 49.

[282] L. Ibáñez, et al. "Agranulocytosis induced by pyrithyldione, a sedative hypnotic drug," *European Journal of Clinical Pharmacology*, Volume 55, February 2000 NIH, p. 764.

[283] Davis, Charles A. and Robert D. Gruener. "Glutethimide – A New Nonbarbiturate Hypnotic," *California Medicine*, Volume 84, No. 4, April 1956 NIH, p. 290.

[284] Dunlap, Sir Derrick. "The Use and Abuse of Psychotropic Drugs," *Proceedings of the Royal Society of Medicine*, Volume 63, December 1970 NIH, Table 2 Hypnotics prescribed in 1968, p. 1280.

1979 found that both 30 mg. temazepam (Restoril) and 500 mg. glutethimide evaluated under "double-blind conditions in a 4-day study in 75 outpatients with a history of insomnia ... were equally effective, and patients receiving either of the active drugs estimated that they fell asleep in about one-half the time of patients on placebo."[285] No physical or ophthalmological changes "attributable to the test medications ... were found, with the exception of a significant increase of 7.0 mm Hg standing systolic blood pressure from baseline in the group treated with glutethimide."[286]

However, in early mice studies glutethimide "caused initial excitation, marked ataxia, and incoordination of movement followed by narcosis and death."[287] By 1981 a therapeutic review by a special expert committee sponsored by the Canadian Department of National Health and Welfare was recommending benzodiazepines for anxiety instead of barbiturates and nonbarbiturate hypnotics:

> Barbiturates and nonbarbiturate sedative-hypnotics (e.g., ethchlorvynol, glutethimide, meprobamate, methaqualone and methyprylon) should not be prescribed for acute reactive anxiety, anxiety neurosis or anxiety disorder since the safer and equally effective benzodiazepines, which are less associated with dependence, are available.[288]

---

[285] Fillingim, J. M. "Double-blind Evaluation of the Efficacy and Safety of Temazepam in Outpatients with Insomnia," *Br. J. clin. Pharmac.*, Volume 8, 1979 NIH, pp. 73S, 77S.

[286] Fillingim, 1979, p. 77S.

[287] Somers, G. F. "Pharmacological Properties of Thalidomide (α-Phthalimido Glutarimide), A New Sedative Hypnotic Drug." *British Journal of Pharmacology*, Volume 15, 1960 NIH, p. 112.

[288] Ban, T. A.., et al. "Therapeutic monograph on anxiolytic-sedative drugs," *CMA Journal*, Volume 124, 1 June 1981 NIH, *Drug Therapy*, p. 1445.

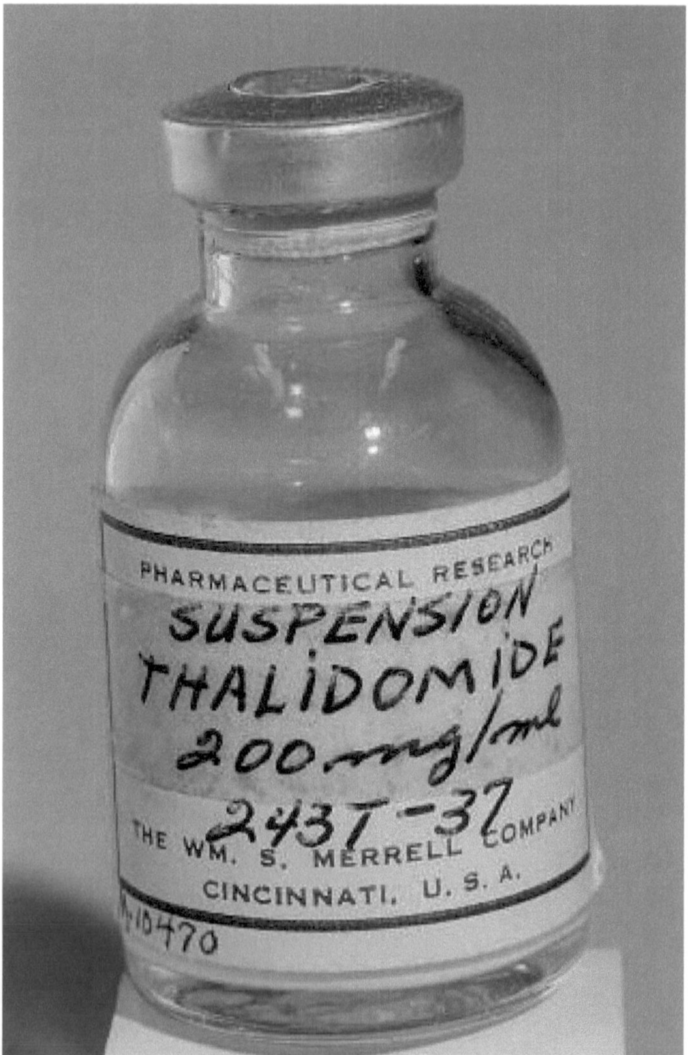

Figure 420. Thalidomide, 200 mg/ml.
Wm S. Merrell Company NMAH.

Thalidomide (Distaval, Contergan, Softenon), another nonbarbiturate hypnotic sedative, was "first synthesized by Kunz, Keller, and Muckter (1956), who also described its main pharmacological properties."[289] Testing in rodents was more than promising, with no serious side effects:

> Thalidomide ... produces no toxic effects when administered orally to animals in massive doses. ... The drug has a quietening effect on the central nervous system, reducing the voluntary activity of laboratory animals and promoting sleep. Unlike the barbiturate drugs it does not cause an initial excitation in mice, incoordination or narcosis. ... It has no deleterious side effects and does not affect the heart, respiration or autonomic nervous system.[290]

Introduced by the German pharmaceutical company Chemie Grünenthal GmbH in 1956, "thalidomide was prescribed as a nonbarbiturate hypnotic sedative able to produce deep sleep without hangover or risk of dependency."[291] Thalidomide was "marketed and distributed in 46 countries around the world using different names. For example, the drug was known as Distaval in the UK and Australia, but was called Softenon in Europe and Contergan in Germany."[292]

Advertised as an effective anti-emetic for pregnant woman suffering from morning sickness, "the drug's popularity was due to its wide availability as it was accessible without prescription and also relatively inexpensive. In Germany it quickly became a top-selling

---

289 Somers, 1960, p. 111.

290 Somers, 1960, p. 111.

291 Rehman, Waqas, et al. "The rise, fall and subsequent triumph of thalidomide: lessons learned in drug development," *Therapeutic Advances in Hematology*, Volume 2, No. 5, 2011 NIH, Introduction, *Historic Perspective*, p. 291.

292 Vargesson, Neil. "Review Thalidomide-Induced Teratogenesis: History and Mechanisms," *Birth Defects Research (Part C)*, Volume 105, 4 June 2015 NIH, Part one: History and Thalidomide Embryopathy, p. 140.

sedative and an estimated 14.6 tons were sold in 1960."[293] The new drug was

> marketed heavily and advertised as completely safe .... Indeed, sample packets of the drug were given out to physicians to distribute freely to patients suffering from morning sickness .... Precisely how many women were given the drug will never be known.[294]

Indeed, the company massively promoted thalidomide as "completely nonpoisonous ... astonishingly safe ... fully harmless ... completely safe for pregnant women and nursing mothers without any adverse effects on mother and child."[295]

This macabre joke kept the product at the height of popularity for another two years. Nevertheless, there appeared reports of adults suffering from serious disorders, an unexplainable epidemic of polyneuritis and the first births of monstrous infants. At the end of 1961 the scandal exploded:

> Dr. William McBride, an Australian obstetrician, and Dr. Widukind Lenz, a German pediatrician and geneticist, made independent observations linking thalidomide use in pregnancy to congenital malformations .... These findings were confirmed by multiple cases worldwide ....[296]

It was not until then that thalidomide was identified as the cause of over 10,000 children who had been born with irreparable malformations. The drug "was confirmed ... to be the cause of the

---

293 Rehman, et al., 2011, p. 291.

294 Vargesson, 2015, p. 140.

295 Evans, Harold. "How men who blighted lives of thousands with thalidomide evaded justice," *The Globe and Mail,* 25 November 2014 [globeandmail.com, hereinafter GM], p. 7/12.

296 Rehman, 2011, pp. 291-292.

largest man-made medical disaster in history ... with huge numbers (over 10,000) of severe birth defects in children. In addition, there were reports of increased miscarriage rates during this period ....”[297]

Birth defects encompassed

> limb and bone abnormalities including amelia, phocomelia, syndactyly and underdeveloped long bones among other deformities ... atresia of the esophagus, duodenum and anus as well as cardiac abnormalities and aplasia of the gallbladder and appendix .... Up to 40% of affected infants died within 1 year.[298]

Many thousands of women had abortions, legally or clandestinely, to avoid the same fate. The survivors “have severe handicaps, and many ... are experiencing early onset age related issues, such as osteoarthritis, joint mobility issues and coronary heart disease, making life more difficult ....”[299]

In Germany Chemie Grünenthal was made aware of the problems with its new drug almost immediately, but only resorted to slightly altering the language of its prospectus:

> Meanwhile several hundred suspected cases were being drawn to the attention of Chemie Grünenthal and in May 1961 six articles critical of the drug were published in German medical journals. ... On 28 July 1961, the company settled a claim out of court [for polyneuritis] .... In the following month, after an article in *Der Spiegel* expressing concern, Chemie Grünenthal asked its licensees to drop the description ‘non toxic’ [quotation marks original] ....[300]

---

[297] Vargesson, 2015, p. 140.

[298] Rehman, 2011, p. 292.

[299] Vargesson, 2015, p. 141.

[300] Teff, Harvey and Colin R. Munro. Thalidomide: the legal aftermath. Westmead, Farnborough, Hants., UK: Saxon House, 1976 AA, Chapter 1 The Case History, Thalidomide and nerve damage, p. 3.

The pediatrician and medical geneticist Dr. Widukind Lenz (1919 – 1995) pressured the company to withdraw Contergan, which they finally did but only after stalling and complaining of bad press. Lenz,

> reputedly the first doctor to identify the association [of thalidomide] with deformity, was almost ready to rule out drugs as the explanation, when he was told by the mother of a deformed child that she had taken *Contergan* during pregnancy. On 16 November, Dr Lenz wrote to Chemie Grünenthal asking them to withdraw *Contergan*, but they were non-committal hoping to satisfy the health authorities merely by inserting the words 'not to be taken during pregnancy' on the label. At a meeting of paediatricians in Dusseldorf on 18 November Dr Lenz revealed his suspicions and on 26 November a newspaper article based on them brought the matter to the attention of the general public. Chemie Grünenthal wrote to the Drug Commission of the German Medical Association: 'Because press reports have undermined the basis of the scientific discussion, we have decided to withdraw Contergan from the market immediately' [italics and quotation marks original].[301]

Chemie Grünenthal nevertheless escaped criminal liability:

> Oddly, no individual nor Grunenthal itself was successfully prosecuted over the disaster. There are reports that Grunenthal may have entered into an agreement with the German Government and the German Federal Prosecutors offices to withdraw a criminal prosecution against them .... It took until 2012 before Grunenthal finally offered an 'apology,' but stopped short of admitting liability, yet little compensation has yet been paid to thalidomide damaged survivors outside Germany .... Grunenthal no longer produces thalidomide, but today is one of the world's largest Pharmaceutical companies producing drugs for pain relief [quotation marks original].[302]

---

[301] Teff and Munro, 1976, The withdrawal of the drug, p. 6.

[302] Vargesson, 2015, p. 141.

In the United States, the drug was never approved due to the efforts of a newly appointed investigator at the Food and Drug Administration, Dr. Frances Kathleen Oldham Kelsey (1914 – 2015). She had been alerted at the end of 1960 to a report in the *British Medical Journal* of "a possible side effect of prolonged use of thalidomide, namely polyneuritis."[303]

> Dr. Frances Kelsey, a physician and pharmacologist, was the FDA officer assigned to review the drug application; she denied approval based on a lack of safety data. ... For her efforts in preventing thalidomide from being marketed and thus averting a major tragedy in the United States, Dr. Kelsey was honored with the President's Award for Distinguished Federal Civilian Service from President John F. Kennedy in 1962 ....[304]

As a result of her work, new laws in 1963 mandating

> greater control and surveillance over the distribution and clinical testing of investigational drugs ... began to appear. The intent of the new procedures is to protect the public ... by ensuring that adequate preclinical studies are done on the drug .... Certainly it should not take many thousands of deformed children to establish the degree of hazard that is associated with thalidomide.[305]

Though it was never approved for sale, it was unfortunately distributed (as it had been in Germany) to doctors for them to trial the new drug on their patients:

---

303 Kelsey, Frances O. "Problems Raised for the FDA by the Occurrence of Thalidomide Embryopathy in Germany, 1960-1961," *American Journal of Public Health*, Volume 55, No. 5, May 1965 NIH, p. 704.

304 Rehman, 2011, p. 292.

305 Kelsey, 1965, pp. 706-707.

[P]re-marketing trials by 1,270 doctors ensured that over 20,000 patients, at least 200 of them pregnant, had taken it. There were in fact ten cases of thalidomide births officially admitted in America, and seven other cases of deformity where thalidomide may have been the cause.[306]

In India impenetrable bureaucracy and a fortuitous political invasion doomed the approval of the new drug before it could do serious damage:

[N]o confirmed case has been reported [and] ... there is no available evidence showing that thalidomide was exported to India. The situation in the Portuguese colony of Goa was different. Although this comparatively small pharmaceutical market was more developed, the registration of drugs was not required. It seems that Grünenthal's exports came to an end a few months after Indian troops occupied the Portuguese territory on 18 December 1961.[307]

In 2023 thalidomide continues to create damaged children in Brazil as it is still used

to successfully treat a wide range of medical conditions, which include leprosy, multiple myeloma, and cancers, as well as Crohn's disease, HIV, and others. ... However, tragically a new generation of thalidomide survivors has occurred in Brazil .... Thalidomide is used to treat complications of leprosy in Brazil, which is sadly common and debilitating. Unfortunately the drug is given to patients who share the medicine with others, and who do not understand or are not informed of the dangers, and damaged children are born. The damage to these children is similar to the damage seen in children between 1957 and 1962.[308]

---

306 Teff and Munro, 1976, p. 7.

307 Wimmelbücker, Ludger and Anita Kar. "A history of thalidomide in India," *Medical History*, Volume 67, No. 3, 2023 NIH, pp. 229, 231.

308 Vargesson, 2015, p. 142.

Neither pyrithyldione, glutethimide nor thalidomide are listed in the 30 March 1961 Single Convention, glutethimide is the only one of the three listed (in Schedule III) of the 21 February 1971 Convention on Psychotropic Substances, none are listed in the schedules of the revised Single Convention as at 18 May 2016, and glutethimide is still the only one of the three listed in the schedules of the revised Convention on Psychotropic Substances as at 13 November 2016.[309]

Figure 421. Dr. Widukind Lenz. Vogel, Friedrich. "Widukind Lenz – An Encomium," *American Journal of Medical Genetics*, Volume 37, Issue 3, November 1990 [onlinelibrary.wiley.com, hereinafter WIL], p. 352.

---

[309] United Nations, 30 March 1961, Schedules, pp. 239-244; United Nations, 1971 UN, List of Substances in Schedule III, unpaged; United Nations, 18 May 2016, pp. 1-8; United Nations, 13 November 2016, List of substances in Schedule III, unpaged.

Figure 422. Joel Fort. Perlman, David. "Joel Fort, psychiatrist who campaigned against orthodoxy, dies," *SF Gate*, 28 August 2015 [sfgate.com, hereinafter SF], p. 2/8.

G. The Addicted Society

It could be said that the addicted society has arrived, to use the expression of American iconoclastic psychiatrist and early cannabis decriminalization advocate[310] Joel Fort (1929 – 2015). Broadly speaking (because those covered do not account for a tenth of the substances in question), the drugs mentioned in this chapter constitute the therapeutic agents available in industrial nations [as opposed to the derivatives of cannabis, coca and the poppy used in traditional societies]. Many of these pharmaceutical products induce tolerance, many are addictive, and some cause great harm. The debatable abstinence syndrome of the amphetamines, for example, is described as a depression followed by a phase of delirium which their deprivation induces when they have been used with prodigality.

Despite the advantages for the medical profession of rapid diagnosis and simplified treatment, to combat tuberculosis with diacetylmorphine, depression with dexamphetamine, obesity with methamphetamine, alcoholism with phenobarbital, cough with methadone, schizophrenia with chlorpromazine, neurosis with meprobamate, anxiety with chlordiazepoxide, unhappiness with diazepam, morning sickness with thalidomide, and insomnia with pyrithyldione along with other originalities of the medical/pharmaceutical business is a good method of establishing intense and unforeseen tolerance, dependence, and addiction if not debilitating side effects, permanent lesions and fatalities. In fact, the shrewdness of the pharmaceutical laboratories date from the very

---

[310] Chawkins, Steve. "Joel Fort dies at 86; iconoclastic psychiatrist testified in Patty Hearst case," *Los Angeles Times*, 27 August 2015 [latimes.com, hereinafter LA], Obituaries, p. 1/5.

beginning of the twentieth century when they were suggesting using cocaine or morphine practically for everything.

Contemplated from any angle, the illegalizing of certain products by adding their names to an international list does not put an end to the presence of addictive drugs, nor with the dependence on legal psychopharmaceuticals generally. Two conclusions appear to impose themselves:

1. The so-called clean society which existed from the end of the Second World War to the middle of the 1960s disposed of many legal chemical resources to procure tranquility, sleep and stimulation, all of them as stupefying and dangerous as the stigmatized drugs, if not more so; and,
2. The spread of therapeutism multiplies the number of persons dependent on some such drug by a factor of ten, so much so that a significant proportion of such persons often do not even know that they are dependent on a drug that can create tolerance and organic lesions.

Consequently, the lack of a large increase in the consumption of prohibited drugs observed during this period does not imply a reduction in the nervousness of contemporary man. What the public has done is trust the government, and what the government has done is trust the pharmaceutical companies, and what the pharmaceutical companies have done is churn the pharmacopoeia, substituting one remedy for another, following a tendency to prefer the synthetic over the natural, the patented over the unpatented, the manufactured over that which grows naturally and can be used with minimal transformations.

Consider Northamerica, for example, around the year 1965. According to the FBN, the number of junkies is somewhere around

45,000 at the beginning of the decade with the number of cokeheads and potheads put together perhaps as many. The number of new opiate addicts reported to the Bureau of Narcotics and Dangerous Drugs in 1965 was 6,012 of whom 5,430 used heroin.[311] This number is obviously insignificant for a country whose population in 1965 is reported to be 194.2 million.[312]

However, let's think in real pharmacological terms, asking ourselves what quantity of legal drugs are consumed there. In 1965 some 2,741,000 pounds of caffeine (both natural and synthetic) were sold there, a value of $5,036,000;[313] the per capita annual consumption of coffee (green beans) in 1965 was 14.8 pounds.[314] In 1965 the country produced 971,000 pounds of barbiturates and 1,548,000 pounds of tranquilizers as well as 29,089,000 pounds of aspirin.[315] In 1967 of an adult population of over 125 million, nearly half of men and a third of women smoked cigarettes.[316] The FDA estimates that in the mid-1960s 8 billion 10 mg. doses of amphetamine were produced.[317] These figures do not include the amount of pethidine consumed (9 tons in 1956) or that of codeine (795,000 lbs. in 2013) or

---

311 Lerner, William, Chief. Statistical Abstract of the United States, 1971, 92nd Annual Edition. Washington, DC: US Bureau of the Census, 1971 [census.gov, hereinafter CG], Recent Trends, Population, Total, incl. Armed Forces abroad, No. 116. Narcotic Addiction – Summary: 1953 to 1969, p. 79.

312 Lerner, 1971, Recent Trends, Population, Total, incl. Armed Forces abroad, p. xiii.

313 Lerner, 1971, Medicinal Chemicals, No. 108. Selected Medicinal Chemicals – Production and Sales: 1945 to 1969, p. 75.

314 Lerner, 1971, No. 123. Civilian Per Capita Consumption of Major Food Commodities: 1940 to 1970, p. 82.

315 Lerner, 1971, p. 75.

316 Lerner, 1971, No. 117. Cigarette Smokers in the Population, by Sex and Age: 1967 and 1968, p. 79.

317 Rasmussen, 2008, p. 977.

meprobamate (870,000 pounds in 1961 only in the UK) or diazepam (the most prescribed medical treatment in the US in 1965 with 44 million prescriptions in 1978), or chlordiazepoxide (the third most prescribed medical treatment in 1965) or glutethimide (582,000 prescriptions in 1968 in the UK, even more in the US).[318]

It is under these domestic pharmacological conditions that the United States decides to launch an assault against the growers of coca, poppy and cannabis around the world. The logic driving the expansion of the pharmacracy is to disseminate their own laboratory preparations as safe medicines, infinitely superior to the plants harvested in the Third World. The American embassies in these so-called backward countries routinely demand those governments suppress the custom of using natural remedies, while offering packaged remedies in exchange.

Urged on by the United States, the Shah of Iran prohibited under penalty of death the cultivation and use of opium in his country, creating a catastrophic situation that obliged him to suspend the measures in 1969. The gynecologist of the royal family, then the Minister of Health, declared to a correspondent from the *Times* that Iran felt ashamed before the hangover of its obscure oriental past:

> Prohibition [of opium] was motivated by prestige reasons. At a time of modernization, which in most developing countries means imitation of Western models, the use of opium was considered a shameful hangover of a dark Oriental past. It did not fit with the image of an awakening, Westernizing Iran that the Shah was creating.[319]

---

[318] Report, "Legal," 1958, p. 5/7; International Narcotics Control Board, 2015, p. 170; Little, 1963, p. 794; López-Muñoz, 2011, p. 558; Kennedy, 1980, p. 1; Dunlap, 1970, p. 1280.

[319] Ghiabi, Maziyar. Drugs Politics: Managing Disorder in the Islamic Republic of Iran. Cambridge, UK: Cambridge University Press, 2019 AA, Chapter 2 A

In 1972, in Southeast Asia

> under intense pressure from the United States Embassy, including the threat to cut off American aid, the Laotian Government last year reversed its traditional policy and banned the production, sale, and consumption of opium, known in Laos as 'flower medicine' [quotation marks original].[320]

When the medieval Christian crusaders invaded the Arab territories, they tried to exchange prostrations to Mecca for communions on the first Friday of the month. The drug crusaders attempt to eradicate the cultivation of poppy, coca and cannabis, while at the same time exporting amphetamines, barbiturates, semisynthetic and synthetic narcotics, tranquilizers, anxiolytics, and nonbarbiturate hypnotics. Further, during this crusade the United States subsidized the export of admittedly dangerous drugs.

In 1964 President Lyndon Baines Johnson (1908 – 1973) in a Special Message to Congress sent his annual report on the price support program for agricultural commodities known as Food for Peace, formally the Agricultural Trade Development and Assistance Act of 1954:

> Today about 40 percent of our government's economic development assistance overseas is in the form of agricultural commodities and local currencies received from their sale. To achieve this record, Food For Peace exports reached a new high in 1964 of 18 million tons of agricultural commodities with an estimated export market value of $1.7 billion.[321]

Genealogy of Drugs Politics: Opiates under the Pahlavi, p. 35.

[320] Szasz, Thomas. Ceremonial Chemistry: The Ritual Persecution of Drugs, Addicts and Pushers. Garden City, NY: Anchor Press, 1974 AA, Part I, Chapter 4 Communions, Holy and Unholy, p. 47.

[321] Johnson, Lyndon B. "Special Message to the Congress on the Food for Peace Program," The American Presidency Project, 31 March 1965 [presidency.ucsb.edu,

One of those subsidized commodities was tobacco grown in the United States. In the ten years between 1954 and 1964 the US subsidized the sale of some 317 million dollars of tobacco to countries around the world, some 16 million in the first half of 1964 alone.[322] For the first ten years this amounted to 436,243,000 pounds of tobacco, 8,818,000 in the first half of 1964.[323]

A pair of editorials in the *New York Times* pushed back:

> As we note above, there are solid economic grounds for dismantling the whole network of Government price supports for agriculture. The place to start is with tobacco, whose chronic use is recognized as injurious to public health. Whether or not to smoke may be a personal decision, but in view of Washington's own concern over the harm caused by cigarettes it should hardly be promoting both the production and consumption of tobacco through artificial subsidies. If the Government can break the tobacco habit, it will be making a major contribution to safeguarding the health of the nation. In addition, it will be speeding the end of the price support program, which has been such an expensive failure.[324]

---

hereinafter APP], pp. 1/6, 2/6.

[322] Reuter, Richard W., Director. The Twentieth Semiannual Report on Activities Carried on under Public Law 480, 83d Congress, as amended, Outlining Operations Under the Act During the Period January 1 through June 30, 1964. Washington, DC: Government Printing Office, 1964 [pdf.usaid.gov, hereinafter USA], Appendix, Programs and Shipment Tables, Title 1 – Agreements Signed, Status of Currencies, and Reports, Table 5. – Dollar value of commodities programmed under Title 1, Public Law 480 agreements signed Jan. 1, 1964 through June 30, 1964, Table 6. – Dollar value of commodities programmed under Title 1, Public Law 480 agreements signed July 1, 1954 through June 30, 1964, pp. 22-25.

[323] Reuter, 1964, Table 7. – Approximate quantities of commodities under Title 1, Public Law 480 agreements signed Jan. 1, 1964 through June 30, 1964, Table 8. – Approximate quantities of commodities under Title 1, Public Law 480 agreements signed July 1, 1954 through June 30, 1964, pp. 26-29.

[324] Editor. "Bigger Agricultural Subsidies ....," *The New York Times*, 1 February 1964 NYT, p. 22.

In spite of a number of reports in the 1960s that the heavy use of cigarettes is a health hazard, the editors noted that

> the Department of Agriculture will be paying out increased subsidies under the law to tobacco producers and will continue to promote the sale of tobacco under the Food for Peace program. ... [T]here is no excuse at all for actively stimulating the production and sale of tobacco with public funds. ... [T]he Administration ... might be doing something better than acquiescing in the Congressional tobacco subsidy.[325]

But the Secretary of Agriculture under the Kennedy and Johnson administrations was not the only one campaigning to increase the consumption of tobacco. Hollywood studios, for example, had been collaborating with tobacco companies to place their products in films since the earliest days of cinema:

> [T]he advent of 'talking pictures' in the late 1920s marked the beginning of the American Tobacco Company's systematic exploitation of film celebrities. Nearly 200 movie actors are known to have simultaneously promoted a tobacco brand and their studios' releases from 1927–51; two-thirds of the top 50 box office stars in Hollywood from the late 1930s through the 1940s endorsed tobacco brands for advertising purposes [quotation marks original].[326]

Indeed, "tobacco imagery is integral to the artistry of American film, citing 'classic' smoking scenes in such films as *Casablanca* (1942) and *Now, Voyager* (1942) [italics, quotation marks original]."[327]

---

325 Editorial Board. "The Tobacco Subsidy," *The New York Times*, Section E, 15 March 1964 NYT, p. 8..

326 Lum, K. L., et al. "Signed, sealed and delivered: 'big tobacco' in Hollywood, 1927–1951," *Tobacco Control*, Volume 17, 2008 [tobaccocontrol.bmj.com, hereinafter TC], Discussion, p. 320.

327 Lum, et al., 2008, p. 313.

Such advertising works. Though they signed the Master Settlement Agreement in 1998 prohibiting tobacco marketing to youth, smoking in the movies

> increased in youth-rated films despite the 1998 MSA .... A population-attributable risk calculation suggests that the movies account for ~390,000 new adolescent regular smokers in the United States annually, enough to replace the 400,000 active smokers that the tobacco industry kills every year.[328]

The MSA does not apply overseas. A cross-cultural longitudinal study in six European countries demonstrated that "an exposure to 1000 smoking depictions [in movies] increases the relative risk of initiating smoking by about 13% [in adolescents]."[329]

Product placement continues for alcohol. Four minutes of screen time for Budweiser in the 1986 *Top Gun: Maverick* "was worth $2.6 million during its theatrical run."[330] The 2002 sequel *Maverick* featured only two and a half minutes of Budweiser products but "Anheuser-Busch reported that net sales increased 7% in the fourth quarter and 5% for the entire year."[331] The Dutch brewers of Heineken

---

[328] Charlesworth, Annemarie and Stanton A. Glantz. "Smoking in the Movies Increases Adolescent Smoking: A Review," *Pediatrics*, Volume 116, No. 6, December 2005 NIH, The Master Settlement Agreement (MSA), p. 1526.

[329] Morgenstern, Matthis, et al. "Smoking in Movies and Adolescent Smoking Initiation: Longitudinal Study in Six European Countries," *American Journal of Preventive Medicine*, Volume 44, Issue 4, April 2013 [AJPMonline.org, hereinafter AJP], Discussion, p. 5.

[330] Brown, Shauna. "Five times Hollywood films have influenced beer sales," *The Drinks Business*, 9 January 2023 [thedrinksbusiness.com, hereinafter DB], Budweiser and Top Gun, p. 1/5.

[331] Brown, 2023, p. 2/5.

reportedly paid $45 million for the product placement in *Skyfall* [2012] ... the first time the international spy had sipped one on screen. That year, the brewers' sales volumes increased by 5.3% and like-for-like volumes went up by 3.7% in Western Europe.[332]

Figure 423. Daniel Craig holds a bottle of Heineken in *Skyfall.* Walsh, Danielle. "What Every James Bond Drank, From Martinis to Heineken," *Bon Appétit*, 9 November 2012 [bonappetit.com, hereinafter BA], p. 2/9.

The obviously lucrative trend is increasing. Researchers found that alcohol brand placements doubled from 1996 to 2015:

---

[332] Brown, 2023, p. 3/5.

In total, 93 percent of R-rated films and 92 percent of PG-13-rated films released during those years featured alcohol being consumed. It isn't just adult films that are heavy on the booze. According to the research, 72 percent of PG-rated films and 46 percent of G-rated films surveyed featured alcohol use. While that number appears to have stayed steady over time, again, brand placements nearly doubled within the 20-year period.[333]

This does not take into account that certain very active stimulants have escaped, and continue to escape, any measure of control. Such is the case with caffeine, an alkaloid somewhat less potent than cocaine, distributed not only in drinks, but in an enormous quantity of pharmaceutical preparations, especially for headache and congestion. Clearly, pharmacological considerations have never been involved in defining what is or is not a prohibited drug.

---

[333] Panko, Ben. "From Budweiser to Heineken, Alcohol Brands Are Rampant in Hollywood Films: Over the past two decades, even G-rated films have amped up the booze labels," *Smithsonian*, 9 May 2017 [smithsonianmag.com, hereinafter SM], pp. 3/6, 4/6.

Figure 424. *Vom Mutterkorn befallene Roggenähre* (Ear of Rye Affected by Ergot). Hagenbach, Dieter and Lucius Werthmüller. *Albert Hofmann und sein LSD*. Aarau, CH: AT Verlag, 2011, p. 97/712.

28
The Pagan Plot (I)

If anything signifies our humanization – a genuine and actual progress – it is the fact that we no longer require excessive oppositions, indeed no opposites at all – we may love the senses, we have spiritualized and made them artistic in every degree; we have a right to all those things which were most maligned until now.[1]
--Friedrich Wilhelm Nietzsche (1844 – 1900)

A. **Exploring the Unconscious**
   1. **The Trials of Walter**
   2. **The Essays of Aldous**
   3. **The Insight of Albert**

B. **Experimenting with Consciousness**
   1. **Mescaline**
   2. **Psilocybin**
   3. **LSD**
   4. ***Amanita muscaria***
   5. **Similitudes**

[1] The Will to Power, tr. Walter Kaufmann and R. J. Hollingdale. NY: *Vintage Books*, 1968 [annasarchive.org, hereinafter AA], Book One: *European Nihilism*, II. History of European Nihilism, 115 (*Jan.-Fall 1888*), pp. 70-71 [humanization and progress italicized in the original]; *Wenn irgend etwas unsre Vermenschlichung ... die am schlimmsten bisher verrufen waren* (Nietzsche, Friedrich. *Der Wille Zur Macht: Versuch Einer Umwertung Aller Werte*. Stuttgart, DE: Alfred Kröner Verlag, 1964 AA, Erstes Buch. Der Europäische Nihilismus, II. Zur Geschichte des europäischen Nihilismus, c) Anzeichen der Erstarkung, 115, pp. 83-84).

C. Arms for the Cold War
- **1. Truth Drugs**
- **2. Behavior Modification**
- **3. Chemical Warfare**

D. Technique versus Chemistry

E. The Pagan Plot Unfolds
- **1. Pharmacological Caution**
- **2. Political Circumspection**
- **3. The Final Revolution**

It never entered into the calculations of the delegates attending the 1961 Single Convention that the provisions of their treaty might endanger the pharmacratic peace prevailing since the end of the First World War. It was a compromise measure, intended to accomplish several purposes at the same time: to maintain and make punishment more robust, to develop solutions more in agreement with the paternalistic remedy of the Welfare State, to answer to the demands of corporations involved in law and medicine, and lastly to moderate the scandalous intoxication of citizens using substances lacking the stigma of being called drugs, though pharmacologically indiscernible from those already stigmatized. Perhaps these were too many goals for a single treaty, which may explain why they left out of their stipulations some of the most widely used psychopharmaceuticals then being used (the barbiturates, the amphetamines, the major and minor tranquilizers and the nonbarbiturate hypnotics), while their entirely debatable scheme of classification placed cannabis, for example, not only in Schedule I but also in Schedule IV ("particularly dangerous" and "liable to abuse and to produce ill effects")[2] along with heroin, one other semisynthetic narcotic (desomorphine), and one synthetic narcotic (ketobemidone).[3]

At the time, pharmacies and drugstores offered a large variety of mind altering substances as a decorous alternative to the malignant pharmacopoeia. But this was only possible due to the competition among three not always compatible ideologies. First, there was the ideology of therapeutism and its experts, characterized by its emphasis

---

2 United Nations. Single Convention on Narcotic Drugs, 1961. NY: United Nations, 31 March 1961 [unodc.org, hereinafter UN], Chapter VI. Narcotic Drugs and Psychotropic Substances, Title 15, Article 2, Section 5 (a), p. 83, Article 3, Section 5, p. 84.

3 United Nations, 31 March 1961, ***List** of drugs included in Schedule **IV***, p. 244.

on rehabilitation rather than repression, though never effectively questioning that repression nor threatening the ethical and political rationale for the crusade. Second, seen from a strictly sociological and scientific level, as to the crusade there was "but one overwhelming conclusion – it does not work."[4] Third, the stereotype of the so-called drug fiend was as deeply rooted in the popular imagination as ever and the antinarcotics brigades had even more agents than before.

There was, then, an almost absolute disconnect among those who made a living from the therapeutist/industrial complex, those who wished to consider the phenomenon empirically, and those attentive to the slogans of the so-called protectors. But now a peaceful divorce becomes impossible, due to a chain of coincidences that will awaken a passionate interest in (until then) the least interesting class of drugs, which instead of offering injections of peace or energy excite an experience of a visionary nature: the entheogens. This chain of coincidences will end up provoking the first large historical outbreak of active resistance to prohibitionism, one of the most relevant social facts in the second half of the twentieth century.

But before embarking upon a description of the actors and their actions in this drama, it's important to keep in mind two things. One is that this so-called plot was hatched in the most cultured circles, practically underwritten by the leading academic institutions of the civilized world when not directly subsidized by the highest echelons of US intelligence agencies. The other is that this so-called conspiracy cannot be divorced from a philosophical reflection upon and an attempt to intervene in the evolution of advanced industrial societies.

---

[4] Skolnick, Jerome H. "Coercion to Virtue: The Enforcement of Morals," *Southern California Law Review*, Volume 41, No. 3, 1968 [heinonline.com, hereinafter HEO], p. 621.

Although the dissidence initially took the form of a pharmacological argument, it quickly became political and cultural in the widest sense of those words. These visionaries never intended merely to continue politics more or less as it had always been done, replacing one government with another, but rather hoped to change what Nietzsche calls the *Grosse Politik*,[5] so that man, now an inhabitant of a technological civilization with all its glories and miseries, could assure himself a degree of autonomy and critical distance before the concrete jungle in which he now lived. Chemical support for this cause was offered not as an end in itself, but as a stepping stone toward the retention of civil liberties and access to forms of enjoyment persecuted or threatened by the development of that same civilization. This project will be upsetting in the extreme for established institutions, as much in the East as in the West, and when its themes take hold among the youth it will come to be considered by some as the most dangerous plague of insanity ever recorded in the annals of history.

---

5 "The time for petty politics is over: the next century will bring the struggle for the domination of the earth – the *compulsion* to great politics [italics original]" (Nietzsche, Friedrich. Beyond Good and Evil: Prelude to a Philosophy of the Future, tr. Judith Norman. Cambridge, UK: Cambridge University Press, 2002 AA, Part 6: We Scholars, Section 208, p. 102); *Die Zeit fur kleine Politik ist vorbei. ... den Zwang zur grossen Politik* (Nietzsche, Friedrich. *Jenseits von Gut und Böse. Vorspeil einer Philosophie der Zukunft*. Leipzig: Druck und Verlag von C. G. Naumann, 1886 AO, Sechstes Hauptstück: wir Gelehrten, 208, p. 148).

Figure 425. A Portrait of Silas Weir Mitchell (1829 – 1914). Photograph by Frederick Gutekunst (1831 – 1917), ca. 1889. Boston Medical Library [nlm.nih.gov, hereinafter NIH].

A. Exploring the Unconscious

At the beginning of the twentieth century there are only scattered, isolated investigations into the entheogens. At twelve noon on 24 May 1896 the physician and poet/scientist Silas Weir Mitchell (1829 – 1914) ate one and a half peyote buttons and lay down in a darkened room: "The display which for an enchanted two hours followed was such as I find it hopeless to describe in language which shall convey to others the beauty and splendour of what I saw."[6] On Good Friday afternoon 1897, the English physician and social reformer Havelock Ellis (1859 – 1939) also experimented with peyote:

> [U]nlike the other chief substances to which it may be compared, mescal [peyote] does not wholly carry us away from the actual world, or plunge us into oblivion; a large part of its charm lies in the halo of beauty which it casts around the simplest and commonest things. It is the most democratic of the plants which lead men to an artificial paradise.[7]

Six months later at 11:45 am on 23 November 1897 the German pharmacologist and chemist Arthur Carl Wilhelm Heffter (1859 – 1925) "performed a careful self experiment with one of the alkaloids that he had isolated from a small cactus,"[8] consuming 150 mgs of his new extract, mescaline.[9]

---

6 Mitchell, S. Weir. "Remarks on the Effects of Anhelonium Lewinii (The Mescal Button)," *The British Medical Journal*, 5 December 1896 NIH, p. 1626.

7 Ellis, Havelock. "Mescal: A New Artificial Paradise," in The Contemporary Review, Volume LXXIII, January – June. London: Isbister and Company Limited, 1898 [books.google.user.com, hereinafter BGU], January, p. 141.

8 Nichols, David E. and Mark A. Geyer. "Preface," The Heffter Review of Psychedelic Research, Volume 1, 1998 [heffter.org, hereinafter HFO], p. viii.

9 *0,15 g Mescalin. hydrochloric* (Heffter, A. "*Ueber Pellote,*" *Archiv fur Experimentelle Pathologie und Pharmakologie*, Vol. 40, 1898 [zenodo.org, hereinafter ZEN], p. 423).

Figure 426. Havelock Ellis (1859 – 1939). The Mansell Collection, New York [britannica.com, hereinafter BRT].

In the late 1920s and 1930s investigations begin anew. Between 1927 and 1934 the German-Jewish philosopher and essayist Walter Bendix Schonflies Benjamin (1892 – 1940) demonstrated interest in drugs of psychic excursion when he and a few friends self-administered high doses of hashish, morphine, eukodal (oxycodone hydrochloride), opium and mescaline: "A last impetus to taking hashish was provided by certain pages of *Steppenwolf* that I read this morning [italics original]."[10] The German-Swiss poet and novelist

[10] Benjamin, Walter. On Hashish, tr. Howard Eiland, et al. Cambridge, MA: The Belknap Press of Harvard University Press, 2006 [issuu.com, hereinafter ISU], Chapter 4 Saturday, September 29 [1928] Marseilles, p. 47; *Einen letzten Anstoß, Haschisch zu nehmen, gaben mir gewisse Seiten im »Steppenwolf«, die ich heute früh gelesen hatte*

Figure 427. Arthur Heffter (1859 – 1925). Photogravure by Erwin Raupp (1863 – 1931), Riffarth & Co. [lautarchiv.hu-berlin.de, hereinafter LAH].

(Benjamin, Walter. Über Haschisch: Novellistisches, Berichte, Materialien. Frankfurt am Main, DE: Suhrkamp Taschenbuch Verlag, 1972 AA, IV Walter Benjamin: 29. September *1928* Sonnabend. Marseille, p. 95).

Hermann Hesse (1877 – 1962) invents Pablo, who has "drugs for stilling pain, for inducing sleep, for begetting beautiful dreams, lively spirits and the passion of love."[11] He offers some opium to Harry: "You are so very unhappy. That is bad. One shouldn't be like that. It makes me sorry. Try a mild pipe of opium."[12]

In one of his first published essays, in 1931 the English author, social critic and philosopher Aldous Huxley (1894 – 1963) decried the lack of amusements available at Cannes, calling for a new drug, one without any ill effects: "It was while disporting myself, or rather while trying to disport myself, in the midst of this apparatus, that I came to my depressing conclusion about the absence of new pleasures."[13] A quarter century later he would find something close.

Although he did not belong to this circle, it's useful here to mention the French artist of the European avant-garde Antoine Marie Joseph Paul Artaud (Antonin Artaud, 1896 – 1948), one of the innovators of modern theater. He lived among the Tarahumaras in the 1930s and related his experiences taking peyote and participating in their dances: "He spat after drinking the Peyote, as we all did. For after the twelve phases of the dance had been performed, and since dawn was about to break, we were passed the ground-up Peyote, which was like a kind of muddy gruel ...."[14]

---

[11] Hesse, Hermann. Steppenwolf, tr. Basil Creighton. NY: Bantam Books, 1963 AA, 'For Madmen Only,' p. 150; *Mittel zum Betäuben ... zum Verliebtmachen* (Hesse, Hermann. *Der Steppenwolf*. Frankfurt am Main, DE: Suhrkamp Verlag, 1961 AO, p. 147).

[12] Hesse, 1963, p. 165; *Sie sind so viel unglücklich. ... Nehmen Sie leichte Opiumpfeife* (Hesse, 1961, p. 164).

[13] Huxley, Aldous. "Wanted, A New Pleasure," in Music at Night & Other Essays. London: Chatto & Windus, 1931 AA, p. 249.

[14] Artaud, Antonin. The Peyote Dance, tr. Helen Weaver. NY: Farrar, Straus and Giroux, 1976 AA, The Peyote Dance, p. 54; *Il cracha après avoir bu le Peyotl ... Peyotl*

Figure 428. Antonin Artaud (1896 – 1948). Agence de presse Meurisse, ca. 1926. As Jacques Dupuis (Gringalet) in the film *Le Juif errant*, director Luitz-Morat [gallica.bnf.fr, hereinafter BNF].

---

broyé, semblable à une sorte de brouet limoneux (Artaud, Antonin. Les Tarahumaras. Décines, Isere, FR: L'Arbalète Marc Barbezat, 1955 BNF, Le Danse du Peyotl, p. 77).

It's important to add to this list the name of the American biologist and father of modern ethnobotany Richard Evans Schultes (1915 – 2001), a professor of botany at Harvard and later the director of its Botanical Museum. Before and during the Second World War he had already published several studies on the indigenous uses of peyote:

> As a result of the physiological activity of its alkaloids, peyote possesses many properties which the natives regard as valuable in the treatment of disease, both spiritual and physical. Indeed, the primary use of Lophophora Williamsi in the religious cult seems to have been based upon the appeal of its supposed curative and stimulating properties.[15]

Schultes never ceased investigating visionary plants in the Old and New Worlds, both as naturalist and anthropologist. His ethnobotanical investigations in South America bore fruit with the rediscovery of other plants with indole alkaloids such as *Banisteriopsis caapi*, and *Psychotria viridis*, used in the brew *ayahuasca* or *yagé*. From the first the active principle harmine[16] will be extracted, from the second dimethyltryptamine[17] [DMT], notably enlarging the catalog of

---

[15] Schultes, Richard Evans. "The Aboriginal Therapeutic Uses of Lophophora Williamsi," *Cactus and Succulent Journal*, Volume XII, No. 11, November 1940 AO, p. 178; see also Schultes, R. E. "Peyote and Plants Used in the Peyote Ceremony," *Botanical Museum Leaflets, Harvard University*, Volume 4, No. 8, April 12, 1937 [samorini.it, hereinafter SAM]; Schultes, R. E. "Peyote (*Lophophora Williamsii*) and Plants Confused with It," *Botanical Museum Leaflets, Harvard University*, Volume 5, No. 5, November 19, 1937 [biodiversitylibrary.org, hereinafter BIO]; Schultes, R. E. "The Appeal of Peyote (*Lophophora williamsi*) as a medicine," *American Anthropologist*, Volume 40, 1938 SAM.

[16] Schultes, Richard Evans. "The Identity of the Malpighiaceous Narcotics of South America," *Botanical Museum Leaflets, Harvard University*, Volume 18, No. 1, 7 June 1957 AO, p. 22.

[17] Blackledge, Robert D. and Charlotte M. Taylor. "*Psychotria Viridis* - A Botanical

psychedelic substances. Though ethnobotany did not begin with Schultes, one could certainly say that his work definitely encouraged it.

Figure 429. Richard Evans Schultes (1915 – 2001), ca. 1941. Harvard Museum of Natural History [hmnh.harvard.edu, hereinafter HMN].

The American biochemist and pharmacologist Gordon A. Alles (1901 – 1963) began studying methylenedioxy-amphetamine (MDA) in the late 1930s because of its chemical similarity to mescaline:

> Mescaline is a multiple methoxy ring-substituted phenethylamine. ... Phenethyl-amine is the basic structure of all compounds which have sympathomimetic activity. ... In 1937 we began a gradual approach to the study of the central nervous system activities of these methylenedioxy compounds. [18]

Source of Dimethyltryptamine (DMT)," *Microgram Journal*, Volume 1, Numbers 1-2, January – June 2003 [researchgate.net, hereinafter RGN], pp. 19, 20.

[18] Alles, Gordon A. "Some Relations between Chemical Structure and Physiological Action of Mescaline and Related Compounds," in Neuropharmacology: Transactions of the Fourth Conference September 25, 26, and 27, 1957, Princeton, N. J., ed. Harold A Abramson. NY: Josiah Macy, Jr. Foundation, 1959 AA, pp. 184,

After taking 126 milligrams of his new salt, Alles recorded externalized visual phenomena as his subjective spatial awareness moved outside his body:

> [A]n abundance of curling gray smoke rings were readily apparent in the environment .... Perceptually, these gray spiraling rings had a complete reality. It seemed quite unnecessary to test their apparent properties because ... passing a finger through their apparent field, caused them to melt away .... Subjective awareness of the body and its functionings became the subject of a detached spatial consideration. The place of detached observation for a time seemed clearly translocated out of the body to a place in the room to the above and right rearward. A couple of times it was compelling to turn my head and look into that corner of the room, in wonder at what part of one could be up there and thoughtfully observing the subjective situation and behavior of the body from that point.[19]

But other than within the confines of certain pharmacological symposiums these early studies do not attract any special attention.

Then the cautious, conservative Swiss chemist Albert Hofmann (1906 – 2008) deliberately ingested 250 micrograms of lysergic acid diethylamide at 4:20 pm on 19 April 1943, today celebrated as Bicycle Day after the perilous bike ride home he took immediately after work. A brilliant doctoral student at the University of Zurich ("where he earned his PhD with distinction after only four years"[20]), he wrote his doctoral thesis *Über den enzymatischen Abbau des Chitins und Chitosans*

202.

[19] Alles, Gordon. "Subjective Reactions to Phenethylamine Hallucinogens," A Pharmacologic Approach to the Study of Mind, Robert M. Featherstone, Alexander Simon, eds. Springfield, IL: Charles C Thomas Publisher, 1959 AA, pp. 242, 243; compare the "great adventure" with LSD of Hofmann and Jünger in 1951, Similitudes, this chapter.

[20] Finney, Nathaniel and Jay S. Siegel. "In Memoriam: Albert Hofmann (1906–2008)," CHIMIA *International Journal for Chemistry*, Volume 62, No. 5, 2008 RGN, p.

Figure 430. Gordon A. Alles (1901 – 1963). California Institute of Technology Archives and Special Collections [collections. archives.caltech.edu, hereinafter CAL].

444.

Figure 431. Albert Hofmann (1906 – 2008). Miller, Norman. "Basel: The Birthplace of Hallucinogenic Science," 14 July 2020 [bbc.com, hereinafter BBC].

[On the Enzymatic Degradation of Chitin and Chitosan] "with only a few months of experimentation – a level of productivity remarkable by any standard."[21] Both "chitin and chitosan have widespread medicinal use."[22]

After graduation Hofmann joined the firm of Sandoz Laboratories in Basel, Switzerland to work on natural products:

> In the spring of 1929, on concluding my chemistry studies at the University of Zurich, I joined the Sandoz Company's pharmaceutical-chemical research laboratory in Basel, as a co-worker with Professor Arthur Stoll, founder and director of the pharmaceutical department. I chose this position because it afforded me the opportunity to work on natural products ....[23]

---

21 Finney, 2008, pp. 444, 447.

22 Finney, 2008, p. 444.

23 Hofmann, Albert. LSD: My Problem Child, Reflections on Sacred Drugs, Mysticism, and Science, tr. Jonathan Ott. Los Angeles, CA: J. P. Tarcher, Inc., 1983

At Sandoz he promptly began to investigate the alkaloids found in ergot of rye (*Claviceps purpurea* or *Secale cornutum*). His boss, the Swiss biochemist Arthur Stoll (1887 – 1971), had already isolated ergotamine in 1918, which Sandoz sold as a remedy for post-partum hemorrhage as well as for migraine but work had halted on the other alkaloids. Competition from foreign labs led Hofmann to propose new research:

Although ergotamine quickly took a significant place in therapeutics (under the trade name Gynergen) as a hemostatic remedy in obstetrics and as a medicament in the treatment of migraine, chemical research on ergot in the Sandoz laboratories was abandoned after the isolation of ergotamine and the determination of its empirical formula. Meanwhile, at the beginning of the thirties, English and American laboratories had begun to determine the chemical structure of ergot alkaloids. ... So I thought it was high time that Sandoz resumed chemical research on ergot alkaloids, unless we wanted to risk losing our leading role in a field of medicinal research, which was already becoming so important.[24]

On 31 January 1960 the English soldier, poet and novelist Robert von Ranke Graves (1895 – 1985) ate psilocybin mushrooms in "Gordon Wasson's apartment overlooking the East River, prepared to set out for Paradise under his guidance."[25] Afterwards he speculated

---

AA, 1. How LSD Originated, p. 2; *Ich trat im Frühjahr 1929 ... über Naturstoffe zu arbeiten* (Hofmann, Albert. *LSD - mein Sorgenkind: Die Entdeckung einer »Wunderdroge«*. München, DE: Deutscher Taschenbuch Verlag GmbH & Co. KG, 2001 [dtv.de, hereinafter DTV], 1 Wie LSD entstand, p. 9/139).

24 Hofmann, 1983, 1. How LSD Originated, First Chemical Explorations, pp. 4-5; *Obwohl Ergotamin schon ... wichtigen Arzneimittelsektor zu verlieren* (Hofmann, 2001, 1 Wie LSD entstand, Erste chemische Arbeiten, p. 10/139).

25 Graves, Robert. "The Poet's Paradise: Address to the Oxford University Humanist Group," in Oxford Addresses on Poetry. Garden City, NY: Doubleday & Co., Inc., 1962 AA, p. 134.

on their influence in the archaic religions of Greece and the pre-Columbians, comparing the experience to the poetic trance:

My single experience of psilocybe was wholly good: an illumination of the mind, a re-education of sight and hearing, and even of touch, as I handled small objects beside me. The perfect sensory control which I could enjoy, confirmed, by analogy, my lifelong faith in the poetic trance: a world where words come to life and combine, under the poet's supra-conscious guidance, into inevitable and true rhythmic statements. But I find one main difference between the two conditions: a mushroom trance is relatively passive; a poetic trance, active – the pen running briskly across paper.[26]

Figure 432. Robert Graves (1895 – 1985) at his house in Mallorca, Spain where he spent his last years.

[26] Graves, 1962, pp. 139-140.

1. The Trials of Walter

During the last years of the Weimar Republic, Walter Benjamin imagined a truly exceptional study of hashish, as he wrote to the Israeli philosopher and historian of religion Gershon Scholem (1897 – 1982): "I do not wish to speak of the projects that had to remain unfinished .... They include ... a truly exceptional book about hashish."[27] Together with physician Ernst Joël (1893 – 1929), neurologist Fritz Fränkel (1892 – 1944), Marxist philosopher Ernst Simon Bloch (1885 – 1977), his cousin, doctor of radiology Egon Wissing (1900 – 1984), as well as wives, a few friends and other colleagues, he began a more or less systematic and scholarly examination of not only hashish but other drugs as well. Sadly, only a little more than a hundred pages, a "loose collection of drug protocols and feuilleton pieces"[28] documenting their experiments were mostly published posthumously.[29] The incomplete nature of the material does not prevent moments of great beauty and subtle reflection: "No one will be able to understand this intoxication; the will to awaken has died."[30]

---

27 Benjamin, 2006, translator's foreword, pp. viii, 145; deutsche-biographie.de; Gershom Scholem, ed. The Correspondence of Walter Benjamin and Gershom Scholem, 1932 – 1940, trs. Gary Smith and Andre Lefevre. NY: Schocken Books, 1989 AO, 4. Benjamin to Scholem, Nice, July 26, 1932, pp. 14-15.

28 Benjamin, 2006, p. viii.

29 However, he did publish two pieces in the early 1930s. "*Mylovice-Braunschweig [Hbf.]-Marseille. Die Geschichte eines Haschisch-Rausch*" appeared in the monthly *UHU* [Eagle Owl], Volume VII, No. 2, November 1930 [arthistoricum.net, hereinafter AHN], beginning on page 90; it appears he also published "a first-person account of his hashish experience in the *Frankfurter Zeitung*" of 4 December 1932 (Boon, Marcus. "Introduction: Walter Benjamin and Drug Literature," in Benjamin, 2006, p. 5).

30 Benjamin, 2006, Protocols of Drug Experiments (1-12), 9: April 18, 1931, p. 79; *Diesen Rausch wird keiner verstehn konnen, der Wille zum Erwachen ist gestorben* (Benjamin, 1972, IX Ernst Joël oder Fritz Fränkel: Protokoll vom 18. April 1931, p. 127).

Figure 433. Walter Benjamin (1892 – 1940), ca. 1929.
Akademie der Künst, Berlin, DE
[adk.de, hereinafter ADK].

The will to awaken had not died by virtue of forgetting (in fact, "[t]he memory of the intoxication is surprisingly clear"[31]), but from the invoking of "immense dimensions of inner experience, of absolute duration and immeasurable space."[32] These experiences give an introductory lesson to "a *profane illumination,* a materialistic, anthropological inspiration [italics original]"[33] into the "mysterious side of the mysterious."[34] The crystallization of the basic character of hashish intoxication is "*the 'secret of wandering.' What defines wandering is not a purposeful movement, not a spontaneity, but a mere, unfathomable being-drawn* [quotation marks, italics original]."[35] But not a being-drawn into mere conformist understanding:

---

[31] Benjamin, 2006, 'Hashish in Marseilles,' p. 118; *Die Erinnerung an den Rausch ist überraschend scharf* [italicized in the original] (Benjamin, 1972, Haschisch in Marseille, p. 45); see also Tiedemann, Rolf and Hermann Schweppenhauser, et al, editors. Walter Benjamin, Gesammelte Schriften, IV – 1. Frankfurt am Main, DE: Suhrkamp Verlag, 1972 AO, p. 410).

[32] Benjamin, 2006, Protocols of Drug Experiments (1-12), 4: September 29, 1928, p. 49; *dieser immensen Dimensionen des inneren Erlebens, der absoluten Dauer und der unermeßlichen Raumwelt* (Benjamin, 1972, IV Walter Benjamin: 29. September *1928* Sonnabend. Marseille, p. 97).

[33] Benjamin, 2006, 'From 'Surrealism' (1929), p. 132; *einer profanen Erleuchtung, einer materialistischen, anthropologischen Inspiration* (Tiedemann, Rolf and Hermann Schweppenhauser, et al, editors. Walter Benjamin, Gesammelte Schriften, II · 1. Frankfurt am Main, DE: Suhrkamp Verlag, 1977 AO, Zweiter band. Zweiter Teil, Literarische und ästhetische Essays (Fortsetzung), Der Sürrealismus, p. 297).

[34] Benjamin, 2006, From 'Surrealism,' p. 133; *Es bringt uns nämlich nicht weiter, die rätselhafte Seite am Rätselhaften pathetisch oder fanatisch zu unterstreichen* (Tiedemann, et al, 1977, p. 307).

[35] Benjamin, 2006, pp. 78-79; *Es wird als das Geheimnis der Wanderung ... nicht eine zweckmäßige Bewegung, nicht eine Spontaneität, sondern ein bloßes unergründliches Gezogenwerden* (Benjamin, 1972, pp. 126-127).

> I recollect a satanic phase. ... My smile assumed satanic features, though it was the expression of satanic knowing, satanic contentment, and satanic calm, rather than satanic destructiveness. ... [T]he great moments of world history are merely costumes beneath which they exchange understanding looks with nothingness, the base, and the commonplace. ... To refuse to be drawn into this understanding is what constitutes the 'satanic satisfaction' of which I have spoken [italics original].[36]

Bloch writes of the differences in the dosages used and the effects experienced in the various sessions: "Today's intoxication compares to the one before as Calvin to Shakespeare. This is a Calvinist intoxication."[37] This neatly expresses the distinction between ritual religion and natural religion, between puritanism and paganism. The alteration in consciousness in the former aspires to forgetfulness of the chains imposed upon spontaneity, while the latter seeks only the relaxation of the soul, even to the point of love:

> And when I recall this state, I would like to believe that hashish possesses the power to persuade nature to repeat the great squandering of our own existence that we enjoy when we're in love. For if, when we first love, our existence runs through Nature's fingers like golden coins that she cannot hold and must squander so that they can thus purchase new being, new birth, she now throws us, without hoping or expecting anything, in ample handfuls toward existence.[38]

---

[36] Benjamin, 2006, Chapter 2 Main Features of My Second Impression of Hashish, *Written January 15, 1928, at 3:30 p.m.*, pp. 23, 24; *Ich erinnere mich an eine satanische Phase. ... In dieses Einverständnis gar nicht hineinbezogen zu sein, das macht dann das »satanische Genügen« aus, von dem die Rede war* (Benjamin, 1972, II Walter Benjamin: Hauptzuge der zweiten Haschisch-Impression, Geschrieben 15. Januar 1928 nachmittags ½4, pp. 69, 70).

[37] Benjamin, 2006, Bloch's Protocol of the Experiment of [January 14, 1928], p. 32; *Der heutige Rausch verhält sich zum vorigen wie Calvin zu Shakespeare. Das ist ein Calvinistenrausch* (Benjamin, 1972, II Walter Benjamin: Hauptzuge der zweiten Haschisch-Impression, Ernst Bloch: Protokoll zu demselben Versuch, p. 76).

[38] Benjamin, 2006, Chapter 4, p. 56; *Und wenn ich dieses Zustands mich erinnere ... uns mit*

The poet, artist and Christian mystic William Blake (1757 – 1827) had more than a century earlier written something similar in one of his letters: "O foolish philosophy! Gratitude is heaven itself. There could be no heaven without gratitude; I feel it and I know it."[39]

The hyperintellectual baggage of Benjamin, Bloch and their medical colleagues forbids expressions of the mystical kind. Though hashish in the beginning excites "a dull feeling of foreboding and uneasiness,"[40] very soon the subject "attains experiences that approach inspiration, illumination."[41] In the end the physician must sit at the feet of the poet: "It is curious that hashish poisoning has not been experimentally studied. The most admirable description of the effects of hashish is by Baudelaire."[42]

Just before the Nazis occupied Paris, Benjamin fled south, crossing over the Pyrennes into Spain, where he was stopped, lacking an exit visa. The night before he was to be imprisoned in a French internment camp, he took "an overdose of morphine tablets."[43] Kafka could have written the epitaph for his unmarked grave: "Oh, hope enough, an infinity of hope – just not for us."[44]

---

vollen Händen dem Dasein hin (Benjamin, 1972, IV, pp. 104-105).

[39] Blake, William. The Letters of William Blake, ed. Archibald G. B. Russell. London: Methuen & Co., 1906 BGU, 30. To William Hayley. London, 14*th January*, 1804, p. 139.

[40] Benjamin, 2006, p. 117; *ist ein dumpfes Ahnungs- und Beklommenheitsgefühl* [italicized in the original] (Benjamin, 1972, Haschisch in Marseille, p. 45).

[41] Benjamin, 2006, p. 117; *Er gelangt auch zu Erlebnissen, die der Eingebung, der Erleuchtung nahekommen* (Benjamin, 1972, p. 45).

[42] Benjamin, 2006, p. 118; *Es ist merkwürdig ... des Haschisch-Rausches stammt von Baudelaire* (Benjamin, 1972, Haschisch in Marseille, p. 46).

[43] Witte, Bernd. Walter Benjamin: An Intellectual Biography, tr. James Rolleston. Detroit, MI: Wayne State University Press, 1985 AO, Chapter IX *The End of the Story* 1940, p. 205.

[44] Witte, 1985, p. 203; *Oh, hoffnung genug, unendlich viel hoffnung – nur nicht für uns* (Brod,

2. The Essays of Aldous

In one of his earliest essays Aldous Huxley exposes with a mixture of jaded elitism and youthful insolence what for a certain segment of society on the French Riviera appeared to be an appropriate topic of conversation in the interregnum between world wars, the invention of a new drug:

> So far as I can see, the only possible new pleasure would be one derived from the invention of a new drug – of a more efficient and less harmful substitute for alcohol and cocaine. If I were a millionaire, I should endow a band of research workers to look for the ideal intoxicant. If we could sniff or swallow something that would, for five or six hours each day, abolish our solitude as individuals, atone us with our fellows in a glowing exaltation of affection and make life in all its aspects seem not only worth living, but divinely beautiful and significant, and if this heavenly, world-transfiguring drug were of such a kind that we could wake up next morning with a clear head and an undamaged constitution – then, it seems to me, all our problems (and not merely the one small problem of discovering a novel pleasure) would be wholly solved and earth would become paradise.[45]

This commentary would not have been unwelcome in pharmaceutical circles when the era of the tranquilizers was just beginning.

Some twenty-five years later Huxley ended up speaking at a pharmaceutical congress discussing the use of various drugs for self-transcendence in the context of relieving the nervous tension of modern life:

Max. "*Der Dichter Franz Kafka*," *Die neue Rundschau*, XXXII ter Jahrgang der FreienBühne, Band 2, 1921 AO, p. 1213.

[45] Huxley, "Wanted, A New Pleasure," 1931, Section IV, pp. 254-255.

Huxley had a vast appetite for knowledge—scientific, cultural, carnal.

Figure 434. Cartoon from James, Clive. "Out of Sight," *The New Yorker*, Volume 79, Issue 4, 17 March 2003 AA, Books, p. 143.

> To relieve tension, a chemical compound does not have to have the characteristics of a tranquilizer. Alcohol, for example, is far from tranquilizing, at least in the middle stages of intoxication. But alcohol has been relieving tension ever since Noah made his epoch-making discovery. Self-transcendence can be achieved by an excitant as well as by a narcotic or a hallucinogen. Tension is relieved, not only by such contemplative drugs as opium, peyote, kava, and ayahuasca, but also by the active, extraverted intoxicants, such as wine, hashish, and the soma of ancient India.[46]

With that lecture (later printed as an essay) he indicated that the *Soma* of his dystopian novel, Brave New World, and the desired euphoriant in 'Wanted' had been discovered. In fact he discusses many (at least with reference to the relief of tension) though none of them allowed one to awaken the next morning with a clear head and unaffected body.

The difference between the two works is one of attitude, with the later work highlighting that any simple euphoriant could become a potential instrument of political oppression through the social technique of herd poisoning:

> But we must never forget that the spellbinders, the rabble-rousers, the potential Hitlers are always with us. We must never forget that it is very easy for such men to turn an innocent orgy into an instrument of destruction, into a savage, mindless force, directed to the overthrow of liberty. To prevent them from exploiting crowd-intoxication for their own sinister purposes, we must be perpetually on our guard.[47]

The near triumph of fascism occurs between these two declarations.

---

[46] Huxley, Aldous. "History of Tension," *The Scientific Monthly*, Volume 85, July – December, 1957 AO, Chemicals for Self-Transcendence, p. 5.

[47] Huxley, "History," 1957, Partial Solutions, p. 8.

Figure 435. Albert Hofmann with sons Andreas (l.) and Dieter (r.) at his home in Bottmingen, Switzerland, ca. 1942. Hagenbach and Werthmüller, 2011, Ehe und Familienglück, Krieg und Frieden, p. 90/712.

3. The Insight of Albert

One of the first great chemical discoveries in the field of entheogenic research almost never happened. In 1943 Albert Hofmann accidentally ingested either through inhalation or transcutaneously lysergic acid diethylamide (LSD – 25):

> Friday, April 16, 1943, I was forced to interrupt my work in the laboratory in the middle of the afternoon and proceed home, being affected by a remarkable restlessness, combined with a slight dizziness. At home I lay down and sank into a not unpleasant intoxicated-like condition, characterized by an extremely stimulated imagination. In a dreamlike state, with eyes closed (I found the daylight to be unpleasantly glaring), I perceived an uninterrupted stream of fantastic pictures, extraordinary shapes with intense, kaleidoscopic play of colors. After some two hours this condition faded away.[48]

The strange sensations he experienced led him to test what he thought would be the least active dose of the new substance on himself the following Monday as part of a series of experiments to evaluate the characteristics of this strange new finding:

> Exercising extreme caution, I began the planned series of experiments with the smallest quantity that could be expected to produce some effect, considering the activity of the ergot alkaloids known at the time: namely, 0.25 mg (mg = milligram = one thousandth of a gram) of lysergic acid diethylamide tartrate.[49]

---

[48] Hofmann, 1983, 1. How LSD Originated, Discovery of the Psychic Effects of LSD, p. 15; *Freitag, 16. April 1943, mußte ich mitten am Nachmittag meine Arbeit im Laboratorium ... Nach etwa zwei Stunden verflüchtigte sich dieser Zustand* (Hofmann, 2001, 1 Wie LSD entstand, Die Entdeckung der psychischen Wirkungen von LSD, p. 17/139).

[49] Hofmann, 1983, 1. How LSD Originated, Discovery of the Psychic Effects of LSD, p. 16; *Ich wollte vorsichtig sein undbegann deshalb ... Lysergsäure-diäthylamidtartrat*

The world's first deliberately planned LSD-25 experiment did not go exactly as planned:

> I had to struggle to speak intelligibly. I asked my laboratory assistant, who was informed of the self-experiment, to escort me home. We went by bicycle, no automobile being available because of wartime restrictions on their use. On the way home, my condition began to assume threatening forms. ... At times I believed myself to be outside my body, and then perceived clearly, as an outside observer, the complete tragedy of my situation. I had not even taken leave of my family .... Would they ever understand that I had not experimented thoughtlessly, irresponsibly, but rather with the utmost caution, an-d [sic] that such a result was in no way foreseeable? ... Another reflection took shape, an idea full of bitter irony: if I was now forced to leave this world prematurely, it was because of this lysergic acid diethylamide that I myself had brought forth into the world. ... Slowly I came back from a weird, unfamiliar world to reassuring everyday reality. The horror softened and gave way to a feeling of good fortune and gratitude, the more normal perceptions and thoughts returned, and I became more confident that the danger of insanity was conclusively past. ... Kaleidoscopic, fantastic images surged in on me, alternating, variegated, opening and then closing themselves in circles and spirals, exploding in colored fountains, rearranging and hybridizing themselves in constant flux. It was particularly remarkable how every acoustic perception, such as the sound of a door handle or a passing automobile, became transformed into optical perceptions. Every sound generated a vividly changing image, with its own consistent form and color.[50]

In fact, he was dealing with a substance bordering upon the extraordinary in many respects. To begin with, it was at the time the

---

(Hofmann, 2001, 1 Wie LSD entstand, Die Entdeckung der psychischen Wirkungen von LSD, p. 17/139).

[50] Hofmann, 1983, 1. How LSD Originated, Self-Experiments, pp. 16-19; *Ich konnte nur noch mit größter Anstrengung verständlich sprechen ... erzeugte ein in Form und Farbe entsprechendes, lebendig wechselndes Bild* (Hofmann, 2001, 1 Wie LSD entstand, Die Entdeckung der psychischen Wirkungen von LSD, p. 19/139).

most powerful psychopharmaceutical ever discovered, with an active dose measured in micrograms; a practically invisible speck could produce an experience of unimaginable intensity:

This self-experiment showed that LSD-25 behaved as a psychoactive substance with extraordinary properties and potency. There was to my knowledge no other known substance that evoked such profound psychic effects in such extremely low doses, that caused such dramatic changes in human consciousness and our experience of the inner and outer world.[51]

No other substance, natural or synthetic, operated at this scale on the nervous system: "[U]ntil then no known substance had displayed even the slightest psychic effect in fraction-of-a-milligram doses. An active compound of such potency seemed almost unbelievable."[52]

Second, no psychopharmaceutical was as remotely lacking in toxicity as lysergic acid diethylamide:

A standard for the toxicity of a substance is the LD50, or the median lethal dose, that is, the dose with which 50 percent of the treated animals die. ... However, if one compares the lethal dose in animals with the effective dose in human beings, which is 0.0003-0.001 mg/kg (0.0003 to 0.001 thousandths of a gram per kilogram of body weight), this shows an extraordinarily low toxicity for LSD. ... Such a procedure is not possible in this case because the lethal dose of LSD for humans is not known.[53]

---

[51] Hofmann, 1983, 1. How LSD Originated, Self-Experiments, pp. 19-20; *Dieser Selbstversuch zeigte ... der äußeren und der inneren Welt und im Bewußtsein des Menschen erzeugte* (Hofmann, 2001, 1 Wie LSD entstand, Die Entdeckung der psychischen Wirkungen von LSD, p. 20/139).

[52] Hofmann, 1983, 1. How LSD Originated, Self-Experiments, p. 20; *Die geäußerten Zweifel waren ... Wirkstoff von einer solchen Potenz schien fast unglaublich* (Hofmann, 2001, 1 Wie LSD entstand, Die Entdeckung der psychischen Wirkungen von LSD, p. 21/139).

[53] Hofmann, 1983, 2. LSD in Animal Experiments and Biological Research, How

Third, the new drug used with assiduity would simply cease to have an effect, regardless of the size of the dosage administered. It was not even minimally addictive. On the contrary, it could be said that LSD could not be abused, for whoever tried to continuously administer the drug would become insensitive to it in a matter of days: "[A]n LSD inebriation, even with the highest doses, lasts no longer than twelve hours, and repeated ingestion leads to tolerance, which means that extra doses are ineffective."[54]

In the fourth place, it was a semisynthetic compound, extracted from a parasite of wild and cultivated cereals. It was abundant in Europe, especially along the Mediterranean coast. The base, the so-called ergot of rye, was an almost ubiquitous fungus.

Sandoz soon introduced for therapeutic use, Delysid (a name Hofmann himself had proposed) with the following suggestions:

INDICATIONS AND DOSAGE

a) Analytical psychotherapy, to elicit release of repressed material and provide mental relaxation, particularly in anxiety states and obsessional neuroses. ...

b) Experimental studies on the nature of psychoses: By taking Delysid himself, the psychiatrist is able to gain an insight into the world of ideas and sensations of mental patients. Delysid can also be used to induce model psychoses of short duration in normal subjects, thus facilitating studies on the pathogenesis of mental disease.[55]

Toxic Is LSD? pp. 25-26; *Ein Maßstab für die Giftigkeit einer Substanz ist die LD50 ... einer LSD-Vergiftung bekannt geworden* (Hofmann, 2001, 2 LSD im Tierversuch und in der biologischen Forschung, Wie giftig ist LSD? p. 23/139).

[54] Hofmann, 1983, 5. From Remedy to Inebriant, Psychotic Reactions, p. 67; *Ein LSD-Rausch ... und wiederholte Einnahme führt zu Toleranz, das heißt, dass dann weitere Dosen unwirksam sind* (Hofmann, 2001, 6 Gefahren bei nicht-medizinischen LSD-Versuchen, p. 44/139).

[55] Hofmann, 1983, 4. Use of LSD in Psychiatry, The Psychic Effects of LSD, pp. 46-47; *Indikationen, Dosierung ... das Studium pathogenetischer Probleme* (Hofmann, 2001, 4 Anwendung von LSD in der Psychiatrie, Die psychischen Wirkungen von LSD, p.

Obscured for decades by psychoanalysis, psychiatry was then a so-called Cinderella science. Thanks to progress in Gestalt psychology, modern, more promising methods examined mental illness with new eyes, without the baggage of morality and cruelty.[56] Mescaline, LSD and later psilocybin were received with great interest by physicians as they represented instruments of incomparably more refinement than anything previous in the chemical arsenal.

But Hofmann was not only a chemist but a humanist with a religiously pagan soul. His family members were followers of the Swiss Christian theologian and reformist Huldrych Zwingli (1484 – 1531) and he was already a passionate reader of the German polymath Johann Wolfgang von Goethe (1749 – 1852) as well as the poet and philosopher Johann Christian Friedrich Hölderin (1770 – 1843). Not surprisingly he understood from the beginning the variety of uses that such a substance could have.

One he did not foresee however was the use of LSD as a simple euphoriant among the general public:

33/139).

[56] The German neurologist and psychiatrist Kurt Goldstein (1878 – 1965) argued for treating the whole person holistically: "[I]t is rather the actual Gestalt of the intrinsic architecture of this building that we try to discover ...." (The Organism: A Holistic Approach to Biology Derived from Pathological Data in Man. NY: American Book Company, 1939 AO, p. 401); the German psychologist and phenomenologist Wolfgang Köhler (1887 – 1967) put forth the major theme of Gestalt psychology, that "the whole is *different* [not greater than] from the sum of the parts [italics original]" (The Task of Gestalt Psychology. Princeton, NJ: Princeton University Press, 1969 AA, Introduction by Carroll C. Pratt, p. 10); the German-American psychologist and 'founder of social psychology' Kurt Lewin (1890 – 1947) observed as early as 1935 that the "fundamental ideas of Gestalt theory ... have become the self-evident foundation of experimental practice" (A Dynamic Theory of Personality: *Selected Papers*, tr. Donald K. Adams and Karl E. Zener. NY: McGraw-Hill Book Company, Inc., 1935 AO, p. 240).

CH. 28 THE PAGAN PLOT (I)

It was obvious that a substance with such fantastic effects on mental perception and on the experience of the outer and inner world would also arouse interest outside medical science, but I had not expected that LSD, with its unfathomably uncanny, profound effects, so unlike the character of a recreational drug, would ever find worldwide use as an inebriant. I had expected curiosity and interest on the part of artists outside of medicine – performers, painters, and writers – but not among people in general. After the scientific publications around the turn of the century on mescaline – which, as already mentioned, evokes psychic effects quite like those of LSD – the use of this compound remained confined to medicine and to experiments within artistic and literary circles. I had expected the same fate for LSD. And indeed, the first non-medicinal self-experiments with LSD were carried out by writers, painters, musicians, and other intellectuals.[57]

---

[57] Hofmann, 1983, 5. From Remedy to Inebriant, Nonmedical Use of LSD, p. 56; *Es lag auf der Hand, daß ein Stoff mit so phantastischen Wirkungen ... Schriftstellern, Malern, Musikern und geisteswissenschaftlich interessierten Personen durchgeführt* (Hofmann, 2001, Vom Heilmittel zur Rauschdroge, Nichtmedizinische Versuche, p. 38/139).

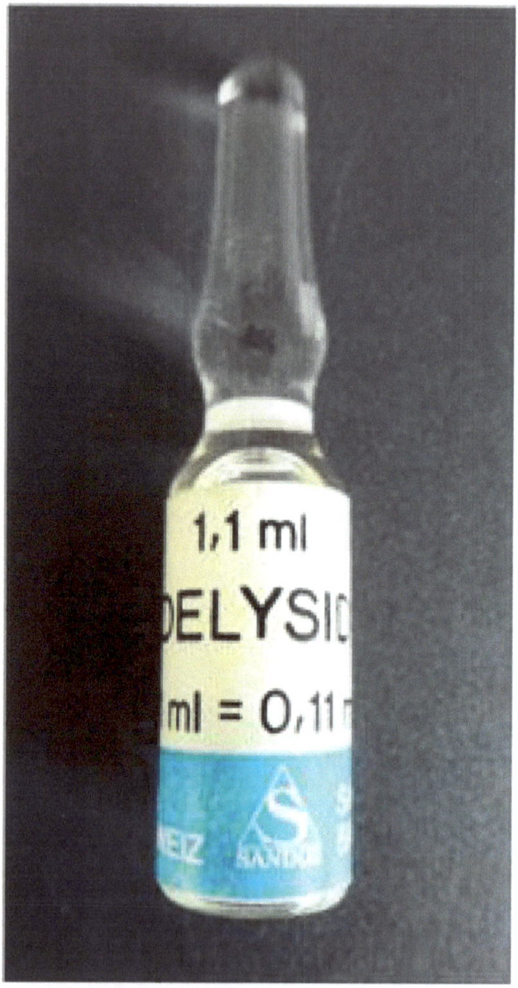

Figure 436. *Original-Ampulle Delysid®.*
Hagenbach and Werthmüller, 2011, p. 119/712.

B. Experimenting with Consciousness

Inevitably, academic research into the entheogens would attract the attention of a number of psychonauts, apostles and scalywags. Mescaline traveled from the chemist's laboratory to the physician's clinic and the author's escritoire. With psilocybin, the path was more circuitous, from a writer's speculation to a researcher's experimentation to a biologist's identification to a chemist's analysis to a physician's trials. LSD followed much the same track as mescaline. Chemical, pharmacological and subjective investigations into *Amanita muscaria* continue.

Figure 437. Henri Michaux (1899 – 1984). Epreuve chromogène, 1939 by Gisele Freund (1908 – 2000) [centrepompidou.fr, hereinafter CPU].

1. Mescaline

In the psychonaut category one could easily place a number of poets, painters and authors. Very precocious and sustained was the attention paid by the Belgian French painter, poet and author Henri Michaux (1899 – 1984) to mescaline as an infinity mechanism:

> *Very* .... It is very .... Everything is very .... *** What is a person saying when he says 'infinite being?' I should be boasting if I spoke more presumptuously about the infinite than about the finite. I never touched anything. I was in an *infinity mechanism.* Everything that appeared was caught in this mechanism [italics, asterisks, quotation marks original].[58]

Certainly, no one can exaggerate the influence of mescaline on literary masters, especially the poet, diplomat and 1990 Nobel Prize winner for literature Octavio Paz Lozano (1914 – 1998), who clearly is describing his own experiences with mescaline while summarizing the explorations of Michaux:

> The self disappears, but no other self appears to occupy the empty space it has left. No god but rather the divine. No faith but rather the primordial feeling that sustains all faith, all hope. No face but rather faceless being, the being that is all faces. Peace in the crater of the volcano, the reconciliation of man – what remains of man – with total presence.[59]

---

[58] Michaux, Henri. Miserable Miracle (*Mescaline*). San Francisco, CA: City Lights Books, 1972 [ejcj.orfaleacenter.ucsb.edu, hererinafter EJC], III. Characteristics of Mescaline, p. 38; *Très .... J'étais dans un mécanisme d'infinité. Tout ... se trouvait pris dans ce mécanisme* (Michaux, Henri. *Misérable Miracle (La Mescaline)*. Paris: Éditions Gallimard, 1972 AO, III. Caractères de la Mescaline, pp. 681-682 [*Très* and *mécanisme d'infinité* italicized in the original]).

[59] Paz, Octavio. Alternating Current, tr. Helen Lane. NY: Arcade Publishing, 1990 AA, Section 2, Henri Michaux, p. 84.

CH. 28 THE PAGAN PLOT (I)

The son of a German pharmacologist, the soldier, author and philosopher Ernst Jünger (1895 – 1998) also showed a poetic interest in the ability of mescaline to chemically modify consciousness:

> Mescaline and its relatives produce an effect that is more brutal and demanding than the effect of the opiates; they transport the user not just to the visionary world and its palaces, but also bring him down into the depths of the subterranean crypts. Extremely archaic visions recover their credibility. Stimulants and narcotics modify time: they expand it or accelerate it. But with mescaline the earth is cloven; the creative power of time returns to the origins.[60]

In the apostle group one must put Huxley. Aldous Huxley took an interest in mescaline after reading an article in the *Hibbert Journal* written by British psychiatrist Dr. Humphry Fortescue Osmond (1917 – 2004) and British neuroscientist John Raymond Smythies (1922 – 2019) discussing the connection between mescaline and schizophrenia:

> No one is really competent to treat schizophrenia unless he has experienced the schizophrenic world himself. This it is possible to do quite easily by taking mescaline. ... A better theory is capable of accounting for more facts [including] ... (c) The nature of the phenomena witnessed under the influence of mescaline. One would have thought that anyone ... would have utilized such a prolific source of material as mescaline offers ....[61]

---

[60] Jünger, Ernst. Approaches: Drugs and Ecstatic Intoxication, unknown translator. Unknown place: unknown publisher, unknown year AO, Ecstatic Intoxication: Homeland and Pilgrimage, Section 38, p. 39/418; *Das Meskalin und seine Verwandten wirken brutaler ... Zeit schaffende Macht wird ursprünglich* (Jünger, Ernst. *Annäherungen: Drogen und Rausch*. Stuttgart, DE: Ernst Klett Verlag, 1970 AA, Section 39, p. 61).

[61] Osmond, Humphry and John Smythies. "The Present State of Psychological Medicine," *The Hibbert Journal: A Quarterly Review of Religion, Theology and Philosophy*, Volume LI, No. 2, January 1953 AA, pp. 138, 141; "It has been known for over fifty

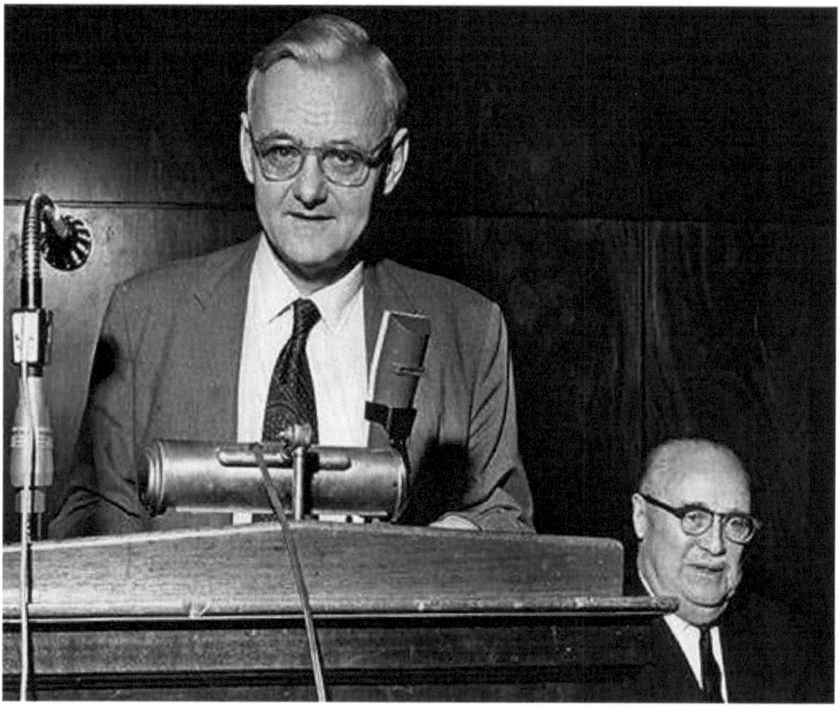

Figure 438. Humphry Osmond (1917 – 2004). Skett, Philippa. "The high life of the self-experimenters," *New Scientist*, 12 August 2004 [newscientist.com, hereinafter NST].

---

years that mescaline ... produces symptoms almost identical with schizophrenia, including catatonia and thought disorder" (Osmond, Humphry and John Smythies. "Schizophrenia: A New Approach" in *The Journal of Mental Science*, Volume XCVIII, No. 411, April 1952 [docdroid.net, hereinafter DOC], The Synthetic Illness, p. 311); as early as 1927 peyote was being considered as an excellent aid in the treatment of certain neuroses: *un excellent adjuvant dans le traitement de certaines névroses* (Rouhier, Alexandre. *Le Peyotl: La Plante Qui Fait Les Yeux Émervéilles*. Paris: Gaston Doin et Cie, 1927 AO, Preface, p. vii).

Osmond was then clinical director of a mental hospital in Weyburn, Saskatchewan[62] where, using "mescalin (the active principle of the cactus peyote – *anhelonium williamsii*), lysergic acid di-ethyl-amide, adrenochrome, adrenolutin, ololiuqui (*Rivea corymbosa*) ... [he] carried out many experiments with all these substances on [himself] and on volunteer subjects [italics original]."[63]

Osmond's first person account describes when he first brought mescaline to Huxley:

> I was working in a mental hospital on the Canadian Prairies over 2,000 miles away. ... Dr John Smythies and I had collaborated in a piece for the *Hibbert Journal* on the present state of psychological medicine. Aldous read it; enjoyed it; and sent us a characteristically friendly and encouraging letter .... He added that he hoped we would visit him when we were next in California. ... The invitation was an honour and an opportunity. I was most curious to meet this notable man .... When the meeting ended, mescalin came up, for I had admitted bringing some with me. Maria assured me that Aldous was looking forward to taking it .... Next morning, as I stirred the water and watched the silvery white mescalin crystals swirling down and dissolving with a slightly oily slick, I wondered whether it would be enough or too much. ... Three days later I flew back to Canada to find the prairies gripped in a late blizzard. I had enjoyed myself and looked forward to Aldous's report, which he worked up into a widely known book – *The Doors of Perception*. From then on we usually saw each other at least once a year and were always writing [italics original].[64]

---

[62] Osmond later accepts a position as Director of the Bureau of Research and Psychiatry at the New Jersey Neuro Psychiatric Institute in Princeton and ends his career as a professor of psychology at the University of Alabama in Birmingham.

[63] Bisbee, Cynthia Carson, et al, eds. Psychedelic Prophets: The Letters of Aldous Huxley and Humphry Osmond. Montreal, Canada: McGill-Queen's University Press, 2018 AA, Appendix Four Humphry Osmond's Statement on Peyote, 5 November 1955, pp. 617, 618.

[64] Huxley, Julian, ed. Aldous Huxley 1894-1963: A Memorial Volume. NY: Harper & Row, 1965 AA, Humphry Osmond, pp. 114, 115, 118, 119.

In the scalywag category is an anomalous character viewed from any angle, Alfred Matthew Hubbard (1901 – 1982), con man, bootlegger, prohibition agent, OSS [Office of Strategic Services, forerunner of CIA] agent, financial magnate, uranium entrepreneur and bankrupt.[65] Though by some accounts he grew up a "shoeless hillbilly"[66] in Kentucky, by 1919 he reportedly made the front page of the *Seattle Post-Intelligencer* for his invention of an "atmospheric power generator."[67] Always interested in emerging technology, he opened an early radio supply store in the 1920s which brought him the attention of the so-called King of Puget Sound Bootleggers who "needed someone who could install communications equipment aboard the fleet of cars, boats and planes used in his bootlegging operation."[68] With the bootlegger's financial backing he also built one of Seattle's first radio stations, KFQX, today's KOMO.[69]

Indicted in 1924 (along with the bootlegger and his entire crew) under the Dry Law for importation, distribution and sale of intoxicating liquors, Hubbard (now broke and divorced) "decided to become an informant in exchange for having his name dropped from the indictment."[70] He also insisted on being appointed as a Prohibition agent:

---

65 Holden, Brad. Seattle Mystic Alfred M. Hubbard: Inventor, Bootlegger and Psychedelic Pioneer. Charleston, SC: The History Press, 2021 AA, Preface, 15/171; Bisbee, 2018, Introduction, p. xl.

66 Holden, 2021, Act I, Chapter 1 The Wizard of Portage Bay, p. 20/171.

67 Holden, 2021, p. 23/171.

68 Holden, 2021, Act I, Chapter 2 Bootlegging and the Birth of Seattle Radio, p. 32/171

69 Holden, 2021, p. 34/171.

70 Holden, 2021, p. 39/171.

Figure 439. Hubbard, during his bootlegging phase, holding a pair of binoculars used to spot Coast Guard ships. Holden, 2021, p. 44/171.

> Hubbard's appointment as an agent was quite unconventional and took a considerable amount of political maneuvering, but with some high-level assistance, the twenty-four-year-old Hubbard was quietly appointed as a Prohibition agent on October 3, 1925. He continued to work as [the bootlegger's] top lieutenant while, unbeknownst to anyone else, he was also having clandestine meetings with the Prohibition Bureau in order to feed them secret bits of information.[71]

It appears he was not averse to working both sides of the street, however, offering "protection against prosecution for the right price."[72] For example, despite "his paltry income as a federal agent, Hubbard had purchased a fancy sports car and owned a couple of speed boats, and he and Rita [his wife] – who sported some eye-catching jewelry – were living in a relatively expensive home."[73] After more incriminating evidence turned up, he was terminated from the Bureau of Prohibition by the end of 1927.

Hubbard then experienced a number of other misadventures, including testifying against his superiors at the Bureau, working as a deputy sheriff, a radio technician for a quickly bankrupt airline, a wiretapper for what later would become the Bureau of Alcohol, Tobacco and Firearms, and again a radio technician for a major booze smuggler (for which he did two years in prison). In 1941 Hubbard found employment "piloting ships to Vancouver, British Columbia, where they were then refitted and sent to England to be used as destroyers in the British navy"[74] as part of the Lend-Lease Act. By 1945, "Hubbard's wartime profits had made him into a millionaire."[75] By one account, while based in Vancouver, "he personally handled

[71] Holden, 2021, p. 40/171.

[72] Holden, 2021, p. 46/171.

[73] Holden, 2021, p. 55/171.

[74] Holden, 2021, p. 66/171.

[75] Holden, 2021, p. 70/171.

several million dollars filtered by the OSS through the American consulate to finance a multitude of covert operations in Europe."[76] After the war he seems to have "had business ties to the mining company directly responsible for providing a significant amount of uranium to the Manhattan Project."[77]

As for how Al Hubbard was introduced to mescaline, one author writes that Hubbard in 1953 read an article by Osmond in the *Hibbert Journal* and became intrigued. Osmond then supposedly flew from Saskatchewan to Hubbard's private island in Vancouver and administered the mescaline, an experience Hubbard later described as: "It was the deepest mystical thing I've ever seen. I saw myself as a tiny mite in a big swamp with a spark of intelligence. I saw my mother and father having intercourse. It was all clear."[78]

Against this, Osmond does not appear to have known of Hubbard before Smythies met him in December 1954:

> John Smythies ... has found a valuable and interesting millionaire, Captain Hubbard, a thickset active (pyknic, not quite sure of the correct Sheldon classification) man who read *The Doors* and was enchanted, he has bought 20 copies so far. He is an airline owner and a uranium king. He is rich, but more important decent. He has taken mescalin and to quote a now hackneyed phrase says that it is the most wonderful thing that ever happened to him. ... He wants to help and I think is likely to do so because he looks upon his function as providing and seeing that money is provided, and not directing how it shall be used [italics original].[79]

---

[76] Lee, Martin A. and Bruce Shlain. Acid Dreams: The Complete Social History of LSD: The CIA, The Sixties, and Beyond. New York: Grove Press, 1985 AO, Chapter 2. Psychedelic Pioneers The Original Captain Trips, p. 43.

[77] Holden, 2021, What was Hubbard's Involvement with the Manhattan Project? p. 157/171.

[78] Holden, 2021, Act II Chapter 5 Tripping the '50s Fantastic, pp. 76-77/171.

[79] Bisbee, 2018, letter dated 7 December 1954 from Osmond to Huxley, p. 143.

2. Psilocybin

The Chase banker Robert Gordon Wasson (1898 – 1986) was avocationally called to ethnomycology thanks to his Russian wife, pediatrician Valentina Pavlova Guercken (1901 – 1958), a self-taught expert on the subject:

All Russians know the mushrooms, not by dint of study as the mycologists do, but as part of our ancient heritage, imbibed with our mother's milk. ... We Russians love the whole mushroom world, and what a world it is! ... This love of Russians for the earthy tribe of mushrooms is, I suggest, a distinctive trait of the Slavs and a significant one.[80]

Valentina introduced Gordon to mushroom collecting, her worshipful, him horrified:

The Catskill Mountains in August are filled with mushrooms, exquisitely beautiful. ... In 1927 I had just married my American husband, and we were spending our first holiday ... near Big Indian. With what astonishment my husband saw me, on our first walk, dart with ecstasy to this fungus and that, and on bended knee strike what seemed to him poses of adoration! With what horror he strove, unsuccessfully, to keep me from bringing home and eating a mess of fragrant *lisichki*! He behaved, as we both at once perceived, like the hen that has hatched ducklings and sees them swim away [italics, exclamation point original].[81]

---

[80] Wasson, Valentina Pavlova and R. Gordon Wasson. Mushrooms, Russia and History, *Volume I*. NY: Pantheon Books, 1957 AA, Chapter I Mushrooms and the Russians, pp. 3, 4.

[81] Wasson and Wasson, Mushrooms, *Volume I*, 1957, pp. 4, 5.

Figure 440. Robert and Valentina Wasson. Illana, C. "*Robert Gordon Wasson: Un Pionero de la Etnamicologia*," *Boletín de la Sociedad Micológica de Madrid*, Volume 31, Octubre 2007 RGN, p. 275.

The complete disconnect between their mycophobic and mycophilic attitudes led the Wassons to exhaustively study everything to do with mushrooms, almost monomaniacally accumulating a mountain of literary and ethnological information. In this endeavor they were guided by Robert Graves who encouraged the Wassons to follow the thread of his own speculations to Mexico. In part due to this advice, the Wassons discovered the traditions related to *teonanacatl*:

On September 9, 1952, Dr. Hans Mardersteig of Verona wrote us that he had observed in the new Rietberg Museum of Zurich a curious stone statuette, about one foot high, representing a mushroom with a human face carved in high relief on the stipe. ... By almost the same post Robert Graves sent us a cutting from a pharmaceutical publication referring to the 16th century use of an inebriating mushroom among the Indians of Mexico. This was our first intimation of a mushroom cult in Mexico. At once we embarked on a double-barreled inquiry, pursuing on the one hand the secret of the mushroom stone and on the other hand the cult of the mushroom in Mexico.[82]

The Wassons began visiting Mexico in 1953.

Graves carefully followed their progress from afar, for which he accorded himself no small part in their discoveries, having spurred on their search for a Mexican mushroom oracle:

My mushroom man is very elated since he actually found the mushroom oracle I sent him after in Mexico, and ate the sacred mushrooms and had them analysed – and there's the next wonder drug to watch out for. He thinks they were what the worshippers ate at the Eleusinian Mysteries to get such terrific visions ....[83]

The oracle Wasson found was, of course, the Mazatec *sabia* María Sabina Magdalena Garcia (1894 – 1985) who remembers the first time the white men attended one of her *veladas*:

---

82 Wasson and Wasson, Mushrooms, *Volume II*, 1957, Chapter Five The Sacred Mushrooms of the Nahua, p. 275.

83 Seymour-Smith, Martin. Robert Graves: His Life and Work. London: Bloomsbury Publishing Plc, 1995 AA. Chapter Twenty-Nine 1953 – 59, IV, p. 462, in a letter to the author dated 24 December 1956; twenty years later, Wasson offered "another mushroom, *Claviceps purpurea*, as holding the secret to the Eleusinian Mysteries" (Wasson, R. Gordon, Albert Hofmann, Carl A. P. Ruck. The Road to Eleusis: Unveiling the Secret of the Mysteries. NY: Harcourt Brace Jovanovich, 1978 AA, Chapter One The Wasson Road to Eleusis, p. 17).

Figure 441. María Sabina. Hagenbach, 2011, p. 213/712.

> The next day, someone brought to my house three white men. One of them was Mr. Wasson. ... Soon, one night, the foreigners attended my velada. ... When the foreigners took the *ninos santos* with me, I did not feel anything wrong. The velada was good. I had different visions. I came to see places that I had never imagined existed. I came to the place of origin of the foreigners. I saw cities. Great cities. Many great houses. ... Before Wasson no one took the little mushrooms simply to find god. Always they took them to cure an illness [tr. gwr, italics original].[84]

Wasson records the date when he ingested for the first time the divine mushrooms as that of 29-30 June, 1955.[85]

But he and his wife continued to accumulate direct evidence for the ceremonies:

> By now we have attended many sessions conducted by shamans in which mushrooms have been used. ... We were the first to attend a *sung* performance, lasting most of the night. We were the first to eat the mushrooms, which we have now done on numerous occasions, in the course of the rite and by ourselves. We were the first to report in detail our experiences, including an account of the hallucinations that the mushrooms cause [italics original].[86]

The reports of the Wassons intrigued both professional mycologists and accomplished chemists. The "dean of French mycologists" Roger Heim (1900 – 1979), director of the *Laboratoire de Cryptogamie* of the *Muséum National d'Histoire Naturelle* joined the

---

[84] *Al día siguiente, alguien trajo a mi casa .... Siempre se tomaron para que los enfermos sanaran* (Estrada, Alvaro. La Vida de María Sabina, La Sabia de los Hongos. Ciudad DF, MX: siglo vientiuno editores, sa, 1977 AA, Vida de María Sabina, pp. 91, 93).

[85] *La noche del 29 al 30 de junio de 1955, cuando asistí por primera vez a una 'velada' cantada por María Sabina en Huautla de Jiménez y, a invitación suya, ingerí por primera vez los hongos divinos* (Estrada, 1977, Presentación, por R. Gordon Wasson, p. 9).

[86] Wasson, Valentina P. and R. Gordon Wasson. "The Hallucinogenic Mushrooms," *The Garden Journal of the New York Botanical Garden*, January-February, Volume 8, Issue 1, 1958 AO, p. 4.

Wassons in 1956. Afterwards, Heim was able to fix "the identity for the first time of seven kinds of mushrooms that are used for divination."[87]

CIA was also intrigued. They sent one of their contract employees Parke, Davis chemist and University of Delaware professor John Alexander Moore (James, 1923 – 1999) to accompany Wasson and Heim. Moore told them their expedition would be funded through a grant from the Geschickter Fund for Medical Research. He did not tell them it was a CIA front.[88]

Moore had a bad trip. It appears that the journey by burro through the Sierras was a near martyrdom for him before he reached his destination. In the words of Wasson describing the journey for *Life Magazine*:

> Those who know these mushrooms are Indians belonging to tribes farthest removed from us culturally, locked in their mountains remote from highways, locked also behind the barrier of their languages. One must win their confidence and overcome their suspicion of white men. One must face the physical discomforts of life and dangers of disease in the Indian villages in the rainy season, when the mushrooms grow.[89]

---

[87] Wasson, V. P. and R. G., 1958, pp. 4, 5; *En vérité, c'est au cours de notre voyage de 1956 en pays mazatèque et chatino que l'identité du Ps. mexicana a pu s'imposer à nos yeux* [italics original] (Heim, Roger and R. Gordon Wasson. *Archives du Muséum National d'Histoire Naturelle, Septième Série, Tome VI*: *Les Champignons Hallucinogènes du Mexique: Éudes ethnologiques, taxinomiques, biologiques, physiologiques et chimiques*. Paris: Éditions du muséum, 1958 [sciencepress.mnhn.fr, hereinafter SCI], Chapitre IV. Étude descriptive et taxinomique des Agarics hallucinogènes du Mexique, Les Psilocybes a) Formes galéroïdes et terricoles à sclérotes *Psilocybe mexicana* Heim, p. 130).

[88] Marks, 1979, p. 114.

[89] Wasson, R. Gordon. "Seeking the Magic Mushroom," *Life*, Volume 42, No. 19, 13 May 1957, pp. 117, 118.

When Moore was in the hut of the shaman María Sabina he was obliged to pretend to be interested in the experience, a session that became for him a true hell. He complained of diarrhea, a bad cold, unfamiliar food, the chanting during the ceremonies and the disorientation caused by the mushrooms themselves.[90]

He returned to Delaware with

> a bag of mushrooms .... Already a thin man, Moore had lost 15 pounds. Over the next week, he slowly nursed himself back to health. He ... started preliminary work in his lab to isolate the active ingredient in the mushrooms. ... [I]f Moore succeeded, it was 'quite possible' that the new drugs could 'remain an Agency secret.' [The] dream of a CIA monopoly on the divine mushroom vanished quickly under the influence of unwanted competitors .... While Moore toiled in his lab, Roger Heim in Paris unexpectedly pulled off the remarkable feat of growing the mushrooms in artificial culture from spore prints he had made in Mexico. Heim then sent samples to none other than Albert Hofmann ... [quotation marks original].[91]

Hofmann was then able to isolate two active principles:

> The active principle of *Psilocybe mexicana* Heim, a mexican mushroom with hallucinogenic properties, has been isolated in crystalline form. The compound has been given the name *Psilocybin*; it possesses indole characteristics and contains phosphorus. A second substance, closely related to *Psilocybin* but found only in traces, has been called *Psilocin*.[92]

---

[90] Marks, John. The Search for the "Manchurian Candidate": The CIA and Mind Control. NY: Times Books, 1979 AA, pp. 114, 115.

[91] Marks, 1979, Chapter 7 Mushrooms to Counterculture, p. 115.

[92] Hofmann, A., Heim, R., Brack, A. and H. Kobel. "*Psilocybin, ein psychotroper Wirkstoff aus dem mexikanischen Rauschpilz Psilocybe mexicana Heim,*" *Experientia*, Volume XIV, No. 3, 1958 [psilocybin-research.com, hereinafter PRC], Summary, p. 109.

Almost immediately the new crystalline compound from Sandoz underwent clinical trials by French neuropsychiatrist and soon-to-be elected member of the *Academie Française* Jean Delay (1907 – 1987), first on normal volunteer subjects, then on those with mental illness.[93] Of the latter, a melancholic became euphoric, a mute catatonic became relatively accessible.[94] Delay speculated that hypothetical therapeutic applications might include a) the reliving of past events, b) a dream state to conduct dream analysis, and c) modifications of mood observed in several cases.[95]

In 1962 Albert Hofmann journeyed with Wasson into the remote mountains of Mexico and both were able to participate in a *velada* with María Sabina, this time using the new psilocybin pills, an experiment without precedent in the annals of pharmacognosy:

> After about another quarter of an hour, the spirit of the pills did begin to yield its effects, which lasted until the crack of dawn. … As we took leave of Maria Sabina and her clan ... the *curandera* said that the pills had the same power as the mushrooms, that there was no difference. This was a confirmation from the most competent authority, that the synthetic psilocybin is identical with the natural product. As a parting gift I let Maria Sabina have a vial of psilocybin pills. She radiantly explained to our interpreter Herlinda that she could now give consultations even in the season when no mushrooms grow [italics original].[96]

---

[93] *des sujets normaux volontaires, puis sur des malades montaux* (Delay, Jean, et al. "*Premiers Essais de la Psilocybine en Psychiatrie* [First Trials of Psilocybin in Psychiatry]," Proceedings of the First International Congress of Neuropsychopharmacology, Rome, September 1958, ed. P. B. Bradley, et al. Amsterdam, NE: Elsevier, 1959, p. 528).

[94] *Une melancolique sous psilocybine est devenue euphorique, une catatonique muette est devenue relativement accessible* (Delay, 1959, p. 531).

[95] *a) la reviviscence d'évènements anciens b) … dans certains cas* (Delay, 1959, p. 531).

[96] Hofmann, 1983, 6 The Mexican Relatives of LSD, A Mushroom Ceremony, pp. 141, 142; *Nach etwa zehn Minuten … Dolmetscherin Herlinda* (Hofmann, 2001, 10 Auf der

Figure 82. The journey, 1962. Hagenbach, 2011, p. 206/712.

Suche nach der Zauberpflanze Ska Maria Pastora, Eine Pilz-Zeremonie, p. 89/139).

In a tangentially related note, Wasson sent Hofmann samples of seeds from a plant with distinctive white, bell-shaped flowers known locally as *ololiuhqui* or *badoh* (*Turbina/Rivea corymbosa*) as well as seeds from a plant with blue, white, purple or pink flowers known locally as *tliltlitzin* or *badoh negro* (*Ipomoea violacea*).[97] Hofmann discovered the main components of both kinds of seeds were "*d*-lysergic acid amide (ergine) and *d*-isolysergic acid amide (isoergine) [italics original]."[98] Hofmann also found ergine [LSA or LAA] was one of the "main alkaloids in ergot growing on the wild grass *Paspalum distichum* L. This grass grows commonly all around the Mediterranean basin and is often infected with *Claviceps paspali*,"[99] supporting Wasson's theory that an ergot potentiated the Eleusinian Mysteries.

---

97 Hofmann, Albert. "The Active Principles of the Seeds of Rivea Corymbosa and Ipomoea Violacea," *Botanical Museum Leaflets, Harvard University*, Volume XX, No. 6, 22 November 1963 [biodiversitylibrary.org, hereinafter BIO], pp. 198, 199.

98 Hofmann, 1963, p. 200; see also *The Psychedelic Review*, Volume 1, No. 3, 1964, p. 302 et seq.

99 Hofmann, Albert. "A Challenging Question and My Answer," in Wasson, et al, Eleusis, 1978, Chapter Two, p. 31.

3. LSD

The first voyages of the Sandoz group (Hofmann, Stoll and soon Jünger) with LSD moved them to the point of considering the substance the most precious of the spiritual gifts discovered by humanity. They viewed the entheogens primarily as medicine and secondarily as aides to creativity. Once again an entheogen moved from the laboratory to the clinical physician and the artist.

The American physician Harold Alexander Abramson (1899 – 1980) initiated the English anthropologist, social scientist and epistemologist Gregory Bateson (1904 – 1980): "*Bateson*: My interest in LSD began when Dr. Abramson gave me 35 μg. about 2 years ago, and was revived the other day by the study just mentioned by Dr. Savage, in which Dr. Adams gave me 100 μg [italics original]."[100]

Although scattered throughout several texts,[101] Bateson's observations on LSD hold a particular interest:

> Under LSD, I have experienced, as have many others, the disappearance of the division between self and the music to which I was listening. The perceiver and the thing perceived become strangely united into a single entity. This state is surely more correct than the state in which it seems that 'I hear the music' [quotation marks original].[102]

---

[100] Abramson, Harold A., editor. The Use of LSD in Psychotherapy: *Transactions of a Conference on d-Lysergic Acid Diethylamide (LSD) April 22, 23, and 24, 1959, Princeton, N.J.* NY: Josiah Macy, Jr. Foundation, 1960 AA, Introductory Remarks, p. 10.

[101] See for example Bateson, Gregory. Steps to an Ecology of Mind: Collected Essays in Anthropology, Psychiatry, Evolution, and Epistemology. Northvale, NJ: Jason Aronson Inc., 1972 AA, Part V: Epistemology and Ecology, Conscious Purpose versus Nature, p. 446, Form, Substance, and Difference, p. 469, Part VI: Crisis in the Ecology of Mind, From Versailles to Cybernetics, p. 478.

[102] Bateson, 1972, Part V: Epistemology and Ecology, Form, Substance, and Difference p. 469.

His experience with the substance doubtlessly influenced one of his fundamental conclusions on the reason-emotion and mind-body dualities: "It is the attempt to *separate* intellect from emotion that is monstrous, and I suggest that it is equally monstrous – and dangerous – to attempt to separate the external mind from the internal. Or to separate mind from body [italics original]."[103]

The poet Irwin Allen Ginsberg (1926 – 1997) recounted his first LSD experience in a letter to his father:

> I went down to Stanford University the other day to be subjected to a research experiment with a new drug – LSD-25 (Lysergic Acid) which Huxley described in his books *Doors of Perception* and *Heaven and Hell.* It was astounding – I lay back, listening to music, and went into a sort of trance state (somewhat similar to the high state of laughing gas) and in a fantasy much like a Coleridge world of Kubla Khan saw a vision of that part of my consciousness which seemed to be permanent and transcendent and identical with the origin of the universe – a sort of identity common to everything – but a clear and coherent sight of it. Rather beautiful visual images also, of Hindu-type gods dancing on themselves. This drug seems to automatically produce a mystical experience. Science is getting very hip. It's a very safe drug – you ought to contact someone at Rutgers who's doing experiments with it and try it – like a comic movie [italics original].[104]

In a revealing 62 minute video recorded at a private party in Los Angeles, the experimental psychiatrist Oscar Janiger (1918 – 2001) recounted the role he played in the dissemination of the entheogenic experience among people with considerable influence, including the use of LSD with Cary Grant:

---

[103] Bateson, 1972, p. 470.

[104] Morgan, Bill, ed. The Letters of Allen Ginsberg. Philadelphia, PA: Da Capo Press, 2008 [terebess.hu, hereinafter TER], Allen Ginsberg [San Francisco, CA] to Louis Ginsberg [Paterson, NJ] May 20, 1959, p. 294/697.

Figure 443. Allen Ginsberg (1926 – 1997), reading "Who be kind to" at the *Festival dei Due Mondi* (Festival of Two Worlds) in Spoleto, Italy, 8 July 1967, for which he was arrested and questioned by the police.

Oscar Janiger: "We ran close to a 1000 people through ... and each of these people were people who had considerable influence in their own right. ... And they were bringing the message out." ...
Timothy Leary: "Who turned on Cary Grant?" ...
Sidney Cohen: "Hartman."[105]
Oscar Janiger: "Hartman did. And then I ... saw him a few times" [transcription gwr].[106]

As to how Al Hubbard was introduced to LSD, two authors write: "Hubbard was introduced to LSD by Dr. Ronald Sandison of Great Britain. During his first acid trip in 1951, he claimed to have witnessed his own conception. 'It was the deepest mystical thing .... It was all clear.'"[107] But this version clearly doubles that of Hubbard's first mescaline trip, and, unfortunately, the first publication by Sandison on the subject of LSD dates to 1954.[108] Another author writes that Hubbard was reading the 1951 *Hibberd* [sic] *Journal* about the behavior of rats given LSD and flew out to Saskatchewan: "Hubbard went and found the person conduction [sic] the experiment, and came back with some LSD for himself."[109]

---

105 Beverly Hills Psychiatrists Dr. Mortimer A. Hartman and Dr. Arthur Chandler administered the drug over sixty times to the movie idol according to Wansell, Geoffrey. The Haunted Idol: The Story of the Real Cary Grant. NY: Quill, William Morrow, 1983 AA, Part Three The Haunted Star, Chapter 10, p. 233.

106 "A Conversation on LSD, Featuring Myron Stolaroff, Sidney Cohen, Al Hubbard, Timothy Leary, Oscar Janiger, Humphry Osmond and Others," V1.1, 16 February 1979, 37:09 to 37:33.

107 Lee and Shlain, 1985, Chapter 2 Psychedelic Pioneers The Original Captain Trips, p. 43.

108 See Sandison, R. A., Spencer, A. M., and J. D. A. Whitelaw. "The Therapeutic Value of Lysergic Acid Diethylamide in Mental Illness," *The Journal of Mental Science*, Volume 100, No. 419, April 1954.

109 Fahey, Todd. "The Original Captain Trips," *High Times Magazine*, November

Unfortunately, there are four serious problems with the latter. First, the *Hibbert Journal* in the early 1950s had a grand circulation of around 3000 copies, mostly in England: "[T]he trend of sales continued downwards ... as printers' costs were rising steeply. The circulation was 3100 in 1952, 2900 in 1954 ...."[110] Second, this "British quarterly that published scholarly commentary on religion and philosophy"[111] was never intended for a lay audience. Third, the story too closely mirrors the actual story of how Osmond brought mescaline not to Al Hubbard's Hollywood Hospital[112] in Vancouver, Canada but to Aldous Huxley's residence in Hollywood, California. Fourth, besides the incorrect dates, spellings and landmasses, Sandison's 1954 article describes his experiments at the Powick Mental Hospital near Worcester, England (not Saskatchewan) with thirty-six psychoneurotic patients (not rats): "The effects of LSD 25 on the behaviour of animals are very different from those observed in man and need not be further considered."[113]

Osmond had met up with Hubbard by 1956: "We had a wonderful time on Al Hubbard's island off Vancouver Island. One of the loveliest places I have ever seen. Sea, mountains, a 15 acre island

---

1991.

110 Ruston, Alan R. The Hibbert Trust: A History. London: The Hibbert Trust, 1984 [unitarian.org,uk, hereinafter UO], 4. The *Hibbert Journal*, p. 41.

111 Holden, 2021, p. 76/171.

112 "Hubbard was actively involved in the Hollywood Hospital, a private clinic ... near Vancouver .... The staff used LSD for the treatment of schizophrenics and alcoholics. Allegedly, a number of Hollywood film personalities were treated there" (Bisbee et al, 2018, p. 274, fn. 39, letter from Aldous Huxley to Humphry Osmond dated 29 June 1956).

113 Sandison, et al, 1954, p. 491.

with every modern convenience including its own sea plane and radio telephone."[114]

Initially, Huxley broadly approved of Smythies' new friend: "So what extraordinary luck that this representative of both these Higher Powers should (a) have become so passionately interested in mescalin and (b) be such a very nice man."[115] Later, however, Huxley had some reservations with Hubbard's methods:

> Your nice Captain tried a new experiment – group mescalinization. It worked ... rather poorly for Hubbard, who tried to run the group in the way he had run other groups in Vancouver, where the drug has worked as a device for raising buried guilts and traumas and permitting people to get on to better terms with themselves.[116]

In particular, Huxley objected to Hubbard's interjection of Catholic morality into the LSD experience:

> Would it not be best to let Al go his way within the Church? It is evidently there that he feels increasingly at home. It is evident, too, that his loyalty to the Church makes him increasingly anxious to use LSD-25 as an instrument for validating Catholic doctrines and for giving new life to Catholic symbols. Of such, perhaps, is the Kingdom of Heaven – but of such is not the kingdom of Scientific Research.[117]

A participant reported that the room used for LSD therapy at Hubbard's Vancouver clinic had three pictures on the walls: Dali's god's-eye view painting of Christ on the cross, Dali's painting of the Last Supper, and a painting of the Buddha by Gauguin, generally promoting a spiritual atmosphere.

---

[114] Bisbee, 2018, Appendix Two, Letter from Osmond to Matthew and Ellen Huxley, dated 16 August 1956, pp. 564-565.

[115] Bisbee, 2018, letter from Huxley to Osmond dated 12 January 1955, p. 151.

[116] Bisbee, 2018, p. 150.

[117] Bisbee, 2018, letter from Huxley to Osmond dated 11 January 1958, p. 365;

What appears to be true is that, although he had no medical training Hubbard did experiment with large doses of LSD in the treatment of alcoholics at his Hollywood Clinic near Vancouver and even co-authored a scholarly paper on the subject:

One of our group [Hubbard] pioneered in the use of a psychedelic experience in alcoholism and evaluated the effect of LSD-25 in a large series of normal subjects. In 1953 he was using an overwhelming-dose experience, at that time up to 500 gamma, in alcoholics and normal subjects. The results were encouraging and led to communications with H. Osmond and A. Hoffer.[118]

Perhaps there does not exist another such bizarre account of chemical voyaging in the history of literature. Criss-crossing the country in his private plane, Hubbard acquired and exchanged all kinds of psychoactive drugs. In the same 62 minute video, Hubbard declares he gave the American psychologist, author and sometime Harvard Professor Timothy Francis Leary (1920 – 1996) LSD as well as CO2:

Al Hubbard: "I gave him [Leary] ... a bottle of 500 tablets."
Timothy Leary: "I know that." ...
Sydney Cohen: "Al, didn't you say you introduced Tim to CO2?"
Timothy Leary: "That's right. That's right. He dragged us all around Boston with these tanks .... He had us all strapped ...."
Al Hubbard: "Some of that stuff ...."
Timothy Leary: "It's fantastic, yeah" [transcription gwr].[119]

Oscar Janiger also attests to Al Hubbard's delivery service:

---

[118] MacLean, J. Ross, et al. "The Use of LSD-25 in the Treatment of Alcoholism and Other Psychiatric Problems," *The Quarterly Journal of Studies on Alcohol*, Volume 22, No. 1, 1961 [jsad.com, hereinafter JSA], pp. 34-35.

[119] "A Conversation," V1.1, 16 February 1979, 01:24 to 01:29, 01:41 to 01:57.

Oscar Janiger: "You know, you're the Johnny Appleseed of LSD, you know, planting it everywhere you get a chance."
Al Hubbard: "Yeah, I sure did." ...
Oscar Janiger: "And I remember old Al Hubbard coming up to the house ... with his leather pouch ... and he opened up his leather pouch and it was all the wampum and great stuff he had and he was trading up. Well, we said, 'What do we have here for the month, now, Al.' And Al said, 'Well, we have this and that, and something new is coming out, how would you like a little of that ....' Remember?"
Al Hubbard: "Yeah, I remember it."
Oscar Janiger: "We were waiting for you. We were waiting for you like a little lady on the prairie waiting for the ... Sears Roebuck catalog." ...
Oscar Janiger: "I must say ... that he never made a lot of money selling that stuff at all. He was, he was a great trader, though. He'd say, 'How about a little of almost pure ... tetrohydrocannabinol oil.' In those days, it was kind of a ... viscous oil. Remember that stuff ...?"
Al Hubbard: "Yeah" [transcription gwr].[120]

Hubbard did introduce many well-known people to their first psychedelic experience with his tireless apostolizing, sharing voyages with politicians, legislators and even an unspecified prime minister.

As for motivation, when questioned Hubbard was circumspect:

Oscar Janiger: "Well, when you started with it all, Al .... You had some kind of purpose or vision in mind, didn't you?"
Al Hubbard: "It cost me a couple hundred thousand dollars. I don't know if that's a good motive or not." ...
Oscar Janiger: "What do you think its best use is for, Al?"
Al Hubbard: "I don't know. ... Just keep waking people up. Let them see themselves for what they are. ... I had four thousand bottles of it to begin with" [transcription gwr].[121]

---

120 "A Conversation," 1979, 04:01 to 04:07, 50:04 to 50:35, 53:45 to 54:03.

121 "A Conversation," 1979, 03:43 to 05:24, 31:29.

Figure 444. *Amanita muscaria.* Wasson, R. Gordon. Soma: Divine Mushroom of Immortality. NY: Harcourt Brace Jovanovich, 1968 AO, Cover.

4. *Amanita muscaria*

Earlier in the twentieth century researchers had drawn limits around the identification of the *Soma* of the Aryan invaders of the Late Bronze Age Indus Valley, "at the same time a god, a plant, and the juice of that plant."[122] French linguist Georges Edmond Raoul Dumézil (1898 – 1986) was able to eliminate mead from consideration: "But, from what we have been able to reconstitute of the cycle of ambrosia, nothing there recalls either the preparation or the manufacture of hydromel [tr. gwr]."[123] French theologian and historian of religion Philippe de Félice (1880 – 1964) summarized what was then known about the substance:

> The liquor about which they speak is always drawn from a plant. This plant grows on the mountains .... What seems to produce the mystical potion is neither the leaves nor the fruit, but always the stems. The juice is either red or clear yellow. It must be filtered or decanted, to eliminate certain elements that are disturbing or that perhaps risk rendering it too toxic. ... [I]t is certainly not for pleasure that one drinks it. The inebriation that it provokes can present grave dangers: the spirit wanders, the drink can even lead to madness. [124]

---

122 Wasson, R. Gordon. Soma: Divine Mushroom of Immortality. NY: Harcourt Brace Jovanovich, 1968 AO, *Part One*, Chapter I The Problem, p. 3.

123 *Mais, d'après ce que ... la fabrication de l'hydromel* (Dumézil, Georges. *Le Festin d'Immortalité: Étude de Mythologie Comparée Indo-Européenne*, *Annales du Musée Guimet, Étude de Mythologie Comparée Indo-Européenne, Tome* 34. Paris: Librairie Orientaliste Paul Geuthner, 1924 AO, III. L'Ambroisie et la Bière, p. 279); O'Flaherty, Wendy Doniger. "The Post-Vedic History of the Soma Plant," in Wasson, 1968, *Part Two* Chapter VIII Later Researches in the Twentieth Century, p. 130.

124 Wasson, Soma, 1968, pp. 134, 135; *La liqueur dont ils parlent ... la folie* (Félice, Philippe de. *Poisons sacrés, Ivresses divines: Essai sur quelques formes inférieures de la mystique*. Paris: Albin Michel, 1936 [RH/0541, New South Wales State Library, hereinafter NSW], Troisième Partie Les ivresses divines dans les religions des peuples indo-

Swiss ethnologist and philologist Karl Meuli (1891 – 1968) observed that many primitive cultures still consumed Amanita: "Widespread throughout all of Siberia, from the Ob [river] to the East Coast, is after all the indulgence of fly-agaric [tr. gwr]."[125]

Supported by their research as well as thirty first-hand accounts and more than a dozen linguistic and ethno-mycological studies, Wasson became convinced that *Soma* was the *Amanita muscaria*: "My candidate for the identity of Soma is *Amanita muscaria* ... the brilliant red mushroom with white spots familiar in forests and folklore throughout northern Eurasia [italics original]."[126]

Naturally, he received some pushback for this controversial hypothesis: "Some Vedic scholars have raised a ballyhoo because we have declared Soma to have been the white-spotted scarlet mushroom."[127] Other candidates that have been proposed include "various kinds of alcohol, the San Pedro Cactus (*Echinopsis/Trichocereus pachanoi*) ... the lotus or water lily-plant (*Nymphaea caerulea*) ... ginseng ... datura (*Datura metel*) ... mandrake (*Mandragora turcomanica*) ... an ergot fungus (*Claviceps paspali*) ... cannabis ... [and] Syrian/mountain rue (*Peganum harmala*)."[128]

---

européens, Chap. I. Soma et Haoma, p. 268).

125 *Durch ganz Sibirien verbreitet, vom Ob bis an die Ostküste, ist schließlich der Genuß des Fliegenschwamms* (Meuli, Karl. "Scythica," *Hermes*, Volume 70, Issue 2, 1935 NSW, p. 146).

126 Wasson, Soma, 1968, Part One Soma: Divine Mushroom of Immortality, II The Fly-Agaric of Eurasia, p. 10.

127 Wasson, R. Gordon, Stella Kramrisch, Jonathan Ott, and Carl A. P. Ruck. Persephone's Quest: Entheogens and the Origins of Religion. New Haven, CT: Yale University Press, 1986 AA, Chapter One Epilogue: The Age of the Entheogens, p. 79.

128 Clark, Matthew. "*Soma* and *Haoma*: Ayahuasca Analogues from the Late Bronze Age," *Journal of Psychedelic Studies*, Volume 3, Issue 2, 2019 [akjournals.com, hereinafter

For a long time the effects of *Amanita muscaria* were said to be due to muscarine. Heim consumed a small quantity of fresh muscarine in 1923, receiving "an agreeable sensation of contemplative well-being [tr. gwr]."[129] But in 1964 a "flycidal constituent from Amanita pantherina (DC.) Fr." was isolated and named "pantherine."[130] The same substance was isolated from *Amanita muscaria* the next year: "This is identical to the pantherine isolated by O. M. Onda [tr. gwr] ...."[131] As of 2017, three substances (especially muscimol and ibotenic acid) have been isolated and are said to be responsible for the psychoactive effects of both *pantherine* and *muscaria*, with still others suspected:

> Bioactive isoxazoles were identified as ibotenic acid, muscimol and muscazole. These substances are responsible for the psychoactive effects of both mushrooms. Muscimol and ibotenic acid are most likely to be the biologically active principles .... Muscazone is less active but other active components are suspected."[132]

AKJ], Theories About the Botanical Identity of *Soma/Haoma*, pp. 106-107.

[129] *l'Amanita muscaria (folie muscarienne), qui renferme la muscarine, alcaloïde toxique ... et qui, consommée fraîche et en petites quantités, peut produire une agréable sensation qui confine au bien-être contemplatif (j'en ai fait l'expérience en 1923, à Briançon)* (Heim and Wasson, *Les Champignons*, 1958, Chapitre VIII Les Effets Psychiques, Auto-expériences préalables, 1. Prèmieres expériences personnelles réalisées avec les Champignons hallucinogènes mexicains, par Roger Heim, p. 278).

[130] Onda, Masayuki, Fukushima, Hiroshi and Masuko Akagawa. "A Flycidal Constituent of Amanita pantherina (DC.) Fr.," *Chemical and Pharmaceutical Bulletin*, Volume 12, Issue 6, 1964 [jstage.jst.go.jp, hereinafter JST], p. 751.

[131] *Dieser ist identisch mit dem von O. M. Onda et al isolierten Pantherin ...* (Eugster, C. H., G.F.R. Müller & R. Good. "*Wirkstoffe aus Amanita muscaria: ibotensaeure und muscazon,*" *Tetrahedron Letters* No. 23, 1965 [file1.lookchem.com, hereinafter FIL], p. 1814).

[132] Patocka, Jiri and Barbora Kocandrlova. "Pharmacologically and Toxicologically Relevant Components of *Amanita muscaria*," *Military Medical Science Letters*, Volume 86, Issue 3, 2017 [mmsl.cz, hereinafter MMS], Chemical Components of *Amanita*

The effects appear to vary with set, setting, dose, person and method of preparation. A small survey in Washington State found accidental users generally find the effects unpleasurable, while intentional users find it enjoyable.[133] A half cup of the mushrooms sliced, sautéed and deliberately ingested by one psychonaut, produced sensations including:

> changes in visual perception ... an 'alive' quality in inanimate objects, mild distortion of size, distance and depth perception ... auditory hallucinations ... slight impairment of motor coordination and balance ... consciousness ... removed and distant from the surroundings ... [and] a great sense of clarity [italics original].[134]

However, a member of the group who ingested half again as much "experienced a complete dissociative reaction, and was unable to communicate with the rest of the group for about five hours."[135]

Modern chemical analysis finds that decarboxylation (by heat, stomach acid) incompletely converts ibotenic acid to muscimol, the "remainder being excreted as free ibotenic acid" in the urine which can then be repeatedly reingested until there is "an insufficient amount of ibotenic acid in the urine to generate a threshhold dose of muscimol by decarboxylation."[136] Wasson idenitified three filters for the preparation of *Soma* in the Rig-Veda: sunlight (heat, drying), lamb's wool and the human body.[137] Coincidentally, Osmond also noticed that "keratin (the

---

muscaria, Isoxazoles, p. 125.

133 Ott, Jonathan. "Psycho-Mycological Studies of Amanita – From Ancient Sacrament to Modern Phobia," *Journal of Psychedelic Drugs*, Volume 8, No. 1, Jan-Mar 1976 AA, Accidental Versus Intentional Use of Psychoactive *Amanita* Species, p. 31.

134 Ott, 1976, Subjective Effects of *Amanita* Intoxication, p. 32.

135 Ott, 1976, p. 32.

136 Ott, 1976, Chemistry and Pharmacology of Psychoactive *Amanita* Species, p. 29.

137 Wasson, Soma, 1968, Part One, Chapter VIII Epithets, Conceits and Tropes for

protein in wool) is very similar to the protein in the central nervous system ... [and] that hallucinogens are possessed of a very great affinity [for wool] and apparently the greater the affinity the more powerful the hallucinogen."[138] Comparing the effects, one discerning user found that whereas the "psychic effects of LSD, psilocybin-containing mushrooms, and peyote" are "similar ... on a continuum of related experience," those of Amanita are "distinctly different."[139]

As an aside, Wasson was again influenced by Robert Graves, the author of I, Claudius (1934) when he supplied a crucial piece of advice on how the emperor Claudius could have been poisoned with a different Amanita:

> We are specially beholden also to Robert Graves, novelist, scholar, and poet, who supplied to us, among other brilliant suggestions, the missing link that we had been seeking in order to round out our own conjecture concerning the death of the Emperor Claudius, and to render that conjecture not merely suggestive but (we make bold to hope) persuasive. We believe that by re-reading the age-worn texts in the light of present-day knowledge, we can state with some assurance exactly what lethal agents were used when, at the behest of the Empress Agrippina, Locusta [the court poisoner] undertook to dispose of Agrippina's august spouse.[140]

Wasson theorized that it was *Amanita phalloides* that did in the Emperor: "For murderers there is only one kind of mushroom worth considering: *Amanita phalloides* [Death Cap]. Almost every one who dies from mushrooms dies from it; and most of those who have eaten it have died from it. Even a small piece of the cap may kill a grown

---

Soma, 4. The Filtres, pp. 51 et seq.

138 Bisbee, 2018, Letter from Osmond to Aldous and Maria, dated 22 December 1953, p. 56.

139 Ott, 1976, p. 32.

140 Wasson and Wasson, Mushrooms, *Volume I*, 1957, Preface, p. xix.

man."[141] But Wasson adds that the poisoners did not stop there. A second drug was then administered, colocynth [*Citrullus colocynthis*]: "Claudius was done in with a one-two knock-out, first a dose of the deadly amanita [*phalloides*], and then a dose of colocynth."[142] Robert Graves "in private correspondence offers us an answer that fits the circumstances perfectly."[143]

---

141 Wasson, R. Gordon. "The Death of Claudius or Mushrooms for Murderers," *Botanical Museum Leaflets Harvard University*, Volume 23, No. 3, 7 April 1972 AO, p. 101.

142 Wasson, 1972, p. 127.

143 Wasson, 1972, p. 124.

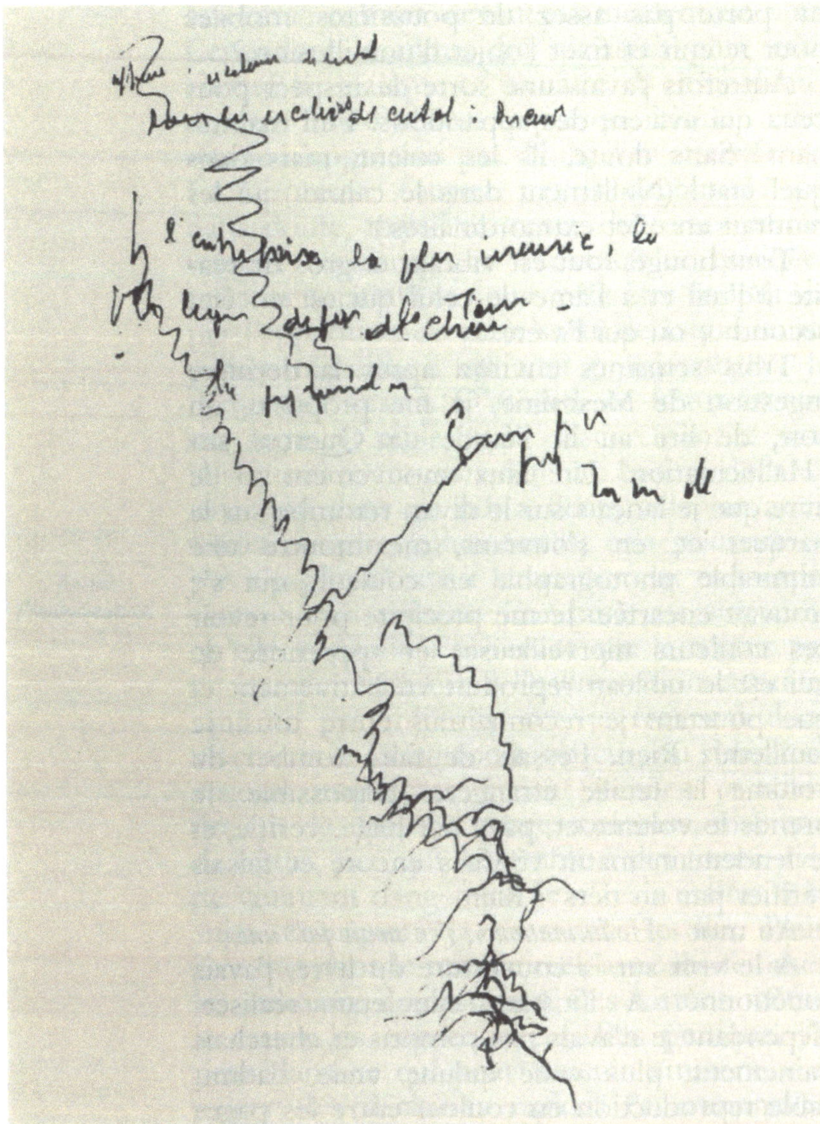

Figure 445. "*Mescaline is a disorder of composition.*" Drawing made on mescaline.
Michaux, Misérable, 1972, II. Avec la mescaline, p. 654, p. 38/242;
Michaux, Miserable, 1972, between pages 32 and 33.

Figure 446. *Schriftzeichnungen, von Walter Benjamin im Meskalinrausch angefertigt* (Drawings by Walter Benjamin under mescaline intoxication). Benjamin, Über, 1972, Protokoll X, Fritz Fränkel: Protokoll des Meskalinversuchs vom 22. Mai 1934, p. 138.

5. Similitudes

In an appendix to his 1952 The Devils of Loůdun, Huxley more broadly discusses "man's deep-seated urge to self-transcendence," especially the "more common Grace-substitutes, into which and by means of which men and women have tried to escape from the tormenting consciousness of being merely themselves."[144] Within the larger mystical context, he opines at that time that such an "anesthetic revelation" can only be purchased at a price:

> William James, in his *Varieties of Religious Experience*, gives instances of 'anesthetic revelations,' following the inhalation of laughing gas. Similar theophanies are sometimes experienced by alcoholics, and there are probably moments in the course of intoxication by almost any drug, when awareness of a not-self superior to the disintegrating ego becomes briefly possible. But these occasional flashes of revelation are bought at an enormous price [italics, quotation marks original].[145]

The vehicles of ebriety he lists for relieving tension are legion. They include alcohol, the natural narcotics, stimulants and hallucinogens, as well as *Soma*, "elementary sexuality which is morally and aesthetically squalid," the "equally disgusting vice of herd-intoxication," "rhythmic movement ... for the purpose of inducing a state of infra-personal and subhuman ecstasy," the "ecstasy-producing rite of rhythmic sound," "vain repetition," "corporal penance," and "horizontal self-transcendence" such as a "hobby," "married love," or identification

---

[144] Huxley, Aldous. The Devils of Loůdun. London: Chatto & Windus, 1952 [mistakenly dated 1922] AO, p. 361.

[145] Huxley, 1952, p. 371; see also James, William. The Varieties of Religious Experience, *A Study in Human Nature*. New York: The Modern Library, 1902 AO, Lectures XVI and XVII Mysticism, p. 370 et seq.

with a "cause wider than their own immediate interests."[146] But for Huxley in 1952, any such easily achieved spiritual awareness "gives place very soon to subhuman stupor, frenzy or hallucination, followed by dismal hang-overs, and ... a permanent and fatal impairment of bodily health and mental power."[147]

The next year on 6 May 1953 he took mescaline at his home in the Hollywood Hills, with Osmond as guide and photographer.[148] A month or so after the experience Huxley wrote to one of the partners at his English publisher about his discovery of an anesthetic revelation without tears:

> It [mescaline] is without any question the most extraordinary and significant experience available to human beings this side of the Beatific Vision; and it opens up a host of philosophical problems, throws intense light and raises all manner of questions in the fields of aesthetics, religion, theory of knowledge. The most extraordinary thing about mescaline ... is that it is almost completely non-toxic. No unpleasant physical results, except a faint seasickish feeling in the beginning, no lowering of intellectual capacity and absolutely no hangover – just a transformation of consciousness ....[149]

As to why Huxley chose to take mescaline first instead of LSD, a man of Huxley's erudition was of course cognizant of the recent work on LSD as well as the previous investigations into mescaline at the turn of the twentieth century. By the mid-1950s

---

146 Huxley, 1952, pp. 361, 363, 365, 367, 369, 370, 374.

147 Huxley, 1952, pp. 371-372.

148 Horowitz, Michael and Cynthia Palmer. Moksha: Aldous Huxley's Classic Writings on Psychedelics and the Visionary Experience. Rochester, VT: Park Street Press, 1977 AA, Foreword by Humphry Osmond, p. viii.

149 Smith, Grover, ed. Letters of Aldous Huxley. NY: Harper & Row, Publishers, 1969 AA, IV *Aun Aprendo*, 1953-1963, No. 632: To Harold Raymond, dated 21 June 1953, p. 678.

scientific research along the broadest lines had already been carried out with LSD in medicine, biology, pharmacology, and psychiatry, and about one thousand papers had already been published. ... Research on mescaline had been done as early as the turn of the century, but interest in this drug had afterwards largely diminished.[150]

Huxley was of course also aware of the earliest experiments with peyote: "You have probably read accounts of the mescaline [peyote] experience – by Havelock Ellis, for example, by Weir Mitchell; and there have been many others."[151] Indeed, the opening sentence of his relatively brief The Doors of Perception[152] references Louis Lewin: "It was in 1886 that the German pharmacologist, Louis Lewin, published the first systematic study of the cactus, to which his own name was subsequently given. *Anhalonium lewinii* was new to science [italics original]."[153]

From the beginning of his correspondence with Osmond, Huxley has options. In his reply to Huxley's initial "appreciative note" on the article in the *Hibbert Journal*, Osmond writes, "I am taking the liberty to send you a copy of a mescal [mescaline] experience of mine" and refers to his experiments with "mescal [mescaline], lysergic acid and new ones we are investigating," while casually mentioning that "I may possibly be at the American Psychiatric Association meeting in Los Angeles this spring (May, I think) and would if at all possible like

150 Horowitz and Palmer, 1977, *Preface* by Albert Hofmann, p. xi.

151 Smith, 1969, 632: To Harold Raymond, dated 21 June 1953, p. 678.

152 The title and the book's opening quote come from one of the better poems by Blake: "If the doors of perception were cleansed everything would appear to be as it is, infinite" (Blake, William. The Marriage of Heaven and Hell. Boston, MA: John W. Luce and Company, 1906 AO, A Memorable Fancy, p. 26).

153 Huxley, Aldous. The Doors of Perception, Includes Heaven and Hell. NY: Harper & Row Publishers, 1954 AA, p. 19/98; see also the version at AO, p. 9.

to call on you."[154] By the next post Huxley then offers him "a bed and bath ... [and] something to eat – though it may be a bit sketchy on the days when we don't have a cook."[155] In a second letter accepting the invitation, Osmond mentions "mescal [mescaline], lysergic acid, harmine, ibogaine or one of our new toys."[156]

But Huxley asks him to bring mescaline, not LSD or any of the other drugs Osmond is using to investigate schizophrenia:

> Hoffmann La Roche has told my young doctor friend that they must send to Switzerland for a supply of mescaline – so it may be weeks before it gets here. Meanwhile do you have any of the stuff on hand? If so I hope you can bring a little; for I am eager to make the experiment and would feel particularly happy to do so under the supervision of an experienced investigator like yourself.[157]

Some have suggested Huxley's blindness as a motivation:

> At sixteen, I had a violent attack of *keratitis punctata*, which left me (after eighteen months of near-blindness, during which I had to depend on Braille for my reading and a guide for my walking) with one eye just capable of light perception, and the other with enough vision to permit my detecting the two-hundred-foot letter on the Snellen Chart at ten feet [italics original].[158]

Osmond recalls his first impression of Huxley in 1953: "He carries a magnifying glass for close work and a little spy glass for long distance .... Yesterday he came down to the meeting and much enjoyed it.

---

154 Bisbee, 2018, 1953 Letter from Osmond to Huxley dated 31 March 1953, pp. 3, 4, 5.

155 Bisbee, 2018, 1953 Letter from Huxley to Osmond dated 10 April 1953, pp. 6, 7.

156 Bisbee, 2018, 1953 Letter from Osmond to Huxley dated 13 April 1953, p. 7.

157 Bisbee, 2018, 1953 Letter from Huxley to Osmond dated 19 April 1953, p. 9.

158 Huxley, Aldous. The Art of Seeing. London: Chatto & Windus, 1943 AA, Preface, p. vi.

Peering through his spy glass and crossing himself when Freud's name was mentioned ...."[159]

Though he may have hoped to see the often reported visions of a mescaline trip, ultimately he did not: "I am a non-visualizer, and got very little in the way of imagery. And yet visions are reported by many of those who have taken the stuff."[160] This of course would not explain the choice of mescaline over LSD since both can be responsible for striking internal visual imagery.

Osmond's friendship with Huxley (a fellow transplanted Englishman) deepened over the last ten years of his life. Evidence is not hard to find. Their letters begin in 1953 with salutations of Dear Dr Osmond" and "Dear Mr Huxley," but after his first mescaline experience they quickly arrive at "My dear Aldous and Maria" and "Dear Humphry."[161] Together, for example, they considered what to call these new substances. Huxley proposed one construction:

> About a name for these drugs – what a problem! I ... find that there is a verb *phaneroein*, 'to make visible or manifest' .... *Thumos* means soul, in its primary usage ....
> To make this trivial world sublime,
> Take half a gramme of phanerothyme [italics, quotation marks original].[162]

Osmond responded with what ultimately stuck:

> "To fathom Hell or go angelic
> Just take a pinch of PSYCHEDELIC.
> (Delos, to manifest)" [capitalization original].[163]

---

159 Bisbee, 2018, unpublished letter of Osmond to his wife Jane, dated 6 May 1953, Preface, p. x

160 Bisbee, 2018, letter from Huxley to Osmond, dated 21 June 1953, p. 20.

161 Bisbee, 2018, pp. 3-20.

162 Bisbee, 2018, letter from Huxley to Osmond, dated 30 March 1956, pp. 265, 266.

Figure 447. Aldous Huxley. Photo from James, "Aldous Huxley," 2003 NYK.

[163] Bisbee, 2018, letter from Osmond to Huxley, dated Early April, 1956, p. 267.

During his last decade Huxley will exhibit extraordinary energy writing articles, attending conventions and analyzing the different aspects of his experience, while investigating it on a personal level. In effect, he became an apostle for entheogens, mescaline in particular, to the point that he was often accused of being an apologist:

> What is really surprising in Huxley's testimonial for mescalin is all that it shows of his own state of mind. Coming from a lesser writer than Huxley, such suggestions for the salvation of mankind could be dismissed as the woolgathering of a misguided crackpot. But coming as they do from one of the current masters of English prose, a man of immense erudition and intellect who usually demonstrates a high moral seriousness, they deserve more careful scrutiny.[164]

Osmond in turn became one of the focal points for the wider diffusion of Huxley's thought among the North American academia.

Two years before the mescaline encounter between the psychiatrist and the writer in Los Angeles, a "great adventure" had taken place "at the beginning of February 1951"[165] between Hofmann and Jünger (who had corresponded with each other since 1947),[166] this time in Europe, and with LSD. During their first LSD trip together, "[i]n mutual astonishment we contemplated the haze of smoke that ascended with the ease of thought from a Japanese incense stick."[167]

---

164 Barrett, Marvin. "Aldous Huxley, Merchant of Mescalin," *The Reporter*, Volume 10, Number 5, 2 March 1954 AA, p. 46.

165 Hofmann, 1983, Chapter 7 Radiance from Ernst Jünger, pp. 150, 151; *Zwei Jahre später, Anfang Februar 1951, kam es zum großen Abenteuer, zu einem LSD-Einstieg mit Ernst Jünger* (Hofmann, 2001, Chapter 11 Einstrahlung von Ernst Jünger, Der erste Einstieg, p. 95/139).

166 Hofmann, 1983, p. 146; *Bottmingen, den 29. März 1947* (Hofmann, 2001, Chapter 11 Einstrahlung von Ernst Jünger, Erste Kontakte mit Ernst Jünger, p. 93/139).

167 Hofmann, 1983, p. 151; *In gemeinsamem Staunen ... von einem japanischen Räucherstäbchen aufstiegen* (Hofmann, 2001, p. 95/139); see Alles, smoke and MDA.

Figure 448. Albert Hofmann and Ernst Jünger, 1990, Montpelier. Hagenbach, 2011, p. 234/712.

Jünger then "assimilated the mentioned spectacle of the incense stick" into the allegorical book he wrote about the experience:

Schwarzenberg burned an incense stick, as he sometimes did, to clear the air. A blue plume ascended from the tip of the stick. ... It revealed itself in the play of this fragrant smoke, which ascended from the slender stick and then branched out into a delicate crown. It was as if his imagination had created it .... Time was active in this creation .... The abundance of space revealed itself in the fiber work, the nerves, which stretched and unfolded in the height, in a vast number of filaments. Now a breath of air affected the vision, and softly twisted it about the shaft like a dancer. ... The beams and lattices of the wondrous flower wheeled around in new planes, in new fields. Myriads of molecules observed the harmony. Here the laws no longer acted under the veil of appearance; matter was so delicate and weightless that it clearly reflected them. How simple and cogent everything was. The numbers, masses and weights stood out from matter. They cast off the raiments. No goddess could inform the initiates more boldly and freely. The pyramids with their weight did not reach up to this revelation. That was Pythagorean luster. No spectacle had ever affected him with such a magic spell.[168]

Huxley, in contrast, did not take LSD until December 1955:

We had our LSD experiment last week ... taking 75 micrograms .... I found the stuff more potent from a physical point of view than mescalin .... The psychological effects ... were identical with those of mescalin, and I had the same kind of experience as I had on the previous occasion [with mescaline] – transfiguration of the external world, and the understanding, through a realization involving the whole man, that Love is the One, and that this is why Atman is identical with Brahman, and why, in spite of everything, the universe is all right.[169]

---

[168] Hofmann, 1983, pp. 152, 152; *Schwarzenberg brannte ... Zauberbann berührt* (Hofmann, 2001, pp. 95, 96/139); Jünger, Ernst. *Besuch auf Godenholm* [Visit to Godenholm]. Frankfurt am Main, DE: Vittorio Klostermann, 1952 AA, 9., pp. 67, 68.

[169] Bisbee, 2018, letter from Aldous to Humphry, dated 23 December 1955, p. 237.

Figure 449. Anaïs Nin at work in Los Angeles, 1963. Photograph, Christian du Bois Larson. Nin, Anaïs. The Diary of Anaïs Nin, 1955-1966, Volume VI, Gunther Stuhlmann, ed. NY: Harcourt Brace Jovanovich, 1976 AO, between pages 142 and 143.

CH. 28 THE PAGAN PLOT (I)

In the 1950s and early 1960s the medical estate was using LSD, mescaline and psilocybin to better diagnose mental illness, as well as for increased understanding of neurology and psychotherapy. At the same time, hundreds of writers and academics were experimenting with the same entheogens. Besides Bateson, Michaux, and Ginsberg, the list includes a who's who of mid-century literati and intelligentsia.

The French born American essayist and novelist Angela Anaïs Juana Antolina Rosa Edelmira Nin y Culmell (Anaïs Nin, 1903 – 1977) tried LSD in the fall of 1955: "After my experience with LSD, a whole day and a whole night of overstimulation, restlessness and the most extreme fatigue, I felt as if my body had received near electrocution by too great a current of vibrations."[170]

The British and American writer Alan Wilson Watts (1915 – 1973) took LSD for the first time in 1958:

> Somewhat more than two years ago (1958) I was asked by a psychiatric research group to take 100 micrograms of lysergic acid .... It seemed ... that my senses had been given a kaleidoscopic character ... Colors became so vivid that flowers, leaves, and fabrics seemed to be illumined from inside. ... Listening to music with closed eyes, I beheld the most fascinating patterns of dancing jewelry, mosaic, tracery, and abstract images. ... The whole experience was vastly entertaining and interesting, but as yet nothing like any mystical experience that I had had before.[171]

The Austro-Hungarian author and journalist Arthur Koestler (1905 – 1983) tried psilocybin in 1961:

---

170 Diary, 1955-1966, Vol. VI, 1976, [Fall 1955], p. 3.

171 Watts, Alan. This is IT and Other Essays on Zen and Spiritual Experience. NY: Vintage Books, 1973 TER, 6. The New Alchemy, pp. 82, 83/102.

The mushroom comes synthesised, in the shape of little pink pills; they look harmless and taste bitter. I swallowed nine of them (18 milligrams of psilocybin), which is a fair-sized dose for a person of my weight. ... I lay down on the couch, and soon began to experience the kind of phenomena which have been repeatedly described by people who experimented with mescalin. When I closed my eyes I saw luminous, moving patterns of great beauty, which was highly enjoyable ....[172]

In a letter to Koestler, Leary related the details of his first mushroom trip in Mexico:

Spent last summer in Mexico. Anthropologist friend arrived one weekend with a bag of mushrooms bought from a witch. Magic mushrooms. ... Wow! Learned more in six hours than in past sixteen years. .... Gone the perceptual machinery which clutters up our view of reality. .... Gone the mental machinery which slices the world up into abstractions and concepts. .... Gone the emotional machinery that causes us to load life with our own ambitions and petty desires.[173]

The American writer and artist William Seward Burroughs III (1914 – 1997) described his experiences on LSD and mescaline:

Interviewer

What do you think of the hallucinogens and the new psychedelic drugs – LSD-25?

Burroughs

I think they're extremely dangerous, much more dangerous than heroin. ... I've tried most of the hallucinogens, without an anxiety reaction, fortunately. LSD-25 produced results for me similar to mescaline. Like all hallucinogens, LSD gave me an increased awareness .... I had my most interesting experiences with mescaline when I got outdoors and walked around – colors, sunsets, gardens. It produces a terrible hangover, though, nasty stuff.[174]

---

172 Koestler, Arthur. Drinkers of Infinity: Essays, 1955 – 1967. London: Hutchinson & Company, Ltd, 1968 AA, "Return Trip to Nirvana," p. 204.

173 Koestler, 1968, pp. 201-202.

174 Knickerbocker, Conrad. "The Art of Fiction XXXVI, William Burroughs, An

The difference between Huxley's single[175] mescaline experience and Jünger's many LSD voyages is overwhelmed by the similarity of their conclusions. Both drugs were able to overcome the Platonic/Christian duality (flesh and spirit, heaven and hell, subject and object), revealing with particular intensity its fundamental incoherence thanks to the visionary trance they provoked. Huxley, on Plato and the separation of Being and becoming:

> Plato seems to have made the enormous, the grotesque mistake of separating Being from becoming and identifying it with the mathematical abstraction of the Idea. He could never, poor fellow, have seen a bunch of flowers shining with their own inner light and all but quivering under the pressure of the significance with which they were charged; could never have perceived that what rose and iris and carnation so intensely signified was nothing more, and nothing less, than what they were – a transience that was yet eternal life, a perpetual perishing that was at the same time pure Being, a bundle of minute, unique particulars in which, by some unspeakable and yet self-evident paradox, was to be seen the divine source of all existence [capitalization original].[176]

But this was all Hofmann could ever have hoped for with his new substance, to collaborate in making more obvious the incoherence of false dualities:

Interview," *The Paris Review*, Issue 35, Fall 1965 [theparisreview.org, hereinafter PRO], p. 17.

175 Huxley continued to dabble in mescaline; see Bisbee, 2018, pp. 216, 217, 244.

176 Huxley, Doors, 1954, p. 22/98; AO, pp. 17-18; though he had not yet taken entheogens, Huxley had already written of ego annihilation *post mortem* similar to that described in the *Bardo Thodol* (see Huxley, Aldous. Time Must Have a Stop. London: Chatto & Windus, 1944 (mistakenly 1916) AO, and Sambhava, Padma. The Tibetan Book of the Dead, tr. Robert A. F. Thurman. NY: Bantam Books, 1994 AA); Wasson suggests Plato "had drunk of the potion in the Temple of Eleusis and had spent the night seeing the great vision" (Wasson, et al, 1978, Chapter One, p. 20).

> There is today a widespread striving for mystical experience, for visionary breakthroughs to a deeper, more comprehensive reality than that perceived by our rational, everyday consciousness. ... I share the belief of many of my contemporaries that the spiritual crisis pervading all spheres of Western industrial society can be remedied only by a change in our world view. We shall have to shift from the materialistic, dualistic belief that people and their environment are separate, toward a new consciousness of an all-encompassing reality, which embraces the experiencing ego, a reality in which people feel their oneness with animate nature and all of creation.[177]

The activity of Huxley in his later years is intricately involved with the entheogens. So much so that to follow this evolution it is necessary to review in some detail his principal writings. However, it is useful beforehand to examine a collateral but relevant development in the evolution of the plot.

---

[177] Hofmann, 1983, Foreword, pp. xi, xii; *Visionäres Erkennen ... Natur und der ganzen Schöpfung* (Hofmann, 2001, *Vorwort*, p. 6/139).

C. Arms for the Cold War

One of the first patients who received LSD was a woman with a diagnosis of hebephrenic schizophrenia (another way of saying disorganized madness)[178] who normally passed the day giggling and laughing at nature. Under the influence of the drug she suddenly became serious:

> Miss B., the second patient who received LSD, was diagnosed a hebephrenic schizophrenic. She had been in the hospital for 15 years. She commonly stood about the ward with her clothes in bizarre disarray, constantly giggling and laughing about the birds and the flowers in May. However, one-half hour after receiving her first 100 *μ*g. dose of LSD the silliness and laughter disappeared entirely. She became very serious, and while much of her communication was incoherent and bizarre, there was no giggling or laughter associated with it. In fact, she seemed quite serious. That morning she called her ward doctor by his correct name for the first time. She said 'Dr. X, this is serious business –, we are pathetic people – don't play with us' [quotation marks original].[179]

Previous studies had already indicated that LSD and analogous drugs could break the precarious equilibrium of certain subjects, though often higher doses were needed "to produce an effect in psychotics than were required by normal subjects …."[180] One chronic

---

[178] Hebephrenia (insanity of youth, due to its common onset in teenagers) is now an obsolete term no longer reflected in the DSM-V, as subtypes do "not adequately reflect the heterogeneity of schizophrenia" (Mattila, Taina et al. "Impact of DSM-5 Changes in the Diagnosis and Acute Treatment of Schizophrenia," *Schizophrenia Bulletin*, Vol. 41, No. 3, 2015 NIH, Omission of Schizophrenia Subtypes, p. 637).
[179] Cholden, Louis S., Albert Kurland, Charles Savage. "Clinical Reactions and Tolerance to LSD in Chronic Schizophrenia," *Journal of Nervous and Mental Disease*, Vol. 122, No. 3, September 1955 AO, p. 217.
[180] Cholden, et al, 1955, p. 211.

regressed schizophrenic patient "expressed a state of acute anguish" while another ended up "seriously calling for help."[181] Because the drug could either intensify or reverse ordinary behavior in schizophrenics,[182] some therapists abstained from using it with these kinds of patients.

It was Sandoz which spread the idea that LSD could create a so-called model psychosis that was both temporary and reversible, a conclusion not yet evident but accepted without hesitation by the majority of researchers, at least in the beginning:

> Because the LSD state manifests many of the characteristics of the schizophrenic reactions, considerable emphasis has been placed on comparing and evaluating this similarity. The experimental value of a drug which could produce a controlled schizophrenic state would be inestimable. It stimulates the imagination to conceive the creation of a model psychosis which can be studied psychodynamically, biochemically and subjectively at once.[183]

By this argument, a patient labeled as schizophrenic suffering a disturbing crisis upon taking LSD did not necessarily indicate that the crisis was brought about by visionary experiences analogous to those produced in persons classified as normal. The same phenomenon could be interpreted as the collapse of defense mechanisms and the armor shielding the personality, being insufferable the inescapable and extemporaneous confrontation between the self and the outside world. Defended by those most interested in the study of LSD and similar drugs, the criterion of a drug that could create a model psychosis (a so-called psychotomimetic) was probably a veiled means of introducing

---

[181] Cholden, et al, 1955, pp. 213, 217.

[182] Cholden, et al, 1955, p. 221.

[183] Cholden, et al, 1955, p. 211.

such agents into psychiatric practice, a ruse that conveniently was not in conflict with prohibitionist ideals.

At the same time there was a sector that really bought into the idea of an experimental psychosis for reasons neither mystical nor therapeutic. On Wednesday, 3 August 1977 the Subcommittee on Health and Scientific Research chaired by Senator Edward Moore Kennedy (1932 – 2009) opened public hearings into the testing of LSD (as well as other drugs and practices) on citizens without their knowledge or consent in various institutions funded by the US government, officially confirming a long history:

> Some 2 years ago, the Senate Health Subcommittee heard chilling testimony about the human experimentation activities of the Central Intelligence Agency. The Deputy Director of the CIA revealed that over 30 universities and institutions were involved in an 'extensive testing and experimentation' program which included covert drug tests on unwitting citizens 'at all social levels, high and low, native Americans and foreign.' Several of these tests involved the administration of LSD to 'unwitting subjects in social situations.' … Then … new records were discovered … [that] reveal a far more extensive series of experiments than had previously been thought. Eighty-six universities and institutions were involved. New instances of unethical behavior were revealed. … The Central Intelligence Agency drugged American citizens without their knowledge or consent. It used university facilities and personnel without their knowledge. It funded leading researchers, often without their knowledge [quotation marks original].[184]

---

[184] Kennedy, Edward. "Project MKULTRA, The CIA's Program of Research in Behavioral Modification," Joint Hearing before the Select Committee on Intelligence and the Subcommittee on Health and Scientific Research of the Committee on Human Resources, United States Senate, Ninety-Fifth Congress, First Session, 3 August 1977. Washington, DC: USGPO, 1977 [nytimes.com, hereinafter NYT], pp. 2, 3.

The hearings came about due to the actions of "one individual, through a Freedom of Information request …."[185] In the early 1970s former State Department analyst John D. Marks (b. 1943) "spurred the agency into finding additional records pertaining to the CIA's program of experimentation with human subjects."[186] The "16,000 pages of documents"[187] including reports and confidential memos allowed other investigators[188] to dive into these activities and describe them in some detail, especially the use of truth drugs, behavior modification and chemical warfare.

---

185 Kennedy, 1977, p. 3.

186 Kennedy, 1977, p. 3.

187 Marks, 1979, p. vii.

188 See for example Lee and Shlain, 1985.

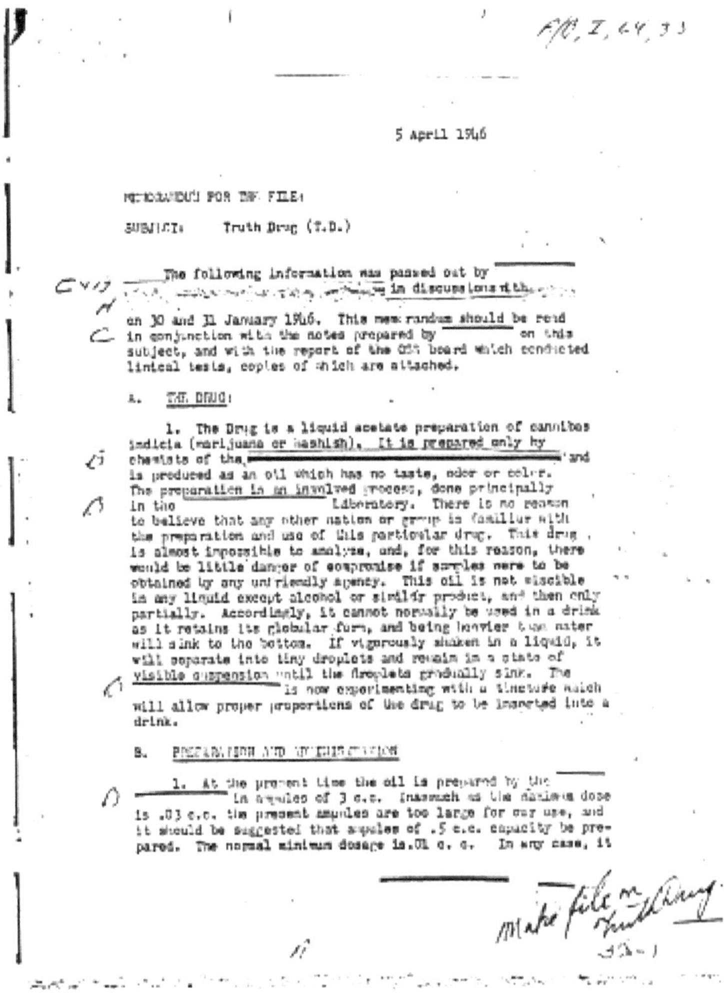

5 April 1946

MEMORANDUM FOR THE FILE:

SUBJECT: Truth Drug (T.D.)

The following information was passed out by [illegible] in discussions with [illegible] on 30 and 31 January 1946. This memorandum should be read in conjunction with the notes prepared by on this subject, and with the report of the OSS board which conducted clinical tests, copies of which are attached.

A. THE DRUG:

1. The Drug is a liquid acetate preparation of cannibas indicia (marijuana or hashish). It is prepared only by chemists of the and is produced as an oil which has no taste, odor or color. The preparation is an involved process, done principally in the Laboratory. There is no reason to believe that any other nation or group is familiar with the preparation and use of this particular drug. This drug is almost impossible to analyze, and, for this reason, there would be little danger of compromise if samples were to be obtained by any unfriendly agency. This oil is not miscible in any liquid except alcohol or similar product, and then only partially. Accordingly, it cannot normally be used in a drink as it retains its globular form, and being heavier than water will sink to the bottom. If vigorously shaken in a liquid, it will separate into tiny droplets and remain in a state of visible suspension until the droplets gradually sink. The is now experimenting with a tincture which will allow proper proportions of the drug to be inserted into a drink.

B. PREPARATION AND [illegible]

1. At the present time the oil is prepared by the in ampules of 3 c.c. Inasmuch as the maximum dose is .03 c.c. the present ampules are too large for our use, and it should be suggested that ampules of .5 c.c. capacity be prepared. The normal minimum dosage is .01 c. c. In any case, it

Make file on truth drug

Figure 450. Memorandum dated 5 April 1946 summarizing the use of cannabis acetate as a truth drug in clinical tests by the OSS, [cia.gov, hereinafter CIA], page one.

1. Truth Drugs

The search for drugs that annulled the will or understanding began before the end of World War Two, stimulated by mescaline experiments undertaken by the Nazis at Dachau and Auschwitz:

> On 2 and 6 October 1944 Ploetner reported … about mescaline experiments on prisoners at Dachau. The aim was a truth drug. … SS Hauptsturmführer Bruno Weber and the pharmacist Viktor Capesius similarly experimented at Auschwitz on the use of psychotropic drugs during interrogation. ... On one occasion three prisoners died.[189]

Nazi doctor Kurt Friedrich Plötner (1905 – 1984) eventually concluded that "mescaline was too unreliable to be a truth drug."[190]

On the American side, intelligence officer, diplomat and director of the OSS William Joseph "Wild Bill" Donovan (1883 – 1959) formed a so-called Truth Drug committee on Halloween,

---

[189] Weindling, Paul. Victims and Survivors of Nazi Human Experiments: Science and Suffering in the Holocaust. London: Bloomsbury, 2015 AA, Part Four Experiments in Perspective, Chapter Sixteen Relentless research, pp. 182-183.

[190] Streatfeild, Dominic. Brainwash: The Secret History of Mind Control. NY: St. Martin's Press, 2007 AA, Chapter 2 Truth Drugs, p. 49/539; Plötner ended up post-war as a university professor and does not appear to have ever been prosecuted; Hubertus Strughold (1898 – 1986), accused of murdering POWs in pressure chamber and freezing experiments at Dachau, was brought to the United States in 1947 where he became known as the 'Father of Space Medicine' (see for example his Compendium of Aerospace Medicine, Volume 1. Brooks Air Force Base, TX: USAF School of Aerospace Medicine, 1977 AO); in particular "Jews were selected" for the air pressure and freezing experiments (Quinn, William W. Dachau, US Army Report, IA, dachauOOunse. Unknown place: Printed by 649th Engr Topo Batallion, May 1945 AO, IV. Dachau Concentration Camp, CIC Detachment, Seventh Army, Memorandum, Experimental Stations, p. 31).

Saturday 31 October 1942 to "investigate the feasibility of using drugs in the interrogation of Prisoners of War."[191] The committee included the soon-to-be president of the American Psychiatric Association Edward Adam Strecker (1886 – 1959) and the commissioner of the Federal Bureau of Narcotics Harry Jacob Anslinger (1892 – 1975) as a liaison officer. It was chaired by Winifred Overholser (1892 – 1964), superintendent of St. Elizabeth's Hospital in Washington, DC, where a number of experiments were to be conducted.[192] From this council came the first directives suggesting thorough investigation of so-called truth drugs as a means of fulfilling the secondary mission of the OSS, to "conduct unconventional warfare."[193]

The OSS tried as so-called truth drugs scopolamine, mescaline and a liquid extract of cannabis. Preliminary experiments narrowed the field to the inhalation of an acetate of cannabis as the delivery method and drug of choice:

---

191 Anonymous. "Report on T. D., 2 June 1943," The Antique Cannabis Book, Second Edition [antiquecannabisbook.com, hereinafter ACB], Chapter Three Censored Medical Studies, The O.S.S. During World War II, Medical Cannabis – As a Truth Serum, p. 1/5; Crewdson, John M. "Files Show Tests for Truth Drug Began in O.S.S.," *New York Times*, Monday, 5 September 1977, NYT, p. 1; Memorandum dated 5 April 1946, Subject: Truth Drug (T. D.), CIA, p. 7/32.

192 Anonymous, "Report," 2 June 1943, p. 1/5.

193 Sacquety, Troy J. "The Office of Strategic Services (OSS): A Primer on the Special Operations Branches and Detachments of the Office of Strategic Services," *Veritas: The Journal of Army Special Operations History*, PB 31-05-2, Volume 3, No. 4, 2007 [arsof-history.org, hereinafter AHO], p. 3; Paddock, Alfred H. US Special Warfare, Its Origins, Psychological and Unconventional Warfare, 1941-1952. Washington, DC: National Defense University Press, Fort Lesley J. McNair, 1982 AA, Introduction, p. 2.

> [T]he acetate derivative was found to be preferable. Various routes of administration were explored …. Of these, inhalation in cigarettes is the only route that can be recommended …. Standard cigarettes … may be loaded with … [the] acetate. The drug is introduced into the cigarette with a 1/4cc tuberculin syringe …. The acetate is injected at maximum viscosity …. Cigarettes prepared as above outlined are perfectly normal in appearance and taste.[194]

Previous trials conducted on Manhattan Project personnel found that swallowing a "concentrated, liquid form of marijuana"[195] caused the subjects to vomit while one wound up in the hospital.

FBN investigator and OSS operative George Hunter White (1908 – 1975) made the first field test of the new drug and delivery method on a mob enforcer on 27 May 1943:

> The subject was one August Del Gracio, who was described in OSS documents as a 'notorious New York gangster.' … [White] administered the drug by inviting Del Gracio up to his apartment for a smoke and a chat. White had been talking to Del Gracio earlier about securing the Mafia's cooperation to keep Axis agents out of the New York waterfront and to prepare the way for the invasion of Sicily. … Naval intelligence officers eventually made a deal in which mob leaders promised to cooperate, and as a direct result, New York Governor Thomas Dewey ordered Del Gracio's chief, boss of bosses, Charles 'Lucky' Luciano freed from jail in 1946 [quotation marks original].[196]

White described the effects of the drug, indicating it "removed any apparent restraint on the gangster who spoke freely in his presence."[197]

---

194 Anonymous, 2 June 1943, pp. 1/5, 2/5.

195 Marks, 1979, Chapter 1 World War II, p. 6.

196 Marks, 1979, pp. 6, 7, and footnote *, page 7; see GHDV2P2, Chapter 26 Latency, B. The Drug Abuse Industrial Complex, b. Political Alliances, pp. 1840 et seq.

197 Jones, M. A. "Office Memorandum to Mr. Nichols, Subject: George H. White (Federal Bureau of Narcotics," United States Government, 28 February 1952 [thememoryhole2.org, hereinafter MHO], U.S. Army and OSS Service, p. 4.

Afterwards he is said to have tried the drug "on suspected Communist soldiers stationed in military camps outside Atlanta, Memphis, and New Orleans."[198]

After taking over from the OSS, CIA set up Operation Midnight Climax, a curious experiment maintained for eight years in which a brothel was outfitted with hidden microphones, cameras and false mirrors. Funded by the US government, the prostitutes laced their clients' drinks with LSD and other substances, allowing the installed devices to follow the particulars of their clients' reactions:

> An unsuspecting John would think he had bought a night of pleasure, go back to a strange apartment, and wind up zonked. ... [T]he women [were normally given] $100 in Agency funds for their night's work .... The program was also referred to as 'Operation Midnight Climax' [quotation marks original].[199]

By 1961 however CIA had generally concluded the same about so-called truth drugs as had Plötner and the OSS:

> The hallucinatory and psychotomimetic drugs such as mescaline, marihuana, LSD-25, and microtine are sometimes mistakenly associated with narcoanalytic interrogation. ... No such magic brew as the popular notion of truth serum exists. The barbiturates, by disrupting defensive patterns, may sometimes be helpful in interrogation, but even under the best conditions they will elicit an output contaminated by deception, fantasy, garbled speech, etc.[200]

---

198 Marks, 1979, p. 7.

199 Marks, 1979, Chapter 6 Them Unwitting: The Safehouses, pp. 98, 99.

200 Anonymous. "'Truth' Drugs in Interrogation," *Studies in Intelligence*, Volume 5, No. 2, Spring 1961, CIA, Conclusions, p. 32; reprinted in Kennedy, 1977, p. 32.

2. Behavior Modification

The abovementioned Dachau physician Plötner also "provided important material for the CIA's mind control experiments with cannabis, mescaline and LSD in the fifties and sixties."[201] Four years after the birth of CIA in 1947, the man who would become its "first civilian director"[202] Allen Welsh Dulles (1893 – 1969) approved a semisecret subdivision known as the "Chemical Division of the Technical Services Staff … responsible for developing, testing, and building the tools of espionage."[203] In 1951 Dulles in turn hired as chief of his new subdivision, Sidney Gottlieb (1918 – 1999) who had received his doctorate in biochemistry from the California Institute of Technology.[204]

On 13 April 1953 (as if synchronized by a kind of poetic logic, less than a month before Huxley had his first experience with mescaline) Allen Dulles approved a new program called MKULTRA "to investigate whether and how it was possible to modify an individual's behavior by covert means."[205] Though most documents pertaining to the program had been deliberately destroyed four years earlier,[206] in 1977 there were discovered some

---

[201] Pross, Christian. "Breaking through the postwar coverup of Nazi doctors in Germany," *Journal of Medical Ethics*, Volume 17, Supplement, 1991 [jme.bmj.com, hereinafter JME], p. 13.

[202] Paddock, 1982, IV. The Interwar Years, Part I: Psychological Warfare, p. 41.

[203] Kinzer, Stephen. Poisoner in Chief: Sidney Gottlieb and the CIA Search for Mind Control. NY: Henry Holt and Company, 2019 AA, Chapter 4 The Secret That Was Going to Unlock the Universe, p. 51.

[204] Kinzer, 2019, Chapter 1 I Needed More of a Challenge, p. 7.

[205] Marks, 1979, Chapter 4 LSD, p. 57.

[206] "on the verbal orders of Dr. Sidney Gottlieb, Chief of TSD. ... Dr. Gottlieb was carrying out the verbal order of then DCI Helms" (Kennedy, 1977, Appendix A,

seven boxes of documents related to Project MKULTRA, a closely held CIA project conducted from 1953-1964. As you may recall, MKULTRA was an 'umbrella project' under which certain sensitive subprojects were funded, involving among other things research on drugs and behavioral modification [capitalization, quotation marks original].[207]

One of the drugs CIA wanted to test was LSD but a single Swiss company, Sandoz owned the patent and the supply. In 1953

a CIA officer was dispatched to Basel to solve this problem. He returned with a report asserting that Sandoz had ten kilograms of LSD on hand, which he correctly called 'a fantastically large amount.' Dulles approved the expenditure of $240,000 to buy it all – the world's entire supply. The two officers he sent to pick it up, however, quickly discovered that their colleague had confused kilograms with grams. Sandoz had manufactured a total of less than forty grams, of which ten were still in stock. This confusion led Gottlieb to decide that MK-ULTRA needed a reliable supply of LSD – and a pledge from Sandoz that it would not sell any to the Soviets. Sandoz was happy to cooperate ... to rid itself of its 'problem child' [quotation marks, capitalization original].[208]

While Gottlieb and Sandoz were having these conversations, an American general suggested to Hofmann's amazement that he should think of the best way to distribute the drug over enemy territory.[209]

Indeed, the Agency had personnel working on surprise attacks using LSD against socialist or leftist politicians in other countries, with the aim of producing indiscernible states of mental insanity.

XVII. Testing and Use of Chemical and Biological Agents by the Intelligence Community, A. The Programs Investigated, 4. MKULTRA, p. 69, original page of report, p. 390).

207 Kennedy, 1977, Prepared Statement of Admiral Stansfield Turner, Director of Central Intelligence, p. 4.

208 Kinzer, 2019, Chapter 5 Abolishing Consciousness, pp. 85, 86.

209 Personal communication from Albert Hofmann.

Revolutionary leaders like the First Secretary of the Central Committee of the Communist Party of Cuba Fidel Alejandro Castro Ruz (1926 – 2016) and Egyptian President Gamal Abdel Nasser Hussein (1918 – 1970) were specific targets. In one such plot, an "aerosol laced with LSD" would "be sprayed in the radio studio from which Castro made live broadcasts that reached millions of Cubans."[210] It appears that "Egyptian president Gamal Abdal Nasser also figured high on the ClA's hallucinogenic hit list."[211]

The President of the American Psychiatric Association from 1952 to 1953, Scottish-born psychiatrist Donald Ewen Cameron (1901 – 1967) reported experiments done on patients at the Allan Memorial Institute, a psychiatric hospital associated with McGill University in Montreal, Canada. His smorgasbord approach brought together virtually all possible techniques of mind control, which he tested individually and together."[212] These techniques included sensory deprivation, isolation, hypnosis, LSD, extreme heat, electroshock, endless repetition of recorded messages, lack of food and "intense red light for eight hours a day over a period of months."[213] Much of this research was funded through the Society for the Investigation of Human Ecology, one of many CIA fronts.[214]

His so-called "psychic driving" therapy entailed "continuously repeated playback" of the patients' own words in "some cases [for] 10 or 20 hours a day for 10 or 15 days" and "sometimes during sleep."[215]

---

210 Kinzer, 2019, Chapter 10 Health Alteration Committee, p. 180.

211 Lee and Shlain, 1985, Part One: The Roots of Psychedelia, Chapter 1 In the Beginning There was Madness ...., p. 36.

212 Marks, 1979, p. 137.

213 Kinzer, 2019, pp. 137, 138.

214 Marks, 1979, Part III. Spells – Electrodes and Hypnosis, Chapter 8 Brainwashing, note, p. 133.

215 Cameron, D. Ewen. "Psychic Driving," *The American Journal of Psychiatry*, Volume

He combined this incessant playback with "sodium amytal," "stimulant drugs, in particular, Desoxyn [methamphetamine hydrochloride]," and in one case by having a patient's "thinking partially disorganized under LSD-25."[216] He compared his approach to "the fire blizzard of World War II" and "the breakdown of the individual under continuous interrogation."[217]

It is curious that ten years earlier Dr. Cameron should have been one of the ten member psychiatric panel appointed by the International Military Tribunal constituted at Nuremberg to judge Deputy *Führer* Rudolph Walter Richard Hess (1894 – 1987) for "Crimes against Humanity."[218] In spite of his "great instability" and a record during incarceration that "included a great variety of symptoms, delusions of persecution, two suicidal attempts, two periods of hysterical amnesia, various bodily symptoms such as abdominal cramps, which apparently are of neurotic origin,"[219] Hess was deemed fit to stand trial: it was "the unanimous conclusion of the undersigned that Rudolf Hess is not insane at the present time in the strict sense of the word."[220] The code of ethical conduct approved at Nuremberg demanded that the "voluntary consent of the human subject is absolutely essential" and that the "experiment should be so conducted as to avoid all unnecessary physical and mental suffering and injury."[221]

112, No. 7, January 1956 AO, pp. 502, 503.

216 Cameron, 1956, pp. 503, 504, 506.

217 Cameron, 1956, p. 508.

218 Manvell, Roger and Heinrich Fraenkel. Hess: A Biography. London: MacGibbon & Kee, 1971 AO, Chapter 5 Nuremberg, p. 156.

219 Editors. "Psychiatric Examination of Rudolph Hess," *Journal of the American Medical Association*, Volume 130, No. 12, 23 March 1946 AO, Editorials, Current Comment, p. 790

220 Editors, 1946, p. 790.

221 Jackson, Robert H. Trials of War Criminals Before the Nuernberg Military

SCIENTIFIC INTELLIGENCE MEMORANDUM

POTENTIAL NEW AGENT FOR UNCONVENTIONAL WARFARE

Lysergic Acid Diethylamide (LSD)
(N, N-Diethyllysergamide)

CIA/SI 101-54
5 August 1954

CENTRAL INTELLIGENCE AGENCY
OFFICE OF SCIENTIFIC INTELLIGENCE

Figure 451. Cover of a CIA report on the use of LSD in unconventional warfare.

Tribunals, Volume II. Nuernberg, DE: USGPO, October 1946 – April 1949 AO, *United States vs Karl Brandt, et al*, XII. Judgment, Count Four, Permissible Medical Experiments, pp. 181, 182.

3. Chemical Warfare

As ambitious as the intelligence agencies, the Army Chemical Corps received generous appropriations from Congress for the development of a so-called non-lethal incapacitant, as part of its study of chemical warfare (CW) agents. A large number of individuals were said to have taken part in these kinds of tests under Army contract at universities or private institutions. One of the drugs studied was LSD, partly because of its inherent safety:

> EA 1729 (lysergic acid diethylamide, LSD25) [is] ... one of the most promising CW [chemical warfare] incapacitating compounds .... It is the most potent of the incapacitating agents studied to date and has the very important attribute of a large safety margin between the incapacitating and lethal doses.[222]

The program had already killed the American tennis pro Harold Blauer (1910 – 1953) with an overdose of 450 mg. of methylenedioxyphenyl-isopropylamine (MDA) administered at the New York State Psychiatric Institute where he had only recently been admitted for "severe depression after a divorce."[223] In 1951 "the Army Chemical Corps and the Psychiatric Institute ... entered into contract ... for the psychological investigation of potential chemical warfare agents ...."[224] The primary purpose for injecting Mr. Blauer was not diagnostic

---

[222] Sim, Van M. I. "Clinical Investigation of EA 1729," U.S. Army Chemical Research and Development Laboratories. Army Chemical Center, MD: Defense Technical Information Center, June 1961 AO, DTIC AD0323701, Introduction, p. 5.

[223] Associated Press. "$700,000 Awarded to Estate of Army Drug Test Victim," *Los Angeles Times*, 6 May 1987 [latimes.com, hereinafter LAT], World and Nation, p. 2/4.

[224] *Barrettt v United States*, 660 F. Supp. 1291, U.S. District Court S.D. New York, 5 May 1987 [storage.courtlistener.com, hereinafter SCL], Opinion, Judge Motley, I. Introduction, II. Facts, *A. The Army's Program*, p. 1295; see also law.justia.com.

or therapeutic but solely to "gather the data the Chemical Corps required for its investigation of the mescaline derivatives as potential chemical warfare agents."[225]

After covering up the tragedy for twenty-five years, the US government awarded Blauer's estate three-quarters of a million dollars for negligently causing his wrongful death.[226] A former soldier who took part in similar studies at the Army Chemical Warfare Laboratories at Edgewood Arsenal in 1957 alleged the drugs left him with a "steadily worsening mental illness."[227] Other so-called therapies were every bit as brutal.

Gottlieb and his colleagues at CIA began to experiment on themselves, at times using other colleagues as unwitting guinea pigs, "sneaking LSD into each other's coffee cups and thereby subjecting themselves to the unknown frontiers of experimental drugs."[228] This ad-hoc experimentation ended tragically in November 1953 when scientists from CIA and the Army Chemical Corps met at their bi-annual three day working retreat at an isolated Boy Scout camp "in the woods of Western Maryland."[229] On the second day, Gottlieb spiked the Cointreau® of bacteriologist and Army biological warfare scientist Frank Rudolph Emmanuel Olson (1910 – 1953) with LSD.[230] When Olson had a bad reaction, Gottlieb sent him to the non-psychiatrist Abramson who brought him "a bottle of bourbon and a bottle of the sedative Nembutal."[231] Ten days after his involuntary dosing Olson

---

225 *Barrettt v United States*, 660 F. Supp. 1291, p. 1299.

226 *Barrettt v United States*, 660 F. Supp. 1291, p. 1323.

227 Associated Press. "Ex-Soldier is Denied Damages for Army LSD Experiments in 1957," *New York Times*, 29 December 1981 NYT, p. 3/4.

228 Marks, 1979, Part II Intelligence or 'Witches Potions,' Chapter 4 LSD, p. 72.

229 Marks, 1979, Chapter 5 Concerning the Case of Dr. Frank Olson, p. 73.

230 Marks, 1979, p. 77.

231 Marks, 1979, p. 80.

fell to the sidewalk from his tenth floor hotel room.[232] The cover-up began immediately, lasted for decades and did not halt MKULTRA.

It was the aforementioned Abramson who explained six years later at a conference that LSD had "certain favorable characteristics for use as an adjuvant to psychotherapy," emphasizing its inherent safety:

> *a)* It is pharmacologically safe; very large doses may be given without tissue damage.
>
> *b)* It is effective in small doses for therapeutic interviews in which the therapist is definitely involved.
>
> *c)* The patient is conscious, cooperative, and better able to integrate material with psychodynamic significance.
>
> *d)* The patient undergoes an essentially elated disturbance in ego function, which is also accompanied by integrative forces, so that it may be thought of as 'hebesynthesis' rather than narcosynthesis.
>
> *e)* The drug may be given repeatedly. There is no evidence of addiction. The pharmacological effects usually wear off within 12 hours.
>
> *f)* Patients usually like the experience of taking LSD in the dose range stated [quotation marks original].[233]

Abramson had already received $85,000 from CIA to use LSD to produce "operationally pertinent materials along the following lines: a. Disturbance of Memory; b. Discrediting by Aberrant Behavior; c. Alteration of Sex Patterns; d. Eliciting of Information; e. Suggestibility; f. Creation of Dependence."[234] The money was passed through the Josiah Macy, Jr. Foundation.[235] A very similar assignment was received by pharmacologist and biochemist Carl Curt Pfeiffer (1908 – 1988) who "conducted LSD experiments for the C.I.A. on prisoners ...

---

232 Marks, 1979, p. 82; Lee and Shlain, 1985, p. 33.

233 Abramson, 1960, "Psychoanalytic Psychotherapy with LSD," p. 55.

234 Marks, 1979, p. 62.

235 Marks, 1979, pp. 64, 65, 118.

between 1955 and 1964. He was paid $25,000 a year through the Geschickter Foundation, he said in a telephone interview."[236] The American toxicologist at the University of Rochester Harold Carpenter Hodge (1904 – 1990), who previously worked on the Manhattan Project, evidently received $25,000 for "tagging the [LSD] molecule with radioactive or with stable isotopes" in order to "design new compounds having like but even more bizarre activities."[237]

Huxley (illegally) tried to contribute to the emotional and spiritual emancipation of his fellow man; CIA (legally) sought in those same substances destructive weapons for internal and external use. A drug that in 1953 promised to be capable of driving normal people insane was by 1959 proposed as a means of strengthening their sanity. This was not only useless but a dangerous threat to national security.

The result is that, in its initial phase, the discovery of LSD did not produce one conspiracy but two clearly different ones. What is certain is that they were two sides of the same coin and what was true of both was something as ambivalent as truth itself. Although the intelligence services wanted to extract truth by force or trickery, and the resurgent pagan conspirators to let truth arise naturally from within, both implicitly agreed that LSD, mescaline and psilocybin went badly with reserve and dissimulation, if not to say lying in general.

---

236 Horrock, Nicolas M. "Private Institutions Used in C.I.A. Effort to Control Behavior," *New York Times*, 1 August 1977 NYT, p. 1.

237 Marks, 1979, pp. 59, 118; Anonymous. "Outline of Proposed Study of the Metabolism of d-Lysergic Acid Diethylamid," MKULTRADOC – 0000017142, p. 17-2, 2/26, p. 1 original, and 17-13, 20/26,

D. Technique versus Chemistry

One of those who eschewed chemistry for technique was the iconoclastic surrealist printmaker, painter and filmmaker Salvador Domingo Felipe Jacinto Dali i Domènech, Marques of Dali of Púbol (Salvador Dalí, 1904 – 1989). He was certainly no stranger to the drugs of the Montparnasse bohemian art scene in the 1930s:

> Cocaine here, heroin there, opium galore, alcohol and pederasty everywhere. Heroin, cocaine, drunkography, opium and pederasty were sure vehicles to ephemeral success. ... For the drug-addicts I furnished a complete theory of hypnagogic images, and I spoke of masks of my invention for seeing dreams in color.[238]

Indeed, rule number nine of his "*Ten rules for him who wishes to be a painter*" is "9. Painter, don't drink alcohol, and chew hashish only five times in your life."[239]

Like Walter Benjamin, he enjoyed investigating the waking dream. But instead of drugs, he relied upon a number of so-called secrets. Number three was sleeping without sleeping, "a repose which walks in equilibrium on the taut and invisible wire which separates sleeping from waking."[240] This involved dozing "in a bony armchair" holding "a heavy key" over a "plate upside down on the floor. ... The moment the key drops from your fingers ... this fugitive moment when you had barely lost consciousness ... is exactly ... what you needed before your virtuous afternoon labors."[241] Supposedly, this so-called

---

238 Dalí, Salvador. The Secret Life of Salvador Dali, tr. Haakon M. Chevalier. NY: Dial Press, 1942 AO, Part Three, Chapter XI. My Battle, p. 295.

239 Dalí, Salvador. 50 Secrets of Magic Craftsmanship, tr. Haakon M. Chevalier. NY: Dove Publications, Inc., 1992 (1948) AA, Chapter One, pp. 64, 65, 66/684.

240 Dalí, 1992, Chapter Two, p. 110/684.

241 Dalí, 1992, Chapter Two, pp. 116, 117/684.

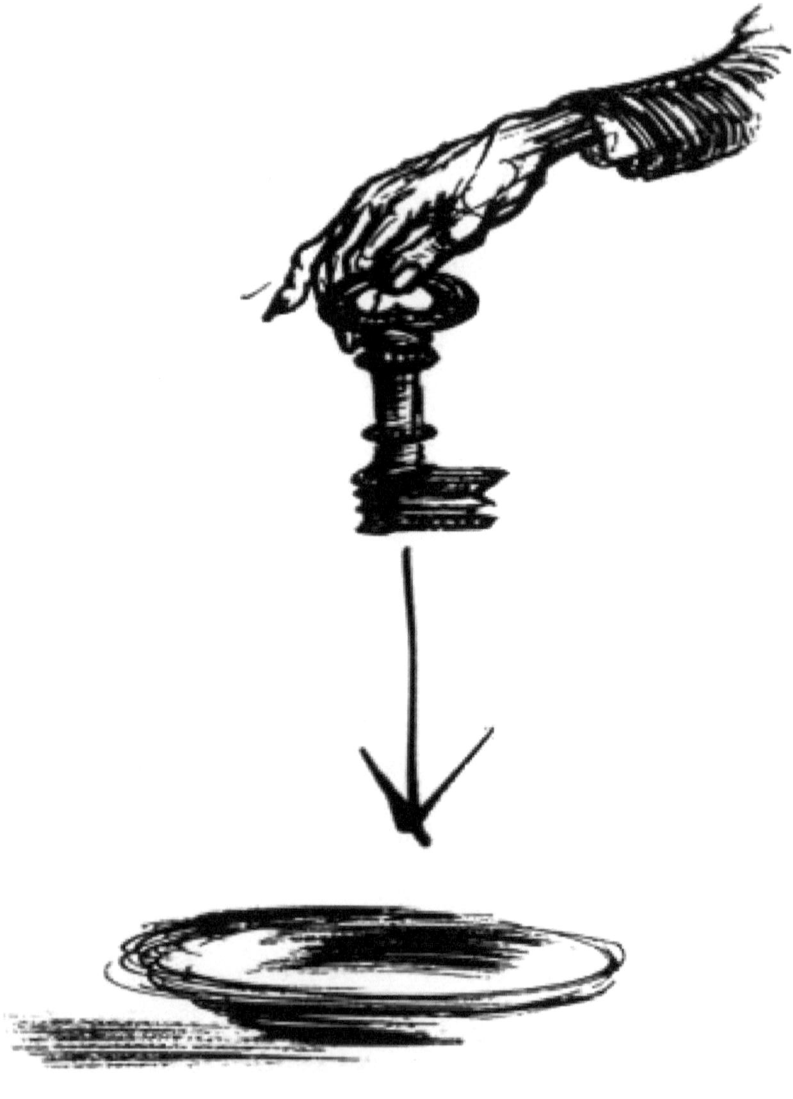

Figure 452. Illustration of the Slumber with a Key.
Dalí, 1992 (1948), p. 120/ 684.

slumber with a key was practiced by "the Capuchin monks of Toledo."[242] He advises the aspiring artist to "execute your work in the half-waking state, lulled by zephers of memories ...."[243]

In his *Apotheosis of the Dollar* (1965) Dalí exhibits another technique, that of *moiré* which he compares to mescaline or LSD and uses to communicate with Martians:

> Interviewer: You've had communications with Martians.
> Dalí: Through the phenomenon of *moiré*. ... And this kind of pattern with which I communicate with the cosmos, is ... *moiré*, this phenomenon when ... two transparent fabrics of the same homogeneity are superimposed to create a kind of unreality. And that corresponds exactly to mescaline or LSD. So the people who take LSD observe the world transformed into a *moiré*. And now all my paintings are based on *moiré* patterns, so that Dalí's audience, which is already very delirious, in addition to its habitual enthusiasm, will become drugged by Dalí [italics original].[244]

Aldous Huxley carefully delineated the differences and similarities between the traditional mystical trance and the new chemically-induced ecstasy, over and above the common euphoria. Either one requires the overcoming of various kinds of fear, demanding courage and sincerity in the same measure, if the voyager is

---

[242] Dalí, 1992, Chapter Two, p. 211/684.

[243] Dalí, 1992, Chapter Three, p. 224/684.

[244] *Vous avez eu des communications avec des Martiens. ... il va devenir drogué par Dalí* ("*Salvador Dalí reçoit à Portlligat,*" Interview with François Barnole, montage de Benoít Grossin, August 1964, L'Édition Spéciale des Actualités Télévisées, RTF [Radiodiffusion-Télévision Française]/ORTF, [dailymotion.com, hereinafter DMC], 5:45 to 6:59/9:09); see also the 09:22 video of 29.08.1964 at ina.fr; "The moire effect is a well known phenomenon which occurs when repetitive structures (such as screens, grids or gratings) are superposed or viewed against each other" (Amidror, Isaac. The Theory of the Moire Phenomenon, Volume I: Periodic Layers, Second Edition. London: Springer-Verlag, 2009 AA, Chapter 1 Introduction, p. 1).

not to descend into horror *à la* Moore. The nucleus of the experience resides in making manifest once again the resplendent in the mundane, the unity of the universe, "the impossible paradox and supreme truth – that perception is (or at least can be, ought to be) the same as Revelation, that Reality shines out of every appearance, that the One is totally, infinitely present in all particulars [capitalization original]."[245]

With the advent of entheogenic chemistry the techniques of achieving enlightenment had now irrevocably been expanded:

> [F]or an aspiring mystic to revert, in the present state of knowledge, to prolonged fasting and violent self-flagellation would be as senseless as it would be for an aspiring cook to behave like Charles Lamb's Chinaman, who burned down the house in order to roast a pig.[246]

Of course, whether these new substances would be able to replace the ancient methods was still an open question:

> The universe is not in the habit of giving us something for nothing. … [C]an we with impunity replace systematic self-discipline by a chemical? It remains to be seen. Of all the consciousness-transforming drugs the most interesting, if not the most immediately useful, are those which, like lysergic acid and mescalin, open the door to what may be called the Outer World of the mind [capitalization original].[247]

Even with his own limited entheogenic experience Huxley felt he had gained a better understanding of mysticism:

---

[245] Huxley, Heaven and Hell, 1956 AO, p. 119; Huxley, 1956, p. 67/98.

[246] Huxley, Doors, 1956 AO, p. 156; Huxley, 1956 AA, pp. 81, 82/98; see the story of Bo-bo in A Dissertation upon a Roast Pig. Boston, MA: D Lothrop Company, 1888 AO by essayist and poet Charles Lamb (1775 – 1834).

[247] Huxley, 1 July 1956, p. 32.

In the course of the last five years I have taken mescalin twice and lysergic acid three or four times. My first experience was mainly aesthetic. Later experiences were of another nature and helped me to understand many of the obscure utterances to be found in the writings of the mystics, Christian and Oriental.[248]

In a letter to an author interested in religion and education, he elaborates on the aid of "gratuitous grace" in achieving salvation:

In my first experiment with mescalin I had a merely aesthetic visionary experience: but since then, with LSD and again with mescalin, I have gone *beyond vision* into many of the experiences described in Eastern and Western literature – the transcendence of the subject-object relationship, the sense of solidarity with all the world so that one actually knows by experience what 'God is love' means: the sense that, in spite of death and suffering, everything is somehow and ultimately All Right. … That a chemical can help people to get out of their own light is distressing to many people; but it happens to be a fact. That the experience is a 'gratuitous grace,' neither necessary nor sufficient for salvation, is certain. Ethical and cognitive effort is needed if the experiencer is to go forward from his one-shot experience to permanent enlightenment. … PS Gratuitous graces are not necessary or sufficient – but they can be very helpful if we choose to let them help us [italics, quotation marks, capitalization original].[249]

The second half of the 1950s is as personally challenging as it is professionally fruitful for Huxley. His first wife Maria Louisa Nys Huxley (1898 – 1955) dies.[250] In 1955 he and his brother, the soon-to-be knighted evolutionary biologist Julian Sorell Huxley (1887 – 1975), take a day trip to see the "experiments with dolphins"[251] being done by

---

248 Smith, ed., 1969, 808: To Fr Thomas Merton, 10 January 1959, pp. 863, 864.

249 Smith, ed., 1969, 818: To Margaret Isherwood, 12 August 1959, p. 874.

250 Bedford, Sybille. Aldous Huxley, A Biography, Volume Two, The Turning Points, 1939-1963. London: Quartet Books, 1979 AA, Part Ten: "I will show you sorrow …," Chapter Four, 1951-1955, p. 187.

251 Huxley, Julian. Memories, Volume II. NY: Harper & Row, Publishers, 1973 AA,

neuroscientist, philosopher and psychoanalyst John Cunningham Lilly (1915 – 2001). Lilly was then with the National Institute of Mental Health (NIMH); in the 1960s he would go on to integrate LSD into his sensory deprivation studies as well as his dolphin research.

Brother Julian describes the busy *Chez* Huxley in Hollywood:

> Aldous was far from leading a hermit's life. While we were with him, there was a stream of visitors – Linus Pauling, Gerald Heard, Christopher Isherwood, Romain Gary (then French consul at Los Angeles, author of that fine book on wild Africa, *Racines du Ciel*) and his wife Lesley Blanch, also a writer (we loved her book, *The Wilder Shores of Love*), Professor Harrison Brown, population expert, Dr William Kiskadden, once a virtuoso surgeon, now turned to population control as a more important problem, Bertalanffi, Alistair Cooke, and others. In all these diverse encounters, Aldous was the fulcrum of the conversation – knowing so much of every subject and putting the intelligent questions it required. He seemed to radiate what journalists now call *charisma*, which added quality to the moment, as we sat around on the terrace of his little house, watching the wide evening sky [italics original].[252]

Chapter X Mostly Transatlantic, p. 175.

[252] Huxley, Julian, 1973, p. 176; Linus Carl Pauling (1901 – 1994), American chemist and peace activist, awarded the Nobel Prize in Chemistry (1954) and the Nobel Peace Prize (1962); Henry FitzGerald Heard (Gerald, 1889 – 1971), historian, science writer and philosopher; Christopher William Bradshaw Isherwood (1904 – 1986), novelist, playwright and screenwriter; Romain Gary (1914 – 1980), French novelist, film director, twice winner of the Prix Goncourt; Lesley Blanch (1904 – 2007), British writer and traveller; Harrison Scott Brown (1917 – 1986), American nuclear chemist and political activist; William Sherrill Kiskadden (Bill, 1894 – 1969), American plastic surgeon and founder (with Aldous and Julian) of the Population Limited Foundation; Karl Ludwig von Bertalanffy (1901 – 1972), Austrian biologist and one of the founders of general systems theory; Alistair Cooke (Alfred, 1908 – 2004), British and American journalist and television personality.

In 1956 he marries the musician, psychotherapist and author Laura Archera Huxley (1911 – 2007),[253] and begins his last novel, Island.[254] He gives a lecture at the New York Academy of Sciences entitled 'The History of Tension'[255] in which he discusses the pharmacology of self-transcendence from the standpoint of an interdisciplinary investigation, publishes the essay 'Adonis and the Alphabet' ('Tomorrow and Tomorrow and Tomorrow'), the non-fiction set of essays Brave New World Revisited, writes a Broadway play titled 'The Genius and the Goddess,' lectures at four cities in Italy, delivers a course of lectures as visiting professor at the University of California at Santa Barbara on 'The Human Situation,' and receives the Award of Merit for the Novel at the American Academy of Arts and Letters in New York.[256]

His letters throughout this period evince great interest in designing experiments in which visionary drugs are used with the blind, artists and the dying:

> Have you ever tried the effects of mescalin on a congenitally blind man or woman? This would surely be of interest. … Sid Cohen has an interesting project which he hopes to get financed – a project that would test the efficacy of graded doses of LSD in affecting the performance of a group of professional artists. … Yet another project – the administration of LSD to terminal cancer cases, in the hope that it would make dying a more spiritual, less strictly physiological process.[257]

---

253 Bedford, 1979, Part Eleven: Soles Occidere Et Redire Possunt ["suns may set and rise again," from Catullus, *Carmina*, Poem 5, E. T. Merrill, ed., perseus.tufts.edu, hereinafter PTE]: 1955-1960, Chapter Three, *Here and Now*, p. 212.

254 Bedford, 1979, Chronology, p. 365.

255 Bedford, 1979, p. 225.

256 Bedford, 1979, pp. 365, 366.

257 Bisbee, 2018, letters dated 2 March 1954, 2 February 1958, pp. 82, 372, 373.

He takes a singular interest in the use of hypnosis to revisit past psychedelic experiences (in this way avoiding the use of drugs):

I suggested to him that he should hypnotize his people before they took LSD and should give them post-hypnotic suggestions aimed at orientating the drug-induced experience in some desired direction, and also at the very desirable goal of enabling subjects to recapture the LSD experience by purely psychological means, after their return to normal consciousness, and whenever they so desired. The fact that this kind of experience occurs in some persons spontaneously indicates that chemicals are not indispensable, and it may be that the unconscious can be persuaded, by means of post-hypnotic suggestions, repeated if necessary again and again, to open the door without the aid of chemical keys.[258]

In 1957 he lunches with Gordon Wasson:

While I was in New York, I lunched with Wasson at his Temple of Mammon. What an odd man! So solemn and humourless! But he has put an immense amount of work into his subject, and the material brought together in his vast tomes is very curious and suggestive. However, he does, as you say, like to think that his mushrooms are somehow unique and infinitely superior to everything else. I tried to disabuse him. But he likes to feel that he had got hold of the One and Only psychedelic – accept no substitutes, none genuine unless sold with the signature of the inventor [capitalization, exclamation points original].[259]

While in New York, he also meets up with the Japanese Zen Buddhist philosopher, principal disseminator of Zen thought to the West, and future winner of the Nobel Peace Prize Daisetzu Teitaro Suzuki (Daisetz, 1870 – 1966): "I also saw dear old Suzuki in New York. What a really wonderful old man!"[260] Suzuki had been teaching

---

[258] Bisbee, 2018, letter dated 1 June 1957, pp. 336, 337.

[259] Bisbee, 2018, letter dated 1 June 1957, p. 337.

[260] Smith, 1969, No. 774: To Dr Humphry Osmond, 1 June 1957, p. 825.

at Columbia University. Their correspondence dates to at least 1949 though Huxley had been reading him from a decade earlier.[261]

By 1958 he is corresponding with Albert Hofmann but they would meet only three years later: "What you say about psillocybin [psilocybin] interests me very much, and I hope that I may have an opportunity of learning more about this new door into the Other World of the mind while I am in Europe this autumn [capitalization, brackets original]."[262]

He even considers writing a kind of guide for psychonauts, based on questions designed to increase insight and reflection:

> As for the guide line for persons taking mescaline or LSD25 – I have been too busy to work this out, but will try to do so before too long. I think the best way of doing the job would be to ask a series of questions. For example, 'Do you now understand what Blake meant when he said, 'Gratitude is heaven itself?' 'Eckhart defined God in operational terms as, 'The denial of all denials.' What is your feeling about this?' 'What does the word 'isness' mean to you as you look at the world around you?' 'Samsara and Nirvana are one – the Absolute is present in every relative and particular event. Eternity manifests itself in every moment of time. How do you feel about these paradoxes?' 'In spite of all appearances to the contrary, God is love and things are somehow all right. What about it?' 'Cleave the wood and you will find me, lift the stone and I am there.' 'What a miracle this is! Drawing water and chopping wood.' 'The meanest flea as it is in God is superior to the highest angel as he is in himself.' It would be possible to put together several dozens of such short questions and statements, to be submitted to the subject in the course of his experience [quotation marks, capitalization original].[263]

---

261 No. 565: To Harold Raymond, 8 May 1949, p. 597; No. 439: To Gordon Sewell, 12 January 1940, p. 449.

262 Smith, 1969, No. 796: To Dr Albert Hofmann, 3 August 1958, p. 853; see note to letter 878, p. 919.

263 Smith, 1969, No. 787: To Dr Humphry Osmond, 11 January 1958, p. 843; see also Leary, Timothy, Ralph Metzner, Richard Alpert. The Psychedelic Experience: A Manual Based on the Tibetan Book of the Dead. New Hyde Park, NY: University

His thinking on entheogens during this period is best described in a 1957 letter to an Oklahoma physician "testing the psychological effects of light doses"[264] of ether and laughing gas:

> It seems evident that anaesthetics, like mescaline and LSD, 'open a door,' which gives access to areas of the mind, of which ordinarily we have no, or very little, or only occasional cognizance. In this area of the mind we may find visionary experience, sometimes terrible, but more often (if we are physically and psychologically healthy) beautiful and illuminating. We may also find what the mystics call 'obscure knowledge' about the nature of the universe, a 'sense of something far more deeply interfused' (in Wordsworth's phrase), a sense that All is present in every particular, the Absolute in every relative. And associated with this obscure knowledge may come a new mode of apprehension, in which the ordinary subject-object relationship is somehow transcended, and there is an awareness of self and the outer world as being one. Such propositions as 'God is love' are realized with the totality of one's being, and their truth seems self-evident in spite of pain and death. With this goes an intense gratitude for the privilege of existence in this universe [capitalization and quotation marks original].[265]

The progressively increasing correspondence with investigators and literary icons from practically the entire world led Huxley to publish in 1958 a systematic and explicit article in the *Saturday Evening Post*, one of the most commercially popular magazines of that epoch. Apart from foreshadowing new peregrinations to the East by pilgrims in search of enlightenment (which will occur punctually in the next

---

Books, 1964 AO, IV. Instructions for Use During a Psychedelic Session, First Bardo Instructions, p. 115 et seq. (reprinted in Moksha, p. 267 et seq).

[264] Smith, 1969, No. 774: To Dr Humphry Osmond, 1 June 1957, p. 825.

[265] Smith, Philip B. Chemical Glimpses of Paradise. Springfield, IL: Charles C Thomas Publishers, 1972 AA, Chapter 6 Fragments, letter dated 20 May 1957, pp. 86, 87.

decade), the text merits being cited at length, as he calls into question whether happiness is compatible with liberty:

> The history of medical fashions, it may be remarked, is at least as grotesque as the history of fashions in women's hats – at least as grotesque and, since human lives are at stake, considerably more tragic. In the present case, millions of patients who had no real need of the tranquilizers have been given the pills by their doctors and have learned to resort to them in every predicament, however triflingly uncomfortable. This is very bad medicine and, from the pill taker's point of view, dubious morality and poor sense. … Too much tension and anxiety can reduce a man's efficiency – but so can too little. There are many occasions when it is entirely proper for us to feel concerned, when an excess of placidity might reduce our chances of dealing effectively with a ticklish situation. … Now let us consider another kind of drug – still undiscovered, but probably just around the corner – a drug capable of making people feel happy in situations where they would normally feel miserable. Such a drug would be a blessing, but a blessing fraught with grave political dangers. … But mightier than either the pen or the sword is the pill. In mental hospitals it has been found that chemical restraint is far more effective than strait jackets or psychiatry. The dictatorships of tomorrow will deprive men of their freedom, but will give them in exchange a happiness none the less real, as a subjective experience, for being chemically induced. The pursuit of happiness is one of the traditional rights of man; unfortunately, the achievement of happiness may turn out to be incompatible with another of man's rights – namely, liberty.[266]

Huxley is speaking of things analyzed in the previous chapter, where the illegalization of certain sedatives and stimulants unleashed a fabulous flood of other sedatives and stimulants, no less toxic or addictive though legally decorous. Here he considers pharmacology's double-edged sword as both threat to and protection of freedom:

---

[266] Huxley, Aldous. "Drugs That Shape Men's Minds," *Saturday Evening Post*, Volume 231, Issue 16, 18 October 1958 AO, pp. 110, 111; Huxley, Aldous. Collected Essays. NY: Harper & Row, Publishers, Inc., 1960 AA, Section IV, Rx for Sense and Psyche, 'Drugs that Shape Men's Minds,' p. 176; see also hofmann.org.

Figure 453. Aldous Huxley in London, 1958. Photograph, W. Suschitzky. Huxley, Julian, ed., 1965, p. 8/92.

It is quite possible, however, that pharmacology will restore with one hand what it takes away with the other. Chemically induced euphoria could easily become a threat to individual liberty; but chemically induced vigor and chemically heightened intelligence could easily be liberty's strongest bulwark.[267]

After examining some of the other drugs then being investigated, the last part of the article is the most combative as it turns on the religious problems that will arise from the so-called new mind changers that will allow for a quotidian mysticism:

From these political and ethical considerations let us now pass to the strictly religious problems that will be posed by some of the new mind changers. … Those who are offended by the idea that the swallowing of a pill may contribute to a genuinely religious experience should remember that all the standard mortifications – fasting, voluntary sleeplessness and self-torture – inflicted upon themselves by the ascetics of every religion for the purpose of acquiring merit, are also, like the mind-changing drugs, powerful devices for altering the chemistry of the body in general and the nervous system in particular. … Now, the life of a hermit, such as Saint Anthony, is a life in which there are very few external stimuli. But as Hebb, John Lilly and other experimental psychologists have recently shown in the laboratory, a person in a limited environment, which provides very few external stimuli, soon undergoes a change in the quality of his consciousness and may transcend his normal self to the point of hearing voices or seeing visions, often extremely unpleasant, like so many of Saint Anthony's visions, but sometimes beatific. … Physiologically costless, or nearly costless, stimulators of the mystical faculties are now making their appearance, and many kinds of them will soon be on the market. We can be quite sure that, as and when they become available, they will be extensively used. … Instead of being rare, premystical and mystical experiences will become common. What was once the spiritual privilege of the few will be made available to the many. For the ministers of the world's organized religions, this will raise a number of unprecedented problems. For most people, religion has always been a matter of traditional symbols and of their own emotional, intellectual and ethical response to those symbols. To men and

[267] Huxley, *Post*, 1958, p. 111; Huxley, Collected Essays, 1960, p. 176; hofmann.org.

women who have had direct experience of self-transcendence into the mind's Other World of vision and union with the nature of things, a religion of mere symbols is not likely to be very satisfying. The perusal of a page from even the most beautifully written cookbook is no substitute for the eating of dinner. … That famous 'revival of religion,' about which so many people have been talking for so long, will not come about as the result of evangelistic mass meetings or the television appearances of photogenic clergymen. It will come about as the result of biochemical discoveries that will make it possible for large numbers of men and women to achieve a radical self-transcendence and a deeper understanding of the nature of things. And this revival of religion will be at the same time a revolution. From being an activity mainly concerned with symbols, religion will be transformed into an activity concerned mainly with experience and intuition – an everyday mysticism underlying and giving significance to everyday rationality, everyday tasks and duties, everyday human relationships [quotation marks, capitalization original].[268]

With the appearance of this text, it could be said that the pagan plot has ceased to be something largely unconscious and ineffable.

In opposition to the prevailing medical/legal fashion that stuffs patients with tranquilizers and stimulants with the goal of stupefaction or exploitation, a different group proposes in the name of health, community solidarity and greater knowledge the adventure of a voyage into inner space. The heterogeneous philosophical orientation of the second group ranges from the Platonism of Gordon Wasson to the pragmatic postures of Graves and Koestler, from the orientalist inclinations of Watts and of Huxley himself to the more Aristotelian constructions of Bateson, Jünger and Hofmann, from the almost technical use by artists like Dalí, Paz and Michaux to the ethnological investigations of botanists like Schultes and Heim or the strictly

[268] Huxley, *Post*, 1958, pp. 111, 113; Huxley, Collected, 1960, pp. 177, 178; hofmann.org; Portuguese friar Saint Anthony of Padua (1195 – 1231); Canadian psychologist sometimes called the 'father of biopsychology' Donald Olding Webb (1904 – 1985).

neurological, psychiatric or psychological investigations of Osmond, Delay, Jünger and Lilly. In common these voyagers had only fruitful experiences with drugs of the entheogenic family, and a conviction concisely expressed by Jünger: "Wine has already changed much, has brought new gods and a new humanity with it. But wine is to the new substances as classical physics is to modern physics."[269]

[269] Hofmann, 1983, letter dated 17 December 1961, p. 161; *Der Wein … modernen Physik* (Hofmann, 2001, 11 Einstrahlung von Ernst Jünger, Drogenproblematik, letter dated 27. Dezember 1961, p. 100/139).

E. The Pagan Plot Unfolds

The 1950s and early 1960s brought a period of experimentation and diffusion. More and more people began to try the new entheogens. Experienced users counseled pharmacological caution and political circumspection.

1. Pharmacological Caution

The best framework for using them was without any doubt the one already in place in those communities where they had always been consumed (especially in Central and South America) with a mixture of respect and preparation (fasting, reflection) adequate to the intensity of the experience to be undertaken. If indigenous peoples used these drugs sacramentally it was because for them the substances were not compatible with an ambiguous psyche or an already drugged metabolism. The ancient hierophants, like the present day shamans, were clear that the impure would be driven mad or to the grave.

As Hofmann observed:

> There are the profound consciousness-altering psychic effects of *peyotl*, *teonanacatl*, and *ololiuqui* which made the Indians of the Latin American countries so respectful and awestruck of these drugs, causing these people to place a taboo on them. Only a ritually clean person, one prepared by a period of prayer and fasting, had the right and qualification to ingest these drugs and then only in such a purified body as their divine nature could develop, whereas the impure felt themselves going insane or mortally stricken [italics original].[270]

Michaux maintained something practically identical, warning of the danger of losing one's soul, even with extensive preparations:

[270] Horowitz, 1977, Preface by Albert Hofmann, p. xii.

Even when prepared by meditation, some felt lost and driven mad, or just tortured, they sulked, they became angry. … One such habitué of mental training, initiated in the practices of Eastern meditation and Zen, was completely lost for a time, unable to find his *center* [italics original, tr. gwr].[271]

In 1959 Huxley corresponds with one of the most famous personalities of the moment, the mystic Trappist monk Thomas Merton (1915 – 1968), discussing the proportion of good to bad entheogenic voyages and warning against recreational use:

Statistically the results of all this experimentation are roughly as follows. About seventy per cent of those who take the drug have a positive experience; the others have a negative experience, which may be really infernal. ... There is a feeling – I speak from personal experience and from word-of-mouth reports given me by others – that the experience is so transcendently important that it is in no circumstances a thing to be entered upon light-heartedly or for enjoyment. … There is, obviously, a field here for serious and reverent experimentation.[272]

Robert Graves also observed the consequences of the uncautious, impious use of Amanita: "The effect of the *amanita muscaria* taken without other intoxicants is to give the taker the most delightful hallucinations, if he is in a state of grace, but horrible nightmares otherwise [italics original]."[273]

---

[271] *Même préparés … en colère. … Tel habitué … à trouver un centre* (Michaux, Henri. *Les grandes epreuves de l'esprit, et les innombrables petites*. Paris: Gallimard, 1966 AA, IX Les Quatres Mondes, p. 202); Michaux refers in a footnote to an experience of Blofeld, John. "A High Yogic Experience Achieved with Mescaline," *Psychedelic Review*, No. 7, 1966 [maps.org, hereinafter MAP], p. 28.

[272] Smith, ed., 1969, 808: To Fr Thomas Merton, 10 January 1959, pp. 863, 864.

[273] Graves, Robert. Difficult Questions, Easy Answers. NY: Doubleday & Company, Inc., 1964 AA/AO, 8 Mushrooms and Religion, p. 97.

2. Political Circumspection

The other thing these literary lions and scientific solons agreed upon was the need to conduct themselves in a rather Eleusinian manner. They tried to avoid any kind of indiscriminate publicity that would treat the entheogens as just one more novelty. These were not to be consumed like other drugs, recreationally, to disinhibit or simply excite.

Humphry Osmond was soon made aware of the political danger and the necessity of presenting the new drugs in a manner acceptable to the relevant social powers. As early as 1953, Osmond was writing to Huxley: "I have been a little uneasy about the publicity we are getting (and we shall get much more)."[274] By 1954 Osmond was getting attacks from without and within: "I told Aldous that there was an interesting attack on us in *Pravda* .... [My] chief male nurse ... began to speak openly about keeping notes for 'higher authorities' on what goes on in the hospital [italics, quotation marks original] ...."[275] The next year the local citizens of Weyburn, Saskatchewan [site of Osmond's mental hospital] were upset: "In the meantime the good citizens of Weyburn snipe away at us. Disliking our activity program and attacking us because our ideas are unfamiliar."[276]

Huxley had also become wary of publicity, especially that newish medium, television:

---

[274] Bisbee, 2018, letter from Osmond to Huxley and Maria, dated 22 August, 1953, p. 33.

[275] Bisbee, 2018, letters from Osmond to Aldous and Maria, dated 27 August 1954 and 3 October 1954, pp. 121, 131.

[276] Bisbee, 2018, letter from Osmond to Aldous, dated 28 July 1955, p. 202.

> I have ... a very bad feeling about TV, particularly in relation to this field. ... As you say in your letter, we still know very little about the psychedelics, and, until we know a great deal more, I think the matter should be discussed, and the investigations described, in the relative privacy of learned journals, the decent obscurity of moderately high-brow books and articles. ... All that TV can do is increase the number of misunderstandings by a thousand-fold ... *Littera scripta manet, volat irrevocabile verbum* [italics original].[277]

Osmond completely agreed: "Newspaper releases are outside science, and, however much they may excite the public they are likely to excite scientists in an equal and opposite direction."[278]

While defending his explosive thesis of so-called applied mysticism before the annual meeting of the American Psychiatric Association, Huxley noted the reluctance of visionaries to report their experiences:

> The mental climate of our age is not favorable to visionaries. Those who have such spontaneous experiences, and are unwise enough to talk about them, are looked on with suspicion and told that they ought to see a psychiatrist. In the past, experiences of this kind were considered valuable and those who had them were looked up to.[279]

Indeed, the political aspect surrounding these new techniques could not be ignored. Considering the progress that pharmacological

---

[277] "The written word remains; what is spoken flees forever" (Bisbee, 2018, letter from Aldous to Osmond, dated 22 July 1956, pp. 283. 284, fn 51).

[278] Bisbee, 2018, letter from Osmond to Aldous, dated 3-8 October 1956, pp. 295, 296.

[279] Huxley, Aldous. "Mescaline and the 'Other World,'" Proceedings of the Round Table on Lysergic Acid Diethylamide and Mescaline in Experimental Psychiatry held at the annual meeting of the American Psychiatric Association, Atlantic City, New Jersey, 12 May 1955, Louis Cholden, ed. NY: Grune & Stratton, 1956 [samorini.it, hereinafter SAM], p. 47.

chemistry had made in the aspect of mere tranquilization, it was important to take care that these discoveries should not be employed as "instrument[s] of statecraft" because, directed "by the wrong people, the coming revolution could be as disastrous, in its own way, as a nuclear and bacteriological war."[280] Huxley predicted the impact of these "extraordinary elixirs" would be at least as important as that other widespread and antique form of finding truth in botany: "What man will ultimately do with these extraordinary elixirs, it is impossible to say. My own guess is that they are destined to play a part in human life at least as great as the past played, up till now, by alcohol, and incomparably more beneficent."[281]

Anaïs Nin, in whose house a number of psychedelic reunions were celebrated, appreciated Huxley's "cool, scientific" descriptions of his journeys but disagreed with Leary's plan to "draw attention to themselves," writing that their experiences were esoteric and should remain so:

> Our parties were meaningful and very special. We shared our esoteric experiences. These experiences should have remained esoteric. All the ancient beliefs, religions, philosophies were at first esoteric. This was not an expression of superiority; it meant that to enter certain realms of knowledge and experience one needed initiations.[282]

---

280 Huxley, Aldous. "Brave New World Revisited: Proleptic meditations on Mother's Day, euphoria and Pavlov's pooch," *Esquire, Magazine for Men*, Volume XLVI, No. 1, Whole No. 272, 1 July 1956 AO, p. 32.

281 Huxley, 1 July 1956, p. 32.

282 Stuhlman, ed., 1966, [Summer, 1963], p. 333.

3. The Final Revolution

However, Huxley was already too well-known and his enthusiasm too great to observe this orientation of cautious reserve. In 1959 he addresses a three-day symposium at the University of California's San Francisco Medical Center whose title "A Pharmacologic Approach to the Study of the Mind" indicates the problem under consideration. His lecture at the conference, in which he hardly spoke of psychedelic drugs, is a meditation on technique and without any doubt one of his best productions.

The point of departure for this man of letters is to overcome the ancient Platonic and Cartesian duality that suffocates nature, deforms the vision of the world and has revealed itself to be unacceptable from the point of view of science. For this he needs a new means of talking about mystical experience:

> Our problem is to adapt a language which is not now suitable to describing the continuum of mind and body, a university of complete continuity. Somehow or other we have to invent the means of talking about these problems in an artistically varied way which shall make them accessible to the general public. Ideally, for example, we ought to be able to talk about a mystical experience simultaneously in terms of theology, of psychology and of biochemistry. This is a pretty tall order, but unless we can do something of the kind, it will remain extraordinarily difficult for people to think about this continuous web of life, to think about it as a continuum, and not in terms of the old Platonic and Cartesian dualism which so extraordinarily falsifies our picture of the world.[283]

With such understanding not only men of letters but scientists and citizens generally must apply technology to human affairs:

---

[283] Huxley, Aldous. "The Final Revolution," Featherstone and Simon, eds., 1959, pp. 219, 220.

Figure 94. Aldous Huxley in California, 1958.
Huxley, Julian, ed., 1965, p. 171/192.

The Final Revolution, as I see it, is the application to human affairs, both on the social level and on the individual level, of technology. Now what is technology? Technology, technique in general, I suppose, is the application in a perfectly conscious and rational way of well-thought-out methods of doing things efficiently. The watchword is 'efficiency' [quotation marks, capitalization original].[284]

Technology for Huxley is something in principle neutral. Left to itself it tends to efficiency in the abstract, to the conclusion of an operation. The decisive problem is to channel it toward one goal or another. Otherwise, one must accept that its exploitation of what is, is self-legitimizing in the name of pure efficiency:[285]

---

[284] Huxley, "The Final Revolution," 1959, p. 220.

[285] The main precedent for this meditation is the philosophy of Martin Heidegger (1889 – 1976) who defined technology as "a way of revealing. ... Always the unconcealment of that which is [*dessen was ist*] goes upon a way of revealing" (Heidegger, Martin. The Question Concerning Technology and Other Essays, tr. William Lovitt. NY: Harper & Row, Publishers, 1977 AO, pp. 12, 25); *Die Technik ist ein Weise des Entbergens. ... Immer geht die Unverborgenheit dessen, was ist, auf einem Weg des Entbergens* (Heidegger, Martin. *Vorträge und Augsätze*. Pfullingen, DE: Verlag Gunther Neske, 1954 AO, Die Frage nach der Technik, pp. 16, 28); a major influence on Heidegger was Jünger: "Beginning in the early 1930s, Martin Heidegger began what would be a life-long engagement with the work of Ernst Jünger .... From this period comes the work that first drew Heidegger's attention, *Der Arbeiter* (*The Worker*, 1932)" (Heidegger, Martin and Ernst Jünger. Correspondence 1949 – 1975, tr. Timothy Sean Quinn. London: Rowman & Littlefield, 2016 AA, Translator's Introduction, p. xi); "Man appears here either as a sorcerer's apprentice conjuring up forces whose consequences are beyond him, or as the creator of an uninterrupted progress rushing towards artificial paradises. However ... man is not bound to technology directly, but rather indirectly. Technology is the manner in which the form of the worker mobilizes the world" (Jünger, Ernst. The Worker, tr. Bogdan Costea and Laurence P. Hemming. Stuttgart, DE: Klett-Cotta, 1981 AA, Section 44, p. 105); *Der Mensch ... die Welt mobilisiert* (Jünger, Ernst. *Der Arbeiter*. Stuttgart, DE:

> Technology tends to grow and develop according to the laws of its own being. It doesn't at all develop according to the laws of our being. The two things are quite separate, and man now finds himself subordinated to this thing which he created, and subject to its laws, which are not at all human laws.[286]

The most immediate and alarming risk is "a further usurpation by the central authority of functions which used to be in the hands of private people."[287] This is due chiefly to two new techniques applied to individuals – propaganda and pharmacological control – which are direct means of aggression toward the human being. Propaganda may

> be defined as opposed to rational argument, argument based upon facts. Argument based on facts aims at producing an intellectual conviction; propaganda aims, above all, at producing reflex action. It is aimed at bypassing the rational choice based upon knowledge of facts and getting directly at the solar plexis, so to speak, and affecting the subconscious. … The technicization of the means of getting at the human unconscious presents an enormous danger to our whole traditional conception of democracy and of liberty. It seems to make complete nonsense of the democratic process, which, after all, is based upon the assumption that voters make rational choices on the basis of facts. … And when one reads … that in this country both political parties employ advertising agents to run the machinery of their campaign, one is alarmed, and one wonders how long the democratic tradition can survive in the teeth of the technical method which is carefully rigged to bypass rational choice, and to affect people on a level below reason, on an almost physiological level.[288]

The same that can be said of propaganda can equally be said of pharmaceutical control, by whose leave the right to consume this or that substance is converted into a great privilege, for which individuals

---

Klett-Cotta, 1981 AA, Die Technik als Mobilisierung der Welt durch die Gestalt des Arbeiters, Section 44, p. 105).

286 Huxley, "The Final Revolution," 1959, p. 223.

287 Huxley, "The Final Revolution," 1959, p. 224.

288 Huxley, "The Final Revolution," 1959, p. 224.

must pay not only a psychological and physical cost but also a social and criminal one. In the same way that progress in the production of all kinds of manufactured goods is only filtered down to the individual by a massive propaganda campaign that confuses and conditions, progress in chemistry tends to remain restricted to the spread of purely conformist drugs, forming part of a military-policial arsenal whose final goal is, as Huxley observed, "brain washing enhanced by pharmacological methods. And this seems to me to be precisely The Final Revolution [capitalization original]."[289]

The last part of this text predicts what some years later will be called countercultural thinking, represented by essayists like the so-called Father of the New Left, philosopher and political theorist Herbert Marcuse (1898 – 1979),[290] the social philosopher Norman Oliver Brown (1913 – 2002),[291] and novelist and social critic Theodore Roszak (1933 – 2011).[292] Huxley posits the problem as technology versus liberty and how to have the best of both:

---

289 Huxley, "The Final Revolution," 1959, p. 226.

290 "[R]epressive sublimation ... operates as the byproduct of the social controls of technological reality, which extend liberty while intensifying domination" (Marcuse, Herbert. One-Dimensional Man: Studies in the ideology of advanced industrial society. London: Routledge & Kegan Paul, 1964 AO, Part 1 One-Dimensional Society, Chapter 3 The Conquest of the Unhappy Consciousness: Repressive desublimation, pp. 75, 76).

291 "*And yet the theory of sublimation is far from clear. This strategic concept reflects all the ambiguities in the relation between psychoanalysis and society*" (Brown, Norman O. Life Against Death: The Psychoanalytical Meaning of History, Second edition. Middleton, CT: Wesleyan University Press, 1985 AA, *Part Four* Sublimation, p. 135).

292 "[T]he rivalry between young and adult in Western society during the current decade is uniquely critical" (Roszak, Theodore. The Making of a Counter Culture: *Reflections on the Technocratic Society and Its Youthful Opposition*. Garden City, NY: *Doubleday & Company, Inc.*, 1969 [monoskop.org, hereinafter MSK], *Chapter I* Technocracy's Children, p. 1).

It is a question of somehow making the best of both worlds so that we can enjoy the results of technology, which are order and efficiency and profusion of goods, and at the same time enjoy what human beings have always held to be of supreme importance, that is to say, liberty and the possibility of spontaneity. … Our problem is to find some way of permitting this spontaneity to come to the surface, and allowing liberty to exist and yet allowing technique to develop to the limits to which it has to develop, and this is an incredibly difficult problem. It is also a problem which is exceedingly urgent. … In the past we have let ourselves be taken by surprise by the developments in technology. … I don't think it was necessary that we should have been taken by surprise by the development of the factory system at the end of the 18th Century and the beginning of the 19th. If we had sat down, if our ancestors had sat down and tried to forsee what was going to happen, I don't think they would have had to subject millions of human beings to an absolutely infernal life, in what Blake called the dark, satanic mill of the period. … And I don't think we have to let ourselves be taken by surprise again.[293]

By the end of 1959 Huxley's ideas have become thoroughly acceptable in major American universities in California and Chicago, as well as at Princeton, Harvard and Yale, which open their doors to this current of thought. At Harvard, professor and clinical psychologist Timothy Leary with psychologist and later author, yoga guru and spiritual teacher Richard Alpert (Ram Dass, 1931 – 2019) formed the Harvard Psychedelic Research Project which held "over 200 visionary-drug sessions" from 1960 to 1963.[294] The founding board included Huxley as well as psychotherapist and researcher on psychedelics and shamanism Ralph Metzner (1936 – 2019), among many others.

Leary was a man of energy, eloquent and enthusiastic, and when Huxley comes in contact with him, it could be said that the initial effort to trace the outlines of the *Grosse Politik* has now become the

---

[293] Huxley, "The Final Revolution," 1959, pp. 226, 227, 228.

[294] Leary, Timothy. High Priest. Berkeley, CA: Ronin Publishing, 1968 AO, Re-Introduction, p. xxv.

germ of a subversive movement within the nation's leading academic institutions. At the Harvard Faculty Club, while laughing over and lunching on non-entheogenic mushroom soup, Leary recalls that

> Huxley offered to sit in on our planning meetings and was ready to take mushrooms with us when the research was under way. From these meetings grew the design for a naturalistic pilot study, in which the subjects would be treated like astronauts carefully prepared, briefed with all available facts, and then expected to run their own spacecraft, make their own observations, and report back to ground control. Our subjects were not passive patients but hero-explorers.[295]

These hero-explorers included divinity students, prisoners, legendary artists and intellectuals and a wide assortment of volunteers.[296]

In the spring of 1960 Huxley makes himself the mortal enemy of the International Psychoanalytical Association when he gives an interview suggesting a single session of LSD may give a person more insight than years of psychoanalysis:

> While one is under the drug one has penetrating insights into the people around one, and also into one's own life. Many people get tremendous recalls of buried material. A process which may take six years of psychoanalysis happens in an hour – and considerably cheaper! And the experience can be very liberating and widening in other ways. It shows that the world one habitually lives in is merely a creation of this conventional, closely conditioned being which one is, and that there are quite other kinds of worlds outside. It's a very salutary thing to realize that the rather dull universe in which most of us spend most of our time is not the only universe there is. I think it's healthy that people should have this experience [exclamation point original].[297]

---

295 Leary, 1968, Trip 4 The Sacrament Solves No Problems: The Dark Paradox, pp. 65, 67.

296 Leary, 1968, Re-Introduction, 1. Einsteinian Relativity, p. xxvi.

297 Wickes, George and Ray Fraser, interviewers. "The Art of Fiction XXIV, Aldous

In May 1960 Huxley had "been in hospital for tests, and been given the diagnosis of a malignant tumour on the back of his tongue."[298] He was prescribed "radium needle treatment" which "was successful – the tumour was knocked out, and Aldous's speech remained perfect. The next ten weeks of convalescence at home were what he called unpleasant."[299] He will soon be diagnosed with laryngeal cancer but instead of retreating into isolation he augments his activity, lecturing indefatigably at universities and foundations, giving interviews and working on his novel: "Even so, he was able to take part in a symposium at Tecate, Mexico, as early as the 24th of June. In July he was at work again on his novel."[300] He continued to collaborate with Leary in experimental sessions in which they employed psilocybin: "I remember Aldous Huxley came over many times."[301]

In a letter from April 1961 Huxley suggests the Harvard professor offer a psychedelic substance to the painter, sculptor and Dada pioneer Max Ernst (1891 – 1976) because

> Ernst sees in a visionary way and is also a first-rate artist capable of expressing what he sees in paintings which are about as adequate to the visionary facts as any I know. It might be interesting to get in touch with him, find out what his normal state is, and then give him mushrooms or LSD and get him to compare his normal experiences with his drug-induced ones.[302]

Huxley," *The Paris Review*, Number Twenty-Three, Spring, 1960 AA, p. 68.

[298] Bedford, Volume II, 1979, Part Eleven, *Chapter Ten* Reprieve, p. 262.

[299] Bedford, 1979, p. 263.

[300] Bedford, 1979, p. 263.

[301] Leary, 1968, Trip 5 You Will Be Hurled Beyond the Good and Evil Game: The Rite to Be Wrong, November 1960, p. 89.

[302] Huxley, Moksha, 1982, Letters, To Dr. Timothy Leary, 13 April 1961, p. 187; Smith, 1969, 861: To Timothy Leary, p. 909.

On the fifteenth of June 1961, his new novel Island now finished[303] he arrived in London.[304] There he taped two long interviews in which he reaffirmed much of his previous work:

> The intensity of the experience is entirely unlike, uh, any ordinary experience …. It's an immense intensification of the world, the, a transfiguration of the external world into incredible beauty and significance. … [I]t's not necessary to salvation but if it can be collaborated with and used in a, an intelligent way it can be an immense help to people. This sense that … in spite of pain, in spite of death, in spite of horror, the universe is in some mysterious sense is all right, capital A, capital R [transcription gwr].[305]

The next month Aldous and Laura "went to Turin on 7th August for a few days with her family …. On their return they stopped at Basle and met Dr Albert Hoffmann [sic] who had first synthesized lysergic acid."[306]

One of the longest and most systematic lectures is one Huxley gave before several hundred delegates who attended the XVI Congress of International Applied Psychology in Copenhagen, Denmark (held August 13 to 19, 1961) about the value of the visionary experience:

---

303 Bedford, 1979, Chronology, p. 366.

304 Bedford, 1979, Part Twelve: Years of Grace 1960 – 1963, *Chapter Two* London – Summer 1961, p. 280.

305 Huxley, Aldous. "Speaking Personally # 2 Aldous Huxley 1961," Interview with John Chandos 11 July 1961 at Ennismore Gardens, recorded at Landsdowne Studios, London, ed. Denis Preston [youtube.com, hereinafter YT], 44:31 to 46:16.

306 Bedford, 1979, Part Twelve, *Chapter Three* An *Amende Honorable* [Reparation], p. 297.

> I suppose in a certain sense one can say the value is absolute. In a sense one can say that visionary experience is, so to say, a manifestation simultaneously of the beautiful and the true, of intense beauty and intense reality, and as such it doesn't have to be justified in any other way. ... [I]f it is co-operated with, if we perceive this has some sort of deep significance and we do something about it, then it may be very, very important in changing our lives, changing our mode of consciousness, perceiving that there are other ways of looking at the world than the ordinary utilitarian manner, and it may also result in significant changes of behaviour.[307]

Shortly thereafter a second text appears, basically a political reflection, halfway between bitterness and hope. He calls the political leaders of the world "the hypnotized prisoners of political and philosophical traditions … grounded in nationalistic idolatry and ideological dogmatism" and "the victims of their society's alienation from present reality," exhibiting the same symptoms of their society's collective neurosis:

> In earlier times, when the rate of technological and demographic change was slow, societies could afford the luxury of their collective neurosis. Today political behavior dictated by obsessive memories of the past (in other words, by venerable traditions that have lost their point, and by old, silly or actually diabolic notions raised to the level of first principles and canonized as dogmas) is apt to be fatally inappropriate.[308]

When this is being written the Kennedy administration is steadily increasing the number of its so-called military advisers in Vietnam, and the Cuban Missile Crisis (16 – 28 October, 1962) will soon be in the news.

---

307 Huxley, Aldous. "1961 Visionary Experience," Moksha, 1982, Part 2 Psychedelic and Visionary Experience, Chapter 33, p. 208.

308 Huxley, Aldous. "1961 Exploring the Borderlands of the Mind," Moksha, Chapter 34, pp. 215, 216; see also Fate Magazine, Volume 15, No. 9, September 1962 [luminist.org, hereinafter LUM], p. 36 et seq.

But more serious than these international crises are the internal crises in developed societies, atheist nations making political ideology a principle of faith, inheritors of a tradition that does not know how to accept the blessings of invention, proud jailers of technology which in reality enslaves them, sustained by habitual drunks that fear going mad with any kind of non-stupefying ebriety. What their citizens really need are not infantile so-called gadgets that change models every year, but a grounding in the permanence of the human condition. At the same time precisely because of this they need the courage to adventure out there where novelty transcends the cobwebs painted with glitter.

In one of his letters to Leary, in which he answers a question about tantric yoga, Huxley mentions the positive side of the final revolution he is predicting:

> As far as one can understand it, Tantra seems to be a strange mixture of superstition and magic with sublime philosophy and acute philosophical insights. … But the basic ideal seems to me the highest possible ideal – enlightenment, not apart from the world … but within the world, through the world, by means of the ordinary processes of living. Tantra teaches a yoga of sex, a yoga of eating (even eating forbidden foods and drinking forbidden drinks). … [T]he therapy is not merely for the abnormal, it is above all a therapy for the much graver sickness of insensitiveness and ignorance which we call 'normality' or 'mental health.' LSD and the mushrooms should be used, it seems to me, in context of this basic Tantric idea of the yoga of total awareness, leading to enlightenment within the world of everyday experience – which of course becomes the world of miracle and beauty and divine mystery when experience is what it always ought to be [quotation marks, capitalization original].[309]

This revolutionary change toward optimism is expressed in the last of his many books – the utopian novel Island – whose elaboration

---

[309] Huxley, Moksha, 1982, Letters, To Timothy Leary, 11 February 1962, p. 235; Smith, 1969, 888: To Timothy Leary, p. 929.

occupied five years. There is a scene where the so-called moksha medicine is both criticized and praised:

'There's nothing blessed about it,' Murugan snapped. 'It's just stupid and disgusting. No progress, only sex, sex, sex. And of course that beastly dope they're all given.'
'Dope?' Will repeated in some astonishment. Dope in a place where Susila had said there were no addicts? 'What kind of dope?'
'It's made out of toadstools. Toadstools!' ….
'But it isn't real,' Murugan insisted. …
'You're like that mynah,' said Dr. Robert at last. 'Trained to repeat words you don't understand or know the reason for, 'It isn't real. It isn't real.' … 'You've been told that we're just a set of self-indulgent dope takers, wallowing in illusions and false *samadhis* [liberation, illumination in Sanskrit]. Listen, Murugan – forget all the bad language that's been pumped into you. Forget it at least to the point of making a single experiment. Take four hundred milligrams of *moksha*-medicine and find out for yourself what it does, what it can tell you about your own nature, about this strange world you've got to live in, learn in, suffer in, and finally die in. Yes, even you will have to die one day … and one's a fool if one doesn't prepare for it [italics, quotation marks original].'[310]

In May 1962 he lectures to scientists at Los Alamos and gives a talk in New York at the American Academy of Arts and Letters; in June his illness recurs, in July he undergoes cobalt treatment and a minor operation, and in August and September he flies to Brussels for a meeting of the World Academy of Arts and Science.[311]

In 1963 he publishes an article for an annual supplement to the Great Books of the Western World on the so-called conquest of space, arguing that conquest requires a dualistic and reductionist worldview:

---

310 Huxley, Aldous. Island. NY: Harper & Row, Publishers, 1962 AA, pp. 137, 139, 142.

311 Bedford, 1979, Chronology, p. 367.

To those whose world view is dualistic and reductionist, the 'conquest' of an infinity of blank space and mindless matter will bring an ever more oppressive sense of human loneliness, insignificance, and futility. … Let us hope, too, that they may come to see themselves not as the murderous and suicidal 'conquerors' of Nature and one another but as purposeful and responsible collaborators with the evolutionary process that is perpetually creating, transforming, and transfiguring the world [quotation marks, capitalization original].[312]

The process of radicalization unfolds in a text prepared for the first anthology of scientific writings on LSD, but which he also sends to *Playboy Magazine* and appears the month of his death. There he does not hesitate to call for large scale experimentation as he draws together into a single hopeful testament the basic lines of all his previous work:

Thanks to the realistic ideas handed down by culture, mankind has survived and, in certain fields, progresses. But thanks to the pernicious nonsense drummed into every individual in the course of his acculturation, mankind, though surviving and progressing, has always been in trouble. History is the record, among other things, of the fantastic and generally fiendish tricks played upon itself by culture-maddened humanity. … A culture cannot be discriminatingly accepted, much less be modified, except by persons who have seen through it – by persons who have cut holes in the confining stockade of verbalized symbols and so are able to look at the world and, by reflection, at themselves in a new and relatively unprejudiced way. Such persons are not merely born; they must also be made. But how? … In the field of formal education, what the would-be hole cutter needs is knowledge. Knowledge of the past and present history of cultures in all their fantastic variety, and knowledge about the nature and limitations, the uses and abuses, of language. … Training on the verbal level needs to be supplemented by training in wordless experiencing. We must learn how to be mentally silent, must cultivate the art of pure receptivity. To be silently receptive – how childishly simple that seems! … By wise activity we can acquire

312 Huxley, Aldous. "Has Man's Conquest of Space Increased or Diminished His Stature?" The Great Ideas Today 1963. Chicago, IL: Encyclopaedia Britannica, 1963 AA, p. 33.

useful analytical knowledge about the world, knowledge that can be communicated by means of verbal symbols. In the state of wise passiveness we make possible the emergence of forms of consciousness other than the utilitarian consciousness of normal waking life.[313] … Always desirable, widespread training in the art of cutting holes in cultural fences is now the most urgent of necessities. Can such a training be speeded up and made more effective by a judicious use of the physically harmless psychedelics now available? On the basis of personal experience and the published evidence, I believe that it can. … How should the psychedelics be administered? Under what circumstances, with what kind of preparation and follow-up? These are questions that must be answered empirically, by large-scale experiment. Man's collective mind has a high degree of viscosity and flows from one position to another with the reluctant deliberation of an ebbing tide of sludge. But in a world of explosive population increase, of headlong technological advance and of militant nationalism, the time at our disposal is strictly limited. We must discover, and discover very soon, new energy sources for overcoming our society's psychological inertia, better solvents for liquefying the sludgy stickiness of an anachronistic state of

---

313 The idea that intelligence constitutes a reducing valve that filters the external world for practical purposes, while intuition represents the opposite, comes from the French philosopher and winner of the 1927 Nobel Prize in Literature Henri-Louis Bergson (1859 – 1941), whose ideas about the human mind Huxley adopts: "It looks as though the most satisfactory working hypothesis about the human mind must follow, to some extent, the Bergsonian model, in which the brain with its associated normal self, acts as a utilitarian device for limiting, and making selections from, the enormous possible world of consciousness, and for canalizing experience into biologically profitable channels. Disease, mescaline, emotional shock, aesthetic experience and mystical enlightenment have the power, each in its different way and in varying degrees, to inhibit the functions of the normal self and its ordinary brain activity, thus permitting the 'other world' to rise into consciousness [quotation marks original]" (Smith, 1969, 623: To Dr Humphry Osmond, letter dated 10 April 1953, p. 668). Hence, formalized intelligence allows us to decompose or analyze things, with the purpose of using them to our private benefit, but only intuition allows us to enter into them directly: "the objects of sense cannot be apprehended by discursive reason, but only by a direct intuition" (Smith, 1969, 518: To Thomas H. McCormack, Jr., letter dated 9 June 1946, pp. 545, 546).

mind. … With their aid, he should be able to adapt himself selectively to his culture, rejecting its evils, stupidities and irrelevances, gratefully accepting all its treasures of accumulated knowledge, of rationality, human-heartedness and practical wisdom. If the number of such individuals is sufficiently great, if their quality is sufficiently high, they may be able to pass from discriminating acceptance of their culture to discriminating change and reform. Is this a hopefully utopian dream? Experiment can give us the answer, for the dream is pragmatic; the utopian hypotheses can be tested empirically. And in these oppressive times a little hope is surely no unwelcome visitant [exclamation point original].[314]

In keeping with his philosophy, Huxley (who had not used psychedelics for two years) asked to be administered LSD as a last rite, and died peacefully after two successive 100 microgram doses.[315] According to his wife Laura, Aldous toward the end was taking very few painkillers:

We had diminished little by little all the drugs as much as possible – only used pain-killers like Percodan, a little Amytal, and something for nausea. He took also a few injections of 2 cc of Dilaudid, which is a derivative of morphine; the doctor says this is a very small intake of morphine.[316]

Laura Huxley describes his last hours:

Then, I don't know exactly what time it was, he asked me for his tablet and wrote, 'Try LSD 100 μ intramuscular.' … It was 11:45 when I gave him his first shot of 100 μ …. I let another half hour pass, and then I decided to give him another 100 μ. … [T]he ceasing of life was not a drama at all, but like a piece of music just finishing so gently in a sempre più piano, dolcemente … and at five-twenty the breathing

---

[314] Huxley, Aldous. "1963 Culture and the Individual," Moksha, 1982, Chapter 39, pp. 249, 250, 252, 255, 256; see also Huxley, Aldous. "a philosopher's visionary prediction," Playboy Magazine, Volume 10, No. 11, November 1963, p. 84 et seq.

[315] Huxley, Laura. "1963 O Nobly Born!" Moksha, 1982, Chapter 40, p. 257.

[316] Huxley, Laura, Moksha, 1982, p. 259.

stopped. … Aldous asking for the *moksha*-medicine while dying is not only a confirmation of his open-mindedness and courage, but as such a last gesture of continuing importance. … Aren't we all nobly born and entitled to nobly dying [quotation marks, italics original]? [317]

As another literary genius said in the 20th century:

It is natural to alleviate the pain of the dying person whose time is running out, but that is not enough. It is our duty to approach; for the last time, the bed-ridden man, alone, the wealth of the world. During those last moments, it is not enough to administer narcotics; rather, what we need are gifts that expand consciousness and make it more acute.[318]

Aldous Huxley died on 22 November 1963. The same day another British writer and scholar died, the theologian Clive Staples Lewis (1898 – 1963). On that same day the thirty-fifth President of the United States John Fitzgerald Kennedy (1917 – 1963) was assassinated.

[317] Huxley, Laura, Moksha, 1982, pp. 263, 264, 266.

[318] Jünger, unknown year, Skulls and Reefs, Section 2, p. 3/418; *Dem Leidenden ... erweitern und schärfen, angebracht* (Jünger, 1970, Section 2, p. 13).

Figure 455. Casady and Leary on the bus. Photo by Allen Ginsberg. Kerr, Euan. "The harsh reality behind the Merry Pranksters 'Magic Trip,'" MPRNEWS [mprnews.org, hereinafter MPR].

29
The Pagan Plot (II)

The second fundamental power is eros; when two individuals love, they seize ground from Leviathan, creating a space it cannot control. Eros will always triumph as the gods' true messenger over all titanic constructs.[1]
-- Ernst Jünger (1895 – 1998)

A. Clinica
1. **Psychotherapy**
2. **Alcoholism**
3. **Palliation**

B. Academia
1. **The Harvard Psilocybin Experiment**
2. **The Concord Prison Experiment**
3. **The Good Friday Experiment**
4. **The New Sacrament**
5. **Opposition**
6. **Paradise Found**
7. **Paradise Lost**
8. **Leary's Theory**
9. **Leary's *Zeitgeist***
10. **The Hunt for the Hierophant**

---

[1] Heidegger, Martin and Ernst Jünger. Correspondence: 1949 – 1975, tr. Timothy Sean Quinn. London: Rowan & Littlefield, 2016 [radicalimagination.institute, hereinafter RAD], Part II "Across the Line," Section 20, p. 97; *Die zweite Grundmacht ist Eros ... über alle titanischen Bildungen* (Jünger, Ernst. Über die Linie. Frankfurt am Main, DE: Vittorio Klostermann, 1950 AA, Section III, p. 39).

C. The Psychedelic Movement
- **1. Hollywood**
- **2. Kesey**
- **3. Peddlers and Cooks**

D. The Acts of Accusation
- **1. Therapeutic Inutility**
- **2. Miscegenation, Apostasy, Insanity, Addiction, Laziness**
- **3. Promiscuity**
- **4. Murder, Suicide, Madness, Teratogeny**

E. The Return of the Pagan

CH. 29 THE PAGAN PLOT (II)

Anaïs Nin (1903 – 1977) recounts in her diary that she and Aldous Huxley (1894 – 1963) disagreed about "the necessity of drugs" for all:

> I also ventured my opinion that if we had been properly trained to appreciate music, painting, poetry, meditation, dreams, we would not have needed drugs, for I had reached such 'states' just listening to music, looking at certain paintings, reading certain books, or in nature at times. But Huxley disagreed vehemently: 'You happen to have direct communication with your unconscious, that is rare, but most people do not and for them drugs are necessary' [quotation marks original].[2]

As we have seen in the previous chapter, Huxley had many times recommended to others maximum discretion and patience, but although he distrusted publicity in the beginning, he never felt that he fed elitist attitudes toward psychedelics. In a letter to Albert Hofmann (1906 – 2008) he defined his project of Applied Mysticism as

> a technique for helping individuals to get the most out of their transcendental experience and to make use of the insights from the 'Other World' in the affairs of 'This World.' Meister Eckhart [ca. 1260 – ca. 1328] wrote that 'what is taken in by contemplation must be given out in love.' Essentially this is what must be developed – the art of giving out in love and intelligence what is taken in from vision and the experience of self-transcendence and solidarity with the Universe [quotation marks, capitalization original] ....[3]

---

[2] Nin, Anaïs. The Diary of Anaïs Nin, 1955 – 1966, Volume VI, ed. Gunther Stuhlmann. NY: Harcourt Brace Jovanovich, 1976 [archive.org, hereinafter AO], (Spring, 1958), pp. 131, 132.

[3] Hofmann, Albert. LSD: My Problem Child, Reflections on Sacred Drugs, Mysticism, and Science, tr. Jonathan Ott. Los Angeles, CA: J. P. Tarcher, Inc., 1983 Chapter 8 Meeting with Aldous Huxley, letter dated 29 February 1962, p. 174; *Technik der ‚angewandten Mystik' ... mit dem Universum aufgenommen haben* (Hofmann, Albert. *LSD - mein Sorgenkind: Die Entdeckung einer »Wunderdroge«*. München, DE: Deutscher

Whether because they rejected the mysticism with which he surrounded the psychedelic experience (the Other World would always be for many people a somewhat tenuous concept) or because they doubted that his Applied Mysticism was democratizable, the detractors of Huxley were many and varied from the beginning, not only in the field of medicine but also within the relatively small group of intellectuals, artists and investigators initially familiar with visionary drugs. Henri Michaux (1899 – 1984) for example rejected Huxley's easy Edens: "*Drugs weary us with their paradises. Let them enlighten us a little instead. Ours is not a century of paradises* [italics original]."[4] Jünger took issue with Huxley's democratic idealism in a letter written at the end of the same year (1961): "I cannot agree with the thoughts of Huxley, that possibilities for transcendence could here be given to the masses. Indeed, this does not involve comforting fictions, but rather realities, if we take the matter earnestly."[5]

The subject was in fact being taken earnestly in any number of ways. Apart from the democratic mysticism of Huxley, LSD was used

---

Taschenbuch Verlag GmbH & Co. KG, 2001 [dtv.de, hereinafter DTV], 12 Begugnung mit Aldous Huxley, p. 178/215; "Master Thomas says the active life is better than the contemplative, insofar as in action one pours out for love that which one has gained in contemplation" (Walshe, Maurice O'C., tr., ed. The Complete Mystical Works of Meister Eckhart. NY: Crossroad Publishing Company, 2009 [academia.edu, hereinafter ACD], Sermon Three, p. 48).

[4] Michaux, Henri. Light Through Darkness, tr. Haakon Chevalier. NY: The Orion Press, 1963 AA, 1. How Drugs Act, p. 3; *Les drogues nous ennuient avec leur paradis. Qu'elles nous donnent plutôt un peu de savoir. Nous ne sommes pas un siècle à paradis.* (Michaux, Henri. *Connaisance par les gouffres*. Paris: Librarie Gallimard, 1961 AO, I. Comment agissent les drogues? p. 9).

[5] Hofmann, 1983, 7. Radiance from Ernst Jünger, Ambivalence of Drug Use, letter dated 17 December 1961, p. 161; *Dem Gedanken Huxleys ... Sache ernst nehmen* (Hofmann, 2001, 11. Einstrahlung von Ernst Jünger, Drogenproblematik, 27 Dezember 1961, p. 166/215).

clinically and experimentally for almost two decades, with results that can only be characterized as remarkable. Up until 1966, when the "promiscuous use of the dream drug"[6] was outlawed in the states of Nevada and California, investigations into this substance had in little more than twenty years produced a bibliography comparable in depth and breadth with many of the other psychopharmaceuticals discovered in the previous century. It was used broadly in psychotherapy (depth psychology [*Tiefenpsychologie*], group therapy, neurological investigations, experimental psychoses, explorations into symbolic archetypes, mysticism, creativity, and rapid diagnostic psychiatry), to treat addictions to alcohol (and other drugs), as well as in palliative care (end-of-life therapy and general analgesia).

6 United Press International reporter. "Control Law Set on LSD," *The Desert Sun*, Volume 39, No. 256, Tuesday, 31 May 1966 [cdnc.ucr.edu, hereinafter CDN], p. 1.

Figure 456. The LSD Psychotherapy Unit at Powick Hospital, 1955
Roberts, Andy. Albion Dreaming: A Popular History of LSD in Britain. London: Marshall Cavendish Publications, 2008, Illustration 3, between pages 111 and 131.

A. Clinica

One of the first published studies (1950) quickly established the efficacy of LSD to dissolve defenses and create favorable conditions for eight patients undergoing conventional psychotherapy:

> With L.S.D. 25 ... some of the patients were then able to re-evaluate the emotional meaning of some of their symptoms, and improved. Most were better able to organize their ideas in relation to real rather than fancied problems and were seen to experience and express relevant emotion.[7]

Two years later, the influential article by Humphry Osmond (1917 – 2004) and John Smythies (1922 – 2019) appeared suggesting the cause of schizophrenia was the inability of the patient's body to control adrenaline, a neurotransmitter with a chemical structure similar to mescaline, causing a self-intoxication: "We therefore suggest that schizophrenia is due to a specific disorder of the adrenals in which a failure of metabolism occurs and a mescaline-like compound or compounds are produced ...."[8] As we saw in the previous chapter, a second article the next year defended a number of unusual positions, such as the utility of a physician using mescaline to understand a schizophrenic patient.[9]

---

[7] Busch, Anthony K. and Warren C. Johnson. "L. S. D. 25 As an Aid in Psychotherapy (Preliminary Report of a New Drug)," *Diseases of the Nervous System*, Volume XI, No. 8, August 1950 [bibliography.maps.org, hereinafter BMP], p. 243.

[8] Osmond, Humphry and John Smythies. "Schizophrenia: A New Approach," *The Journal of Mental Science*, Volume XCVIII, No. 411, April 1952 [docdroid.net, hereinafter DOC], The Synthetic Illness, p. 314.

[9] Osmond, Humphry and John Smythies. "The Present State of Psychological Medicine," *The Hibbert Journal: A Quarterly Review of Religion, Theology and Philosophy*, Volume LI, No. 2, January 1953 AA, pp. 138, 141; see Chapter 28, 1. Mescaline, p. 2049.

More generally it was hypothesized early on that a better understanding of the alkaloids would lead to a better understanding of the chemistry of the central nervous system, perhaps improving the cerebral faculties, a supposition which has largely been proven to be true:

> All alkaloids are neurotransmitters and active agents in the nervous system. Many alkaloids from natural plants and also modified alkaloids can impress euphoric, psychotomimetic and hallucinogenic properties on humans. Some of them can influence narcosis, states of stupor, unconsciousness, or arrested activity. Some of them in moderate doses dull the senses, relieve pain and induce sleep.[10]

Another of the hypotheses in vogue during the 1950s was that LSD and its simple indolic analogues (serotonin, tryptamine, psilocin, psilocybin) altered synapse time, allowing a greater or lesser volume of information to the nerve centers, another now largely accepted hypothesis:

> Only alkaloids can promote or inhibit activity of ion channels and their active pumps. Therefore, these channels are important in an alkaloid signaling system. This mechanism is connected directly or indirectly to receptor proteins. Alkaloids such as dopamine, histamine or serotonin are well-known neurotransmitters with their own receptors. The stimulation of a neurotransmitter system (especially ion channels) is caused by an influx of Na+-ions. This large-scale and rapid influx activates a so-called voltage gate of Na+ and K+-channels, which is essential for alkaloids. Neurotransmission is one of the most important biological characteristics of alkaloids.[11]

---

10 Aniszewski, Tadeusz. Alkaloids – Secrets of Life: Alkaloid Chemistry, Biological Significance, Applications and Ecological Role. Amsterdam, NL: Elsevier, 2007 AO, Chapter Three Biological Significance of Alkaloids, 4. Narcotics, p. 169.

11 Aniszewski, 2007, Chapter 3, 1.1 From stimulators to inhibitors and destroyers of growth, p. 144.

1. Psychotherapy

One psychopharmacological investigator classified the three main techniques of LSD therapy as psycholytic, psychedelic and hypnodelic.[12] Psycholytic LSD therapy uses small or medium doses with individuals or groups over considerable periods of time with the aim of opening up their patients and preparing them for better communication with their therapist or the larger group:

> [T]his technique is the most common form of LSD therapy currently employed in Europe. ... Each patient retires to a private room in the clinic; psychiatric help is available. When the drug effect begins to decrease, the patients meet in a group therapy session, do some art work, and discuss the experiences of their LSD session. With this technique, relatively small doses of LSD are employed (100 to 150 μg.) in each of the 15 to 20 drug sessions. The patients are also treated in individual or group psychotherapy, so that they come to the clinic once or twice a week, not necessarily for an LSD session, but to discuss with their therapist material emerging during drug sessions [italics original].[13]

Psychedelic LSD therapy employs high doses (300 to 600 μg):

> A large dose of the drug (300 to 600 μg.) is employed .... Usually, only a single drug session is given, or a few at most. What is sought is not an abreactive effect [reliving an experience with less emotion], but rather a mystical or transcendental type of experience with a concomitant rapid personality reorganization. ... [T]he orientation is that of a conversion experience; the therapist expects a single large dose of the drug to bring about the therapeutic effect [italics original].[14]

---

[12] Levine, Jerome. "LSD – A Critical Overview," in Black, Perry, ed. Drugs and the Brain: *Papers on the Action, Use, and Abuse of Psychotropic Agents*. Baltimore, MD: Johns Hopkins Press, 1969 AA, Chapter 22, p. 305.

[13] Levine, 1969, p. 305.

[14] Levine, 1969, p. 306.

Hypnodelic LSD therapy (rarely used) initiates the sessions by hypnotizing the patient in order to optimize the experience:

> [I]t utilizes hypnosis to control the LSD experience .... [I]f the patient is hypnotized, or at least subjected to a hypnotic induction procedure, in the period between the time of LSD administration and the onset of LSD effect, he can be effectively guided during the LSD experience. This is believed to enhance the therapeutic benefit of the drug session.[15]

LSD therapy has proven to be indisputably useful, given the overwhelming amount of testimony in an already extensive bibliography accumulated by the middle of the 1960s, even considering only "English-language publications."[16] In 1967, one investigator tabulated that over "2,000 publications have appeared in the scientific press, concerning the treatment of thirty to forty thousand patients."[17] Since that time more reports have come in from around the world:

> [T]he literature has continued to grow and now includes book-length works as well as the shorter reports published in journals and anthologies. ... Reports of therapeutic successes have come from hundreds of psychotherapists working in many of the countries and cultures of the world.[18]

---

[15] Levine, 1969, p. 306.

[16] Unger, Sanford M. "LSD and Psychotherapy: A Bibliography of the English-Language Literature," *The Psychedelic Review*, Volume 1, No. 4, 1964 [maps.org, hereinafter MAP], p. 442; see also Weil, Gunther M., et al, eds. The Psychedelic Reader. NY: The Citadel Press, 1971 AA.

[17] Buckman, John. "Theoretical Aspects of LSD Therapy," in Abramson, Harold A., ed. The Use of LSD in Psychotherapy and Alcoholism. Indianapolis, IN: The Bobbs-Merrill Company, Inc., 1967 AA, III Psycholytic Therapy, Panacea of self-deception, p. 96.

[18] Masters, Robert E. L. and Jean Houston. "Toward an Individual Psychedelic Psychotherapy," in Aaronson, Bernard and Humphry Osmond, eds. Psychedelics: *The Uses and Implications of Hallucinogenic Drugs*. Garden City, NY: Doubleday &

The Second International Conference on the Use of LSD in Psychotherapy held at Amityville, Long Island, New York from 8 to 10 May, 1965 (besides the numerous participants from the United States) attracted 19 investigators in the field of psychiatry from eight foreign countries.[19] One of them reported that at the conclusion of a course of psycholytic LSD therapy, his patients exhibited greater emotional and social maturation:

> [T]he patients relate that they feel personally free and exempt from various pathological dependencies they suffered from previously. They often speak about rebirth and new life, about a new beginning. Even if the series is interrupted or terminated, the patients go on to discover new genetic relations and the process of accelerated emotional and social maturation which was inhibited for a long time by unfavorable circumstances of their life histories continues.[20]

In other words, from the therapist's standpoint LSD can reveal to their patients new possibilities for restructuring their lives:

> The basic rationale behind using psychedelic drugs in psychiatric treatment is now fairly widely agreed. It is accepted that the effect of psychedelics like LSD is, so to speak, temporarily to put the individual back into the crucible – to melt down existing forms and allow much that is otherwise contained deep in the interior to float to the surface, to reveal new possibilities, and to render the patient malleable enough for restructuring.[21]

Company, Inc., 1970 AA, Part VII. Therapeutic Applications, p. 323.

19 Aaronson and Osmond, eds., Psychedelics, 1970, Registered Participants, pp. xvii-xxi.

20 Grof, Stanislav. "Use of LSD 25 in Personality Diagnostics and Therapy of Psychogenic Disorders," in Aaronson and Osmond, 1970, III. Use of LSD in Psychotherapy, p. 177.

21 Wells, Brian. Psychedelic Drugs. NY: Jason Aronson, 1974 AA, 4 Therapeutic Applications, Modes of Use, pp. 63, 64.

So widespread was LSD therapy that even in a country relatively isolated from the rest of the world like Spain, in the late 1950s there were at least three communications about LSD therapy. One from 1956 lists an extensive bibliography (*copiosa bibliografía*) and adds data on thirty-six subjects given doses of between 30 and 160 gamma, noting that the drug increased anti-social behavior in psychotics (schizophrenics) but surprisingly there was no such accentuation of symptomatology in neurotics.[22] Another study from 1958 using doses between 25 and 50 gammas reported variable reactions depending on the personality of the patient, one discovering the face of his mother-in-law hidden behind a vase of flowers in a painting while another patient experienced great terror.[23]

The prevailing regulations in the former Czechoslavakia demanded that therapists who wished to practice this therapy should have some personal experience:

> It is significant that Czechoslovakia allows doctors to use the psychedelic drugs in experiments or practice providing they have had special training, including observation of at least thirty administrations and have taken the drugs at least five times themselves.[24]

---

[22] *En los psicópatas se ha exaltado el comportamiento antisocial, la agresividad, etc. En los neuróticos nos sorprendió que no se acentuara la sintomatología previa a la administración de la LSD ...* (Ruiz-Ogara, C., et al. "*Psicosis Lisérgica*," *Revista de Psiquiatria y Psicologia Médica de Europa y América Latinas*, Tomo II Anos 1955-1956, ed. L. Acevedo, et al. Barcelona, ES: Redacción y Administración, 1956 [samorini.it, hereinafter SAM], pp. 566-572, 585); see also Sarro Burbano, Ramón. "*Farmacos y psiquiatria*," *Medicina Clínica*, Volume 26, No. 3, 1956.

[23] *Las reacciones son muy variables ... experimentó gran terror* (Rof Carballo, J. and A. Gonzalez Morado. "*Experiencia clínica con la dietilimida del ácido lisérgico (DAL)*," *Boletín del Instituto de Patología Médica*, Volume XIII, No. 10, Octubre 1958 SAM, pp. 273, 275).

[24] Clark, Walter Houston. Chemical Ecstasy: Psychedelic Drugs and Religion. NY:

In some cases the therapist takes LSD with the patient:

> Because it is difficult to learn about interpersonal relationships in an individual session, some therapists begin to take the drugs with their patients to maximize the empathic process. ... It is not always sufficient to call out from the forest's edge to rescue someone lost. One must sometimes go in himself.[25]

Naturally, as psychiatrists belong to different schools, they oriented their practices with LSD accordingly. The Freudians looked for early childhood sexual trauma, the Jungians preferred to highlight images from the collective unconscious, the Rankians birth trauma and so forth:

> [A]lthough the explanation given by different therapists will vary, each interpretation has a definite relationship to the life pattern of the patient. A Freudian may express it in terms of unresolved Oedipal complexes, a Jungian will speak of archetypes, a Rankian of separation anxiety, and a Sullivanian of oral dynamisms. ... It is curious how under LSD the fondest theories of the therapist are confirmed by his patient. Freudian symbols come out of the mouths of patients with Freudian analysts. Those who have Jungian therapists deal with the collective unconscious and with archetypal images. The patient senses the frame of reference to be employed, and his associations and dreams are molded to it.[26]

Sheed & Ward, 1969 AA, Chapter 7. Drugs and Personality Change, p. 97, citing "Information obtained from Stanislav Grof, M. D., of the Pschiatric Research Institute, Prague, and Johns Hopkins University" (p. 114).

25 Blewett, Duncan. "The Psychedelics and Group Therapy," in Aaronson and Osmond, 1970, Part VII. Therapeutic Applications, *Use of Psychedelics by the Therapist in Therapy*, pp. 353, 354.

26 Cohen, Sidney. The Beyond Within: The LSD Story. NY: Atheneum, 1965 AA, Chapter 9 Psychotherapy with LSD: Pro and Con, pp. 182, 183.

But the vast majority of investigations and treatments describe something extremely unusual in psychiatry (except in cases of obvious cruelty, not completely infrequent),[27] which was to count on the patient not only to understand the characteristics of the drug and to give her consent, but also to have confidence in and trust her own feelings and deepest values, instead of those suggested by the therapist. As one psychiatrist observed, most therapists with any experience with the drug adopted the Socratic method, which instead of teaching one thing or another tries to bring to light knowledge so to speak forgotten or buried within the patient:

> This LSD treatment experience combines the conscious use of psychotherapeutic techniques and principles, with direct life experience, all intensified by the LSD 'enlightenment' effect. The therapy model outlined has been designed to give the patient explicit support, instruction and assurance. He is told that his inner motives and feelings are valuable and can be trusted, that the powerful and protective therapist desires that he should have them and approves them, and that in this crucial interpersonal situation, love, protection and appropriate gratification are available [quotation marks original].[28]

---

[27] Administering LSD to psychotics, or any involuntary use, could be considered cruelty, especially in large doses. One therapist, for example, suggested keeping the patient awake and in a state of anxiety with methamphetamine the night before a treatment session with LSD: "LSD's effectiveness is enhanced by combining it with intravenous methylamphetamine, 15-30 mg. This is either given when the patient goes to bed on the night before treatment, or at the same time as the drug. Giving methylamphetamine at bedtime ensures that the patient has a sleepless night, during which time he ruminates about his problems and begins treatment in an anxious and suggestible state of mind" (Dally, Peter. Chemotherapy of Psychiatric Disorders. London: Logos Press Limited, 1967 AA, V. Hallucinogenic Drugs, Therapeutic Uses of LSD, p. 124).

[28] Downing, Joseph. "Attitude and Behavior Change Through Psychedelic Drug Use," in Tart, Charles T., ed. Altered States of Consciousness. Garden City, NY: Doubleday & Company, Inc., 1969 AA, Chapter 28, p. 450.

Figure 457. Dr. Sidney Cohen.

The basic perspective is not so much to achieve the conformity of each individual with certain social norms as it is to get her to see that the effort to adjust to convention could be inhibiting a more valid and less egocentric way of living.

LSD therapy appears to be advisable for many kinds of personality disorders and neurotic conditions, including those resistant to treatment, and even more so in those suffering from the scourge of an overly severe moral conscience, or a lack of confidence and self-esteem. The most spectacular successes show up in those Sidney Cohen (1910 – 1987) called the "lost" people, isolated and lacking in motivation:

> People suffering from an excessively strict conscience, those who have lost confidence and self-esteem, and those who are unable to overcome the grief of a personal loss are the best candidates. Generally depressions due to situational factors are favorably influenced. Those 'lost' people who are unable to find meaning in existence are particularly good candidates [quotation marks original].[29]

It has even been used with neurodevelopmental disorders. One child psychiatrist reports having successfully treated autistic children with doses of LSD ranging from 25 gamma weekly to 150 gamma daily:

> We used LSD on 89 children from January 1961 to July 1965, when Sandoz no longer made it available for research purposes. ... We hope to go back to using LSD because we have found that it is one of the most effective methods of treatment we have for childhood schizophrenia. It tends to normalize the labile, boundaryless physiological, perceptual and psychological functions in schizophrenic children, and helps them to a more normal physiological, psychological and social adjustment.[30]

---

[29] Cohen, 1965, p. 195.

[30] Bender, Lauretta. "Children's Reactions to Psychotomimetic Drugs," in Efron, Daniel H., ed. Psychotomimetic Drugs. NY: Raven Press, 1970 SAM, pp. 268, 270.

In any case, the accumulated experience also allows an agreement as to the type of patients or disorders for which this kind of therapy is not advisable. It is inadvisable, for example, for those described as eternal adolescents or in cases of persons extremely depressed, hysterical, paranoid or psychotic:

> Some patients are completely unsuitable for a trial with the LSD type of therapy. The eternal adolescent who has never grown up or functioned effectively is a poor candidate. The extremely depressed, the hysterical and the paranoid personalities are poor risks because of the danger of accentuating their depressive, hysterical or paranoid tendencies. Although occasional claims have been made that psychotic patients have been helped, the consensus is that LSD is not for them. The borderline psychotic is a precarious patient because of the danger that he may decompensate and fall into a full-blown psychosis.[31]

But the so-called dangers of LSD therapy are minimal: "[W]hen the drugs are administered by those therapists and researchers who are most effective, the 'dangers' are negligible. This is borne out by studies involving many thousands of patients and experimental drug subjects [quotation marks original]."[32]

Almost all the studies affirm that only an infinitesimally small number of LSD experiences were negative. In 1959 two researchers demonstrated that unfavorable reactions to LSD and similar drugs could be avoided with "careful screening and handling" of subjects, including brief preliminary interviews, low doses and a supportive, non-inquisitorial setting:

---

[31] Cohen, 1965, p. 195.

[32] Masters and Houston, 1970, p. 326.

> We have consistently found in our work with LSD in 'normal' subjects that the quality of the drug response is largely a function of personality; so much so that one can often predict, on the basis of a control interview, how a subject will react after taking LSD. ... We do not wish to leave the impression that we consider personality to be the only factor determining the quality of the LSD reaction. It is a major variable, but there are others. These are chiefly two: (1) dosage and (2) the interpersonal environment [quotation marks original].[33]

Further, in 1960 a vast survey of adverse reactions to LSD experimentation brought to light some interesting data. Of the "almost five thousand individuals [some normal and some in psychotherapy] who had received either LSD or mescaline on more than 25,000 occasions" at doses ranging from 25 to 1500 mcg., only 0.08 percent of normals and 0.18 percent of patients had a psychotic reaction lasting over 48 hours, while among patients only 0.12 percent tried suicide and 0.04 percent succeeded.[34] The percentage of consummated suicide is below that for many conventional psychiatric treatments.[35]

---

[33] Klee, Gerald D. and Walter Weintraub. "Paranoid Reactions Following Lysergic Acid Diethylamide (LSD-25)," in Bradley, P. B., et al., eds. Neuropsychopharmacology: Proceedings of the First International Congress of Neuropsychopharmacology, held in Rome, September, 1958. Amsterdam, NE: Elsevier, 1959, pp. 459, 460.

[34] Cohen, Sidney. "Lysergic Acid Diethylamide: Side Effects and Complications," *Journal of Nervous and Mental Disease*, Volume 130, No. 1, January 1960 [psychonautdocs.com, hereinafter PSD], pp. 30, 36, Table 1 *Estimated Rates of Major Complications Associated with LSD*.

[35] See for example König, Daniel, et al. "Suicide risk after discharge from in-patient psychiatric care: A 15-year retrospective cohort study of individual patient data," *Journal of Affective Disorders*, Volume 354, 2024 [pdf.sciencedirect.com, hereinafter SCD]; Walsh, G., et al. "Meta-analysis of suicide rates among psychiatric in-patients," *Acta Psychiatrica Scandinavica*, December 2014 [researchgate.net, hereinafter RGN].

Figure 458. Weyburn Mental Hospital, Saskatchewan. Dyck, Erica. "Psychedelic Research in 1950s Sasketchewan," 2019 [thecanadianencyclopedia.ca, hereinafter TCC].

2. Alcoholism

Abram Hoffer (1917 – 2009) and Humphry Osmond were some of the first to administer high doses of LSD to patients with long histories of dipsomania, with the goal of getting them to touch bottom, freeing repressed memories and creating a situation propitious for new learning processes. Although the trials did not include long term follow up studies, of the almost 1000 patients treated with psychedelic therapy in Saskatchewan, British Columbia, Baltimore and elsewhere approximately half abandoned completely or significantly reduced their consumption of alcoholic beverages:

> Psychedelic therapy refers to a form of psychotherapy in which hallucinogenic drugs are used in a particular way to facilitate the final goal, which for alcoholics is sobriety. The drugs may be mescaline, LSD, psilocybin, and many others, as well as combinations. ... Delirium tremens is one of the common toxic states. It occurred to us that LSD might be used to produce models of dt's. Many alcoholics ascribed the beginning of their recovery to 'hitting bottom,' and often 'hitting bottom' meant having had a particularly memorable attack of dt's. ... The one striking conclusion is that every scientist using psychedelic therapy with alcoholics found the same proportion of recoveries. Whether the experiments were considered controlled or not, about 50 per cent were able to remain sober or to drink much less. This seems to be a universal statistic for LSD therapy [quotation marks original].[36]

In larger or smaller doses, alone or in combination with other drugs, psychedelic therapy was used with apparent success by many other researchers. An LSD study with a follow up of from six months to a year of 61 alcoholics with "poor prognosis" found that thirty "of

---

[36] Hoffer, Abram. "Treatment of alcoholism with psychedelic therapy," in Aaronson and Osmond, eds., Psychedelics, 1971 SAM, pp. 359, 360, 361.

the alcoholics ... were much improved" and sixteen others "showed some improvement."[37] A fifty year old man

> whose drinking caused him to lose both his job and his wife ... received a preliminary course of psychotherapy lasting several weeks before receiving LSD ... [resulting in] a spiritual awakening .... Eighteen months later, the follow up team reported that the patient ... was totally abstinent, and had returned to his previous job. He effected a reconciliation with his family, and maintained a degree of peaceful equanimity; his depression continued to improve.[38]

In social interaction studies of eight alcoholics administered LSD, five were still sober a year later:

> [M]any comments about reliving of past experiences and increased insight were made by the subjects, though, deliberately, no attempt at therapeutic use of the experience was made by the investigators. Despite this, 1 year after the interaction studies were completed, five of the eight alcoholics were still sober.[39]

In 1968 one researcher even speculated that "the egocentric problems of the alcoholic may be specifically tailored for this 'ego-dissolving, ego-building' technique [quotation marks original]."[40]

---

37 MacLean, J. Ross, et al. "The Use of LSD-25 in the Treatment of Alcoholism and Other Psychiatric Problems," *The Quarterly Journal of Studies on Alcohol*, Volume 22, No. 1, 1961 [jsad.com, hereinafter JSA], pp. 34-35.

38 Savage, Charles, et al. "Therapeutic Applications of LSD," in Drugs and the Brain: *Papers on the Action, Use, and Abuse of Psychotropic Agents*, Perry Black, ed. Baltimore, MD: Johns Hopkins Press, 1969 AO, Part IV. LSD, Chapter 23, pp. 311, 312

39 Cheek, Francis E. and Carolyn M. Holstein. "Lysergic Acid Diethylamide Tartrate (LSD – 25) Dosage Levels, Group Differences, and Social Interaction," *Journal of Nervous and Mental Disease*, Volume 153, No. 2, 1971, p. 146.

40 Freedman, Daniel X. "On the use and abuse of LSD," *Archives of General Psychiatry*, Volume 18, No. 3, March 1968, p. 340.

Figure 459. Dr. Abram Hoffer (1910 – 1987), University of Saskatchewan, University Archives & Special Collections, Photograph Collection, A-10368, TCC.

A recent (2020) systematic review of eight "randomized-controlled clinical trials" involving hundreds of patients over several decades was able to conclude that LSD can in fact help alcoholics at least as much as naltrexone:

> [A]lcohol use disorder patients may benefit from LSD treatment. Other studies with a lower quality control group (patients did not receive a treatment comparable to the treatment group) also found significant differences in favor of LSD treatment in alcoholism .... Likewise, according to a retrospective analysis of studies published in the late 1960s, LSD is a potential therapeutic agent for the treatment of chronic alcoholism .... A recent meta analysis ... of six of the clinical trials chosen for this review showed the superiority of LSD over placebo in the treatment of alcoholism .... This study found that a LSD single dose was comparable in terms of effectiveness with the daily intake of naltrexone, acamprosate, or disulfiram in alcoholism treatment ....[41]

On the other hand, a 1966 incompletely double blind study of thirty patients with "a long history of excessive and uncontrolled drinking" found a substantial improvement in abstinence but the

> lysergide [LSD] group did not differ from the others in gain in total abstinence or in their longest period of abstinence, nor did they have fewer post-treatment occasions on which drinking or drunkenness occurred. Further, lysergide did not seem to reduce or eliminate symptoms such as morning drinking, getting drunk on working days, blackouts, preoccupation with alcohol, neglect of meals, or drinking only for the effects of alcohol. Nor did lysergide seem to increase the alcoholics' involvement in therapy.[42]

---

[41] Fuentes, Juan José, et al. "Therapeutic Use of LSD in Psychiatry: A Systematic Review of Randomized-Controlled Clinical Trials," *Frontiers in Psychiatry*, Volume 10, Article 943, 21 January 2020 [frontiersin.org, hereinafter FRP], pp. 1, 10.

[42] Smart, Reginald G., et al. "A Controlled Study of Lysergide in the Treatment of Alcoholism," *Quarterly Journal of Studies on Alcohol*, Volume 27, Issue 3, September 1966 AA, pp. 470, 474, 478.

There do not appear to have been many systematic trials of LSD in cases of addiction to other drugs (opiates, barbiturates, and so forth), although the results obtained from its use with alcoholism certainly suggests such trials might be useful. In one 1965 study of seventy inpatient "post-narcotic drug addicts" in Lexington, Kentucky, at "both the two-week and two-month post-therapy intervals, hypnodelic [hypnosis and LSD] treatment consistently produces more improvement than any of the other treatment methods."[43] A 1973 investigation of seventy-eight "chronic heroin abusers" found that LSD therapy "in combination with a brief period of inpatient residence, may be capable of making a contribution to the rehabilitation of chronic heroin abusers."[44] It is possible, however, that this apparent dearth of randomized, controlled clinical trials may be due to extra-medical motivations, i.e., the attitude of the legislator toward LSD.

---

43 Ludwig, Arnold J. and Jerome Levine. "A Controlled Comparison of Five Brief Treatment Techniques Employing LSD, Hypnosis and Psychotherapy," *American Journal of Psychotherapy*, Volume 19, No. 3, July 1965 [sci-hub.ru, hereinafter SCI], pp. 417, 431.

44 Savage, Charles and O. Lee McCabe. "Residential Psychedelic (LSD) Therapy for the Narcotic Addict," *Archives of General Psychiatry*, Volume 28, June 1973, pp. 808, 813.

3. Palliation

A series of trials of LSD as an analgesic for terminal patients and those suffering insupportable pain excited much interest. Two anesthesiologists at Chicago's Cook County Hospital selected "50 gravely ill patients" suffering from

> cancer of the breast with metastasis, 10; herpes zoster with severe burn, 1; cancer of the cervix with metastasis, 13; gangrene of foot or leg, 10; cancer of the pancreas with metastasis, 2; cancer of the pancreas, 2; cancer of the liver, 2; cancer of the tonsils and larynx with metastasis, 4; cancer of the lung with metastasis, 6.[45]

The patients were then administered

> dihydromorphinone HCl, 2 mg. and meperidine HCl, 100 mg. in double-blind fashion. Upon the complaint of pain, the patient received either drug initially. Upon the subsequent complaint of pain, and at least 6 hours later, the patient received the other drug in a randomized design. At least 6 hours after the second administration and upon the complaint of pain, the patient received 100 mcg. of LSD-25.[46]

Pain levels were evaluated according to "(1) the observer's opinion of the pain intensity, (2) the patient's statements, (3) the objective signs of pain distress (thrashing, crying, etc.), (4) statements from neighboring beds and house staff."[47] The results were that "[d]ihydromorphinone compared favorably with meperidine in the intensity and length of

---

[45] Kast, Eric C. and Vincent J. Collins. "Study of Lysergic Acid Diethylamide as an Analgesic Agent," *Anesthesia and Analgesia ... Current Researches*, Volume 43, No. 3, May-June 1964, pp. 285, 288.

[46] Kast and Collins, 1964, pp. 288, 289.

[47] Kast and Collins, 1964, pp. 289, 290.

analgesic action, and LSD-25 showed a protracted and more effective action than either of the other drugs."[48]

In a second study a single dose of 100 mcg LSD-25 was administered to 128 patients "selected from Cook County Hospital. All were preterminal, meaning that death could be foreseen within one to two months. All suffered from malignant diseases with metastases."[49] The patients were not told upfront they would be receiving LSD though they quickly figured out something was wrong:

> The patients also become immediately aware that something incisive has happened to them. ... As soon as these were noted, they were told that they had received a potent medicine, that they would feel peculiar, and that this feeling would pass shortly. This was done to obviate additional anticipation of panic and fear.[50]

Perhaps because of the initial lack of transparency, thirty percent of the patients did not wish to repeat the experience,[51] yet results for the others included both a notable lack of preoccupation with the fear of death as well as a reduction in insomnia:

> Under LSD, patients were so strikingly unconcerned about death or any other anticipatory concern .... The patient was able to state that death was near, that the situation was hopeless, but felt that this did not matter. ... The first night after LSD administration was almost invariably a good one. After that we noted a meaningful reduction of sleep disturbances up to about ten nights, which is also the time when concern about the morbid condition returned.[52]

---

[48] Kast and Collins, 1964, p. 291.

[49] Kast, Eric. "Pain and LSD-25: A Theory of Attenuation of Anticipation," in Solomon, David, ed. LSD: The Consciousness-Expanding Drug. NY: G. P. Putnam's Sons, 1966 [libraryofrickandria.com, hereinafter LOR], Chapter 14, p. 243.

[50] Kast, 1966, p. 244.

[51] Kast, 1966, p. 244.

[52] Kast, 1966, pp. 247, 248.

In a third series of experiments reported a few years later, 100 gamma of LSD-25 were administered to the dying as palliative care:

Eighty patients suffering from terminal malignant disease with an estimated life expectancy of weeks or months were selected. ... An interview was conducted in which the patient's condition and prognosis were discussed .... After the interview we gave 100 μg of LSD hypodermically to insure uniformity of absorption. ... The patients were interviewed daily for the subsequent three weeks [italics original].[53]

In spite of the initial improvement, very few of these terminally ill patients could tolerate the full experience

for more than ten hours without having some frightening image that necessitated termination. However ... only 10 per cent, or eight patients, did not wish to repeat the administration .... The relatively high percentage of patients whose experience was terminated can be accounted for by the fact that these were debilitated patients who tired easily.[54]

Nevertheless, the vast majority of the patients (72 percent) not only were ready to repeat the experience but also felt an improvement in feelings, mood and sleep patterns:

While the depression returned to a certain extent, a definite lifting of the mood was noted for approximately two weeks .... The happy, oceanic feeling so often experienced by normal subjects was also evident among preterminal patients. It could be noted up to twelve days following the administration of LSD .... Parallel to the general improvement in the patient's feelings, mood, and conflict situation, sleep patterns improved for approximately twelve to fourteen days ....[55]

---

[53] Kast, Eric C. "A Concept of Death," in Aaronson and Osmond, Psychedelics, 1970, Part VII. Therapeutic Applications, pp. 373, 374.

[54] Kast, 1970, p. 375.

[55] Kast, 1970, pp. 375, 376, 378, 380.

Overall, the effects could be described as both transient and profound:

> Although short-lived and transient, this happy state of affairs was a welcome change in their monotonous and isolated lives, and recollection of this experience days later often created similar elation. ... In human terms, however, the short but profound impact of LSD on the dying patient was impressive. In summary, the drug effect consisted of a lessening of the patients' physical distress and a lifting of their mood and outlook that lasted about ten days.[56]

Similar results were obtained in a separate trial of 17 terminal cancer "patients in a pilot study with no control group" with similar results in that "one-third (the same percentage of people Huxley considered susceptible of having a so-called bad or an indifferent trip) of the patients were not particularly helped, one-third were helped somewhat, and one-third were helped dramatically."[57] Other researchers into end-of-life LSD therapy with seven patients reported beneficial findings. After a single psychedelic session one woman with metastatic breast cancer said, "I became poignantly aware that the core of life is love."[58]

---

[56] Kast, 1970, p. 381.

[57] Pahnke, Walter N. "The Psychedelic Mystical Experience in the Human Encounter with Death," *Psychedelic Review*, Volume 11, Winter 1970/1971 MAP, pp. 7, 8.

[58] Savage, et al., in Black, 1969, p. 315; see also perhaps the most well-known work on the subject: Grof, Stanislav and Joan Halifax. The Human Encounter with Death. NY: E. P. Dutton, 1977 AA.

Figure 460. Timothy Leary lecturing on his book, The Interpersonal Diagnosis of Personality, 1950s Harvard. Ilnytzky, Ula. "What a trip: Timothy Leary's files go public in New York," 18 September 2013 [centralmaine.com, hereinafter CMC].

B. Academia

In the United States these therapies had their academic genesis in the most prestigious university in the country. At Harvard, a group of psychologists began to follow up on the work of Jean Delay (1907 – 1987) who had used Sandoz psilocybin in a clinical setting in France. In 1958 Delay studied the reactions induced by the periodic administration of the recently isolated and extracted drug psilocybin in doses between 5 and 14 mcg to (among others) thirteen young normal volunteers (*normaux volontaires*) whose background was decidedly middle and upper class (*d'un niveau socio-culturel moyen ou supérieur*).[59]

The scholarly reputation of the director of the soon-to-be-established Harvard Psilocybin Project, psychologist Timothy Leary (1920 – 1996), had originally been based on his specialized research in fields then in the vanguard of the social sciences in the 1950s, personality diagnosis and behavior modification:

> The field of study Tim had chosen was an academic growth industry. Much as World War I had introduced widespread psychological testing to select personnel within the armed forces, World War II had created an overwhelming need for clinical psychologists to treat those who had returned home suffering from the aftereffects of battle.[60]

Perhaps the most interesting aspect of his early work was measuring the utility of psychotherapy in a large hospital, contrasting

---

[59] Delay, J., et al. "*Les effets somatiques de la psilocybine,*" in Abély, Paul, editor-in-chief. *Annales Médico-Psychologiques*, Tome Premier. Paris: Masson & Cie, Éditeurs, 1959 SAM, Seance du 27 Avril 1959, p. 893; see GHDV4P2, Chapter 28, 2. Psilocybin, p. 2063.

[60] Greenfield, Robert. Timothy Leary: A Biography. NY: Harcourt, Inc., 2006 AA, The Berkeley Circle: Berkeley, California, 1941-1958, Chapter Seven, p. 67.

the progress of a group of treated patients with those patients already diagnosed but awaiting treatment. Both groups improved equally, demonstrating the complete ineffectiveness of any of the treatments in use.[61] One reviewer called Leary's 1957 five hundred and eighteen page tome laying out his analysis in dense statistical detail "[p]erhaps the most important clinical book to appear this year ...."[62]

In 1959 he took a year's sabbatical from his job as "Director of Psychological Research for the Kaiser Foundation Hospital" to work on a follow up book:

> I had brought with me a trunk full of psychological data, thousands of test scores and numerical indices which demonstrated with precision why psychotherapy did not work. ... I ... sat sweating in a small room in a Spanish house adding and subtracting long columns of figures. Hour after hour. ... Each laborious calculation was proving that psychology was just a mind-game, an eccentric head trip on the part of psychologists, and that psychotherapy was an arduous, expensive, ineffective, unimaginative attempt to impose the mind of the doctor on the mind of the patient.[63]

He hoped that this ambitious work would on the one hand demolish the tricks and techniques of clinical psychology, and on the other find "existential-transactional" methods to study natural events as they unfold, without prejudice:

---

[61] See Leary, Timothy. Interpersonal Diagnosis of Personality: A Functional Theory and Methodology for Personality Evaluation. NY: John Wiley & Sons, 1957 AO.

[62] Snyder, William U. "Psychotherapy," in Annual Review of Psychology, Volume 9, Farnsworth, Paul R. and Quinn McNemar, eds. Palo Alto, CA: Annual Reviews, 1958 AO, Theoretical Contributions, p. 353.

[63] Leary, Timothy. High Priest. Berkeley, CA: Ronin Publishing, 1995 AO, Trip 1 Death of the Mind: Abysmal Prelude, pp. 4, 6.

I was dissatisfied with the theory and methods of psychology and trying to develop an existential-transactional approach to the study of human events. Existential means you study natural events as they unfold without prejudging them with your own concepts. ... Transactional means you see the research situation as a social network, of which the experimenter is one part.[64]

Returning to Harvard, he "was offered a suite of offices on the third floor"[65] of the Center for Research in Personality to continue his work by the director, David Clarence McClelland (1917 – 1998), who was convinced that what Leary was advocating for was "the future of American psychology" and that he was not alone in calling for a shake-up in the dogmatic methods of the profession:

There are several hotshots in our profession – like Benjamin Spock, Carl Rogers, Abraham Maslow, Harry Stack Sullivan, Milton Gloaming – urging that we emphasize inner potential and personal growth through self-reliance, so patients avoid dependence on authoritarian doctors and dogmas.[66]

At that time Leary was not interested in psychopharmacology. A good friend recommended psilocybin mushrooms, but Leary was put off with all the esoteric talk "about William Blake revelations, mystical insights, and transcendental perspectives produced by the strange fungi. I ... warned him against the possibility of losing his scientific credibility if he babbled this way among our colleagues."[67] Looking back with a perspective of another quarter century, Leary saw himself at the time as being very square:

---

[64] Leary, High Priest, 1995, Trip 2 God Reveals Himself in Mysterious Forms: The Sacred Mushrooms of Mexico, p. 13.

[65] Greenfield, 2006, God and Man at Harvard: Cambridge, Massachusetts, 1958-1963, Chapter Ten, p. 106.

[66] Leary, 1990, Chapter 1 Search for the Key, p. 18.

[67] Greenfield, 2006, p. 103.

> I've always considered myself very square. ... I always try to hang around the hippest person in the area, and I continue to do that. I feel that, I really feel that I'm square, and I have very little sense of aesthetics and I try to hang around the most sophisticated, beautiful people in the world so I hope some of it will radiate off on me [transcription gwr].[68]

In contrast, one of Leary's more staid Harvard colleagues remembers Leary as being "surprisingly" anti-everything: "Leary, even then, in 1959, was surprisingly radical, surprisingly anti-middle class. His whole career had been a kind of flight from middle-class values, relationships, people, scenes, everything."[69]

Huxley, who in 1952 had ruled out ever finding an anesthetic revelation without tears, took mescaline in 1953 and found one. Leary, who in 1959 had condemned his friend's babbling about Mexican mushrooms, took them in 1960 and became fascinated:

> I was first drugged out of my mind in Cuernavaca, August 1960. I ate seven of the Sacred Mushrooms of Mexico and discovered that beauty, revelation, sensuality, the cellular history of the past, God, the Devil – all lie inside my body, outside my mind. ... In the summer of 1960 Cuernavaca was the site of considerable activity by American psychologists ... vacationing on research grants and working in the lush valley of Morelos in sight of the snowy peaks of the legendary volcanoes. ... The happenings of that summer in quiet Cuernavaca were to set up reverberations which have echoed now for years. Many of the scientists who were working and vacationing there that season have had their lives dramatically changed, and none of them will ever completely escape from the mysterious power, the challenge, the paradox of what started to unfold [capitalization original].[70]

---

[68] "A Conversation on LSD, Featuring Myron Stolaroff, Sidney Cohen, Al Hubbard, Timothy Leary, Oscar Janiger, Humphry Osmond and Others," V1.1, 16 February 1979, 08:30 to 08:57.

[69] Slack, Charles W. Timothy Leary, the Madness of the Sixties and Me. NY: Peter H. Wyden, 1974 AO, p. 55.

[70] Leary, High Priest, 1995, Trip 2, pp. 12, 13.

Leary's equivalent of Wasson's María Sabina was an "old woman, backbent, gray stringy hair, black shawl, eyes down, creaking stiffly, Señora Juana."[71] The *curandera* procured the mushrooms and "popped two of them in her mouth"[72] to prove they were safe and show him the dose. Even so, the Harvard psychologist was skeptical:

> By now they had been eaten by a few scientists, a few poets, a few intellectuals looking for mystical experiences. They produced wondrous trances. Oh yeah? What does he mean by that? ... I picked one up. It stank of forest damp and crumbling logs and New England basement. Are you sure they are not poisonous? ... They tasted worse than they looked. Bitter, stringy. Filthy. I took a slug of Carta Blanca and jammed the rest in my mouth and washed them down.[73]

Sixteen pages and seven mushrooms later Leary returned:

> And that was the trip. It was the classic visionary voyage and I came back a changed man. You are never the same after you've had that one flash glimpse down the cellular time tunnel. You are never the same after you've had the veil drawn. In the seven years since eating seven mushrooms in a garden in Mexico I have devoted all of my time and energy to the exploration and description of these strange deep realms.[74]

In those days enthusiasm was not considered in itself a sign of clouded judgment except by the uninitiated.

Twenty-five years later, one historian described the effect on the conservative Harvard faculty of their fellow scientists returning from Mexico babbling about ecstasy as like something out of a horror movie:

---

[71] Leary, 1995, Trip 2, p. 16.

[72] Leary, 1995, p. 16.

[73] Leary, High Priest, 1995, Trip 2, pp. 17, 18.

[74] Leary, 1995, Trip 2, p. 34.

[I]t was like watching a science fiction novel unfold before your eyes. The plot went something like this: good solid scientists embark upon interesting research program involving native drugs. Come back babbling about love and ecstasy and insisting you haven't understood anything until you've been there, to the Other World, beyond the Door. It was a little like *Invasion of the Body Snatchers*, a cult movie favorite of the Fifties, in the sense that every day the crowd in Leary's shoebox office grew larger, graduate students and junior faculty members, all with these soft intense voices and glowing eyes, talking about the death of the mind, the birth of the uncensored cortex [capitalization, italics original].[75]

---

[75] Stevens, Jay. Storming Heaven: LSD and the American Dream. NY: The Atlantic Monthly Press, 1987 AO, Chapter 12. The Harvard Psilocybin Project, p. 136; see also the 1988 Perennial Library edition, p. 110.

Figure 461. Hallucinations at Harvard. Ram Dass "The First Encounter," 1964 [ramdass.org, hereinafter RDO].

1. The Harvard Psilocybin Experiment

At Harvard's Center for Research in Personality, Leary and later devotee of yoga and Eastern spirituality Richard Alpert (Ram Dass, 1931 – 2019) prepared a program of psychedelic investigation that guided "over 200 [or 300] visionary-drug sessions" from 1960 to 1963.[76] In one of their first experiments they administered psilocybin to 175 healthy volunteers with an average age of around 30:

> During the course of this first naturalistic study psilocybin was administered to 175 Ss [subjects], of which 127 were men and 48 were women. The median age was 29.5 years, with 70 per cent of the Ss falling in the range 22 to 35 years. All Ss were volunteers and unpaid. ... The actual median dosage in the present study was 16 mg. of psilocybin. The total range was from four mg. to 100 mg. and the interquartile range was from 12 mg. to 20 mg.[77]

The backgrounds of these experimental subjects included alumni and postgraduates of Harvard, professors from other universities, artists and writers of the so-called beat generation, and a heterogeneous selection of other personalities: "As to occupation, Ss [subjects] included graduate students, professional writers and artists, academic psychologists, musicians, housewives and inmates of a correctional institution."[78]

---

76 Leary, High Priest, 1995, Re-Introduction, p. xxv; "Over 300 drug experiments had been conducted and there had not been one bad trip" (Leary, Timothy. Flashbacks: A Personal and Cultural History of an Era: An Autobiography. NY: G. P. Putnam's Sons, 1990 AA, *Part 1 Metamorphosis: The End of the Old*, Chapter 16 Ambushed by the Harvard Squares, Spring 1962, Harvard University, p. 125).

77 Leary, Timothy, Litwin, George H., and Ralph Metzner. "Reactions to Psilocybin Administered in a Supportive Environment," *Journal of Nervous and Mental Disease*, Volume 137, Issue 6, December 1963, Subjects, Dosage, p. 563.

78 Leary, et al., 1963, p. 563.

All survived without serious side effects and did not become addicted:

All Ss [subjects] are alive and healthy. No lasting physical effects were reported or observed. ... No psychological casualties were reported. ... There was no tendency toward addiction. ... [T]here is no evidence for physical or psychological dependence. There were no withdrawal symptoms or serious hangovers. Indeed, after one or two very profound or 'shattering' insight experiences, Ss typically tended to regard further ingestions with some ambivalence [quotation marks original].[79]

More than half of the subjects felt thoroughly enriched from the experience, and ninety percent wanted to repeat it:

[I]n the kind of setting provided, which was seen as 'supportive' by 78 per cent of Ss [subjects], the majority of the initial mushroom experiences are reported to be positive and useful. Seventy per cent reported pleasant or ecstatic experiences; 88 per cent learned something or had insights; 62 per cent reported that the experience changed their lives for the better; 90 per cent stated that they wished to repeat the experience [quotation marks original].[80]

Could this be, ultimately, a method for accomplishing psychedelic therapy?

---

[79] Leary, et al., 1963, Results, p. 563.

[80] Leary, et al., 1963, Questionnaire Results, *Main effects*, p. 564.

Figure 462. Massachusetts State Prison Warden's House, Concord Reformatory, Concord, Massachusetts. Massachusetts Historical Commission, CON. 451 [MHC-Macris.net, hereinafter, MHC].

2. The Concord Prison Experiment

In March 1961 Leary began a brave experiment that eventually involved "thirty-five convicts and fifteen Harvards"[81] at the Massachusetts Correctional Institute in Concord with the purpose of reducing recidivism through psilocybin therapy. In his very first session in the prison infirmary, Leary felt enormous fear sitting next to a "Polish embezzler," both just having taken psilocybin:

> I said to him with a weak grin, How are you doing, John? He said, I feel fine. Then he paused for a minute and asked, How are you doing, Doc? ... I said, John, I'm afraid of you. His eyes got bigger, then he began to laugh. ... Then I heard him say, Well that's funny, Doc, 'cause I'm afraid of you. We were both smiling at this point, leaning forward. Doc, he said, why are you afraid of me? I said, I'm afraid of you, John, because you're a criminal. He nodded. I said, John, why are you afraid of me? He said, I'm afraid of you, Doc, because you're a mad scientist. Then our retinas locked and I slid down into the tunnel of his eyes, and I could feel him walking around in my skull and we both began to laugh.[82]

After that first session, Leary recorded:

> We laughed in triumph. All of us, Harvardites and convicts, had passed a crucial test. We had put our faith in human nature and the drug experience on the line. A bit of pagan magic had occurred, and none of us would ever forget that brief day of grace. It was a heroic moment in our lives.[83]

---

[81] Leary, High Priest, 1995, Trip 10, And the Prisoners Will Become Priests: The Convicts Break-Out, Spring 1961, p. 206.

[82] Leary, 1995, Trip 9 The Sacrament Can Liberate the Imprisoned: The Sacred Mushrooms Go To Jail, March 1961, pp. 183, 184.

[83] Leary, Flashbacks, 1990, Chapter 11 Prisoners to Prophets, March 1961, Harvard University, p. 87.

Leary observed the hardened criminals begin to move toward love, ecstasy and generosity of soul:

> [T]he convicts ... had changed. Showed less depression, hostility, antisocial tendencies, more energy, responsibility, cooperation. The objective indices so dear to the heart of the psychologist had swung dramatically and significantly in the direction of increased mental health. ... We had kept twice as many convicts out on the street as the expected number. We had halved the crime rate.[84]

This supposed early success was put down to the enthusiasm of the experimenters and their support and understanding of the prisoners.

But although the Warden and the prison psychologist were initially supportive, those who had been paroled began to return:

> The warden laughed. He liked me and felt protective toward our hopes. Well, we're getting some of your men back. Kelly returned today in handcuffs. He was one of your men, wasn't he? Yes, Kelly had come back to the prison and so were some others returning. They had not committed new crimes. They were returning cheerfully, peacefully, quietly, not making it on the outside. Dropping-out.[85]

Leary wrote a postscript: "[W]e were reborn in the old costumes and picked up the tired games. ... The spark we had lit within each one of us was there and we guarded it, but the sun-flame had not yet burst forth."[86]

For several decades, the Concord Prison Experiment was "generally accepted to have had somewhat beneficial results" or "to have been an astonishing success."[87] However, Leary's claim of halving the crime rate was false:

---

[84] Leary, High Priest, 1995, Trip 10, pp. 194, 209.

[85] Leary, 1995, p. 209.

[86] Leary, 1995, p. 211.

[87] Doblin, Rick. "Dr. Leary's Concord Prison Experiment: A 34-Year Follow-Up

> Leary compared the recidivism rates of his experimental group after they had been out of jail an average of ten months (32%) with the recidivism rates of a base rate group (56%) who had been out of Concord Prison an average of 30 months, a fact he did not specify. ... Recidivism is, among other factors, a function of how long someone has been out of prison, with rates rising over time: more time out of prison presents more opportunities for criminal behavior and police apprehension. ... When the appropriate comparison between the experimental and control group is made for the identical period of 10 months post-release, the recidivism rate for the control group turns out to be 34.3%, compared to 32% for the experimental group. ... The 2.3% reduction is not significant and is the same as a finding of no treatment effect.[88]

Coming from one with his statistical prowess, this was an astonishing lapse in judgment. Further, Leary claimed those who returned had not committed new crimes but only technical parole violations, a distinction that is "largely meaningless since the majority of what Leary considered 'parole violations' were caused by incidents that later led to convictions for new crimes [quotation marks original]."[89]

Psychologist Ralph Metzner (1936 – 2019) who was "probably more deeply involved in the project and in the writing-up of the results than anyone besides Leary" admitted thirty-five years later that he

> fell victim to the well-known 'halo effect,' by which researchers tend to see their data in as positive a light as possible. ... In this sense, I'm grateful to have this late opportunity to acknowledge a chastening correction. ... It's an integral part of the scientific method that when mistakes are found, they are reported and corrected [quotation marks original].[90]

Study," *Journal of Psychoactive Drugs*, Volume 30, Issue 4, Oct-Dec 1998 MAP, Reported Outcome of the Original Experiment, p. 420.

[88] Doblin, 1998, Reanalysis of the Reported Short-Term Recidivism Success, p. 422.

[89] Doblin, 1998, Parole Violations or New Crimes? p. 423.

[90] Metzner, Ralph. "Reflections on the Concord Prison Project and the Follow-Up Study," *Journal of Psychoactive Drugs*, Volume 30, Issue 4, Oct-Dec 1998, pp. 427, 428.

Figure 463. The Rose Window, Marsh Chapel, Boston University. Charles J. Connick, glass artisans. Photo by Cydney Scott [bu.edu, hereinafter BUE].

Figure 464. "*Walter Norman Pahnke E Il Libro Dimenticato*," by Administrator, 8 February 2017 [viaggionel mistero.it, hereinafter VEM].

3. The Good Friday Experiment

Working under the direction of Leary, "an advanced graduate student in the Ph.D. program of the Harvard Divinity School" Walter Norman Pahnke (1931 – 1971) decided to do as his thesis dissertation a "medically supervised, double-blind, pre- and post-tested, controlled" experiment to see if the "mystic experience as described by Christian visionaries" could be brought about by psilocybin.[91] On 20 April 1962 (Good Friday), twenty seminary students from Andover-Newton Theological School assembled in the basement of Marsh Chapel at Boston University to listen to "a two-and-one-half-hour religious service which consisted of organ music, four solos, readings, prayers, and personal meditation ...."[92] As part of the experimental design, the twenty students would be divided into five small groups:

> In each group there would be four divinity students two of whom would be given psilocybin ... and the other two a placebo .... Each group would be guided by two members of our Harvard project – psychedelic veterans – one of whom would take psilocybin and one of whom would get the placebo.[93]

The study was designed to be and began as double-blind:

---

[91] Leary, High Priest, 1995, Trip 14 When Will You Be Ready to Admit You Are a Divine Messenger? The Sacrament Goes to Church, Spring 1962, p. 291.

[92] Pahnke, Walter. "Drugs and Mysticism: An Analysis of the Relationship between Psychedelic Drugs and the Mystical Consciousness," a thesis presented to the Committee on Higher Degrees in History and Philosophy of Religion, Harvard University, Cambridge, MA, June 1963 MAP, Chapter IV Experimental Design, Non-Drug Factors, p. 87.

[93] Leary, 1995, p. 304.

Double-blind technique was employed. The subjects had been told that some of them would receive psilocybin and some would be controls, but they did not know that two of the subjects in each group would receive psilocybin, nor that the other two members, as controls, would receive a control substance, nicotinic acid. They had been told that one of their two leaders would receive a small dose of psilocybin.[94]

But Leary, who participated as one of the leaders, quickly figured out who had taken the psilocybin and who had not:

It's a ridiculous ritual to run a double blind study using psychedelic drugs. After thirty minutes everyone knows what has happened, who has taken the sacrament. ... It was easy to tell who had taken the psychedelics. Ten students sat attentively like good worshipers. Facing the altar. Silent. The others were less conventional. Some lay on the benches – one lay on the floor. Some wandered around the chapel murmuring in prayer and wonderment. One chanted a hymn. One wandered to the altar and held his hands aloft. One sat at the organ bench and played weird, exciting chords. One wanted to go out.[95]

The data showed those who took the psilocybin had a "statistically significant, <u>different</u> [underlining original]"[96] experience:

[T]he participants who ate the mushrooms had mystic religious experiences and the control group didn't. The statistical results were clear cut. Our administration of the sacred mushrooms in a religious setting to people who were religiously motivated provided a scientific demonstration that spiritual ecstasy, religious revelation, and union with God were now directly accessible. Mystical experience could be produced for and by those who sought it.[97]

---

[94] Pahnke, 1963, Drug Preparation, pp. 96, 97.

[95] Leary, <u>High Priest</u>, 1995, p. 311.

[96] Pahnke, 1963, VII. General Discussion and Conclusions, Summary and Discussion of Data, p. 220.

[97] Leary, <u>Flashbacks</u>, 1990, Chapter 14 Miracle of Good Friday, p. 108.

Over a quarter century later, a "methodological critique and long-term follow-up study" of sixteen of the original twenty subjects, "nine from the control and seven from the experimental group" who retook the same questionnaire as previously, revealed that their opinions of the original experience had hardly changed:

> The average scores for the eight categories of the mystical experience and the scores for persisting positive and negative changes in attitude and behavior have changed remarkably little for either the controls or the experimentals despite the passage of between twenty-four and twenty-seven years between the two tests. The questionnaire seems to be reliable and indicates that time has not substantially altered the opinions of the subjects about their experiences.[98]

It also revealed that Pahnke had not disclosed data that should have been reported: "Pahnke failed to report the administration of the tranquilizer thorazine to one of the subjects who received psilocybin. ... In addition, Pahnke underemphasized the difficult psychological struggles experienced by most of the psilocybin subjects."[99] Indeed, the experiment in psilocybin-induced mysticism seemed to have worked too well:

> [One] subject was reported to be deeply moved by a sermon [which] ... emphasized that it was the obligation of all Christians to [proselytize]. This subject was reported to have gone outside of the chapel possibly intending to follow the exhortation. A struggle ensued when the group leaders, worried for his safety, tried to bring him back .... Pahnke tranquilized him with a shot of thorazine. He was then brought back into the chapel and remained calm for the duration of the experiment.[100]

---

[98] Doblin, Rick. "Pahnke's 'Good Friday Experiment:' A Long-Term Follow-Up and Methodological Critique," *The Journal of Transpersonal Psychology*, Volume 23, No. 1, 1991 MAP, pp. 1, 2, 11.

[99] Doblin, 1991, Discussion, p. 24.

[100] Doblin, 1991, *A Significant Omission*, pp. 23, 24.

A more recent (2006) double-blind study with two month follow up of thirty-six well educated, psychologically stable "hallucinogen-naïve" volunteers with an average age of 46 who regularly engaged in spiritual or religious activities given either methylphenidate or psilocybin confirmed the findings of Pahnke:

> [C]ompared to methylphenidate, psilocybin produced significantly greater elevations in ratings of positive attitudes, mood, social effects, and behavior; ... [R]atings of the personal meaningfulness and spiritual significance of the experience and whether the experience changed their sense of well being or life satisfaction ... were significantly higher after psilocybin than after methylphenidate. It is remarkable that 67% of the volunteers rated the experience with psilocybin to be either the single most meaningful experience of his or her life or among the top five most meaningful experiences of his or her life ....[101]

Indeed, the number who felt they had a meaningful mystical experience was even higher than reported by Pahnke, attributed in part to longer preparation and the individualized (versus group) setting with sleep mask and music, demonstrating that

> psilocybin, when administered under comfortable, structured, interpersonally supported conditions to volunteers who reported regular participation in religious or spiritual activities, occasioned experiences which had marked similarities to classic mystical experiences and which were rated by volunteers as having substantial personal meaning and spiritual significance. Furthermore, the volunteers attributed to the experience sustained positive changes in attitudes and behavior that were consistent with changes rated by friends and family.[102]

---

[101] Griffiths, R. R. et al. "Psilocybin can occasion mystical-type experiences having substantial and sustained personal meaning and spiritual significance," *Psychopharmacology*, Volume 187, No. 3, Aug 2006 AA, Abstract, *Persisting Effects Questionnaire*, pp. 268, 276.

[102] Griffiths, et al., 2006, pp. 279, 281.

Figure 465. Michael Hollingshead at his Cambridge, Massachusetts apartment, Christmas 1974. Roberts, Andy. Divine Rascal: On the Trail of LSD's Cosmic Courier, Michael Hollingshead. London: Strange Attractor Press, 2019, Chapter XI You Take the High Road, p. 190.

4. The New Sacrament

A curious chameleon-like character Michael Hollingshead (Michael John Shinkfield, 1931 – 1984) burst onto the scene in late 1961 with a sixteen ounce "mayonnaise jar full of LSD-infused [confectioner's sugar] paste."[103] At 14, due to a serious "unknown incident," he was taken out of his home (where his father, "a heavy drinker ... frequently indulged in domestic violence" against his coerced, terrified co-dependent mother) and was sent away to a school for "maladjusted boys of very high intelligence" where he learned to "deceive and outwit" his therapists.[104] After National Service in the RAF, he taught English in Denmark, wrote radio shows and travel guides, married, and had a son; when friends visited "he would often play mind games, frequently bragging about non-existent achievements and over exaggerating past exploits."[105] In 1950s London, already an alcoholic, he "discovered he had a taste for heroin and began to buy from"[106] Beat poet and author Alexander Whitelaw Robertson Trocchi (1925 – 1984).[107] Those who knew Hollingshead considered him a "no-good, two-bit English con man" and advised Leary not to have "anything to do with him."[108] Initially taken in, even genial scalywag Alfred Matthew Hubbard (1901 – 1982)[109] soon considered him

---

103 Roberts, Divine Rascal, 2019, Chapter I. Introduction, p. 9, Chapter III. An Englishman in New York, p. 38; see also AA.

104 Roberts, 2019, Chapter II. Sorrow and Dreams, pp. 19, 20, 23.

105 Roberts, 2019, pp. 26, 27.

106 Roberts, 2019, p. 28.

107 See GHDV4P2, Chapter 26 Latency, B. The Drug Abuse Industrial Complex, c. The Dope Fiend, pp. 1864 et seq.

108 Leary, High Priest, 1995, Trip 12, p. 240; Roberts, 2019, p. 51.

109 See GHDV4P2, Chapter 28 The Pagan Plot (I), B. Experimenting with Consciousness, 1. Mescaline, pp. 2052 et seq.

"thoroughly dishonest and a most convincing liar."[110] Alpert "thought Hollingshead was a sociopath ...."[111] Metzner termed what Hollingshead did, "mind fucking."[112] "[T]wenty-eight-year-old blond heiress" and "international jet-setter"[113] Peggy Mellon Hitchcock (1933 – 2024) thought him ridiculous:

> It seems to me that Michael had set himself up as a guru, dispensing LSD to the world. I found him to be ridiculous. ... He was very funny, but he was also very pretentious. He wasn't malicious, but I would never trust his judgment, as he was lacking in common sense.[114]

By late 1961 Hollingshead had "inveigled himself" into Leary's household: "With his wit, cunning and charm – all underpinned by his ability to function on high doses of LSD – Hollingshead could easily gain many people's trust and confidence, allowing him to exploit loopholes or weaknesses in their personalities."[115] In New York, he divorced, remarried, changed his name, and cold-called Leary, saying "I have been working with Professor G. E. Moore at Oxford. Mr. Moore sends his fondest greetings, by the way."[116] English philosopher and Cambridge professor George Edward Moore (1873 – 1958) had died three years earlier. At lunch at the Harvard Faculty Club, he spun an

---

110 Roberts, 2019, p. 76.

111 Roberts, 2019, p. 65.

112 Dass, Ram and Ralph Metzner. Birth of a Psychedelic Culture: Conversations about Leary, the Harvard Experiments, Millbrook and the Sixties. Santa Fe, NM: Synergetic Press, 2010 AA/AO, Part 2 First Zihuatanejo Retreat Summer 1962 to Psychedelic Training Program Summer 1963, p. 73.

113 Leary, Flashbacks, 1990, p. 126.

114 Dass and Metzner, 2010, p. 43.

115 Roberts, 2019, Chapter IV Meetings with Remarkable Men, pp. 58, 65.

116 Leary, High Priest, 1995, Trip 12, £sd-The Drop-Out Drug: The Sacrament Administered by a Divine Rascal, Fall 1961, p. 234.

erotic tale of a levitating bank clerk that left Leary "half an hour late to a Faculty meeting," his "untouched" cigarette with "an inch-long ash."[117] Three days later, while Leary was en route to the airport, Hollingshead manufactured a last minute rescue-me crisis, declaring that he was suicidal and Leary "was the only person in the world who could help him."[118] Leary lent him his car to drive to New York, pick up his new wife, and "stay on the third floor" of Leary's home.[119] Ten days later she left "because of his [Michael's] insistence that she persuade her father to cash in some savings bonds."[120] Michael insinuated himself into the house even further, playing baseball with Leary's children, and even "began to act as an '*amanuensis*,' helping Leary with his paperwork and general office duties, a role which Leary was happy for Hollingshead to take on [italics, quotation marks original]."[121] In early 1962 Leary would employ Hollingshead to "help run sessions at the Concord State Prison."[122] In May 1962 his name appears with Leary and Alpert as one of five co-authors of a scholarly reply to a fear-mongering article on the use of LSD as one of many "psychotropic" weapons: "Your brain is your own. Intelligent, open collaboration can expand your mind – with words and with drugs. Only ignorance and misinformation can allow someone else to control it – with their own words or with their drugs or with their imaginary fears."[123] In early December 1961[124] the "divine rascal" Hollingshead introduced a reluctant, recalcitrant Timothy Leary to LSD.

---

[117] Leary, 1995, Trip 12, p. 237.

[118] Leary, 1995, p. 238; Roberts, 2019, p. 50.

[119] Leary, 1995, p. 238.

[120] Leary, 1995, p. 241.

[121] Roberts, 2019, p. 56.

[122] Roberts, 2019, p. 65.

[123] Leary, Timothy, George Litwin, Michael Hollingshead, Gunther Weil, and Richard Alpert. "The Politics of the Nervous System," in *Bulletin of the Atomic Scientists: The*

The change of sacrament meant a change of *Weltanschauung*. Psilocybin had been an experience centered on warmth, laughter, spiritual communion, and love:

> The 'love' aspect of psilocybin was in part due to the relatively small doses (six to eight milligrams) that we generally used in our studies. The psilocybin experiences were reasonably mild; there were very few extreme reactions. Largely, people felt a softening and melting of their ego boundaries; they came closer together in the group. They spoke ... about the closeness they felt, the oneness, the unity of all people and all mankind. ... It was 'ego softening' [quotation marks original].[125]

Larger doses could lead to fear and a true experience of ego death and resurrection:

> We had decided to take a very high dose of psilocybin. I took 60 milligrams and George Litwin took 80 milligrams. ... Pushing the edges, trying to see what it's like. ... I was afraid, because I had taken such a large dose. I had in-built fear about what was going to happen to me. ... I felt trapped in a kind of deadly mechanical spider's web. ... I seemingly couldn't move, or think and wondered if I was dead or alive?[126]

But high doses of LSD tapped into elemental vibration:

Magazine of Science and Public Affairs, Volume 18, No. 5, May 1962 AA, pp. 26, 27.

[124] Leary, 1995, Trip 12, p. 244; or "November" (Leary, High Priest, 1995, p. 256); or Spring 1962 (Leary, Flashbacks, 1990, Chapter 16 Ambushed by the Harvard Squares, Spring 1962, p. 117); or "with Alan Watts on Easter Sunday of 1961" (Roberts, 2019, p. 58); or late fall 1961 (Hollingshead, Michael. The Man Who Turned On the World. NY: Bland & Briggs, Ltd., 1973 [psychedelic-library.org, hereinafter PSL], Chapter 1. A Lovin' Spoonful, September 1961, pp. 5, 9/139).

[125] Dass and Metzner, 2010, Part I The Harvard Psilocybin Project 1960 – 1962, George Litwin, pp. 30, 31.

[126] Dass and Metzner, 2010, RM, p. 29.

Meanwhile, my cosmic odyssey went on and on. One myth after another, lived out and traced back to the basic flash in the silent, impersonal, whirring of primal vibrations, beyond sense, beyond cell, beyond seed, beyond life. The latticework shuttling of energy patterns. All forms, all structure, man made and organic, were seen clearly in their molecular and particle nature. All structure was an illusion. Every form was a momentary stage prop for the great theater of illusion, continually changing. ... My previous psychedelic sessions with psilocybin had opened me up to the sensory levels of consciousness, pushed consciousness out to the membrane frontier, contact points of eyeball and light, ear canal and sound. Psilocybin had sucked me down into nerve nets, into the somatic organs, heart pulse, and air breath, had let me spiral down the DNA ladder of evolution to the beginning of life on this planet. But LSD was something different. [It] flipped consciousness out beyond life into the whirling dance of pure energy, where nothing existed except whirring vibrations, and each illusory form was simply a different frequency. It was the most shattering experience of my life.[127]

Five years later, Leary would write that from that moment he knew that he would leave Harvard and eventually American society:

I have never forgotten it. Nor has it been possible for me to return to the life I was leading before that session. I have never recovered from that shattering ontological confrontation. I have never been able to take myself, my mind, and the social world around me as seriously. Since that time five years ago I have been acutely aware of the fact that everything I perceive, everything within and around me is a creation of my own consciousness. ... Since that first session with Michael I was never able to commit myself to the game of Harvard or even to the game of rehabilitation. ... From the date of this session it was inevitable that we would leave Harvard, that we would leave American society, and that we would spend the rest of our lives as mutants, faithfully following the instructions of our internal blueprints, and tenderly, gently disregarding the parochial social insanities.[128]

---

[127] Leary, High Priest, 1995, Trip 12, £sd-The Drop-Out Drug: The Sacrament Administered by a Divine Rascal, Fall 1961, pp. 253.

[128] Leary, High Priest, 1995, pp. 256, 257.

Figure 466. Jack Kerouac and Allen Ginsberg. Photo by Robert Frank, 3rd Ave & East 9th St., NYC, 1964 The Allen Ginsberg Project [allenginsberg.org, hereinafter AGO].

5. Opposition

Ultimately, however, the choice to leave Harvard was no longer Leary's. It was in the hands of his academic colleagues for whom his investigations had provoked a mixture of discomfort, suspicion and fear. Like Huxley, Leary received pushback from without as well as within academia.

Beat poet Jean-Louis Lebris de Kérouac (Jack Kerouac, 1922 – 1969) remained "aloof from and critical of the drug-culture lifestyle."[129] In the fall of 1960 in a dingy New York apartment, Kerouac's first psilocybin experience hardly shook him. He

> continued to drink and rant like a sailor in a port-town bar, striding around the room, jumping on chairs, declaiming funny, poetic gibberish. ... [He] continued to shout and guffaw with alcoholic exuberance. ... Throughout the night Kerouac remained unmovably the Catholic carouser, an old-style Bohemian without a hippie bone in his body. Jack Kerouac opened the neural doors to the future, looked ahead, and didn't see his place in it. Not for him the utopian pluralist optimism of the sixties.[130]

Beat poet Irwin Allen Ginsberg (1926 – 1997) on the other hand proposed to democratize entheogens, unlacing the therapeutic corset, using psilocybin and mescaline to consummate the sexual as well as the political revolution. Ginsberg was an enthusiastic and happy tripper. During his first psilocybin experience in December 1960 he wandered into Leary's study stark naked except for his glasses, brainstorming about calling literary icons and world leaders, having had his own Marsh Chapel-like revelation:

---

[129] Leary, Flashbacks, 1990, Chapter 9 Literary Elites and Black Hope, p. 63.

[130] Leary, 1990, pp. 65, 67.

> 'I'm the Messiah. I've come down to preach love to the world. We're going to walk through the streets and teach people to stop hating.' ... 'Come on,' Allen said, 'we're going out to the city streets to tell the people about peace and love. And then we'll get lots of important leaders on a big telephone to settle all this about the Bomb once and for all.' ... '[W]e'll call Kerouac on Long Island and Kennedy and Khrushchev and Bill Burroughs in Paris and Norman Mailer' [quotation marks original].[131]

Meanwhile, Leary no doubt was thinking of next month's phone bill.

Junky poet William Seward Burroughs (1914 – 1997) hosted Leary and Ginsberg in Tangiers in August 1961. Burroughs described his first psilocybin experience as "less than beatific."[132] Leary's objective appraisal agreed:

> 'Bill, how are you doing?' I asked. 'I'm not feeling too well. I was struck by juxtaposition of purple fire mushroomed from the Pain Banks. Urgent Warning. There are many hostile territories in the cerebral hemispheres. I think I'll stay here in this shriveling envelope of larval flesh. I'm going to take some apomorphine.' He heaved but nothing came up. 'One of the nastiest cases ever processed by this department,' I said to Ginsberg, quoting Dr. Benway from *Naked Lunch* [quotation marks, capitalization, italics original].[133]

After his "first sexual experience" under the influence of psilocybin in early 1962, Leary consulted Aldous Huxley as to

> what he thought about the erotogenic nature of psychedelic drugs. His [Huxley's] immediate reaction was agitation. 'Of course this is true, Timothy, but we've stirred up enough trouble suggesting that drugs can stimulate aesthetic and religious experiences. I strongly urge you not to let the sexual cat out of the bag' [quotation marks original].[134]

---

131 Leary, 1990, Chapter 6 Politics of Ecstasy, pp. 48, 49.

132 Leary, Flashbacks, 1990, Foreword by William S. Burroughs, p. 7.

133 Leary, 1990, Chapter 13 Hostile Territories, p. 96.

134 Leary, 1990, Chapter 15 The Ultimate Aphrodisiac, Spring 1962, p. 114.

Huxley proposed instead that they remain strictly within the medical model and avoid any mention of the carnal.

But Leary dreamed of his own "Grand Plan" for consciousness expansion:

> [W]e started plotting the neurological revolution, moving beyond scientific detachment to social activism. We would no longer be psychologists collecting data. We would create data. ... The Grand Plan seemed quite logical. First we would initiate and train influential Americans in consciousness expansion. They would help us generate a wave of public opinion to support massive research programs, licensing procedures, training centers in the intelligent use of drugs. It was at this moment that we rejected Huxley's elitist perspective and adopted the American egalitarian open-to-the-public approach [capitalization original].[135]

Director McClelland called an interdepartmental meeting on 14 March 1962 "to air the grievances."[136] At the meeting one professor from a different department objected to the controversial methods of Leary and Alpert, saying they violated the academic community's values:

> [T]his work violates the values of the academic community. The whole program has an anti-intellectual atmosphere. Its emphasis is on pure experience, not on verbalizing findings. It is an attempt to reject most of what the psychologist tries to do. I'm also sorry to say that Dr. Leary and Dr. Alpert have taken a very nonchalant attitude toward these experiments – especially considering the effects these drugs might have on the subjects. I am not at all impressed by the way they are administering this project.[137]

---

[135] Leary, Flashbacks, 1990, p. 50.

[136] Leary, 1990, p. 121.

[137] Lattin, Don. *The* Harvard Psychedelic Club: *How Timothy Leary, Ram Dass, Huston Smith, and Andrew Weil Killed the Fifties and Ushered in a New Age for America*. NY: HarperCollins Publishers, 2010 AO/AA, Chapter Four Crimson Tide, p. 89, 80/239;

The result was that a "committee was formed to oversee" their work.[138] Further, "to allay bureaucratic fears" Leary and Alpert had to agree to turn over their "supply of psychedelic drugs to ... [the] director of the Harvard Medical Service" which would refuse "to release the drugs without checking with the watchdog committee."[139] Leary writes that the two researchers were still considered respectable scientists: "We had a solid phalanx of support throughout the faculty."[140]

Confidence in their professional ethics, however, declined when they supplied their own psilocybin for the Good Friday Experiment.[141] Further, they disagreed that "psilocybin and LSD were dangerous drugs that should [only] be administered by physicians in a medical setting."[142] But this was an attack against the twin institutions of both Church and Medicine at the same time, and they knew it:

> We were involved, not in a controversial research project, but in a classic religious struggle. ... The stakes of the game were no longer academic prestige or scientific renown but the souls of the protagonists. The psychedelic drugs are sacraments, and like all sacraments that work, they demand your all. They demand that you live up to the revelation. Like all sacraments, the psychedelic drugs threaten society and that part of your own mind that is attached to the current social taboos.[143]

---

see also Smith, Robert E. "Psychologists Disagree on Psilocybin Research," *The Harvard Crimson*, 15 March 1962 [thecrimson.com, hereinafter TCC].

138 Leary, Flashbacks, 1990, p. 125.

139 Leary, High Priest, 1995, pp. 306, 307.

140 Leary, 1990, p. 125; both were protégées of David McClelland, but Ram Dass years later said McClelland "didn't like Tim" while Ralph Metzner said "Tim's drug research was too radical for McClelland. He was freaked out by that" (Dass and Metzner, 2010, RD, RM, p. 84).

141 Leary, 1995, p. 308.

142 Leary, 1990, pp. 121, 122.

143 Leary, High Priest, 1995, pp. 317, 318.

Figure 467. View from Hotel Catalina Beach Resort, Zihuatanejo, Mexico. Photo 4/100 [mexicoresorts.org, hereinafter MRO].

6. Paradise Found

Social pressure pushed Leary and friends "towards the classic solutions of the new religious cult. Exile and monastic retreat. There were twenty to thirty of us who were dedicating most of our energies to the sacrament ...."[144] Since the academic situation was clearly worsening, by the spring of 1962 they decided to "avoid further confrontation ... [and] move the project to Mexico for the summer."[145] They found a small

> fishing village a hundred miles north of Acapulco called Zijuatanejo. It turned out to be idyllic. The rundown airstrip and the unpaved highway kept all but the most daring travelers away. ... The village was small and sleepy. A bumpy dirt road curved along sea cliffs, deadending at the Hotel Catalina, a complex of terraced one story cottages overlooking the magnificent deserted bay with its mile-long private beach. The stone staircases zig-zagging down to the shore were bordered by insanely colorful tropical flowers. Painted birds chirped shamelessly from lush trees. At night the stairs, the cottages, and the open-air bar/dining area were lit by strings of rainbow lights.[146]

Any cutbacks in their freedom to investigate had ceased since Leary's group no longer had to depend on the official supply of psilocybin: "Since psilocybin was becoming more and more difficult to obtain in large quantities, we used LSD ...."[147] Leary had "brought out a glass jar of LSD sugar paste which Michael Hollingshead had given me as a farewell present."[148]

---

[144] Leary, High Priest, 1995, p. 320.

[145] Leary, Flashbacks, 1990, pp. 125, 126.

[146] Leary, 1990, p. 126.

[147] Leary, 1990, p. 141.

[148] Leary, 1995, p. 322

Metzner remembers that first idyllic summer as "just a group of about twenty or twenty-five. Just experiencing."[149] Leary recalls:

> Every day there were trippers walking along the beach, body surfing, meditating, or lazing in hammocks strung along the terrace. At night the grounds were alive with color, fires burned in the sand, guitars and flutes filled the air. Small groups clustered together discussing previous voyages. We felt that we were involved in a fascinating historical event – the first research project in which experimentally induced mystical experiences were being woven into the fabric of daily work and play. We saw ourselves as pioneers developing modern versions of the traditional techniques for philosophic inquiry and personal growth.[150]

At the end of their six week retreat, Leary organized a baseball game with the local village:

> The baseball game which Tim organized, Harvard versus the Zihuatanejo home team, was definitely the grand finale of our stay. Timothy was a great fan of baseball, which was the most popular game in Zihuatanejo. We all agreed that by ending the summer with a baseball game, we would end our stay on a high note. Our Harvard team all took LSD (unbeknownst, of course, to our opponents). Our team's sense of timing was greatly enhanced, and to our dismay, we started winning. We did not want to win, of course, since our goal was to generate a feeling of good will with the town. As I remember I only played one or two innings. Almost everyone else somehow managed to play out what seemed like a very long nine innings. The home team of Zihuatanejo won, to everyone's delight.[151]

Leary remembers the game ending in a tie:

---

[149] Dass and Metzner, 2010, Part 2, First Zihuatanejo Retreat – Summer 1962, RM, p. 55.

[150] Leary, Flashbacks, 1990, p. 141.

[151] Dass and Metzner, 2010, Peggy Hitchcock, p. 57.

CH. 29 THE PAGAN PLOT (II)

The crowd went wild when the village team, in a heroic comeback, tied the score. No one was in a mood for extra innings. We all cheered, embraced, and drank beer and tequila. The party spread throughout the town. Everyone urged us to come back next year. And we planned to. The six weeks at Zihuatanejo had given us a glimpse of utopia.[152]

[152] Leary, Flashbacks, 1990, p. 143.

Figure 468. Dr. Andrew Weil [drweil.com, hereinafter DRW].

7. Paradise Lost

Back at Harvard, it soon became clear that the university was no longer interested in sponsoring psychedelic research so Leary and friends formed their own non-profit, the International Federation for Internal Freedom (IFIF) in January 1963. Its stated paradoxical purpose was

> to encourage, support and protect research on psychedelic substances and ... to take responsibility for serious studies in the area. We are fully aware that institutions, however libertarian their purpose, tend to restrict and inhibit the development of spiritual freedom. They often end in external control of internal freedom. This danger we seek to avoid. This paradoxical tension we recognize and accept.[153]

IFIF started "publishing the *Psychedelic Review* ... and sponsored the Summer Training Program in Mexico the following summer."[154]

By May 1963 Harvard had dismissed both Leary and Alpert. Leary was let go for what might be called dereliction of duty: "The official reason for my sacking was that I failed to show up for classes. A phony rap: I had completed all my course work."[155] Alpert was "ousted for something more romantic. He got caught in the middle of a love triangle involving an undergraduate editor on the Harvard *Crimson*,"[156] Andrew Thomas Weil (b. 1942), today an advocate for integrative medicine. Alpert had turned on his undergraduate lover but

---

153 Dass and Metzner, 2010, II. Organization, p. 77.

154 Dass and Metzner, 2010, RM, p. 79.

155 Leary, 1990, Chapter 20 Earthly Paradise, May 1963, p. 166.

156 Leary, 1990, p. 166.

didn't turn on Andy, and that cost me. Andy Weil wrote an article in the *Harvard Crimson*, condemning me because I was giving drugs to undergraduates. ... My claim to fame was that I was thrown out of Harvard. They always say it was because of the drugs but it wasn't only the drugs, it was also my homosexuality. Because I wouldn't have turned on those undergraduates if it wasn't for my sexual benefit, I'm sorry to say [italics original].[157]

Weil's denunciation advanced his own career but worms do turn: "I also found myself a couple years after I left Harvard in a position that seemed to me very parallel to that of Alpert's, where I became the focus of a lot of institutional paranoia and I saw that my life had gone in a kind of parallel way."[158] At that point years later, when it was Weil who was blocked from doing a drug study, he called up Alpert and said, "I'm in the same situation you were in at Harvard."[159] Said Metzner of Weil: "I've heard him say that when he was applying to do the research with psychoactives and being turned down, he was told that if he would just cast his research to the negative about psychedelics then he could get whatever funding he wanted."[160]

The second summer (1963) at Zihuatanejo was planned as "a whole program for the public."[161] Richard Alpert (Ram Dass) and Ralph Metzner reminisce about the second season nearly a half century later:

RD The second Zihuatanejo retreat we took very seriously. We were going to transfer our entire operation there.

---

[157] Dass and Metzner, 2010, pp. 87, 89.

[158] Forte, Robert. "*The Harvard Crimson Story*: An Interview with Andrew Weil," in Timothy Leary: Outside Looking In, Robert Forte, ed. Rochester, VT: Park Street Press, 1999 AA, p. 308.

[159] Dass and Metzner, 2010, RD, p. 88.

[160] Dass and Metzner, 2010, RM, p. 88.

[161] Dass and Metzner, 2010, RM, p. 55.

RM It had become clear it was not possible to offer that kind of program to the public in the United States whereas Mexico has a tradition of alternative health programs of all kinds. So, we rented the Hotel Catalina again and sent out brochures to our IFIF mailing list. ... I remember the banner headline in the *San Francisco Chronicle*, $200 for a tropical paradise, three or four guided LSD sessions included, for a month. We had more sign-ups than we could handle [italics original].[162]

Anaïs Nin begged them not to go:

I begged Leary not to go to Zihuatanejo to form a commune. I know Mexico's small towns; even Acapulco at one time was puritan Catholic. They were offended by the behavior of the tourists. Instead of seclusion in idyllic surroundings, the commune would draw attention to themselves. I was invited to go but sensed the error. Journalists followed. The village was appalled by the naked figures on the beach, by the opiumized behavior of the visitors. ... The dangers came from the Mexican puritanism and the permitting of publicity. I knew the destructive force of publicity, the inherent caricature, the malicious effect of the press. Publicity destroyed the Mexican experience. From a symbol of the liberation of the imagination, Leary became the symbol of dropping out, of disaffection from the culture, of separation from so-called American values (work, survival).[163]

Inevitably the police arrived:

The Federales were polite and friendly; two men in suits and white shirts. They told us we were being expelled because of all the bad publicity. Personally, they said they did not believe the rumors and felt we were good people. One of them even expressed interest in taking LSD. But they said we had twenty-four hours to leave: The technical reason was that we were on tourist visas and were running a business.[164]

---

162 Dass and Metzner, 2010, Part 2, Psychedelic Training Program – Summer 1963, RD, RM, pp. 92, 93.

163 Nin, 1976, Summer 1963, p. 333, Fall 1963, p. 343.

164 Dass and Metzner, 2010, RM, p. 95

Nin's diary reproduces one of the least negative press stories:

Life was lovely, casual, and open at Zihuatanejo, the disbanded LSD colony on the west coast of Mexico .... The colonists, screened from thousands of applicants, paid $200 a month for food and lodging, lived in one of several bungalows above a beautiful white beach, dotted with palm trees and cabanas. ... The LSD companions, including one member of the IFIF staff, would swallow liquid LSD and plunge into the dream world of visions, mind-expansion, self-awareness, and mystical ecstasy. ... The dosage was heavy: 100 to 500 micrograms. More than 300 micrograms is considered an overwhelming dose by most experienced pharmacologists and psychiatrists. ... Thus, enough LSD to cover the head of a pin can send one off like an Atlas rocket. As the hours wore on, the group ... would exchange visions, cry out at sudden insights of omnipotence and glory, listen to a motley collection of records. ... Even when immigration officials, embarrassed by stories of the LSD paradise in the Mexican press, moved in to close the IFIF colony on June 12, nobody was upset. ... They all left for Mexico City on Sunday, June 16, on a special DC-3 chartered by immigration officers. The Zihuatanejo experiment had begun on May 1. ... [An observing physician opined:] 'But I do not agree with them that LSD should be available to all who want it. It is a potent, potentially dangerous drug, and should be used on an experimental basis only, by qualified professional researchers' [quotation marks original].[165]

Peggy Hitchcock in September 1963 then stepped in to relocate the commune once more:

Luckily, my twin brothers, Billy and Tommy, who had just turned twenty-one, had come into considerable money. They had decided to invest in a large thousand acre property, in Millbrook, New York .... Several houses already existed on the property. One of them was a very large, turreted, rambling Victorian home ... but which had not been inhabited for sometime.[166]

---

165 Nin, 1976, pp. 334, 335, 336, citing Dusheck, George. "Paradise Lost by Mexico LSD Colony," *San Francisco News Call-Bulletin*, 2 July 1963.

166 Dass and Metzner, 2010, Peggy Hitchcock, p. 59.

Figure 469. Leary and Metzner at Millbrook.

Leary could not have asked for better:

It was a magical location, twice five miles of fertile ground with an imposing gatehouse complete with sallyport and huge portcullis. From the gatehouse a mile-long drive under rows of maple trees led to the mansion, four stories high with two towers. Gleaming white, with sixty four rooms inside, it was surrounded by elegant lawns, stables, and an ornate two-story chalet, which held a bowling alley. ... We would go low-profile and, in secluded isolation, continue our research into altered states. ... We called ourselves the Castalia Foundation, emulating the fellowship of mystic scientists in Hermann Hesse's *The Glass Bead Game* [italics original].[167]

Millbrook was a temporary refuge, a "space colony" where

[w]e saw ourselves as anthropologists from the twenty-first century inhabiting a time module set somewhere in the dark ages of the 1960s. On this space colony we were attempting to create a new paganism and a new dedication to life as art. It felt right and was, come to think of it, my boyhood dream come true.[168]

But Leary was under no illusions: "The world of conflict and political struggle seemed far removed, but trouble was lurking outside, grim, unrelenting."[169] Even though LSD and psilocybin were still legal, Leary's days as a free citizen were numbered.

---

[167] Leary, Flashbacks, 1990, Chapter 22 Life on a Grounded Space Colony, pp. 187, 188.

[168] Leary, 1990, p. 190.

[169] Leary, 1990, p. 190.

Figure 470. Konrad Lorenz with one of his grey geese. Schwarz-Weiß-Porträt [deutschlandfunk.de, hereinafter DLF].

8. Leary's Theory

One of the fundamental concepts the Austrian zoologist and ethologist (awarded the Nobel Prize in Physiology or Medicine in 1973) Konrad Zacharias Lorenz (1903 – 1989) extracted from his observations of animal behavior was that of imprinting (*Prägung*). Imprinting explains a wide range of conduct which occurs in the early stages of existence that can neither be considered volitional nor instinctive. The first moving object perceived by a Greylag gosling, for example, becomes its mother even if it does not belong to any avian species:

> [*W*]*hen a Greylag gosling is taken into human care directly after hatching* ... all of the instinctive behaviour patterns directed towards the parents are at once elicited by the human foster-parent. In fact, it is necessary to employ specific safety precautions to induce young Greylag goslings which have been *artificially* brooded in an incubator to follow a mother Greylag goose which is leading other goslings. The artificially-hatched goslings *must not be allowed full sight of a human being* between hatching and transfer to the mother goose, since otherwise the following drive will immediately become attached to human beings [italics original].[170]

Further this initial identification influences the entire range of the animal's subsequent actions and, it appears, cannot be forgotten:

---

[170] Lorenz, Konrad. Studies in Human and Animal Behaviour, Volume I, tr. Robert Martin. Cambridge, MA: Harvard University Press, 1970 AA, Companions as Factors in the Bird's Environment, III Imprinting of the object of species-specific instinctive behaviour patterns, p. 125; *Ganz anders jedoch ... Menschen eingestellt ist* (Lorenz, Konrad. *Der Kumpan in der Umwelt des Vogels: Der Artgenosse als auslösendes Moment sozialer Verhaltensweisen*. München, DE: Deutscher Taschenbuch Verlag, 1973 AA, III. Die Prägung des Objektes arteigener Triebhandlungen, p. 41).

[T]he recognition response cannot be 'forgotten'! ... The justification for such a pronouncement is based upon the fact, observed in many cases, that birds which have been hand-reared by a human being and have come to direct their conspecific [belonging to the same species] and instinctive patterns towards the human frame do not alter their behaviour in the slightest, even when kept together with conspecifics and away from human beings for many years [italics, quotation marks original].[171]

Starting from this Lorenzian concept, Leary's basic idea was that psychedelics allow one to undo the pre-determined imprinting of character automatically adopted in one's early years, making possible a different choice of attitudes and patterns of behavior: "It always works this way after a good trip. Your old reality fades a bit, and you incorporate a new reality. This identification is not metaphorical. It is neurological."[172] He called this process "re-imprinting" and noticed his subjects transferring their attraction to the guide after their psilocybin sessions:

It was almost inevitable that the guide of the session would be seen as God and lover. When the mind is suspended you project on the calm person who has turned you on, all the attributes of divinity and eternal malehood. We called this process of new attraction-repulsion *re-imprinting*. ... Allen Ginsberg has been my soul brother since his trip. In the first two months of our Harvard psychedelic research seven women followed me home much as the baby ducklings followed Conrad Lorenz and announced their love [italics original].[173]

After his first LSD trip, Leary felt the effect first-hand, re-imprinting on Michael Hollingshead:

---

171 Lorenz, 1970, p. 127; *Sie kann nämlich nicht vergessen werden! ... mit Artgenossen zusammenhält* (Lorenz, 1973, p. 43).

172 Leary, Flashbacks, 1990, Chapter 11 Prisoners to Prophets, p. 87.

173 Leary, High Priest, 1995, Trip 7 You Have to Go Out of Your Mind to Use Your Head: Arthur Koestler's High Climb, January 1961, p. 154.

After the session a new relationship with Michael developed. My LSD-charged brain portrayed Michael as an agent for some higher intelligence, a wise alien who could spin through a million realities a minute. He was some sort of a god. A raffish sad clown of a god but unmistakably divine. I watched his every move, seeking clues about the meaning of the space/time scenarios that he juggled so knowingly. I felt sheepish that I had not recognized Michael's extraordinary powers before the session and tried to make up for my neglect. This picture of Michael as a superior alien gradually diminished. The effect of the session seemed to last about seven days.[174]

Parallel with the exploration of outer space was that of the investigation of inner space, both seen as part of the human expansion of consciousness encapsulated in "Turn on, tune in, drop out," Leary's catchy, mellifluous and oft repeated slogan in the 1960s:

'Turn on' means to contact the ancient energies and wisdoms that are built into your nervous system. They provide unspeakable pleasure and revelation. 'Tune in' means to harness and communicate these new perspectives in a harmonious dance with the external world. 'Drop out' means to detach yourself from the tribal game. Current models of social adjustment – mechanized, computerized, socialized, intellectualized, televised, Sanforized [mechanically pre-shrunk, as in blue jeans, versus loom state; by extension natural, individualized, unique] – make no sense to the new LSD generation, who see clearly that American society is becoming an air-conditioned anthill. In every generation of human history, thoughtful men have turned on and dropped out of the tribal game and thus stimulated the larger society to lurch ahead [quotation marks original].[175]

Leary presented Huxley's proposals in popular, less intellectual and esoteric language, as a spontaneous rejection of an anachronistic way of life and social organization, all of which appealed mainly to the young. Only when irrationally blocked by repressive measures did this

---

[174] Leary, Flashbacks, 1990, Chapter 16 Ambushed by the Harvard Squares, p. 119.

[175] Leary, Timothy. The Politics of Ecstasy. Berkeley, CA: Ronin Publishing, 1998 AA, Chapter 7 She Comes in Colors, p. 141.

take on dramatic overtones. The goal was to avoid environmental degradation, wars of aggression, manipulation by political propaganda, submission to technology, WASP [White, Anglo-Saxon Protestant] morality and the silent poisoning of the soul with stupefying, venomous drugs, all thanks to a return to a simpler way of life and sexual liberation. The politics of ecstasy was as peacefully idyllic for its adherents as it was deliriously threatening for the Establishment. Leary ingenuously predicted victory in the short term, practically without struggle, for this new psychedelic enrichment of human life:

> It will enable each person to realize that he is not a game-playing robot put on this planet to be given a Social Security number and to be spun on the assembly line of school, college, career, insurance, funeral, good-bye. Through LSD, each human being will be taught to understand that the entire history of evolution is recorded inside his body; the challenge of the complete human life will be for each person to recapitulate and experientially explore every aspect and vicissitude of this ancient and majestic wilderness. Each person will become his own Buddha, his own Einstein, his own Galileo. Instead of relying on canned, static, dead knowledge passed on from other symbol producers, he will be using his span of 80 or so years on this planet to live out every possibility of the human, prehuman and even subhuman adventure. As more respect and time are diverted to these explorations, he will be less hung up on trivial, external pastimes. And this may be the natural solution to the problem of leisure. When all of the heavy work and mental drudgery is taken over by machines, what are we going to do with ourselves – build even bigger machines? The obvious and only answer to this peculiar dilemma is that man is going to have to explore the infinity of inner space, to discover the terror and adventure and ecstasy that lie within us all.[176]

The way to establish this new regime was a mix of pacifism and resolution, supported by the force of argument of its earliest defenders,

---

[176] Leary, 1998, Chapter 7, p. 159.

those belonging to the intellectually and economically most privileged strata of American society. As one psychologist observed in 1964:

> A major finding is that – up until now at least – LSD seems mainly to be used by professionals, intellectuals, or other middle-class people – in other words, by people who are successful, socially favored, respected, and generally conforming. The use of the drug by these people does not lead to behavior that is generally considered antisocial or immoral. If LSD use represents for them some kind of revolt, it is a quiet one.[177]

In the beginning, Leary was not proposing an aggressive reckoning but only the patient, illustrative work to achieve the small, legal modifications necessary to bring about this utopia. It was enough to restore to adults the immemorial right to self-medication of the entheogens, without fear of what would happen to the consumption of other drugs. If the State did not put obstacles in the way of consuming cannabis and other psychotropic drugs, only an insignificant minority would bother to recreationally ingest the true stupefacients. After completing (with Ralph Metzner and Richard Alpert) in 1964 an updated manual for psychonauts based on the *Bardo Thodol*,[178] Leary began to enjoy unparalleled popularity on college campuses.

The only philosopher who had then awakened comparable popular attention in the United States was the political theorist Herbert

---

177 Sanford, Nevitt. "Foreword" in Blum, Richard and Associates. Utopiates: The Use and Users of LSD 25. NY: Atherton Press, 1964 AA, p. xiii.

178 Leary, Timothy, Ralph Metzner and Richard Alpert. The Psychedelic Experience: A Manual Based on the Tibetan Book of the Dead. New Hyde Park, NY: University Books, 1971 AA; the original Tibetan title appears to be *The Great Book of Natural Liberation Through Understanding in the Between* (*Bardo thos grol chen mo*) (Thurman, Robert A. F., "Preface," in Sambhava, Padma. The Tibetan Book of the Dead, tr. Robert A. F. Thurman. NY: Bantam Books, 1994 AA, p. 17/321); see also Evans-Wentz, W. Y., tr. The Tibetan Book of the Dead. London: Oxford University Press, 1957 AO.

Figure 471. Herbert Marcuse, 1968 [britannica.com, hereinafter BRC].

Marcuse (1898 – 1979). His One-Dimensional Man (1964), despite its radical differences with the work of Leary and friends, also proposed a realizable utopia. Advanced industrial societies, wrote Marcuse, betray their own possibilities, specifically that "possibility of a qualitatively different historical practice which might destroy the existing institutional framework."[179] Instead of producing a new kind of slave unconscious of his own chains (having lost contact with his true interior critical self and thus compelled to perpetuate false necessities), such a utopian "transcendent" project, "in order to falsify the established totality" must show:

> (a) it offers the prospect of preserving and improving the productive achievements of civilization; (b) it defines the established totality in its very structure, basic tendencies, and relations; (c) its realization offers a greater chance for the pacification of existence, within the framework of institutions which offer a greater chance for the free development of human needs and faculties.[180]

Like Leary, Marcuse recognized that these false necessities "anchor" the individual to society: "The people recognize themselves in their commodities; they find their soul in their automobile, hi-fi set, split-level home, kitchen equipment."[181] Unlike Leary, Marcuse managed to clearly define the underlying political contradiction: "Freedom from the necessity of human intervention [*Eingriffs*] – this is the principle of technological rationalism. Today this is entangled in

---

[179] Marcuse, Herbert. One-Dimensional Man: Studies in the ideology of advanced industrial society. London: Routledge, 2007 AA, Part III The Chance of the Alternatives, Chapter 8 The Historical Committment of Philosophy, pp. 224, 225.

[180] Marcuse, 2007, pp. 224, 225.

[181] Marcuse, 2007, Part I One-Dimensional Society, Chapter 1 The New Forms of Control, p. 11.

the power structure [*Herrschaftsapparat*], perpetuating the very necessity whose abolition it makes possible [tr. gwr]."[182]

The growing opposition to the Vietnam War comprises the common backdrop. Like Leary, Marcuse supports forms of civil disobedience (such as burning military draft cards) based on the principle that laws and orders can only be obeyed when they are faithful to certain values:

> Over and above their legitimacy in constitutional terms, the extent to which established law and order can legitimately demand (and command) obedience and compliance largely depends (or ought to depend) on the extent to which this law and this order obey and comply with their own standards and values. ... [A]s these values are betrayed, compromised, denied in the social reality ... the existing society has become illegitimate, unlawful: it has invalidated its own law.[183]

These are the years when revolution is proposed, a revolution precisely against the technocrats. On this subject the discourses of the psychologist with a priestly vocation and those of the philosophical sociologist are almost indiscernible:

> The obvious contradiction between the liberating possibilities of the technological transformation of the world, the light and free life on the one hand and the intensification of the struggle for existence on the other, generates among the underlying population that diffused aggressiveness which, unless steered to hate and fight the alleged national enemy, hits upon any suitable target: white or black, native or foreigner, Jew or Christian, rich or poor.[184]

---

[182] *Freiheit von der ... Aufhebung sie ermöglicht* (Marcuse, Herbert. *Kultur und Gesellschaft 1*. Frankfurt am Main, DE: Suhrkamp Verlag, 1968 AA, Vorwort, p. 18).

[183] Marcuse, Herbert. An Essay on Liberation. Boston, MA: Beacon Press, 2000 AA, III. Subverting Forces – In Transition, pp. 77, 78.

[184] Marcuse, 2000, pp. 50, 51.

Although transitory, the convergence between psychedelic use and political agitation can be clearly observed in the declarations of political activist Carl Preston Oglesby Jr. (1935 – 2011), the President of one of the largest leftwing organizations, Students for a Democratic Society (SDS), from 1968 to 1969:

> The acid experience is so concrete. It draws a line right across your life – before and after LSD – in the same way you felt that your step into radical politics drew a sharp division. People talked about that, the change you go through, how fast the change could happen on an individual level and how liberating and glorious it was. Change was seen as survival, as the strategy of health. Nothing could stand for that overall sense of going through profound changes so well as the immediate, powerful and explicit transformation that you went through when you dropped acid. In the same way, bursting through the barricades redefined you as a new person. It's not necessarily that the actual content of the LSD experience contributed to politically radical or revolutionary consciousness – it was just that the experience shared the structural characteristics of political rebellion, and resonated those changes so that the two became independent prongs of an overarching transcending rebellion that took in the person and the State at the same time.[185]

In reality, Marcuse and Leary were not the only contemporaneous essayists with unforeseen points of contact. Something very analogous could be said of Marcuse and sociologist Norman Oliver Brown (1913 – 2002), the author of a notable historical essay on Puritan mentality,[186] as well as Leary and the writer and

---

[185] Lee, Martin A. and Bruce Shlain. Acid Dreams: The Complete Social History of LSD: The CIA, The Sixties, and Beyond. NY: Grove Press, 1985 AA, Chapter 5 The All-American Trip, Acid and the New Left, p. 108, citing interview with M. Lee, 24 April 1979.

[186] Brown, Norman O. Life Against Death: *The Psychoanalytical Meaning of History*, second edition. Middleton, CT: Weslayan University Press, 1985 AA, *Part Five*: Studies in Anality, Chapter XIII The Excremental Vision, pp. 194, 197; Francisca

popularizer of Eastern disciplines Alan Wilson Watts (1915 – 1973) who became a vehement enthusiast for psychedelic drugs.[187] Accused of being pernicious influences on their students, both Leary and Marcuse left their teaching posts at Harvard and Brandeis, respectively, though Marcuse found another at the University of California, San Diego (UCSD); neither ceased to be controversial.

Perujo (1934 – 2014) translated Brown's original title into Spanish as "Love and Death" to highlight the Freudian lecture (*subraya la lectura freudiana*) central to the work (see *Eros y Tánatos: El sentido psicoanalítico de la historia*. Barcelona, ES: Santa y Cole, 2007 AA, Nota del Editor); Freud speculates there is "a death instinct as well as Eros" (Freud, Sigm. Civilization and its Discontents, tr. Joan Riviere. London: Hogarth Press, 1930 AO, VI., p. 97); *Also außer dem Eros einen Todestrieb* (Freud, Sigm. *Das Unbehagen in der Kultur*. Wien, AT: Internationaler Psychoanalytischer Verlag, 1930 AO, VI., p. 92); on "the recurrent dynamic of the struggle between Eros and death instinct" see Marcuse, Herbert. Eros and Civilization: *A Philosophical Inquiry into Freud*. NY: Vintage Books, 1955 AA, Chapter 5 Philosophical Interlude, p. 97.

187 See Watts, Alan. The Joyous Cosmology: Adventures in the Chemistry of Consciousness. NY: Vintage Books, 1962 [holybooks.com, hereinafter HYB].

Figure 472. March against the Vietnam war.

Figure 473. Woodstock.

9. Leary's *Zeitgeist*

Besides opposition to its war in Vietnam, the US government faced a growing number of internal conflicts including demands for drug decriminalization, calls for black civil rights, university protests and even some very active terrorist organizations. According to a Congressional subcommittee, between January 1969 and April 1970

> the country suffered 4,330 bombings – 3,355 of them incendiary, 975 explosive – resulting in 43 deaths and $21.8 million in property damage. In addition, there were 1,175 attempted bombings and 35,129 bomb threats. And the trend has shown no sign of abating.[188]

In the US the hippie movement was in full swing. The word had been coined by a feature writer for the *San Francisco Examiner* in 1965 to describe "the aimless – the long-haired hippies."[189] Four months later, various student leaders and Ken Kesey's Pranksters convoked the first California Trips Festival. The fifteen thousand gathered there can be compared to the half million at Woodstock. The East and West Coasts routinely sprouted centers of subculture which put a spotlight on the movement. With elements of the Dionysian procession, the Children's Crusade, and the Muslim Hajj, young people from all over the country set off on their own spiritual journeys, guided

---

[188] Greene, Wade. "The Militants Who Play With Dynamite," *New York Times*, Volume CXX, No. 41,182, Sunday 25 October 1970 [nytimes.com, hereinafter NYT], Section SM, p. 20.

[189] Fallon, Michael. "Bohemia's New Haven," *San Francisco Examiner*, 7 September 1965 [blog.littlehippie.com, hereinafter BLH], p. 8, col. 3; see also Fallon, Michael. "A New Paradise for Beatniks," *San Francisco Examiner*, 5 September 1965 [newspapers.com, hereinafter NPC], p. 7.

by nothing more than Leary's vaporous mantra of "Turn on, Tune in, Drop Out."

The groups and communities who take psychedelics also call for the decriminalization of cannabis. In a few decades, cannabis passes from a drug infrequently smoked by poor immigrants to a favorite intoxicant of enlightened middle class university students: "In the relatively short period from the thirties to the sixties, marihuana use moved from the fringe or marginal members of society, the outsiders, to youthful, educated, affluent 'insiders' of the society [quotation marks original]."[190]

More than "one hundred surveys" of cannabis use were conducted between 1965 and 1971, showing large increases both in the numbers of those who had tried the drug as well as in the numbers of those who were currently using it:

> The surveys, taken together, demonstrate significant overall increases, since about 1965, in the proportion of Americans who have tried marihuana at least once and those who currently use the drug. ... The findings show that 14% of the youth (12 to 17 years of age) and 15% of the adults (18 years and over) in the national sample reported they had tried marihuana at least once .... Projecting from this nationally representative sample to the total U.S. resident population in 1970, we now estimate that 3,360,000 youth and 20,700,000 adults or a total of roughly 24 million Americans have tried (ever used) marihuana.[191]

---

190 Shafer, Raymond P., chairman. appendix marihuana: a signal of misunderstanding The Technical Papers of the First Report of the National Commission on Marihuana and Drug Abuse, Volume I. Washington, DC: U.S. Government Printing Office, 1972 AO, Part Two Social Aspects, I. Marihuana Use in American Society, p. 249.

191 Shafer, 1972, Surveys of Marihuana Use, p. 250, *The Incidence and Prevalence of Marihuana Use*, Persons Who Have Tried Marihuana, p. 251.

A slightly censored version of the 1944 LaGuardia Report[192] on cannabis use (with certain technical portions removed) was republished, becoming a popular 1966 paperback:

> [S]everal lengthy technical sections of the Report (relating to a detailed breakdown and analysis of methods and procedures employed in the study) have been eliminated. The editor has in no way, however, added to or altered any of the original wording of the text, nor have any of the findings and conclusions been omitted.[193]

Shortly thereafter many books and articles appeared defending the drug's utility. Writers of the Beat Generation, especially Allen Ginsberg, declared cannabis could enhance aesthetic appreciation:

> Marijuana is a useful catalyst for specific optical and aural aesthetic perceptions. I apprehended the structure of certain pieces of jazz and classical music in a new manner under the influence of marijuana, and these apprehensions have remained valid in years of normal consciousness.[194]

William S. Burroughs, who became celebrated relating his experiences as an opiate addict, maintained at a 1961 symposium organized by the American Psychological Society that the levels of reality evoked by marijuana and hashish were a positive aid to the development of the aesthetic experience. They were "very useful to

---

[192] See Mayor LaGuardia's Committee on Marihuana. The Marihuana Problem in the City of New York. Metuchen, NJ: Scarecrow Reprint Corporation, 1973 AO.

[193] Solomon, David, ed. The Marihuana Papers. Indianapolis, IN: The New American Library, 1966 AA, Book Three: Scientific Papers, Chapter One The Marihuana Problem in the City of New York, Mayor LaGuardia's Committee on Marihuana, pp. 278, 279.

[194] Ginsberg, Allen. "First Manifesto to End the Bringdown," in Solomon, ed., 1966, Book Two: Literary and Imaginative Papers, Chapter Seven, p. 244.

the artist, activating trains of association that would otherwise be inaccessible," adding that they and other entheogens not only supplied a key to unlock creative processes but also a roadmap to discover non-chemical methods of expanding consciousness: "It would seem to me that cannabis and the other hallucinogens provide a key to the creative process, and that a systematic study of these drugs would open the way to non-chemical methods of expanding consciousness."[195]

Editorials in prestigious medical journals advised taxing it:

> [T]he question was raised whether the marihuana problem might be abolished by removing the substance from the list of dangerous drugs ... and giving it the same social status as alcohol by legalising its import and consumption. This suggestion is worth considering. Besides the undoubted attraction of reducing, for once, the number of crimes that a member of our society can commit, and of allowing the wider spread of something that can give pleasure, a greater revenue would certainly come to the State from taxation than from fines.[196]

After comparing the strong connections between alcohol and violent crime, rape, aggravated assault and death with the nonexistent connections between cannabis and same, one pediatrician recently reiterated a popular sentiment from the 1960s when he wrote:

---

[195] Burroughs, William S. "Points of Distinction Between Sedative and Consciousness-Expanding Drugs," in Solomon, ed., 1966, Book Three, Chapter Five, pp. 445, 446.

[196] Anonymous. "Pop 'Pot,'" *The Lancet*, Volume 282 (orig. vol. 2), No. 7315, Saturday 9 November 1963 AA, p. 989.

When someone asks me whether I'd rather my children use pot or alcohol, after sifting through all the studies and all the data, I still say 'neither.' Usually, I say it more than once. But if I'm forced to make a choice, the answer is 'marijuana' [quotation marks original].[197]

Leary had become the poster child for this period of drug experimentation and rapid social change. His experiments with psilocybin and LSD had caused a number of seminary students and clerics to abandon their religious orders (while strengthening their faith) and to question the absurdity of chastity and celibacy. To persecute his apostles and defenders was exactly the same as persecuting Christian or pagan mystics, pure disguised religious intolerance, because this movement (as numerous studies had expressed in detail) was structurally identical to any other religious reform movement that had appeared throughout history, often with a leader of messianic temperament and "practices and experiences" initially seen as mystical:

---

[197] Carroll, Aaron E. "Alcohol or Marijuana? A Pediatrician Faces the Question," *The Incidental Economist* 18 March 2015 [theincidentaleconomist.com, hereinafter TIE]; Similar sentiments were reported in the 1960s as well: "The chairman of the New Jersey Narcotic Drug Study Commission in 1966 called LSD 'the greatest threat facing the country today ... more dangerous than the Vietnam war'" [quotation marks original] (Brecher, Edward M., et al. Licit and Illicit Drugs. Boston, MA: Little, Brown and Company, 1972 AA, Chapter 50 How LSD was popularized, 1962-1969, p. 369); personal recollection.

But whatever a man's temperament may be, no religion makes a full appeal to him unless it indicates some way by which he may experience what is believed to be an authentic commerce between man and the Ultimate. It is in their pursuit of the Ultimate that certain temperaments have played such a notable part in religion, especially in those practices and experiences which are labelled mystical [capitalization original].[198]

To this Leary added what had been lacking to unleash both the prohibition of and unconditional adherence to the psychedelic movement: LSD not only served to find the divine in oneself but was also the most potent aphrodisiac ever discovered. Still not content, he accused the police and the authorities of promoting the consumption of heroin and other addictive drugs by persecuting the hallucinogens. His advocacy and accusations did not go unnoticed.

Figure 474. The Fabulous Furry Freak Brothers.

[198] Spinks, G. Stevens. Psychology and Religion: An Introduction to Contemporary Views. Boston, MA: Beacon Press, 1963 AA/AO, Chapter XI Religious Experience, Experience and Temperaments, p. 158.

Figure 475. Leary and Eldridge Cleaver, Algiers Airport, October 1970. Elder, Sean. "Revisiting the Violent, Sometimes Wacky World of America's 1970s Radical Underground," *Newsweek*, 20 April 2015 [newsweek.com, hereinafter NWC].

10. The Hunt for the Hierophant

In December 1965, "after apparent denial of entry into Mexico"[199] Leary, his teenaged daughter and son, and two other passengers were detained at the International Bridge when a search of their vehicle uncovered a small amount of cannabis. Without hesitation Leary told the customs officer that he assumed responsibility for the substance. In court Leary argued his pharmacological practices were protected not only as a scientific investigator but also under the First Amendment's guarantee of religious liberty exactly like those regarding peyote in the Native American Church:

> I took the stand to defend my First Amendment right as a scientist and as an initiated Hindu to use marijuana as a research tool and a sacrament. To authenticate my stature as a drug researcher we introduced in evidence letters of support from Massachusetts prison officials. To affirm religious use of grass we produced dozens of letters from theologians, plus Exhibit C, a snapshot of Nanette and me standing in front of a legal ganja shop in Calcutta.[200]

His arguments were ignored.

In March 1966 Leary "was convicted of transporting and failing to pay a tax on less than half an ounce of marijuana by a Federal Court jury in Laredo, Texas ...."[201] He was sentenced to thirty years. Considering he was not yet 46 at the time, this was evidently life imprisonment. This excessive and unwarranted sentence by the Texas tribunal outraged a large part of American society and radicalized others.

---

199 *Leary v United States*, 395 U.S. 6 (1969) [supreme.justia.com, hereinafter SJC], p. 6

200 Leary, Flashbacks, 1990, Chapter 29 The Peat Moss Caper, p. 241.

201 Lerner, Stephen D. "Leary Gets 30 Years on Marijuana Charge," *The Harvard Crimson*, 12 March 1966 TCC.

Leary was released pending his appeal to the Supreme Court and for the next three years he took part in a number of public acts of resistance to the laws, including the massive Gathering of the Tribes, or the Human Be-In. Along with an excellent sense of humor (which he maintained intact through it all), Leary's actions almost always included moments of theosophical clowning. But at the Be-In, even

> Tim Leary, despite fears that he might be a tad too professorial, kept it short. ... And then he had paused to absorb the spectacle, those twenty thousand tripping human beings .... What could he possibly tell them that they hadn't already intuited in their first flash of LSD clairvoyance. So he had abandoned his prepared speech and after leading the crowd in 'tune in, turn on, drop out,' had sat down and spent the rest of the afternoon playing pattycake with a little girl [quotation marks original].[202]

Occupying a theoretical position midway between irony and prudence, he advocated in serious political forums great caution with the use of LSD, admitting that it was a drug that should not be freely available but should be submitted to rigorous control, like cannabis. This control should take the form, he suggested in Congressional testimony, of licenses to operate various vehicles: to use cannabis and its derivatives a driver's license should be enough, while to use LSD and other psychedelics would require a higher degree of skill, similar to that required for driving a semi or flying an airplane:

> Dr. LEARY. ... I believe that the criteria for marihuana, which is the mildest of the psychedelic drugs, should be about those which we now use to license people to drive automobiles, whereas the criteria for the licensing of LSD, a much more powerful act, should be much more strict, perhaps the criteria now used for airplane pilots would be appropriate.[203]

---

[202] Stevens, 1988, p. 260.

[203] Leary, Timothy. "Statement of Timothy Leary, LSD Experimenter, Testifying on Behalf of the Castalia Foundation of Millbrook, N.Y.," The Narcotic Rehabilitation

Some were not surprised when in 1969 the Supreme Court unanimously reversed the Texas court's decision with an acquittal that had not been seen since the 1920s: "There was general consensus that the federal marijuana law, which had been slipped through Congress in 1927 as a tax statute, would be thrown out when my case reached the Supreme Court."[204] The reversal was based upon nothing less than considering that the Marihuana Tax Act was technically unsustainable. Three decades after its passage, Justice John Marshall Harlan II (1899 – 1971), writing for the entire court, ruled that the Act demands a person declare and pay taxes on an illegal substance, thereby exposing himself "to a 'real and appreciable' risk of self-incrimination ... [quotation marks original]."[205]

This provoked understandable consternation in the American media, even considering its long history of repressive hysteria. In Leary it provoked an attack of maniacal enthusiasm, even considering his long history of drug advocacy. When he learned of his acquittal, Leary quixotically declared his candidacy for the Governor of California, "the candidate of a new party whose name was FERVOR, an acronym of Free Enterprise, Reward, Virtue and Order. Among other things, FERVOR proposed selling marijuana in state stores."[206]

But the forces of order had two spare cartridges in case the decision went against them. First, the Texas court decided to try him on other grounds and, with an unusual alacrity, sentenced him to ten

---

Act of 1966 Hearings before a Special Subcommittee of the Committee on the Judiciary United States Senate Eighty-Ninth Congress Second Session. Washington, DC: U.S. Government Printing Office, 1966 BGU, Friday, 13 May 1966, p. 241; Stevens, 1988, p. 226.

204 Leary, Flashbacks, 1990, Chapter 30 Altered States, p. 248.

205 *Leary v United States*, 395 U.S. 6 (1969) [tile.loc.gov, hereinafter TLG], Opinion of the Court, Section C, p. 16.

206 Stevens, 1988, p. 282 [Leary! Thou shouldst be living at this hour].

years in prison. Second, one year earlier a Laguna Beach police officer had found "two planted marijuana roaches and five specks of marijuana dust in Leary's coat pocket,"[207] amounting to "two half-smoked cigarettes,"[208] or "a couple of marijuana joints in the ashtray ...."[209] A number of authors dispute the amount, mention that a kilo, two pounds or even four pounds were discovered; however, it's difficult to believe that a person on bail facing thirty years in prison would be carrying a kilo of the prohibited drug when he could easily find it in small quantities for personal use almost anywhere in the country. The Superior Court judge denied bail, sentenced him to another ten years, and called Leary a "pleasure-seeking, irresponsible, Madison Avenue"[210] publicist for LSD and cannabis.

Against this, Leary argued he was the victim of gross entrapment and loudly protested at the time of the arrest that the officer "had planted the drugs."[211] With this accusation, now it was no longer a case of an unjust sentencing, but a choice to condemn the police for serious felonies (conspiracy to incriminate a citizen, making false statements, and so on) or to condemn him instead: "The jury came back with the verdict: we were all guilty of the wizard crime, possession. Then the judge pulled the shocker. I was remanded to jail

---

[207] Anonymous. "Bad Trip for Learys," *The Crimson*, TCC, 17 March 1970.

[208] Leary, Timothy. "Memorandum of the Appellant Timothy Leary" Supreme Court of the United States, 1970 [hofmann.org, hereinafter HOF].

[209] Schou, Nicolas. Orange Sunshine: The Brotherhood of Eternal Love and Its Quest to Spread Peace, Love, and Acid to the World. NY: St. Martin's Press, 2010 AA, Chapter 7 Legend of a Mind, p. 165

[210] Anonymous. "Leary Sentenced on Coast in Second Marijuana Case," *New York Times*, 17 March 1970 NYT, p. 39, col. 1.

[211] Schou, 2010, p. 165.

immediately without appeal bond – unheard of and clearly unconstitutional."[212]

His imprisonment had far reaching implications. Losing the case seemed to the leaders of the New Left, Black Liberation and student protest movements not only another surrender of constitutional liberty but also the beginning of a new witch hunt, with catastrophic consequences for both the reformist and revolutionary factions within each group. Hence, the ex-professor was converted into a martyr of a cruel inquisition by his unconditional supporters and a symbol of institutional barbarism for the protest movement generally:

> Many prominent people signed the statement of support – Steve Allen, Eric Bently, Peter Fonda, Jules Feiffer, Angier St. George Biddle Duke, Irving Kristol, Norman Mailer, Anaïs Nin, Norman Podhoretz. The Defense Fund office hummed with activities – pamphlets, mailings, phone calls, public appearances – all to raise money for my lawyers, who were fighting another team of attorneys paid for by our taxes.[213]

An influential part of the press amplified his arguments, becoming more aggressive when he was imprisoned than when he was free pending appeal.

Taking advantage of a transfer to a minimum security facility, he decided to escape, a decision that shocked some of his friends:

> It was shocking to discover, in later months, that many Americans, indeed many of my liberal friends, were offended when I took the midnight express out of prison. ... But consider my situation: I was a forty-nine-year-old man facing life in prison for encouraging people to face up to new options with courage and intelligence. The American government was being run by Richard Nixon, Spiro Agnew, John

---

[212] Leary, Flashbacks, 1990, Chapter 34 Twenty-four Steps to Freedom, p. 288.

[213] Leary, Flashbacks, 1990, p. 243.

Ehrlichman, Robert Haldeman, G. Gordon Liddy, John Mitchell, J. Edgar Hoover, and other cynical flouters of the democratic process. There was no question in my mind: it was my duty to escape. Would you have let men like these keep you in prison for life for your ideas?[214]

The extent to which he was being attacked and persecuted is mirrored in the ensuing incredible series of adventures. With generous funds donated by the Brotherhood and the help of a terrorist group, the Weathermen Underground ("the manic reckless guerrilla tribe, scourge of the FBI"[215]), Leary escapes and flees to Algeria where another public enemy Leroy Eldridge Cleaver (1935 – 1998) of the Black Panthers had also taken refuge:

The next day Eldridge introduced us to ... an attractive woman around thirty-five, who was the Panthers' liaison with the FLN, the ideological left faction of the Algerian government. After a meeting with the officials, she informed us that we would be offered political asylum.[216]

After a brief stay there (in reality, it is difficult to imagine attitudes more remote from one another than psychedelics, the Black Panthers, and the Algerian FLN), he flew to Switzerland where he briefly met with Hofmann,[217] and discovered he "had been indicted in Orange County on nineteen counts of drug dealing. I was labeled ... as the Godfather of the largest drug smuggling organization in the world, the Brotherhood of Eternal Love. My bail was set at five million dollars."[218]

---

[214] Leary, Flashbacks, 1990, p. 289.

[215] Leary, Flashbacks, 1990, p. 297.

[216] Leary, Flashbacks, 1990, Chapter 35 The Exiles, p. 303.

[217] Leary, Flashbacks, 1990, Chapter 36 Landlocked in the Alps, pp. 314, 315.

[218] Leary, Flashbacks, 1990, Chapter 37 Captured in Kabul, p. 325.

A few months later he flew to Afghanistan. While embarking at the airport in Kabul he was tricked into surrendering his passport to an Afghani official and then immediately detained by an American embassy official for lack of documentation:

In the Kabul air terminal a young woman, dressed in uniform, identified herself to us as an Afghan immigration official. She asked for our passports and disappeared with them. Then a pleasant young man from the American Embassy came over and said, 'You are being placed under arrest.' 'For what?' I said. 'Because you have no passports,' he replied, logically enough [quotation marks original].[219]

He spent the next year in the inescapable prison of Folsom, "a real fortress with high granite walls and turrets ... a stone dungeon built by Chinese labor."[220] In April 1974, he was transferred to Vacaville Prison, where he worked (*à la* Kesey) as a trusty in "a hospital for the criminally insane."[221] He was finally released, and on "or about July 4, 1976, the bicentennial anniversary of the American Revolution, I reassumed my own name and identity, Timothy Leary, autobiographer, ready to continue broadcasting."[222]

---

219 Leary, Flashbacks, 1990, Chapter 37 Captured in Kabul, p. 328.

220 Leary, Flashbacks, 1990, Chapter 38 Folsom Prison, p. 335.

221 Leary, Flashbacks, 1990, Chapter 39 Escape Plot, p. 346.

222 Leary, Flashbacks, 1990, Chapter 41 Freedom? p. 388.

Figure 476. Mary Pinchot Meyer, aboard Sequoia, 29 May 1963. Kim, Leena. "Inside the Unsolved Murder of JFK's Mistress Mary Pinchot Meyer," *Town and Country*, 25 May 2020 [townandcountrymag.com, hereinafter TAC]. Photo by Robert Knudsen, White House JFK Presidential Library and Museum, Boston, Massachusetts.

C. The Psychedelic Movement

But Huxley's cat had long since escaped the dark confines of its clinical/academic bag. Henry Luce and Timothy Leary and Michael Hollingshead would make sure of that. By the beginning of the 1960s, the wealthy and politically connected were experimenting with the then still legal psychotropics, especially LSD.

Some who took either psilocybin or LSD were characterized by their notoriety and economic opulence like Peggy Hitchcock or the "painter, socialite and feminist martyr" Mary Eno Pinchot Meyer (1920 – 1964),[223] reputedly one of the many lovers of President John

---

223 Leary, 1990, Chapter 27 Dissipative Structures, p. 224; no one has ever been convicted of her murder on the Chesapeake and Ohio Canal towpath in Georgetown (Washington, D. C.) on 12 October 1964. A staff writer for *The Washington Post* writes that the *National Enquirer* alleges (using as their "principal source" James Truitt who was paid for his story and whose financial affairs were managed by a "court-appointed conservator" from 1969 to 1972 because a physician certified he "was suffering from a mental illness that was 'such as to impair his judgment and cause him to be irresponsible'") that "President Kennedy conducted a two-year love affair with a Washington artist [Pinchot] and smoked marijuana with her in a White House bedroom" (Oberdorfer, Don. "JFK Had Affair With D.C. Artist, Smoked 'Grass,' Paper Alleges," *The Washington Post*, Issue 80, Monday 23 February 1976 AA, [proquest.com, hereinafter PQT], pp. 1, A9, Col. 1); Leary alleges that Mary Pinchot approached him to "learn how to run an LSD session" in the Spring of 1962 (Leary, Flashbacks, 1990, p. 128); Leary also alleges that around 1 December 1963 that Mary Pinchot called him "drunk or drugged or overwhelmed with grief" saying, "'They couldn't control him [JFK] any more. He was changing too fast'" (Leary, 1990, p. 194); Peter Janney alleges that his own father was part of a "conspiracy" to "terminate" her life (Janney, Peter. Mary's Mosaic: The CIA Conspiracy to Murder John F. Kennedy, Mary Pinchot Meyer, and Their Vision for World Peace. NY: Skyhorse Publishing, 2013 AA, Preface to Second Edition, p. xi); a jury found "twenty-five-year-old day laborer" Ray Crump Jr. "not guilty" of her murder (Burleigh, Nina. A Very Private Woman: The Life and Unsolved Murder of

Fitzgerald Kennedy (1917 – 1963). While visiting them in their home in Arizona, Sidney Cohen turned on the *Time, Life*, and *Fortune* magazine magnate Henry Robinson Luce (1898 – 1967) and his wife, the socialite, writer, diplomat and politician Claire Boothe Luce (1903 – 1987):

> The Luces took a 'trip' under Cohen's guidance. Clare reported an enhanced appreciation of colors in her paintings, while the tone-deaf Luce heard music so bewitching that he walked out into the cactus garden and conducted a phantom orchestra. He also discovered that ordinary objects such as tableware took on new dimensions of beauty. Although the Luces apparently repeated the experiment several times later, they were fortunate in having had no bad trips. Luce in fact was so impressed that he turned up in New York to present the managing editors of Time, Life and Fortune with copies of a book on psychedelic drugs along with an enthusiastic talk about the subject's story possibilities – a suggestion quickly adopted by Time and Life, the latter being the first 'family' magazine to cover it [quotation marks original].[224]

Presidential Mistress Mary Meyer. NY: Bantam Books, 1998 AA, pp. 15, 273).

[224] Swanberg, W. A. Luce and His Empire. NY: Charles Scribner's Sons, 1972 AA, Chapter XXXIV, 2. I'm from Oskaloosa, p. 463.

Figure 477. Cary Grant and Sophia Loren.

1. Hollywood

Great curiosity in visionary drugs is provoked among the general public when a major metropolitan newspaper reveals that the actor Archibald Alec Leach (Cary Grant, 1904 – 1986) had taken LSD more than seventy times with various psychiatrists. Grant was notoriously circumspect about his private life: "This was the star everyone in Hollywood knew *never* talked about himself, avoided the columnists and who, so the jokes ran, was 'always on, and when he isn't on he's depressed' [italics, quotation marks original]."[225]

But while filming *Operation Petticoat* in Key West, Grant made an endorsement of LSD therapy to the Hollywood correspondent for the *New York Herald Tribune*, Joe Hyams (1923 – 2008):

> 'I have been born again,' he told Hyams confidentially as they sat on the deck of the pink-painted submarine that was the heart of the picture. 'I have been through a psychiatric experience which has completely changed me. It was horrendous. I had to face things about myself which I never admitted, which I didn't know were there. Now I know that I hurt every woman I ever loved. I was an utter fake, a self-opinionated bore, a know-all who knew very little' [quotation marks original].[226]

This caused a sensation in the film colony. Shortly thereafter there was more experimentation with LSD in Hollywood than in any other part of the country. LSD received "its first major burst of publicity" in Hollywood, in part due to the story by Hyams:

---

[225] Wansell, Geoffrey. The Haunted Idol: The Story of the Real Cary Grant. NY: Quill, William Morrow, 1983 AA, Part Three The Haunted Star, Chapter 11, p. 245.
[226] Wansell, 1983, p. 245.

After my series came out, the phone began to ring wildly. Friends wanted to know where they could get the drug. Psychiatrists called, complaining their patients were now begging them for LSD. Every actor in town under analysis wanted it. In all, I got close to eight hundred letters.[227]

Enthusiasts gathered together to take the new drug, holding

far-into-the-night parties at which the guests might include Aldous and Laura Huxley, Marlon Brando, John Saxon, Lew Ayers, Anais Nin, Zen master Joshu Sasaki, and a fascinating cast – this is Hollywood – of psychiatrists, physicians, artists, writers, dancers, and hippies who, in this context, somehow managed not to bore each other.[228]

By 1963 small communities begin to appear in New York, Boston, San Francisco and Los Angeles where LSD is consumed in a manner similar to how peyote is consumed in the Native American Church, although those partaking of the communion are not necessarily indigenous:

In New York the drug is bartered freely in Greenwich Village coffeehouses. In Boston, communal homes have been established where LSD communicants can share insights gained through better living with chemistry. In San Francisco black marketeers ply a busy trade smuggling the drug in from Canada, while in Los Angeles drug cultists gather to plan for the idyllic day when there will be LSD therapists (similar to the ones now working in Europe) with cubicle-lined offices filled with happily hallucinating patients. Like winter colds and Asian flu, LSD is sweeping the nation, and its eager exponents assure us it will soon be as much a part of the American culture and diet as Mom's apple pie.[229]

---

227 Gaines, Bob. "LSD: Hollywood's Status-Symbol Drug," *Cosmopolitan*, Volume 155, Issue 5, November 1963 [fr.annas-archive.org, hereinafter FRA], p. 78.

228 Watts, Alan. In My Own Way: an autobiography, 1915 – 1965. Novato, CA: New World Library, 1972 AA, Chapter 13 Breakthrough, pp. 298, 299.

229 Gaines, 1963, Hollywood Had It First, pp. 78, 79.

Figure 478. Ken Kesey. Tanner, Stephen L. Ken Kesey. Boston, MA: Twayne Publishers, 1983, frontispiece.

2. Kesey

But as decisive or more for the psychedelic movement must be considered the activities of Kenneth Elton Kesey (Ken, 1935 – 2001), who discovered LSD almost by accident. While in the creative writing program at Stanford, he "volunteered for drug experiments being conducted at the Veterans' Hospital in Menlo Park [California],"[230] unaware it was secretly being underwritten by the CIA's MK-ULTRA program:

> [U]p there at the top of the LSD distribution system could be found the men of MKULTRA. ... From 1959 on, Dr. Leo Hollister was testing LSD at that same hospital. ... Thus, hoping to improve on CIA and military-funded work, Hollister tried drugs out on student volunteers, including a certain Ken Kesey, in 1960.[231]

There, Kesey was offered "small cash stipends (under $100)"[232] to be a lab rat (guinea pig), ingesting (amid the placebos and the ferocious pharmaceuticals like Ditran) "a number of hallucinatory drugs"[233] which expanded his perspective of the world: "I was taking mescaline and LSD. It gave me a different perspective on the people in the mental hospital, a sense that maybe they were not so crazy or as bad as the sterile environment they were living in."[234] In the words of

---

230 Tanner, Ken Kesey, 1983, *Chapter One* From Oregon to California, p. 14;

231 Marks, John. The Search for the 'Manchurian Candidate:' The CIA and Mind Control. NY: Times Books, 1979 AA, Part II Intelligence or 'Witches Potions,' Chapter 7 Mushrooms to Counterculture, p. 120.

232 Perry, Paul. On the Bus: The Complete Guide to the Legendary Trip of Ken Kesey and the Merry Pranksters and the Birth of the Counterculture. NY: Thunder's Mouth Press, 1990 AA, Part I: Origins, Drug Experiments Lead to the Writing of Cuckoo's Nest, p. 11.

233 Tanner, 1983, p. 14.

234 Faggen, Robert. "The Art of Fiction CXXXVI: Ken Kesey," *The Paris Review*,

his pop biographer, the novelist Thomas Kennerly Wolfe, Jr. (Tom, 1931 – 2018), it wasn't the "White Smocks" but the young writing student who had discovered something secret:

> It was quite a little secret to have stumbled onto, a hulking supersecret, in fact – the triumph of the guinea pigs! In a short time he ... had tried the whole range of the drugs, LSD, psilocybin, mescaline, peyote, IT-290 the superamphetamine, Ditran the bummer, morning-glory seeds. They were onto a discovery that the Menlo Park clinicians themselves never – mighty fine irony here: the White Smocks were supposedly using *them.* Instead the White Smocks had handed them the very key itself. *And you don't even know, bub ... with these drugs your perception is altered enough that you find yourself looking out of completely strange eyeholes. All of us have a great deal of our minds locked shut. We're shut off from our own world. And these drugs seem to be the key to open these locked doors* [italics, capitalization original].[235]

He then took a job as the "night attendant on the psychiatric unit"[236] investigating everything available inside and outside the hospital to get an in depth look at the available psychiatric resources. He even "arranged to be given a clandestine electroshock therapy (EST) in order to write about that experience."[237] He collected all these impressions together in his first "brilliant ... boisterous, ribald ... powerful ... unforgettable ... impressive" novel.[238]

Volume 36, No. 130, Spring 1994 AA, p. 71.

[235] Wolfe, Tom. The Electric Kool-Aid Acid Test. NY: Bantam Books, 1969 AA, Chapter IV What Do You Think of My Buddha? pp. 39, 40; Wolfe, 2008 AO, p. 45; Wolfe, 1999 [voidnetwork.gr, hereinafter VOI], p. 73/669.

[236] Leeds, Barry H. Ken Kesey. NY: Frederick Ungar Publishing Co., 1981 AA, 1. Biography: The Hallucinogenic Outlaw, p. 2.

[237] Leeds, 1981, p. 3.

[238] Kesey, Ken. One Flew Over the Cuckoo's Nest. NY: Signet Books, 1962 AA, cover blurbs from *Time*, *Library Journal*, *Life*, the *N. Y. Herald Tribune*, and the *San Francisco Examiner.*

Figure 479. Jack Nicholson in *One Flew Over the Cuckoo's Nest.*

The book turned out to be a revolutionary parable, where the epic tone and meticulous attention to detail articulated the themes of the countercultural protests of the 1960s. Kesey's main character is Randle McMurphy and it's difficult to write a better description of the character and summary of the book than Wolfe:

He is a big healthy animal, but he decides to fake insanity in order to get out of a short jail stretch he is serving on a work farm and into what he figures will be the soft life of a state mental hospital. He comes onto the ward with his tight reddish-blond curls tumbling out from under his cap, cracking jokes and trying to get some action going among these deadasses in the loony bin. They can't resist the guy. They suddenly want to *do* things. The tyrant who runs the place, Big Nurse, hates him for weakening ... Control, and the System. By and by, many of the men resent him for forcing them to struggle to act like men again. Finally, Big Nurse is driven to play her trump card and finish off McMurphy by having him lobotomized. But this crucifixion inspires an Indian patient, a schizoid called Chief Broom, to rise up and break out of the hospital and go sane: namely, run like hell for open country [italics, capitalization original].[239]

The first several passages were written under the influence of peyote but only pencils write novels:

[P]sychedelics are only keys to worlds that are already there. The images are not there in the white crystals in the gelatin capsule. Drugs don't create characters or stories any more than pencils do. They are merely instruments that help get them on the page. ... It's impossible for me to write on LSD .... I did write the first several pages of *Cuckoo's Nest* on peyote, and I changed very little of it. It had little effect on the plot, but the mood and particularly the voice in those first few pages remained throughout the book [italics original].[240]

---

[239] Wolfe, 1969, pp. 43, 44.

[240] Faggen, 1994, p. 71.

The publication in February 1962 "made his literary reputation immediately."[241] The novel was acclaimed by critics, became a New York stage play and was made into an award-winning film.

His second novel published in 1964, "in the fullest sense a work of the new consciousness,"[242] some critics considered a masterpiece while others received it coldly and criticized its immoderation, as if the author was on something, which he was: "There were also some sections of *Sometimes a Great Notion* written when I was taking mushrooms. Again, the effect is more on mood and voice than on vision. But for the most part, I don't write under the influence of LSD or other drugs [italics original]."[243]

Otherwise, the second book (which also became a film) resounded with the themes of the previous: individualism, a return to nature espoused by the Greeks and Nietzsche, the essential radical American writers (Jefferson, Whitman, Thoreau), and the rejection of the dehumanization imposed by State control:

> It was about the head of a logging clan, Hank Stamper, who defies a labor union and thereby the whole community he lives in by continuing his logging operation through a strike. It was an unusual book. It was a novel in which the strikers are the villains and the strikebreaker is the hero. The style was experimental and sometimes difficult. And the main source of 'mythic' reference was not Sophocles or even Sir James Frazer but ... yes, Captain Marvel [quotation marks original].[244]

But the conflict in the second novel was no longer about administrative health versus real health, but a tale of a family of

---

[241] Wolfe, 1969, pp. 44, 45

[242] Kesey, Ken. Sometimes a Great Notion. NY: Bantam Books, 1972 (1964) AA, cover blurb by Charles A. Reich.

[243] Faggen, 1994, p. 71.

[244] Wolfe, 1969, pp. 45, 46.

lumberjacks fighting alone to fulfill a contract against a local lumber union. Instead of the fashionable conflict between left and right, tradition and progress, the dilemma was to keep one's word or to join an organization maintained by coercively selling others security.

By then Kesey had become the self-described "Non-navigator" of a small company of self-described "freaks" known as the Merry Pranksters after he bought a "1939 International Harvester school bus" already rigged out with "bunks and benches and a refrigerator and a sink for washing dishes and cabinets and shelves and a lot of other nice features for living on the road. Kesey bought it for $1,500 – in the name of Intrepid Trips, Inc."[245] The plan was for fifteen men and women to take both a chemical and a geographical excursion together across the country. Among them was the writer Neal Leon Cassady (1926 – 1968), who Kerouac had mythologized as the beatnik Dean Moriarity ("the perfect guy for the road because he actually was born on the road"),[246] and who acted as elder and driver:

> KESEY Cassady was an elder to me and the other Pranksters, and we knew it. He was literally and figuratively behind the wheel of our bus, driving it the way Charlie Parker worked the saxophone. When he was driving he was improvising an endless monologue about what he was seeing and thinking, what we were seeing and thinking and what we had seen, thought and remembered. Proust was his literary hero, and he would quote long passages from Proust and Melville from memory, lacing his revelations with passages from the Bible. He was a great teacher, and we all knew it and were affected by him.[247]

Cassady also observed Homeric features in their Non-navigator.

---

[245] Wolfe, 1969, Chapter VI The Bus, pp. 60, 65.

[246] Kerouac, Jack. On the Road. NY: The Viking Press, Inc., 1957 AA, Part One, 1, p. 5.

[247] Faggen, 1994, p. 67.

Figure 480. Furthur.

Soon the vehicle was painted in primary colors, outfitted with an open-air attic and filled with layers of fluorescent mandalas, disguises, masks, magnetic tapes, speakers, microphones, musical instruments and semen-stained mattresses, while its inhabitants filmed tens of thousands of feet of a movie that proved almost impossible to edit.[248] Outside, the bus had a "destination sign in the front" that read: "'Furthur,' with two *u*'s ... [with] a sign in the back saying 'Caution: Weird Load' [italics, capitalization original]."[249] Inside, it had "ten or fifteen American flags walking around" which were the Pranksters decked out "in white coveralls of the sort airport workers wear, only with sections of American flags sewn all over, mostly the stars against fields of blue but some with stripes running down the legs"[250] as if they felt they needed to advertise their patriotism.

On 14 June 1964[251] the beat-up rattletrap of a bus began its epic journey from California to New York, making great detours and provoking by turns admiration and resentment. The bus did not omit a scandalous stop at Millbrook: "Ginsberg and Alpert were part of IFIF, the International Federation for Internal Freedom. ... Our group on the bus was known as ISIS, the Intrepid Search for Inner Space."[252] Leary and friends were attempting the same "fantastic experiment in human consciousness" but in a different manner, with transcendental meditation and macrobiotics, all of which seemed hilarious to the mischievous Pranksters:

---

248 See for example: *Intrepid Traveller and His Merry Band of Pranksters Look for a Cool Place: A Work in Progress by Ken Kesey, Episode One A Journey to the East* [youtube.com, hereinafter YT], Kesey Intrepid Traveller-1.

249 Wolfe, 1969, pp. 61, 63; Wierd Load was in front, and sometimes the front sign was spelled Further (see Magic Trip 2011 YT).

250 Wolfe, 1969, Chapter I Black Shiny FBI Shoes, p. 11.

251 Perry, 1990, Part II: The Trip, p. 43.

252 Faggen, 1994, p. 68.

The Pranksters thought of themselves and Leary's group as two extraordinary arcane societies, and the only ones in the world ... [T]he Learyites ... are friendly, but ... there is a general ... *vibration* ... of: We have something rather deep and meditative going here, and you California crazies are a sour note. ... Where was Leary? ... Well, word came down that Leary was upstairs in the mansion engaged in a very serious experiment, a three-day trip, and could not be disturbed. Kesey wasn't angry, but he was very disappointed, even hurt. It was unbelievable – this was Millbrook, one big piece of uptight constipation, after all this [italics original].[253]

First impressions and bad timing did not help:

RAM DASS: There was no forewarning whatsoever that the Pranksters were going to show up at Millbrook. ... The night before ... [w]e had all done acid and it turned out to be a very intense and profound trip. We sat by the fire, all of us huddled together. There was a lot of intimacy and profundity and it was a very deep trip that had gone on all night long. By seven or eight in the morning, everybody was in a mellow, delicate, vulnerable space and drifting off to bed for the day. It was at this very moment that the bus drove up. ...
RON BEVIRT: So we rolled in there, and set off a green smoke grenade that blew green smoke right through the open windows into their house. And their house was kind of enveloped in green smoke. It was like the Huns coming to visit Camelot. ...
BABA RAM DASS: ... They caught us about twelve hours too late; it was nothing more than that. If they had come the night before, it would have been an entirely different story for all of us for the rest of our lives. But that's the way it is. I live in a world where there is no error, so that is what was meant to happen.[254]

Afterwards, Leary went straight to bed:

---

[253] Wolfe, 1969, Chapter IX The Crypt Trip, pp. 93, 94, 95; Owsley encountered "a similarly lukewarm reception" (Greenfield, Robert. Bear: The Life and Times of Augustus Owsley Stanley III. NY: St. Martin's Press, 2016 AA, Chapter 10 Print the Legend, p. 88).

[254] Perry, 1990, Part II: The Trip, pp. 93, 101, 102.

TIMOTHY LEARY: I had just fallen in love with a woman who later became my wife, so, needless to say, that was number one on my consciousness. Not only was I lovesick, but I had also come down with a heavy flu. So I went right to my room and went to bed. ... I didn't know this was history being made, a meeting of the acid tribes.[255]

At Millbrook, Leary's group was exploring classical mysticism, derived from Huxley's syncretic perennial philosophy:

PHILOSOPHIA PERENNIS ... the metaphysic that recognizes a divine Reality substantial to the world of things and lives and minds; the psychology that finds in the soul something similar to, or even identical with, divine Reality; the ethic that places man's final end in the knowledge of the immanent and transcendent Ground of all being – the thing is immemorial and universal. Rudiments of the Perennial Philosophy may be found among the traditionary lore of primitive peoples in every region of the world, and in its fully developed forms it has a place in every one of the higher religions [capitalization original].[256]

At La Honda (Kesey's new California home), the Pranksters were instead following characters from *Captain Marvel* and *Captain America* comic books as well as science fiction novels like those by the American aeronautical engineer Robert Anson Heinlein (1907 – 1988), English futurist Sir Arthur Charles Clarke (1917 – 2008), American author and critic Edward Hamilton Waldo (Theodore Sturgeon, 1918 – 1985), and American saga narrator Franklin Patrick Herbert, Jr. (Frank, 1920 – 1986).[257] The fictional shamanism of American

---

[255] Perry, 1990, pp. 96, 97.

[256] Huxley, Aldous. The Perennial Philosophy. London: Chatto & Windus, 1947 AO, Introduction, p. 1.

[257] See Stranger in a Strange Land. NY: Ace Books, 1961 AA, [avalonlibrary.net, hereinafter ALN]; Childhood's End. NY: Harcourt, Brace & World, Inc., 1953 AA; More Than Human. NY: Farrar, Straus and Giroux, Inc., 1953 AA; and, Dune.

anthropologist Carlos César Salvador Arana (Castaneda, 1925 – 1998)[258] rounded out their intellectual, mystical universe, not unlike the inventory of a 1960s alternative bookstore in San Francisco's Haight-Ashbury district:

Another thought that would have struck a visitor to the Psych Shop in early 1966 was how esoteric most of the reading was. Among the fiction, Herman Hesse was the obvious best seller – sales of *A Journey to the East*, *Steppenwolf*, and *Siddhartha* would make Hesse the largest-selling German author in America by the end of the Sixties – closely followed by the science fiction novels (*Stranger in a Strange Land*, *Childhood's End*, etc.) that the Pranksters had found so illuminating. Balancing the fiction was a section of technical works on the psychedelic experience, Leary, Huxley, Watts, plus a variety of Eastern and occult texts, ranging from the *Tibetan Book of the Dead* to the *Zohar*. Aldous Huxley would have been overjoyed at this intermingling of East and West, but he might have been a trifle disturbed at the amount of occult chaff that was getting mixed in with the grains of perennial philosophy. Although Huxley had predicted that LSD would awaken the Baby Boom's slumbering appetite for spiritual meaning, he hadn't anticipated what would happen once this hunger began searching for something to feed upon … in the Haight, the perennial philosophy came heavily spiced with astrology, numerology, alchemy, black magic, voodoo; a crazy quilt of arcane practice and contemporary jargon that affronted the trained Western intellect's need to formalize, to abstract out a workable map from anarchic reality [italics, capitalization original].[259]

Both Alpert and Leary say they learned much from that single meeting with the Pranksters:

Philadelphia, PA: Chilton Book Company, 1965 AA, respectively.

[258] See to begin, The Teachings of Don Juan: A Yaqui Way of Knowledge. Berkeley, CA: University of California Press, 1968 AA.

[259] Stevens, 1988, p. 239.

RAM DASS: There were great philosophical differences between us and the Pranksters, even though both groups were searching for something. I think that the Pranksters, at that time, were making more of a social-political statement than we were. Millbrook was primarily a research-oriented space that was trying to understand human consciousness.
TIMOTHY LEARY: ... The genius of the tribal system is that each one has its own totem and its own gods. ... We learned from their tribal nature. A sense of humor ran through everything that the Kesey people did. They had a rollicking, good-natured, hit-the-road quality that we needed. We learned from that.[260]

When the Pranksters returned to La Honda, California in August 1964, the pagan festivals known as the Acid Tests were spontaneously born, with light shows, the bus movie, LSD and music by the Grateful Dead[261] specifically tailored for the events:

For the members of the Grateful Dead, it was first of all an opportunity to play the way they wanted. 'We knew we had something,' [six-string bass guitarist Phil] Lesh said later, 'but we didn't know how deep it was. We directed and focused it through these parties' [quotation marks original].[262]

By the second Acid Test, the events had a slogan:

The second Acid Test happened on December 4, 1965, in San Jose, on the night of a Rolling Stones concert. At the concert, the Pranksters passed out crayon-lettered handbills for a house party. Their cryptic message was a street address and the words: 'Can YOU Pass the Acid Test?' ... [T]he Grateful Dead played until the police broke up the party [quotation marks, capitalization original].[263]

---

260 Perry, 1990, pp. 97, 102.

261 Perry, 1990, Part III: The Acid Tests – And Beyond, pp. 109, 114, 115.

262 McNally, Dennis. A Long Strange Trip: The Inside History of the Grateful Dead. NY: Broadway Books, 2002 AA, Chapter 10 The Bus Came By (11/13/65 – 25/66), p. 112.

263 Perry, 1990, p. 115.

Figure 481. The Grateful Dead. *Billboard*, 5 December 1970, BGU, p. 9.

Figure 482. Poster announcing a 1966 event in Los Angeles (Hollywood), with admissions from one to two dollars.

Like Leary would be nine months later, Kesey was arrested and imprisoned for marijuana possession at a time before LSD was prohibited: "In April 1965, Kesey was arrested for possession of marijuana. In the ensuing year of appeals and court appearances, the Pranksters continued and escalated their manic escapades and use of hallucinogenic drugs."[264]

One such escapade was the equivalent of the experiment made by Leary with prisoners and psilocybin. A weekend of fraternization between the freaks and the Hell's Angels began on 7 October 1965. Employing a drug unknown to their violent guests (whose normal pharmacological menu was alcohol and amphetamines), the celebration held obvious risks for the hosts. However, the experiment produced results as unexpected for them as it had been for Leary's prisoners.

Tom Wolfe: "The beer made the Angels very happy and the LSD made them strangely peaceful and sometimes catatonic, in contrast to the Pranksters and other intellectuals around, who soared on the stuff."[265] Hunter S. Thompson (1937 – 2005):

> Contrary to all expectations, most of the Angels became oddly peaceful on acid. With a few exceptions, it made them much easier to get along with. The acid dissolved many of their conditioned reflexes. There was little of the sullen craftiness or the readiness to fight that usually pervades their attitude toward strangers. The aggressiveness went out of them; they lost the bristling, suspicious quality of wild animals sensing a snare. It was a strange thing, and I still don't quite understand it ....[266]

---

264 Leeds, 1981, p. 6.

265 Wolfe, 1969, p. 153.

266 Thompson, Hunter S. Hell's Angels: A Strange and Terrible Saga. NY: Random House, 1967 AO, Chapter 21 The Dope Cabala and the Wall of Fire, p. 142/169.

Who were not so peaceful were the neighbors from the nearest town, who would have launched an attack with pitchforks and torches had it not been that the place was already surrounded by police cars:

> As it happened, nine marijuana charges against the Kesey menagerie were dropped on Friday; this was duly noted in the Saturday papers, which appeared in La Honda just about the time Kesey was posting a sign on his gate saying: THE MERRY PRANKSTERS WELCOME THE HELL'S ANGELS. The sign, in red, white and blue, was fifteen feet long and three feet high. It had a bad effect on the neighbors. When I got there, in the middle of the afternoon, five San Mateo County sheriffs' cars were parked on the highway in front of Kesey's property. About ten Angels had already arrived and were safely inside the gate; twenty others were said to be en route. The pot was boiling nicely. I had brought my wife and small son along, and we wanted to go down to the beach for a short meal before joining the festivities. Several miles down the road I stopped at the general store in San Gregorio, a crossroads community with no real population but which serves as a center for the surrounding farms. The store was quiet back around the tool, produce and harness sections, but up front at the bar, things were loud and edgy. The folks were not happy about the goings-on up the road. 'That goddamn dope addict,' said a middle-aged farmer. 'First it's marywanna, now it's Hell's Angels. Christ alive, he's just pushin our faces in the dirt!' 'Beatniks!' said somebody else. 'Not worth a pound of piss.' There was talk of divvying up the ax handles in the store and 'goin up there to clean the place out.' But somebody said the cops were already on the job: 'Gonna put em in jail for good this time, every damn one of em ....' So the ax handles stayed in the rack [capitalization, quotation marks original].[267]

Before the stupefied eyes of the constabulary, hundreds of half-naked and outlandishly dressed people danced and showed open affection to one another, while stroboscopic lights and loudspeakers mounted in trees covered in fluorescent paint beat time to rock music and bizarre speeches. It prefigured the disco era, except that it was explosively libertarian and free. Law enforcement had to limit

---

[267] Thompson, 1995, p. 138/169.

themselves to observation, while demanding driver's licenses and registration from the unheard of bestiary that kept arriving from the highway.

After more arrests for possession of cannabis, Kesey took advantage of provisional liberty to flee to Mexico:

> On January 17, 1966, a judge found Kesey guilty of the April 1965 charge of possession of narcotics. Two days later, while awaiting appeal, he was again arrested for possession .... Facing a probable five-year jail sentence, Kesey fled to Mexico and remained a fugitive for the better part of 1966.[268]

At the end of the year he was back in jail:

> Kesey's nine-month flight to avoid prosecution was a comedy of errors. ... Word of his exile in Puerto Vallarta leaked, and he fled in disguise to Mazatlan .... After several close calls, notably an episode in which he escaped from Mexican Federales by jumping aboard a passing freight train, Kesey secretly reentered the United States in late September 1966, posing as a drunken cowboy singer riding a horse. ... In October, he was captured on a freeway and arrested by the FBI.[269]

In the face of furious judges and the kind of chaotic, progressively corrupt Eleusis which California had become, Kesey copped a plea. Kesey's lawyers argued for leniency because, as they told the judge, he had returned voluntarily to tell his followers to go beyond that "pestilent habit of taking LSD" due to his having seen the light, a vision,

---

[268] Leeds, 1981, p. 7.

[269] Leeds, 1981, pp. 8, 9.

a certain vision Mr. Kesey has had, of 'beyond acid,' an inspiration, a miracle, a light he has seen .... Mr. Kesey has a very public-spirited plan .... He has returned voluntarily from exile in his safe harbor, to risk certain arrest and imprisonment, in order to call a mass meeting of all LSD takers, past, present and potential, for the purpose of telling them to move beyond this pestilent habit of taking LSD ... [quotation marks original].[270]

Indeed, Kesey suggested at the disjointed, sparsely attended Acid Test Graduation held on Halloween, 31 October 1966 that he had taken the road to discover interior truth, no longer needing chemical support, having used it only to cross over the lines of understanding and routine existence:

Kesey spoke calmly and subtly about his experiences with drugs. He said LSD was innocense [sic] – a garden of eden – but it was only a door that you go through enter a room stay a while and leave through the same door – at this point some cops came into the garage to have a look.[271]

Few believed in his sincerity and few agreed to follow his advice:

Ken Kesey returns from Mexico as if from the dead ... and then he is caught and jailed and released and the Federal prosecutor drops the charges against him though he faces two other convictions. The rumours start flying ... is Kesey copping out? ... Does he want to create a big freak out, a big bummer? Does he want to make a bundle of bread and ship the pranksters, himself and his bus to Europe or pay off the cops or beat the rap?[272]

---

[270] Wolfe, 1969, Chapter XXVII The Graduation, p. 332.

[271] Anonymous writer. "Ken Kesey and the Great Pumpkin," *The San Francisco Oracle*, Number 3, Ken Kesey's Graduation Party, November 1966 in Cohen, Allen, ed. The San Francisco Oracle Facsimile Edition: The Psychedelic Newspaper of the Haight-Ashbury 1966-1968. Berkeley, CA: Regent Press, 1991 AA, col. 3, p. 3/47.

[272] Anonymous, 1991, col. 1, p. 3/47.

Whether heartfelt or not, his tale of a road to Damascus awakening worked to his legal advantage:

> After two trials ended in hung juries, Kesey pleaded *nolo contendere* to a lesser charge ('knowingly being in a place where marijuana was kept'), dropped his appeal for the original charge of possession, and in June 1967 began to serve both sentences concurrently .... Released in November 1967, he moved with his family to Pleasant Hill, Oregon ... [italics, quotation marks original].[273]

If Leary saw LSD as a sacrament within a salvationist cult, Kesey started profane festivals where the drug was taken for its own sake, to experience the joy of the moment, life being actively lived.[274] Along with their extraordinary abilities to manage people, perhaps the main point of contact between them was a common rejection of the pure logic of dominion generically termed the System. Otherwise, it is their disparities that shine through. Leary exhibited elements of messianism, with an oscillation from academy to temple, while Kesey rejected the pedantic as much as the salvific. Hence, he did not sacralize any drug, for even those most useful for counterpunching were only transitorially useful, appropriate for pole-vaulting over one's own passive learning.

What remains of his legacy is the ideal of the holy counterpunch, the rejection of the Big Nurse (minion of the Combine), and the different sensory, temporal, historical, social, psychological and emotional time lags (brainwashing) which needed to be overcome:

---

[273] Leeds, 1981, p. 9.

[274] See for example Mariano Antolin Rato. "*Los psiquedelicos reconsiderados*," *El Viejo topo*, No. 29, 1 Feb 1979, pp. 44-53.

A person has all sorts of lags built into him, Kesey is saying. One, the most basic, is the sensory lag, the lag between the time your senses receive something and you are able to react. One-thirtieth of a second is the time it takes, if you're the most alert person alive, and most people are a lot slower than that. ... We are all of us doomed to spend our lives watching a *movie* of our lives – we are always acting on what has just finished happening. It happened at least 1/30th of a second ago. We think we're in the present, but we aren't. The present we know is only a movie of the past, and we will really never be able to control the present through ordinary means. That lag has to be overcome some other way, through some kind of total breakthrough. And there are all sorts of other lags, besides, that go along with it. There are historical and social lags, where people are living by what their ancestors or somebody else perceived, and they may be twenty-five or fifty years or centuries behind, and nobody can be creative without overcoming all those lags first of all. A person can overcome that much through intellect or theory or study of history and so forth and get pretty much into the present that way, but he's still going to be up against one of the worst lags of all, the psychological. Your emotions remain behind because of training, education, the way you were brought up, blocks, hangups and stuff like that, and as a result your mind wants to go one way but your emotions don't ... [italics original].[275]

Kesey's Acid Tests gave birth to the Human Be-In, or Gathering of the Tribes on 14 January 1967 in San Francisco's Golden Gate Park. A press release for the event urged love and eschewed fear:

Berkeley political activists and the love generation of the Haight-Ashbury will join together with members of the new nation who will be coming from every state in the nation, every tribe of the young (the emerging soul of the nation) to powwow, celebrate, and prophesy the epoch of liberation, love, peace, compassion and unity of mankind. The night of bruited fear of the American eagle-breast-body is over. Hang your fear at the door and join the future. If you do not believe, please wipe your eyes and see [italics original].[276]

---

[275] Wolfe, 1969, pp. 129, 130.

[276] Anthony, Gene. The Summer of Love: Haight-Ashbury at its Highest. San Francisco, CA: Last Gasp, 1995 AA, The Human Be-In, Press Release, January 12,

Figure 483. Poster by Rick Griffin, 1967.

1967, p. 147.

Perhaps some twenty thousand people rallied on the Polo Fields

in celebration of a new spirit of consciousness. That fact caused a considerable stir. The social and political implications divided large numbers of people at a time when the war in Vietnam had already badly shaken the country. The Haight-Ashbury and the Human Be-In scared some people and for others it became an inspiration.[277]

Free food was provided by "the valiant band of St. Francises ... who called themselves Diggers" and security was provided by the Hell's Angels who spent most of the time relaying announcements concerning lost children:

'The Hell's Angels have a little girl here behind the platform and she has curly hair. She says her name is Mary. She wants to see her mother.' For that particular tribe of young men on motorcycles had also appeared at the Be-In .... They were well equipped for the task of serving as a clearing house for lost and strayed children, since they had walkie-talkies and were well organized. ... Late in the afternoon ... we felt as if we were looking at a heavenly nursery, that indeed the formidably dressed young men were angels; and the children looked so happy and admiring of their benefactors that it was difficult to imagine that any of the mothers were urgently needed that afternoon [capitalization, quotation marks original].[278]

The Haight-Ashbury Free Clinic featured a chill-out station to rescue, reorient or sedate those in difficulties: "*The waiting room at the Free Clinic in the Haight-Ashbury remained open around the clock. ... A Calm Center in the Free Clinic was specially set up for psychedelic space pilots who needed help in finding their way back down to earth* [capitalization, italics original]."[279]

---

[277] Anthony, 1995, p. 165.

[278] Perry, Helen Swick. The Human Be-In. NY: Basic Books, Inc., Publishers, 1970 AA, Chapter 6 '*The Beginning is the Human Be-In,*' pp. 5, 87, 88.

[279] Anthony, 1995, The Free Clinic, p. 71.

Furthur, Kesey's old bus also gave birth, to an infinity of vehicles driven by apprentice pranksters all over the world, many of which competed in the Great Bus Race held in Aspen Meadows, New Mexico 21 June 1969:

> The buses are Kesey's renowned Further, with a skeleton crew of Farmsters aboard, and the Hog Farm's fleet: Road Hog, Hospital Bus, Kitchen Bus, etc. The Motherfuckers' tight little bus is around but not in the race. ... The survivors of the trial run line up. They're immense, these faded colorful wrecks filled with folly. People are climbing off, others are climbing on. It's a test of passengers as much as drivers. The mood is pure: fatalistic optimism.[280]

Who won is still being debated. Or, in the words of the editor: "The Great Bus Race May Never End."[281]

---

280 Anonymous writer. "The Great Bus Race," The Last Whole Earth Catalog: Access to Tools, Stewart Brand, ed. Menlo Park, CA: Nowels Publications, 1971 AO, Nomadics, p. 245.

281 Brand, Stewart. "The Great Bus Race May Never End," 1971, p. 245.

Figure 484. Owsley Stanley and Jerry Garcia. Photo, Rosie McGee. [owsleystanleyfoundation.org, hereinafter OSF].

3. Peddlers and Cooks

The law illegalizing LSD in California did not come into effect until 6 October 1966:

California has made unauthorized possession or knowing use of the drug a misdemeanor punishable by a maximum of 1,000 dollars or a year in jail. Illegal manufacture, possession, possession for the purpose of sale, or sale of LSD constitutes a felony punishable by imprisonment of one to five years for the first offense.[282]

The Haight-Ashbury district of San Francisco ironically celebrated the new prohibition with the Love Pageant Rally, a symbolic Boston Tea Party on "666" (October 6, 1966):

Declaring that the long arm of the State was reaching into their psyches, the hippies welcomed the new law with a sort of Boston tea party – plenty of drugs, free food, and music – which took place in a narrow strip of park paralleling Haight Street known as the Panhandle. The get-together had a name, the Love Pageant Rally, and to everyone's surprise and delight, several thousand extravagantly garbed hippies turned out ....[283]

They even penned their own Declaration of Independence: "[W]e hold these experiences to be self evident, that all is equal, that the creation endows us with certain inalienable rights, that among them are: the freedom of body, the pursuit of joy, and the expansion of consciousness ...."[284]

---

282 Rosborough, Brian Alexander. "LSD: A Challenge to American Drug Law Philosophy," *Florida Law Review*, Volume 19, Issue 2, Article 5, 1966 [scholarship.law.ufl.edu/flr, hereinafter FLR], The Legal Status of LSD, pp. 318, 319.

283 Stevens, 1988, p. 252.

284 Anonymous, 1966, in Cohen, ed., 1991, p. 12/28.

Nearly two million doses of LSD would be seized that year, including a truck outfitted with a mobile laboratory:

> [B]etween May 1, 1966, and April 30, 1967, the Bureau of Drug Abuse Control had seized approximately 1.6 million doses .... On March 31, a 1958 International Harvester truck [and trailer] ... had been stopped ... and in the cab the police found a plastic bag containing 800 milligrams of LSD. ... [W]hen they opened the back doors and looked inside: the trailer was ... a mobile LSD lab.[285]

Naturally, the new law ensured clandestine alchemists and distributors would be needed to fill the already substantial recreational market.[286] Often they ended up creating in the process various amounts and kinds of impurities. These impurities may have led to the first LSD trial in US history.[287]

One of the earliest in the business was Augustus Owsley Stanley III (Bear, 1935 – 2011),[288] followed by Robert Timothy Scully (Tim, b. 1944), Nicholas Francis Hiskey (Nicholas Sand, 1941 – 2017),

---

285 Stevens, 1988, p. 267; the lab appears to have belonged to Sand.

286 Anonymous writer. "A Prophesy of A Declaration of Independence," *The San Francisco Oracle* #1 Love Pageant Rally, 20 September 1966 in Cohen, ed., 1991, p. 12/28.

287 Bernard Allen Roseman (b. 1934) and James Bernard Copley (1926 – 2000) sold impure LSD to a clinician and were convicted in 1964 not of possession or manufacture (still legal at that time), but of a new FDA regulation on importing and selling a misbranded new drug.

288 On 21 December 1967 Owsley was caught with 217 grams of LSD (roughly 750,000 hits of 300 gamma), and defended himself alleging this was his own private reserve for personal use: "When the trial ended, the judge sentenced him to three years in prison and fined him three thousand dollars" (Stevens, 1988, p. 279). According to an agent of "the newly formed Bureau of Drug Abuse Control (BDAC)," capturing him had "cost more than a million dollars in time and a dozen vehicles" (Stevens, 1988, pp. 215, 279).

and Ronald Hadley Stark (1938 – 1984), who sold or gave away for cost a number of strains of LSD, including the so-called orange sunshine.[289] Owsley fabricated enormous quantities and put his LSD at the disposition of Kesey when the Pranksters returned from their wandering bus journey: "In league with Owsley ... Kesey arranged several public 'acid tests' at which LSD was distributed free to all [quotation marks original]."[290]

The responsibility of supplying the tribes fell upon an effective group, the Brotherhood of Eternal Love, who imported tons of marijuana and hashish from South America and Asia, while giving away LSD at ridiculously low prices as a loving distribution of the sacrament. The way Leary tells it, the Brotherhood of Eternal Love began as

> a group of about eight or ten uneducated kids .... They were actually juvenile delinquents. ... And they went into this house in the Hollywood Hills where there was a party going on, and came in with their guns and masks .... And they said, 'We want acid.' And by the time they got back to Laguna Beach, the acid hit and they went in the water and ... they said they threw their guns in and they saw God [quotation marks original].[291]

The headquarters of the Brotherhood was established on a remote California farm, where they lived with their families in Indian teepees, growing fruits and vegetables for their own consumption:

---

[289] They also produced other drugs including methedrine, STP and DMT. ALD-52 was a legal fiction used as a defense at one of their trials.

[290] Leeds, 1981, Chapter 1 Biography: The Hallucinogenic Outlaw, p. 7.

[291] Rosenbaum, Ron. "Back in the High Life: Timothy Leary, the acid sixties guru, is now tuned in to L.A.'s social circuit," *Vanity Fair*, Volume 51, No. 4, April 1988 [archive.vanityfair.com, hereinafter AVF], pp. 144, 154.

They bought a three-hundred-acre plot at the arid base of the Santa Ana Mountains to provide a safe haven for their extralegal activities. The Brotherhood occupied a run-down farmhouse surrounded by a circle of seven teepees and grew their own vegetables, which their wives and girlfriends dutifully cooked. ... They stayed high all the time, smoking as much as thirty joints per day per person and dropping acid whenever the spirit moved them.[292]

The head of the organization, John Murl Griggs (1943 – 1969)

looked to Leary for guidance, revering the older man as a guru. At the time, the High Priest of LSD was urging everyone to start their own church. This seemed like an excellent idea to Griggs. The Brotherhood of Eternal Love, consisting of approximately thirty original members, was formally established as a tax-exempt entity in October 1966, ten days after LSD was made illegal in the state of California. The articles of incorporation announced the group's objective: 'to bring to the world a greater awareness of God through the teachings of Jesus Christ, Buddha, Ramakrishna, Babaji, Paramahansa Yogananda, Mahatma Gandhi, and all true prophets and apostles of God, and to spread the love and wisdom of these great teachers to all men' [quotation marks original] ....[293]

It was the Brotherhood who bore a significant portion of the funding for Leary's legal defense: "[W]hen Leary was fighting his Texas conviction, the Brotherhood gave his defense fund ten thousand dollars."[294]

But while LSD was the Brotherhood's sacrament, smuggling cannabis paid the bills. They came to embody the new public enemy number one in the US, according to the authorities:

---

[292] Lee/Shlain, 1985 AA, p. 240.

[293] Lee/Shlain, 1985, AA, p. 237.

[294] Lee/Shlain, 1985, AA, p. 237.

> But their primary occupation was smuggling: the Brotherhood were probably the best dope smugglers in America. ... The Brotherhood's primary focus was marijuana and hashish; they never took a profit on LSD, since they saw that part of their operation as a charitable spreading of the sacrament. ... But ... the Brotherhood ... also [became the] BDAC's [Bureau of Drug Abuse Control] number-one target.[295]

Griggs reportedly died from ingesting an overdose of something illegal (PCP, psilocybin crystals, in some versions) and then refusing medical attention, as the hospital would have reported whatever they would have found in his bloodstream. He died quietly. Supposedly, his last words were, "It's between me and god." One of the judges in one of the many trials wrote:

> put a fancy name on it, call it a psychedelic movement, call it the Brotherhood of Eternal Love, call it the wonderful Hells Angel movement – whatever you wanted to call it, they all ended up in one thing. They all ended up in the degradation of mankind, the degradation of society.[296]

Although the original group was made up of perhaps thirty members, one of the federal accusations maintained that at its largest it was composed of seven hundred and fifty individuals spread across five continents, trafficking in marijuana, hashish, hash oil, cocaine and LSD earning them some two hundred million dollars. But even the prosecutors could not dispute that this so-called outlandishly dressed hippie mafia donated a large part of their profits to giving away LSD. At only one rock concert in Anaheim, California, it is said they gave away gratis over a hundred thousand doses, and that they sent to Vietnam for the use of the troops millions. The ordinary street price for a dose of 250 gamma was two dollars.

---

[295] Stevens, 1988, Chapter 26 Too Many Gurus, p. 280.

[296] Stevens, 1987, Book Three: The Pure Void, Chapter 26 Too Many Gurus, p. 352.

As for the alchemists themselves, Owsley and Scully were recognized talents already in high school, who manufactured LSD for clearly extra-economic motivations. Sand (who began by making DMT in his bathtub in Brooklyn) was more financially prudent and less meticulous in the purity of his product. After Owsley was arrested, Scully and Sand received financial backing from Leary's patron, millionaire William Mellon Hitchcock (Billy, 1928 – 1989) in order to obtain essential ingredients (ergotamine, e.g.) and set up laboratories.

As the raw materials became scarce around the world (and after the death of Griggs), the pace of manufacturing and supply was maintained by the mysterious Stark. One day he showed up at the Brotherhood's ranch with a kilo of pure LSD, claiming to have a secure source of the raw material and an excellent laboratory in Paris. What he really had (as became known later) was an actual chemist, Richard Hilary Kemp (b. 1943), who had figured out a way to reproduce ergot in cryogenic tanks, rediscovering a finding by Sandoz in the 1950s to produce the drug by the ton if that became necessary.

In contrast with Scully and Sand, arrested by 1973, Stark managed to disappear at the opportune moment. He passed a good deal of his time in Sicily, surrounded by friends from the *Cosa Nostra*, representatives from various national secret agencies, and political extremists from both left and right, when not sojourning in Lebanon. In 1975 on an anonymous tip he was captured in a hotel in Bologna, Italy with some five kilos of morphine and cocaine. On him were found various documents relating to the fabrication of LSD, as well as several letters bearing the letterhead of the US embassy in London addressed to the underground laboratory he and Kemp had in Brussels.

Once in prison, he managed to infiltrate the leftist terrorist organization the Red Brigades by way of their leader Renato Curcio (b.

1941), proving his worth to the warden by giving advance warning of some of their attacks. In prison he continued to receive visits from American, English and Lebanese diplomats, as well from the Italian Secret Service, and came into contact directly with General Vito Miceli (1916 – 1990), later implicated in a series of neofascist attempted coups. Although he appeared as one of the principals accused in the trials against the Brotherhood, the US government never sought his extradition, and he was sentenced in Italy to fourteen years for drug trafficking.

However, he appealed his sentence presenting himself as Khouri Ali, a Palestinian revolutionary, in perfect Arabic explaining that he was part of an international terrorist organization. Described as a tortured genius by the president of the appeals court, this new revelation was investigated by a judge who died days later in a mysterious accident. The Italian prosecutor then accused him of armed banditry and it looked like he might spend the rest of his life in prison. But four months later he was released by orders from a judge who based his decision on a scrupulously enumerated series of proofs that he belonged to the CIA.

In 1982 he was detained again in Holland, accused of trafficking hashish, heroin and cocaine, and deported to the United States, where without publicity he was released from custody in San Francisco after only a few months of incarceration. The federal department of justice refused to indict him on the basis that too much time had passed to prosecute the case. Two years later he died, so it is said, from a heart attack.[297] There was no autopsy.

---

[297] Lee/Shlain, 1985 AA, pp. 248-251, 279-287.

Figure 485. Fray Toribio de Benavente (Motolinía). Villa Roiz, Carlos. "*¿Quien fue Fray Toribio de Benavente, 'Motolinía'?*" *Desde la Fe*, 2 August 2019 [desdelafe.mx, hereinafter DDL].

D. The Acts of Accusation

Although the new crusade against LSD was accepted without difficulty by large sectors of the population, the traditional prohibitionist scheme needed important tweaks to confront this new threat. Fray Toribio de Benavente (Motolinía, 1482 – 1565) witnessed in the sixteenth century the natives of New Spain eat this bitter food called *teonanacatl* in order to adore their cruel god:

> They have another way of getting drunk even more cruel, with fungi or small mushrooms .... In a short while they see a thousand visions .... These they call in their language, *teonanacatl*, or flesh of the gods, or of the demon they adore. With this bitter delicacy they commune with their cruel god [tr. gwr, italics original].[298]

Now the food not only was not bitter, it was also imperceptible to the naked eye. If one of its crystals could be seen without a magnifying glass, it would without any doubt be an overdose, perhaps ten to fifty times greater than average. One gram of this drug (which a gifted alchemist could make from then still available precursors) could cause 10,000 people to trip out, and a kilo could intoxicate San Francisco.

The attempt to control the production and distribution of this substance with arguments and procedures thought sufficient for opium or cocaine was completely illusory. It did not require cultivation, it was not a drug of the puerile races exported to America, and its first illegal manufacturers worked in the departments of chemistry and pharmacy of the country's principal universities. They were dealing with a drug

---

[298] *Tenían otra manera de embriaguez que los hacía más crueles ... con aquel amargo manjar su cruel dios los comulgaba* (Benavente (Motolinía), Fray Toribio de. *Historia de Los Indios de la Nueva España*. Madrid: Real Academia Española, 2014 AO, Primera Parte, Capítulo Segundo, p. 27).

practically given away for free, which advanced students and alchemists produced for feeding the tribe. "Unholy communions," the anti-psychiatrist psychiatrist Thomas Stephen Szasz (1920 – 2012) called these gatherings:

> Those who reject the doctrines of our principal religions and who cultivate instead various heretical faiths, congregate at pot and acid parties and at gatherings where heroin and other even more esoteric and forbidden drugs are used; and they too have elaborate ceremonies symbolizing the counter-virtues of marijuana and LSD, incense and Oriental mysticism, and so forth. These are the unholy communions of our age.[299]

---

299 Szasz, Ceremonial Chemistry, 1974, I. Pharmakos: The Scapegoat, Chapter 4. Communions Holy and Unholy, p. 41.

1. Therapeutic Inutility

LSD and psilocybin were now declared to be therapeutically useless, lacking any interest for investigators not employing mice or monkeys. Evidently more preoccupied by controlling scientific investigation rather than controlling street use, the authorities first conducted an official purge of human trials of LSD and psilocybin. Sandoz was commanded to turn over all existing reserves of their stocks on American soil to the National Institute of Mental Health (NIMH) who had previously committed to authorize only projects viewed favorably by the Food and Drug Administration (FDA). The latter, in turn, defined these drugs as experimental drugs restricted to use with animals, and in so doing effectively prohibited their use in medical practice: "[T]he result was that all researchers using experimental drugs would now have to clear their research projects with Washington. No longer would it be possible to mail a form to Sandoz and receive in return LSD or psilocybin."[300] Closing off experimental knowledge with these drugs, in early April 1966 Sandoz decided

to sever all corporate ties to its problem children, LSD and psilocybin. On April 7, Sandoz telephoned the FDA and announced that they were terminating all research contracts and would be willing to turn over their entire supply of the two drugs to the federal government. LSD had become a public relations disaster: Sandoz received dozens of phone calls from journalists and doctors every time it made the news, each requesting a copy of its LSD bibliography, which was now nearly ten inches thick. Researchers were ordered to return all supplies of LSD and psilocybin to Sandoz, and then resubmit their research proposals to the NIMH for reapproval.[301]

---

[300] Stevens, 1988, Chapter 14 The Politics of Consciousness, p. 146.

[301] Stevens, 1988, Chapter 21 Psychotic Reaction, p. 224.

The commissions charged with approving grants and subsidies also authorized a regulation automatically excluding any work by scientists taking the drug themselves, which had been one of the early suggestions by Sandoz: "By taking Delysid himself, the psychiatrist is able to gain an insight into the world of ideas and sensations of mental patients."[302]

But shutting the doors on academic research only opened them wider to a black market (that had been operating for some time with good intentions) which now began to be invaded by very toxic substitutes like STP and PCP:

STP (2,5 dimethox-4-methylphene-thylamine – the initials stood for 'Serenity, Tranquility, Peace') was developed in 1964 by an experimental chemist working for the Dow Chemical Company .... STP made its debut in the Haight when five thousand tabs were given away during a solstice celebration marking the onset of the Summer of Love. ... [T]he crowd of eager pill poppers ... gobbled the gift as if it were an after-dinner mint, and a lot of people were still tripping three days later. ... STP was just one of the bizarre drugs that were pumped into the willing arteries of the acid ghetto. According to doctors who worked at the Haight-Ashbury Free Clinic, there was a rash of adverse reactions when a compound purporting to be THC (a synthetic version of marijuana) inundated the Haight. The drug was actually phencyclidine, or PCP – otherwise known as 'angel dust' – which had originally been marketed as an animal tranquilizer by Parke-Davis [quotation marks original].[303]

Further, the LSD was adulterated on occasion with rat poison and amphetamine: "Much of the LSD turning up on the street was fortified with some sort of additive, usually speed or strychnine ... or in some cases insecticide."[304]

---

302 Stevens, 1988, Chapter 1 A Bike Ride in Basle, p. 14.

303 Lee and Shlain, 1985, Chapter 7 The Capital of Forever, The Great Summer Dropout, p. 147.

304 Lee and Shlain, 1985, p. 148.

Figure 486. Robert Francis Kennedy, 5 June 1965, Bettman Archive.

But this was only one example of what happens when a substance suddenly mutates overnight by legislative decree. As if the correct or incorrect use of X-rays in particular cases would allow one to generalize as to its medical relevance, LSD was transfigured into a satanic substance, as mandrake was converted into a sign of diabolic apostasy during the Middle Ages, invoking the phenomenon of false consciousness in an entire community. While even the so-called stupefacients had an exception for medical or scientific use, what shortly before had been the pride of psychopharmacology was now transformed suddenly into impure miasma, devoid of any interest or function.

Understandable astonishment at this legislative legerdemain was well reflected in a meeting of a 1966 Senate subcommittee. Senator Robert Francis Kennedy (NY, 1925 – 1968), whose spouse had received completely satisfactory psychedelic therapy at Hubbard's Hollywood Sanitarium in Vancouver, BC., limited himself to intervening cautiously, risking the label of appearing to be pro-LSD:

> Here is a drug which has been available for well over 20 years. Research on its effects and possible therapeutic uses has been going on for a long time. ... Experiments indicate that LSD may be useful in treating alcoholics – one of the largest groups of the handicapped. It has been helpful in some cases as an adjunct to psychotherapy for mentally ill people. ... I fear that with so much emphasis over the period of the last several months on the damage and the dangers of LSD, that these rather sensational stories have deterred the Government from doing the kind of research that really might be helpful in dealing with the problems of the illegal use of LSD, and of the use of LSD for beneficial purposes.[305]

---

305 Senator Kennedy, Organization and Coordination, 1966, Statement of Hon. Robert F. Kennedy, U.S. Senator from the State of New York, Need for Inquiry into the Federal Role, p. 2; Studies to Determine Scope of LSD Use, p. 72.

Kennedy pointedly asked representatives from both the National Institute of Mental Health (NIMH) and the Food and Drug Administration (FDA) as well as the Assistant Secretary for Health and Scientific Affairs why legitimate research using LSD was being terminated:

> Senator KENNEDY. ... I come back to the major question that I raised then, that if they were worth while 6 months ago, why aren't they worth while now? ... If those projects were worth while and were financed by NIMH prior to 4 months ago why weren't they worth while afterward? ... I am asking why, if it was worth while making the studies before, it is not worth while now?[306]

The bureaucrats avoided answering specific questions but Kennedy continued to insist, almost badgering one witness: "We keep going around and around, you and I. ... If I could get a flat answer about that I would be happy. Is there a misunderstanding about my question?"[307] The bureaucrats' vague excuses included "shortness of time ... tremendously inconvenienced ... and acceptable scientific plan."[308] But while they spoke of being attentive to scientific integrity and their ethical and moral responsibilities, not one admitted to or questioned the experiments done by the secret intelligence services on uninformed human guinea pigs.

Though officially LSD would now be therapeutically useless, some were finding it unofficially quite useful. One intrepid author demonstrated intellectual rigor by taking street vendor LSD with his

---

306 Senator Kennedy, Organization and Coordination, 1966, Studies to Determine Scope of LSD Use, p. 72; Breakdown of Research Projects, p. 73; Reasons for Terminations of Studies, p. 75.

307 Senator Kennedy, Organization and Coordination, 1966, Urgent Need to Continue Investigations, p. 73.

308 Dr. Yolles, Organization, 1966, p. 73; Mr. Goodrich, Organization, 1966, p. 74.

wife before ending his chapter on hallucinogens, with "not at all bad" results:

It is difficult to explain how long and gritty and unsatisfying the LSD experience was. For several months we used it as a comparison for anything unpleasant; yet the results were not at all bad. We both felt that it made us more sensitive to shape and colour, and that it made us more dispassionate about other experiences and relationships, more direct about our day-to-day intentions. None of these effects was profound, but LSD seemed to jolt us forward over a stretch of maturing we'd probably have covered anyway. Like a tough expedition; one came away from it saying, 'If I can cope with that, I can cope with a lot of other things too.' ... For us the LSD experience was less important than the carpets it lifted and the structure of our minds we saw below [quotation marks original].[309]

Nearly contemporaneous was the experience of the partner of one of the founders of the *Paris Review*, a typical example of a difficult but educational mescaline trip:

I gave her mescaline on an autumn night of wind and rain. On her first drug trip, D freaked out; that is the drug term, and there is no better. She started to laugh, and her mouth opened wide and she could not close it; her armor had cracked, and all the night winds of the world went howling through. Turning to me, she saw my flesh dissolve, my head become a skull – the whole night went like that. Yet she later saw that she might free herself by living out the fear of death, the demoniac rage at one's own helplessness that drug hallucinations seem to represent, and in that way let go of a life-killing accumulation of defenses. And she accepted the one danger of the mystical search: there is no way back without doing oneself harm. Many paths appear, but once the way is taken, it must be followed to the end.[310]

The next adventure went better:

---

309 Laurie, 1967, Chapter 8 Hallucinogens, p. 109.

310 Matthiessen, Peter. The Snow Leopard. NY: Viking Press, 1978 AA, Chapter I. Westward, p. 46.

> I remember an April afternoon in 1962, when we had taken LSD together. She came out onto the terrace of a country house and drifted toward me, down across the lawn. D had black hair and beautiful wide eyes; in the spring breeze and light of flowers, she looked bewitched. ... There was no need to speak, the other knew to the last word what would be said. Struck dumb by this telepathy, our mouths snapped shut at the same instant, then burst into smiles at the precise timing of this comic mime of our old fights; delighted, we embraced and laughed and laughed. And still not one word had been spoken; only later did we discover that all thoughts, laughter, and emotions had been not similar but just the same, one mind, one. Mind, even to this: that as we held each other, both bodies turned into sapling trees that flowed into each other, grew together in one strong trunk that pushed a taproot deeper and deeper into the ground. And yet, and yet .... At no time did the 'I' dissolve into the miracle [quotation marks original].[311]

These are testimonies of difficult experiences. The first is from a couple with no desire to repeat it, and the second from a couple that continued to experiment. They contrast with the opinions of those who have no personal experience with the entheogens. And they help present the full range of therapeutic possibility.

[311] Matthiessen, 1978, pp. 46, 47.

Figure 487. Commune, 1960s.

2. Miscegenation, Apostasy, Insanity, Addiction, Laziness

We turn first to an English jurist observing the use of cannabis in a be-bop club in London in the 1950s:

> After several weeks I have just completed exhaustive inquiries into the most insidious vice Scotland Yard has ever been called upon to tackle – dope peddling. Detectives on the assignment are agreed that never have they had experience of a crime so vicious, so ruthless and unpitying and so well organised. Hemp, marijuanha [sic] and hashish represent a thoroughly unsavoury trade. One of the detectives told me: 'We are dealing with the most evil men who have ever taken to the vice business.' The victims are teen-age British girls and, to a lesser extent, teen-age youths .... The racketeers (or peddlers) are 90 per cent. coloured men from the West Indies and West coast of Africa .... As the result of my inquiries, I share the fears of detectives on the job that there is the gravest danger of the reefer craze becoming the greatest social menace this country has known. The other day I sat in a tawdry West End Club. I was introduced by a member, a useful contact both to me and the police. Drinks sold were nothing stronger than lukewarm black coffee, 'near' beer or orangeade. I watched the dancing. My contact and I were two of six white men. I counted 28 coloured men and some 30 white girls. ... Girls and coloured partners danced with an abandon – a savagery almost – which was both fascinating and embarrassing. ... My contact indicated photographs on the walls. They were of girls in the flimsiest drapings. 'They are, or were, members,' I was told. We went outside. I had seen enough of my first bebop club, its coloured peddlers, its half-crazed uncaring young girls. ... 'The day will come,' said the dusky Jesse, 'when this country will be all mixtures if we don't watch out. There will be only half-castes' [quotation marks original].[312]

The text has structural similarities with a first-hand description from a French journalist of one of Hollywood's unique hippie churches in the 1960s:

---

312 Johnson, Donald McI. Indian Hemp: A Social Menace. London: Christopher Johnson, 1952 AA, Chapter 4 Indian Hemp in England, pp. 44, 45, 48.

The one I saw in Hollywood had once been a very large store fronting on the street. It was called 'His Place,' and it was open only from nine o'clock at night till morning. In the big display window, a huge, brightly lit Christ reposed on his cross, and various texts of the new faith were set out. ... What a spectacle! At the entrance a crowd of bearded, barefoot, and long-haired hippies, dressed in baroque costumes, encircled a tall receptacle hissing out steam, not from holy water, but from coffee, free to all. ... In the middle of the church, a giant black cross lay flat on the floor. Couples, lolling at random on top of and around the cross, spoke to one another in low voices, or slept, or cuddled, or copulated. Everything was bathed in an unpleasant half-light. These couples enlaced on the cross were, in fact, iconoclasts. ... Actually, the adherents to this old/new order deny that their practices are sacrilegious. They propose that love in all its forms, spiritual or physical, would not shock Christ, who was, at the same time, love and love made material. The act of flesh should not be offensive to the one who created it. ... But now the hippies have made up new and baroque cults in which prayer is conducted in hallucinogenic stupor, where communion is sanctified, not with a wafer, but with a sugar cube of LSD, and in which the god Sex is the object of worship. The hippie churches have indeed evoked their constitutional right to drugs in the practice of their religion, and the issue has been carried to the Supreme Court ... [quotation marks original].[313]

A Belgian toxicologist is said to have added:

The United States has been the scene of supposedly scientific *collective* psychedelic gatherings by supposedly sane people. Sadly, this unchecked quest for greater self-knowledge leads not to wisdom but to neurosis. These amateur Socratics debate like devils in holy water. Authentic scientific curiosity can also lead to imprudence. Are they sure they are immune from these traitorous drugs [italics original]?[314]

---

[313] Labin, Suzanne. Hippies, Drugs and Promiscuity, tr. Stephanie Winston. New Rochelle, NY: Arlington House, 1972 AO, Chapter 2 The Sense Revolution in the United States, *Drugs as Religion*, pp. 31, 32, 33, 34; *Celle que j'ai vue à Hollywood se trouve située ... en appellent à la Cour Suprême* (Labin, Suzanne. *hippies, drogues et sexe*. Paris: La Table Ronde, 1970 [gallica.bnf.fr, hereinafter BNF], pp. 34, 35, 36, 37).

[314] See Varenne, Gaston. *L'abus des drogues*. Bruxelles, BE: C. Dessart, 1971.

Each of these three professional opinions does not differ from those of the man in the street or for that matter the drug police. All three are completely convinced that certain psychoactive substances (those prohibited) are drugs in the moral sense with the ability to cause treason, and that certain other psychoactive substances (those not prohibited) are only metaphorically drugs since in reality they are food and medicine. But with these and similar arguments one activates the mechanism of the self-fulfilling prophecy. Any delirious conduct (which in another time would have caused the subject to be branded insane) begins to be explained easily and rapidly as a result of the taking of some psychedelic drug, ignoring the anterior history of the subject and the chemical nature of what he had just ingested.

Soon the label of delirious drug addict becomes rooted in the minds of some of the very same users who (after omitting the minimal precautions as to company and occasion) end up succumbing to more or less conscious fears of being driven mad, entering into experiences of intense panic. Since the label of temporary insanity allows for an irresponsibility equal to or greater than that of junkie, there were not lacking many thousands of aspirants for the title of LSD addict. Sadly, by 1956, experiments made at Lexington demonstrated that within a few days individuals were incapable of perceiving that they were continuing to receive a strong dose of LSD each morning: "When LSD was given daily, tolerance was evident after administration for only three days."[315]

LSD users were also accused of lacking ambition. Indeed, some simply lost any interest in their traditional careers, as happened with a jockey and a law student:

---

315 Isbell, Harris, et al. "Studies on Lysergic Acid Diethylamide (LSD – 25)," *A.M.A. Archives of Neurology and Psychiatry*, Volume 76, November 1956, Summary, p. 477.

One former disk jockey in the sample said that he had lost his employment after using LSD and had no ambition to start work again. A law student, not in the sample, told us that LSD (taken in a medical-experimental situation after screening by psychological testing) had opened up new vistas to him. He had 'a perspective of the whole world now' and his legal studies were very dull and uninteresting by comparison. This abandonment of ambition, reduction in goal-striving, and inability to perceive one's own work performance accurately after taking LSD, has also been documented [quotation marks original].[316]

[316] Ungerleider, J. Thomas, et al. "The Dangers of LSD: Analysis of Seven Months' Experience in a University Hospital's Psychiatric Service," *Journal of the American Medical Association*, Volume 197, No. 6, 8 August 1966, Comment, p. 111.

Figure 488. Poster promoting cannabis as an aphrodisiac.

3. Promiscuity

Before hallucinogens became a social threat, it was commonly believed that they neither stimulated nor inhibited, but only modified the consciousness of the user according to her expectations, setting and dosage:

> The subjective effects apparently depend on at least three kinds of variable: the properties and potency of the drug itself; the basic personality traits and current mood of the person ingesting it, and the social and psychological context, including the meaning to the individual of his act in taking the drug and his interpretation of the motives of those who made it available.[317]

The academic and scientific investigators agreed, for example, that although it was not an aphrodisiac in the true sense, LSD could be used in the treatment of frigidity, timidity, inhibitions and poor sexual relations:

> While the published case histories of frigidity cures with LSD have been emphasized, LSD has similar effects and results in the treatment of male impotence. [L]ess attention has been paid to the causes and treatment of this condition. Since here again the disabling agents that lead to impotence are anxiety, unconscious blocks, fear and inhibition, LSD can bring about an effective cure.[318]

Ethnobotanically, it appears that "no drug has yet proved capable of behaving as a *specific* sex stimulant. Exceptions to this rule may, however, exist amongst the psychedelic drugs ... [italics

---

[317] Barron, Frank, Murray E. Jarvik, and Sterling Bunnell, Jr. "The Hallucinogenic Drugs," *Scientific American*, Volume 210, No. 4, April 1964 AA, p. 33, col. 2.

[318] Stafford, P. G. and B. H. Golightly. LSD: The Problem-Solving Psychedelic. NY: Award Books, 1967 AA/AO/[druglibrary.org, hereinafter DLO], Chapter IV Everyday Problems, Frigidity, Impotence, Homosexuality and Perversion, p. 84.

original]."[319] The botanist and physician Francisco Hernández (1530 – 1587) in the notes from his 1571 to 1575 expedition to *Nova Hispania* described *ololiuhqui* (morning glory seeds) as being an aphrodisiac: "Moreover, eaten, it excites lust [*deuoratum verò, venerem excitat*, tr. gwr]."[320] Iboga was also considered by some tribes to be an aphrodisiac: "The bark of the root *Tabernanthe iboga* ... was used by the natives of West Africa and the Congo to increase resistance against fatigue and tiredness and as an aphrodisiac."[321] There is also some data from the Amazon basin about *yagé*, which some tribes considered capable of distending the clitoris and causing an erect phallus:

> Throughout the region drained by the many tributaries of the Amazon, natives prepare a drink from the stems of the *Banisteria caapi* vine. It is a potion of many names – yagé, ayahuasca or caapi. ... But caapi ... happens to be one of the few hallucinogens for which an aphrodisiac property is claimed; clitoral distention and penile engorgement have been described.[322]

The medical establishment, however, formally agreed with official policy, denying any aphrodisiac qualities in the drug, yet at the same time affirming them. One physician, for example, accused Leary

---

319 Wells, Psychedelic, 1974, Chapter 7 Sex and Sexuality, p. 137.

320 Hernandez, Francisci. *Rerum Medicaum Novae Hispaniae Thesaurus seu Plantarum Animalium Mineralium Mexicanorum*, ed. Nardo Antonio Recchi. Roma: Ex typographeio Vitalis Mascardi, 1651 AO, Liber Quintus, Cap. XIV De OLILIUHQUI seu planta orbicularium foliorum, p. 145; Schultes, Richard Evans. A Contribution to Our Knowledge of Rivea Corymbosa: The Narcotic Ololiuqui of the Aztecs. Cambridge, MA: Botanical Museum of Harvard University, 1941 SAM, II. The History and Identification of Ololiuqui, pp. 6, 7.

321 Hoffer, A. and Osmond, H. The Hallucinogens. NY: Academic Press, 1967 AO, Chapter IV. Indole Hallucinogens Derived from Tryptophan, Iboga Alkaloids, p. 468.

322 Cohen, 1965, Chapter 2 The Search, pp. 22, 23.

of lying when he predicted marvellous copulations with LSD, and a moment later could not help relating a lurid unsupported story that it was useful to make victims vulnerable to orgiastic activity:

> [T]he one thing LSD was not, was a physical aphrodisiac. ... This is not to say that people do not have sexual intercourse under the influence of LSD. The drug has been given to girls, sometimes without their knowledge, to put them in a position of such confusion and passivity that they could then be subjected to any sort of sexual activity including group orgies.[323]

A second was not fazed by the paradox, saying that, against the opinion of Leary, LSD had no influence on the libido, although once the idea of sex is suggested, people engaged in inconceivable orgies; a third ignored distinctions and affirmed that the presence of other parties does not at all inhibit the games of these drug addicts that have sex in public parks, in places filled with people and with various couples in the same bed.[324] Perhaps the most dramatic anecdote is from the first doctor:

> For example, one young woman took LSD and was subsequently lying in the middle of a public street, her dress pulled up, her legs far apart, moaning over and over again, 'Come on God, fuck me.' But the mental eroticism ordinarily has no physical counterpart [quotation marks original].[325]

To be fair, it could be said that we are asking two different questions. One inquires into the aphrodisiac effect of certain substances, and the other the influence of psychedelics on sexuality. It

---

[323] Louria, 1968, p. 146.

[324] See Varenne, Gaston. _L'abus de drogues_. Oudergem, Brussels, BE: Editions Mardaga, 1971.

[325] Louria, 1968, p. 146.

is evident that, from the beginning, some groups simply adopted a non-Christian posture, understanding that particular religion as a condemnation of the flesh in favor of the spirit.

Writing about life in the Haight-Ashbury district of San Francisco in 1967, one journalist recorded that free love had less to do with drugs and more to do with a general philosophy of life:

> Max is telling me how he lives free of all the old middle-class Freudian hang-ups. 'I've had this old lady for a couple of months now ... and I come in three days late and tell her I've been with some other chick, well, maybe she shouts a little but then I say, 'That's me, baby,' and she laughs and says, 'That's you, Max.' Max says it works both ways, 'I mean, if she comes in and tells me she wants to have Don, maybe, I say, 'OK, baby, it's your trip' [quotation marks original].[326]

The tenets of this philosophy are otherwise without mystery. An Indian sociologist who studied the hippie subculture in Yorkville, Toronto, Canada in the 1960s found it was not without its own rules regarding sexuality:

> On to this concern with human relationships has been grafted the concept of free love. Relationships, while important, are generally transitory. Sexual relations are seen as an aspect of human relationships and hippies enter into them easily without the concern for lasting fidelity with people in the 'straight' world. ... If you like the person, a relationship is formed and sexual relations follow naturally. The important factor is that relationships are not intended to be binding before sexual relations can ensue [quotation marks original].[327]

---

326 Didion, Joan. "The Hippie Generation: Slouching Towards Bethlehem," *The Saturday Evening Post*, Volume 240, Issue 19, 23 September 1967 AA, p. 27, col, 2.

327 Smart, Reginald G. and David Jackson. The Yorkville Subculture: A Study of the Lifestyles and Interactions of Hippies and Non-Hippies, prepared from the field notes of Gopala Alampur. Toronto, CA: Addiction Research Foundation, 1969 AO, II The Four Major Groups, (ii) The Hippie, p. 14.

Whether or not it was based on love, a binding social relationship with someone was not established without first establishing a sexual relationship, a custom which in the end has become rooted in a large part of the Western world as a model of simplicity and reasonableness.

With respect to the aphrodisiac qualities of entheogens generally, this appears to be a good time to compare the results of "an informal survey of about 200 users" of cannabis conducted in 1969 by a Stony Brook [State University of New York] sociologist. The great majority of those interviewed said that the drug had no automatically erotic effect, although female subjects especially said it did act "as a sexual stimulant when they're with someone with whom they're already" intimate:

> More than a third of the respondents said that marijuana has no effect on their sexual desire. ... But 44 per cent – a strong plurality – replied that marijuana definitely increases their sexual desire. ... An overwhelming majority – 68 per cent – replied that marijuana increases their sexual enjoyment; that their orgasmic pleasure is heightened by the drug. Yet most scientists claim that in physiological terms marijuana lacks an aphrodisiac effect.[328]

One empiricist asked "what experienced users feel about marijuana intoxication" and sex:

> The majority of the users indicated that marijuana greatly enhances sexual pleasure. Relevant characteristic effects were: *new qualities to touch and taste* (with *new smell qualities* being common0 – what one might consider the intimate senses—and *new, pleasurable qualities to orgasm.* It was common for the user to *feel more need and desire for sex*, and ... to *feel more sexual desire if the situation was appropriate* [italics original].[329]

---

[328] Goode, Erich. "Marijuana and Sex," *Evergreen Review*, Volume 13, No. 66, May 1969 AA, pp. 19, 20.

[329] Tart, Charles T. On Being Stoned: A Psychological Study of Marijuana Intoxication. Palo Alto, CA: Science and Behavior Books, 1971 AA, Part III:

Another observer "who has spent a considerable amount of time evaluating cannabis as a member of the British Government's Advisory Committee on Drug Dependence" concluded that "the lurid stories of teenage drug and sex orgies which are so commonly believed are actually complete"[330] myths:

> For many years cannabis has been associated with sensuousness, carnality, debauchery and sexual gratification. Many of the reports in the press have made their exposures of drug taking sound positively pornographic, suggesting that an evening which begins with cannabis is likely to end with a sexual orgy.[331]

Indeed, the major investigating bodies found no such thing:

> The Indian Hemp Commission reported that cannabis did not lead to sexual misconduct. The Mayor of New York's Committee on Marihuana reported that the drug did not stimulate sexual desires. The White House Commission states: 'Although marihuana has long held the reputation of inciting individuals to commit sexual offences and other anti-social acts, evidence is inadequate to substantiate this.' Supporters and opponents of cannabis law reform tend to agree that the drug does not stimulate sexual desire [quotation marks original].[332]

Relationships, Chapter 31 Summary, Sexuality, p. 289.

330 Wells, 1974, p. 140.

331 Schofield, Michael. The Strange Case of Pot. Harmondsworth, Middlesex, UK: Penguin Books Ltd., 1971 AA, Chapter 11 Sex, *Conflicting Reports*, p. 123.

332 Schofield, 1971, p. 124.

Figure 489. Dr. Jeffrey R. MacDonald, 1970 [images.seattletimes.com, hereinafter IST].

4. Murder, Suicide, Madness, Teratogeny

Plowing the same furrow even deeper, supposedly a man stabbed his mother over a hundred times and was absolved as being temporarily insane because he said he had done it under the influence of LSD:

> There have been several homicides attributed to LSD. The most notorious of these was the killing of Mrs. Florence Cooper, a fifty-seven-year-old schoolteacher who was stabbed one hundred and five times by her thirty-two-year-old son-in-law, a former medical student. The killer claimed that he had taken LSD, and had no knowledge of the crime; he was subsequently acquitted on the grounds of temporary insanity.[333]

In another anecdote, an "American who killed a girl in London in 1968 while both were on an LSD 'trip', had the charge reduced from one of murder to manslaughter, but was convicted on that count though the Court acknowledged that he would have had no knowledge of his action [quotation marks original]."[334] In neither of these cases did the courts consider it necessary to prove the actual ingestion of the drug, or even that the subject had it in his possession.

Before the prohibition, as previously indicated, many polls indicated that in psychiatric practice LSD was a medicine as safe as any, as data from over 30,000 patients attest:

---

[333] Louria, 1968, Chapter 8 LSD: Abuse and Disillusion, p. 151.

[334] Bergel, Franz and D. R. A. Davies. All about Drugs. London: Thomas Nelson and Sons Ltd, 1970 AA, Chapter 8 The Hallucinogens: LSD and the Products of the Sacred Cactus, p. 139.

> By 1965, there had appeared in scientific journals more than two thousand papers describing treatment, of thirty to forty thousand patients, with psychedelics ... Finally, psychedelic therapy has been assailed as too dangerous. Very definitely, the evidence does not bear this out; and in fact, when the drugs are administered by those therapists and researchers who are most effective, the 'dangers' are negligible. This is borne out by studies involving many thousands of patients and experimental drug subjects [quotation marks original].[335]

While acknowledging the complications associated with the drug, two other researchers found "very few toxic or psychologic complications," "no confirmed instance of attempted or completed suicide," and few "psychotic reactions persisting longer than 2 days ...."[336] With respect to the Native American Church, their extensive religious practices with peyote (over a quarter million persons) demonstrates the astonishing predominance of the safe and completely peaceful use of very active visionary drugs.

But after the incarceration of Kesey and Leary, there are innumerable notices in the press about people jumping out of windows, killing and being driven permanently mad due to lysergic acid diethylamide, peyote, psilocybin and so forth. One spoke of a Swiss physician who drowned in a lake, another of a Norwegian woman who stabbed her would-be seducer, a third of people who lost their minds in an original and entertaining manner, but most popular were the assassinations ordered by the criminal cult leader Charles Miles Manson (1934 – 2017). Leary, who met the psychopath in Folsom prison, said he called for the murders because "acid" could make the "kids ... do anything" and because the Bible told him so:

---

335 Masters and Houston, 1970, Part VII Therapeutic Applications, pp. 323, 326.

336 Cohen, Sidney and Keith S. Ditman. "Complications Associated with Lysergic Acid Diethylamide (LSD-25)," *Journal of the American Medical Association*, Volume 181, No. 2, 14 July 1962, p. 161.

[Manson] 'When I got out of prison in '65, I was amazed. Thousands of kids just waiting to be programmed. Give them acid and they'd do anything.'
[Leary] 'Charles, have you ever been interviewed by psychologists or experts about how you did it? ... You did what every intelligence agency in the world dreamed of. You programmed people to go out on assassination missions. ... Why did you do it?'
[Manson] 'I'm a Christian, man. The Bible's my manual. The Bible gives you the program. It tells you right there in Revelation that the women are the cause of all man's problems' [quotation marks original].[337]

Not only Manson but an indeterminable number of other individuals mounted systems of mental vampirism and ego dominance over young disoriented people who had come to California looking for a psychedelic initiation. The co-founder of a spiritual commune in Tennessee known as 'The Farm,' Stephen Gaskin (1935 – 2014) remembers the would-be Hollingshead-like gurus on the streets of San Francisco: "The whole catalog of craziness, like Adler's ideas of ego-dominance and stuff, was exposed by acid. There was such a thing as people who were into ego-dominance. That was all they cared about was whether they dominated you."[338]

But the assassinations of the Manson clan had their counterpart in atrocious crimes perpetrated under the cover of social prejudice. The clearest example was the murder of a pregnant woman and her two small daughters, attributed by the father and spouse of the victims, the Army Special Forces physician Jeffrey Robert MacDonald (b. 1943), to a satanic group of drugged out hippies: "MacDonald told the police ... he was awakened by the screams of his wife and daughters, then was attacked by three men and a woman with long blond hair and a floppy hat who carried a lighted candle and chanted 'acid is groovy;

---

[337] Leary, Flashbacks, 1990, Chapter 38 Folsom Prison, p. 337.

[338] Gaskin, Stephen. Haight Ashbury Flashbacks. Berkeley, CA: Ronin Publishing, 1990 AO, p. 51.

kill the pigs.'"[339] The news produced a wave of wrath all over the country.

However, Captain MacDonald, who maintains his innocence to this day, was eventually convicted as the only one who could have perpetrated this monstrous crime:

> Prosecutors still contend that the evidence shows MacDonald used a knife and an ice pick to kill them before stabbing himself with a scalpel. They say he donned surgical gloves and used his wife's blood to write the word 'PIG' over their bed to imitate that year's Charles Manson murders [quotation marks, capitalization original].[340]

A friend testified that they had "discussed the ritualistic murders of the actress Sharon Tate and three of her friends only a couple of days before," a story which had appeared in the "current issue of *Esquire* magazine."[341] To imagine him writing with the blood of his own wife introduces a foreboding moral connotation to the expression WASP (White Anglo-Saxon Protestant).

Among those responsible for public health, no one wanted to understand that the prohibition of medical and religious use would promote the dissemination of every kind of poison; that even in the rare instances of unadulterated drugs, it would be impossible to avoid acquiring them except via the hands of someone else of dubious responsibility; and, that they were often consumed spontaneously in inadequate settings. In the large festivals (Monterey, Woodstock, Altamont, Wight) there were dozens of intoxications due to cuts

---

339 Richer, Alanna Durkin. "'Acid is groovy; kill the pigs'; Man convicted of killing pregnant wife, daughters says drug-fuelled hippies were the real killers," *Toronto Sun*, 17 January 2017 [torontosun.com, hereinafter TTS].

340 Richer, 2017, TTS.

341 Waldron, Martin. "Friend Says Captain Discussed Tate Killing Before Family Died," *New York Times*, 20 February 1970 NYT, p.38, col. 2.

[adulterations] of atropine, strychnine and phencyclidine (PCP), a fact proven from the toxicological analysis of the unconsumed samples left behind. When the authorities treated intoxications without being able to analyze the rest of the substance, they always maintained that the intoxication was caused by a psychedelically pure substance.

In LSD-Mein Sorgenkind [LSD: My Problem Child] Hofmann relates how between 1964 and 1966 there were not only enthusiastic claims for the drug but also "reports of accidents, mental breakdowns, criminal acts, murders, and suicide under the influence of LSD. A veritable LSD hysteria reigned."[342] When one tried to track down the basis of these reports, they were almost always "sensationally exaggerated by the mass media."[343] Hofmann of course did not try to dismiss an indeterminate number of administrations of LSD that unfolded into unfortunate episodes, even in suicides or crimes, but it is enough to compare the number of savage acts committed under the influence of alcohol and the suicides propitiated by the sedatives and somniferants. Without any exaggeration, the figure for the crimes and suicides attributable to these legal drugs in only one day grossly exceeds the analogous acts attributable to LSD over more than ten years, even attending to the most alarmist literature. This finding is even more significant considering that from 1970 no less than fifteen million people in the world had used LSD at least once.

Donald B. Louria (1928 – 2021), the Head of the Cornell Infectious Diseases Laboratory at Bellevue Hospital in New York City has perhaps been the most well-known medical professional compiling tragedies due to LSD. He is also the one who with the most firmness has maintained its pathogenic nature. Unfortunately, he is not a stickler for the facts.

---

342 Hofmann, 2001, Chapter 5 From Remedy to Inebriant, pp. 61, 62.

343 Hofmann, 2001, p. 67.

For example, he quotes from "noted neurologist, Dr. Roy Grinker, writing in the *Archives of General Psychiatry* in 1963" that LSD cannot only provoke a temporary psychosis but also a permanent one, even though the user has no previous clinical history, is perfectly sane, and the experience takes place in an adequate setting:

The drugs are indeed dangerous even when used under the best precautions. There are increasing numbers of reports that temporary or even permanent harm may be induced in spite of apparently careful pre-therapeutic screening of latent psychosis and careful precautions during the artificial psychosis. Here again is the story of evil results from the ill-advised use of a potentially useful drug due to unjustified claims, indiscriminate and premature publicity and lack of proper professional controls.[344]

The first two sentences are pure invention by Louria; Grinker did not write them. Only the last sentence can be found verbatim in Grinker's editorial in the May 1963 issue of the *Archives of General Psychiatry*, with the substitution of the word "useful" for the word in the original, "valuable."[345] Louria's inventive additions are contradicted by an article in the same issue which acknowledges the adverse effects of the drug but reiterates that LSD is a useful research tool:

Adverse effects can occasionally follow the administration of D-lysergic acid diethylamide (LSD). Complications such as prolonged psychotic reactions, severe depressive and anxiety states, or intensified sociopathic behavior are much more likely to occur after the unsupervised or inexpert use of this drug. When properly employed, LSD is a relatively safe and important research tool.[346]

---

[344] Louria, 1968, Chapter 8 LSD: Abuse and Disillusion, p. 148.

[345] Grinker, Roy R. "*Editorials*: Lysergic Acid Diethylamide," *Archives of General Psychiatry*, Volume 8, Issue 5, May 1963 AA, p. 425.

[346] Cohen, Sidney and Keith S. Ditman. "Prolonged Adverse Reactions to Lysergic Acid Diethylamide," *Archives of General Psychiatry*, Volume 8, Issue 5, May 1963 AA, Summary, p. 480, cols. 1, 2.

But adverse effects can also follow the casual, unsupervised use of naturally-occurring LSD congeners as well. The results of "casual ingestions of a psychochemical [morning glory seeds, called by the Aztecs *badoh* or *ololiuhqui*] whose properties were not well studied" varies considerably:

> Some individuals appeared to have no reaction whatsoever, others obtained a full blown LSD-like response. Side effects were rather frequent, nausea, vomiting, diarrhea, drowsiness, numbness of the extremities and muscle tightness have been described.[347]

In an extreme incident, three weeks after chewing "300 Heavenly Blue seeds (equivalent to 200-300 mcg. of LSD-25)" a 24 year old university student "dressed, drove his car to a nearby hill, hurtled down at a speed estimated at 90-100 miles an hour and crashed into a house at the bottom."[348]

Louria also narrates the blind teenagers case that came to the world's attention at the beginning of 1968. Again, the good doctor is less than precise with the facts of the case, placing the event in California [Pennsylvania] and numbering the victims at four [six]:

> And in California, four young students between the ages of eighteen and twenty-four stared at the sun while under the influence of LSD. Ordinarily, this would produce substantial discomfort, compelling an individual to close or avert his eyes. But these students felt no pain, continued to stare and permanently injured part of the retina, resulting in partial blindness.[349]

---

347 Cohen, Sidney. "Suicide Following Morning Glory Seed Ingestion," *American Journal of Psychiatry*, Volume 120, No. 10, April 1964 AA, p. 1024.

348 Cohen, 1964, p. 1025.

349 Louria, 1968, p. 154.

What was true was that in January 1968 the governor of Pennsylvania Raymond P. Shafer (1917 – 2006) announced to the press that six undergraduates had gone blind in 1966 from staring directly at the sun while under the influence of LSD. The very next day he reversed himself, calling the report a hoax:

> Gov. Raymond P. Shafer of Pennsylvania labeled as a hoax today the report that six college students were blinded by the sun while they were under the influence of LSD. The Governor, who yesterday told a news conference that he was convinced the report was true, said his investigators discovered this morning that the story was 'a fabrication' by Dr. Norman Yoder, commissioner of the Office of the Blind in the Pennsylvania State Welfare Department [quotation marks original].[350]

The nation's newspapers picked up the sensational story which had provoked the immediate interest of journalists and investigators interested in knowing the identity of the students and the degree of harm suffered by each. Their curiosity was not satisfied. Getting out in front of the foreseeable stories debunking the myth, Governor Shafer, who would two years later be named by President Richard Milhous Nixon (1913 – 1994) as the chairman of the National Commission on Marihuana and Drug Abuse (NCMDA), said the inventive commissioner was

> unavailable for comment [and] ... had admitted the hoax. ... Dr. Yoder was admitted to the Philadelphia Psychiatic Center this afternoon at his own request. ... The Governor's investigators ... described Dr. Yoder as 'distraught and sick' and apparently motivated 'by his concern over illegal LSD use by children' [quotation marks original].[351]

---

[350] Anonymous. "Governor Shafer Calls LSD Blindings a Hoax: Story of Six Students Who Stared at Sun is Laid to a Pennsylvania Official," *New York Times*, Volume 117, Issue 40,172, Friday 19 January 1968 AA, p. 22, col. 2.

[351] Anonymous, 1968, p. 22, col. 2.

It would not be necessary to comment further on the custom of personally fulfilling one's own prophecy had it not been that the next day a state senator declared the commissioner, described as a "prominent and highly respected state official," was telling the truth: "[T]he story gained credibility on Tuesday when State Senator Benjamin R. Donolow [a former narcotics agent] of Philadelphia said at a news conference that the story was true. He declined to name the students or their college."[352]

The senator's assertion is almost as interesting for the historian as that of the commissioner. Instead of telling their friends and other Americans about the dangers of a madness-inducing drug, the six mythical boys preferred to remain blind in secret rather than reveal their own names and compromise a dutiful public official, since the stigma of using (newly illicit) LSD was more undesirable than anything else. Considering the phenomenon as a whole, it is difficult not to agree with Thomas Szasz:

> These explanations hardly account for the enthusiastic acceptance of Dr. Yoder's story by the Pennsylvania state officials and the nation's press. The fact is that Dr. Yoder said what everyone wanted to hear and believe – namely, how terribly dangerous LSD really was.[353]

What everyone wanted to hear and believe was repeated regarding chromosomal abnormalities. After analyzing the white blood cells of "a population of illicit users of LSD and other drugs,"[354] some

---

352 Anonymous, 1968, p. 22, col. 4.

353 Szasz, 1974, III. Medicine as Social Control, Chapter 9 Missionary Medicine: Holy Wars on Unholy Drugs, p. 133.

354 Irwin, Samuel and Jose Egozcue. "Technical Comment," on "Chromosome Damage Not Found in Leukocytes of Children Treated with LSD-25," *Science*, Volume 159, Issue 3816, 16 February 1968 [science.org, hereinafter SCO], p. 749,

doctors announced to the media that the drug possessed teratogenic properties and was capable of producing genetic malformations. The world press echoed this immediately.

Although some specialized journals denied it, their reports received no publicity at all. One of the first physicians to reject the myth was the neuropsychiatrist Lauretta Bender (1897 – 1987), who worked for years with LSD and autistic children. Using a control group, she discovered "chromosome breakages of less than 2 percent of those examined were found in the children who had received LSD-25 and also in those who had not."[355] Nor is such breakage rare:

> The fact is ... chromosome breakage in white blood cells is a response which may occur in the presence of many other substances such as radioactivity, certain virus infections, and even aspirin and caffeine .... The British 1970 Advisory Committee on Drug Dependence ... judged that the existing evidence for LSD causing genetic abnormalities which might be transmitted on to future generations was very incomplete and that the genetic evidence was, in any case, very one-sided – only presenting the alarming cases and opinions.[356]

A 1968 review of the current scientific literature on the subject of LSD and chromosomal damage concluded:

---

col. 2.

[355] Bender, Lauretta and Siva Sankar. "Technical Comment," on "Chromosome Damage Not Found," *Science*, 1968, p. 749, col. 1; Wells, 1974, Chapter 5 Pathogenic Aspects, p. 106.

[356] Wells, 1974, p. 106.

All persons who take LSD are exposed to its chromosomal effects, although the evidence for a harmful effect on chromosomes from small doses is insufficient. Until questions concerning the normal level of chromosome abnormalities, the minimal sample size required for dependable analysis and the contribution of drugs other than LSD to abnormalities are answered, this evidence will be difficult to establish.[357]

A second review article three years later concluded that LSD did not cause genetic damage, was not a teratogen or carcinogen:

From our own work and from a review of the literature, we believe that pure LSD ingested in moderate doses does not damage chromosomes in vivo, does not cause detectable genetic damage, and is not a teratogen or a carcinogen in man. Within these bounds, therefore, we suggest that, other than during pregnancy, there is no present contraindication to the continued controlled experimental use of pure LSD.[358]

The matter remained definitively clarified upon knowing that the initial information on the effects of LSD did not come from simple users of LSD exclusively but were instead polydrug users:

Nearly all the subjects used or abused drugs other than LSD. These drugs included alcohol, amphetamine ... heroin ... mescaline ... MDA, MMDA ... nicotine ... psilocybin, and ritalin. ... In fact, most subjects were multiple drug users, abusers, or addicts exposed to toxic substances of unknown composition and potency.[359]

---

[357] Smart, Reginald G. and Karen Bateman. "The Chromosomal and Teratogenic Effects of Lysergic Acid Diethylamide: A Review of the Current Literature," *Canadian Medical Association Journal*, Volume 99, 26 October 1968 NIH, p. 810.

[358] Dishotsky, Norman I. et al. "LSD and Genetic Damage: Is LSD chromosome damaging, carcinogenica, mutagenic, or teratogenic?" *Science*, Volume 172, Issue 3982, 30 April 1971, Summary and Conclusion, p. 439, col. 3).

[359] Dishotsky et al., 1971, p. 434, cols. 1, 2.

In fact, much of this data was already in the possession of the 1966 Senate subcommittee charged with studying the possible illegalization of visionary drugs. It is also significant that one of its members Senator Abraham Alexander Ribicoff (Dem. CT, 1910 – 1998) stepped over the line between fantasy and reality. The senator argued something basically analogous to the motive behind which the Pennsylvania state senator had defended the lies of the Pennsylvania state commissioner:

> Only when you sensationalize a subject matter do you get reform. Without sensationalizing it, you don't. That is one of the great problems. You scientists may know something, a Senator may know something, but only when the press and television come in and give it a real play because it hits home as something that affects all the country, do you get action.[360]

It is not necessary to state that Congress decreed that LSD lacked any therapeutic use.

It might have come to a different conclusion, had the legislators listened to the interventions of the ill-fated brother of the late president, had they been introduced to the substance at some previous moment, had they at least trusted the opinion of persons with some experience with the substance, or had they heeded the warning from the representative from the NIMH:

> Senator, I have a very strong feeling that, if we make the possession of LSD illegal, it will drive it further underground and make what perhaps is the beginning of a flaunting of authority and experimenting with something new perhaps a more pathologic process and a more strongly accented act of rebellion.[361]

---

[360] Ribicoff, Abraham. Organization and Coordination, 1966, Sensationalism Brings Action, p. 50.

[361] Doctor Yolles, Organization and Coordination, 1966, Stringent Limits on Possession, p. 37.

Figure 490. Album Cover. Ehrich, Florian. "*50 Jahre, Sgt. Pepper's Lonely Hearts Club Band*," 1 June 2017 [deutschlandfunk.de, hereinafter DLF].

IV. The Return of the Pagan

From the middle 1960s to the middle 1970s drug consumption in the US was linked broadly with a return to rural life, ecology, sexual liberation, pacifism, humanist psychology and the counterculture. Globally there was a simultaneous abandonment of bourgeois and proletariat ideals in the name of a kind of individualistic paganism (gilded, for all that, with cooperativist elements) which demanded mankind use its technological progress instead of being used by it. If 1966 can be considered a critical year, 1968 will remain in the memory as the paradigm. This is the moment when millions of economically advantaged young people from developed countries take to the road as world travellers; others marginalize themselves without geographical displacement, preferring to live off the leavings than to give into the siren song of consumerism promoted by the so-called Establishment.

The motivation for this new paganism was expressed with eloquent frankness by the winner of the 1937 Nobel Prize in Physiology or Medicine Albert Imre Szent-Györgyi Nagyrápolt (1893 – 1986). When a journalist asked him in 1970 what he would do if he were twenty years old again, he replied:

> I would share with my classmates rejection of the whole world as it is – all of it. Is there any point in studying and work? Fornication – at least that is something good. What else is there? Fornicate and take drugs against this terrible strain of idiots who govern the world.[362]

The completely predictable response from America's ruling class was to prepare for the post-war purification by reinforcing the

---

[362] Reinhold, Robert. "Biologist Doubts Man's Survival in a World Run by 'Idiots,'" *New York Times*, Volume CXIX, No. 40,935, Friday 20 February 1970 NYT, p. 43, col. 1.

repressive/therapeutist industrial complex. With the ongoing conflict in Vietnam at its apogee, in 1971 "the use of heroin by GI's in Vietnam became, for the first time, a matter of grave concern."[363] President Nixon declared dramatically that not the war but the abuse of drugs was public enemy number one:

> In the judgment of some soberminded politicians, the spread of heroin addiction could have the effect of precipitating an American pullout from Southeast Asia. The President moved last week to head off any such repercussions, declaring a 'national emergency' and initialling the most intensive antidrug program yet undertaken in the U.S. Said Nixon: 'America's Public Enemy No. 1 is drug abuse' [quotation marks original].[364]

In 1972 the US Congress approved by 366 votes to 0 a federal attack on the abuse of drugs which would cost a billion dollars over three years and create the Drug Enforcement Administration (DEA):

> In 1972, the House voted unanimously to authorize a '$1 billion, three-year federal attack on drug abuse.' The Drug Enforcement Administration (DEA) began operations the following year .... The DEA was tasked with enforcing all federal drug laws, as well as coordinating broader drug interdiction activities. Under the direction of the DEA, what is now known as the War on Drugs quickly expanded in scale and scope [quotation marks original].[365]

---

363 Wald, Patricia M. and Peter Barton Hutt. "The Drug Abuse Survey Project: Summary of Findings, Conclusions, and Recommendations," in Dealing with Drug Abuse: *A Report to the Ford Foundation*, chaired by Wald and Hutt. NY: Praeger Publishers, 1972 AA, The Present Problem and Efforts to Control It, The Nature and Extent of Drug Abuse, pp. 6, 7.

364 Anonymous. "The New Public Enemy No. 1," *Time Magazine*, Volume 97, No. 26, 28 June 1971 [time.com, hereinafter TIM], p. 20, col. 1.

365 Coyne, Christopher J. and Abigail R. Hall. "Four Decades and Counting: The Continued Failure of the War on Drugs," *Policy Analysis*, Number 811, 12 April 2017 [cato.org, hereinafter CTO], p. 6, col. 2, p. 7, col. 1, citing '$1 Billion Voted for Drug

Spending would double the first year: "As the tables indicate, the government will spend about $417,601,000 on drug-abuse activities in fiscal 1972, almost double the amount spent in fiscal 1971."[366]

Up until that moment, drugs had given place to subcultures, but never to a complete alternative culture, defended by millions that occasionally demonstrated their power from time to time by coming together in musical festivals like Woodstock or Wight. It is difficult to believe that without LSD and analogous substances the so-called hippie movement would ever have existed; inversely, without the psychedelic movement these drugs would never have been listed in the satanic pharmacopoeia, with restrictions even more severe than upon the official stupefacients. Admittedly, this deals with a complex sociological phenomenon, perhaps too recent to admit an equanimical analysis.

However, even with the small distance proportioned to us by the passage of only a few years, one can barely understand the mix of wonder, fury and impotence expressed by the puritanical, publishing and political estates toward rock music. Much of their ire seemed to be directed at a single group and a single album by that same group. The John Birch Society launched a campaign in 1966 against the music of the Beatles, "convinced that the Beatles were themselves part of a communist plot to brainwash young people in the United States and the rest of the free world."[367] In a series of recorded telephone

---

Fight,' *Syracuse Herald Journal*, 16 March 1972.

[366] Goldberg, Peter B. and James V. DeLong. "Federal Expenditures on Drug-Abuse Control," in Wald, Hutt (1972), Total Federal Expenditures, p. 302.

[367] Roberts, Michael James. Tell Tchaikovsky the News: Rock 'n' Roll, the Labor Question, and the Musicians' Union, 1942 – 1968. Durham, NC: Duke University Press, 2014 AA, Chapter Four A Working Class Hero is Something to Be, pp. 171, 172.

messages, "the John Birch Society and other ultra-conservative groups" charged that

Communist scientists have discovered that music with a broken meter in the treble, played over in an insistently regular beat which increases to the point of frenzy can produce hysterical effects to [sic] young people, as if they were trying to rush madly in two directions at once. ... Is it any wonder the Communists have banned Beatle music and yet enthusiastically promote it in the United States ....[368]

Released in 1967, their album *Sgt. Pepper's Lonely Hearts Club Band*

played a large part in expanding the counterculture in America. ... Although John Lennon had publicly denied it, the second track on *Sgt. Pepper's*, 'Lucy in the Sky with Diamonds,' was a song about an acid trip. ... According to McCartney, 'It [LSD] opened my eyes. We only use one-tenth of our brains .... Just think what we could accomplish if we could tap the hidden part' [quotation marks, italics original].[369]

The venerable BBC banned the final track of the album, "A Day in the Life" because of the lyrics, "I'd love to turn you on." The director of sound broadcasting wrote to the chairman of the Beatles' record company, EMI on 23 May 1967:

We have listened to it over and over ... and we cannot avoid coming to the conclusion that the words, 'I'd love to turn you on,' ... could have a rather sinister meaning. ... 'Turned on' is ... currently much in vogue in the jargon of the drug-addicts [quotation marks original].[370]

---

368 Anonymous. "Beatles Unwitting Agents of Red Subversion, Sez One Right-Wing Group," *Variety*, Volume 244, No. 3, Wednesday, 7 September 1966 AA, p. 2, col. 4, p. 54, col. 3.

369 Roberts, 2014, pp. 193, 194, citing *Queen Magazine* and Thompson, Thomas. "The New Far-Out Beatles," *Life*, 16 June 1967.

370 Taysom, Jay. "Why the BBC Banned 'A Day in the Life' by the Beatles," *Far Out*

Figure 491. The Beatles. *Our World*, Sunday 25 June 1967 television broadcast to 24 countries, 400 to 700 viewers.

Magazine, Friday, 5 March 2021 [faroutmagazine.co.uk, hereinafter FOM]; see also the typewritten letter at beatlesbible.com.

Even three years after its release the former governor of Maryland and then vicepresident Spiro Theodore Agnew (1918 – 1996), in a speech to 1000 Republicans at the ... Sahara Hotel" in Las Vegas, Nevada, repeated the charge that American young people were being "brainwashed" by among other things rock music, specifically citing the Lennon/McCartney tune "With a Little Help from My Friends" from the same album:

> The Beatles' tune, he said, included these lines: 'I get by with a little help from my friends, I get high with a little help from my friends ....' Mr. Agnew said that it was ... 'a catchy tune, but until it was pointed out to me, I never realized that the 'friends' were assorted drugs' [quotation marks original].[371]

But not only this group but practically all musical groups were acting as unconditional propagandists for psychedelics.

It was as if suddenly *le club des hashischins* had opened an infinity of branch offices in the developed world and all of them were mercilessly conspiring against the reigning values and norms. At the same time this appeared to be a peaceful and creative venture which produced commercial novelties in music, the plastic arts, literature, clothes, artisanry, fashion, language, ceremonies and interpersonal conduct. In fact, these novelties were so profitable that they were only rejected in passing and later adopted on a massive scale, as soon as they could be adapted to fit into the consumerist dynamic.

This occurred when the effect of the austerity measures taken in the wake of the OPEC petroleum crisis (1973) substantially reduced the means available for going on the road with minimal guarantees of survival. It was also when the psychedelic community suffered the

---

[371] Naughton, James M. "Agnew Assails Songs and Film That Promote a 'Drug Culture,'" *The New York Times*, Volume CXIX, No. 41,142, Tuesday 15 September 1970 NYT, p. 18, col. 2; front page details from slounik.by.

infiltration of a basically miserable mass, attracted by the promises of gurus and irresponsibility, protected in the beginning by the stupor of the repressors and a large number of sympathizers. In fact, the twilight of the affluent society marked the twilight of its alternative.

Psychedelia as a way of life was a somewhat puerile option, but in matters of style it enjoyed formidable success. It is possible that this commercial assimilation would later lead to the posterior gradual decline of the original communities, and (without great holocausts) their disappearance. Curiously, not only traditional conservatives but also progressives (after a first epoch of unconditional agreement between psychedelics and radical politics) recognized the use of these drugs as a desertion from traditional politics. At a 1967 symposium the French-American leftist scholar and political activist John Gerassi (Tito, 1931 – 2012) encouraged withdrawal from society but also critiqued it as unlikely to succeed:

> And so we pull out and we become diggers, hippies, drug addicts .... What does this lead to? Well, it is disruptive and therefore it is to be encouraged. ... But is it effective? I have nothing against hippies, I have nothing against diggers. ... But can they be successful?[372]

A year later an anonymous writer in an alternative newspaper summarized the academic debate this way: "'Don't give Che Guevara LSD, he might stop fighting.' So I said, 'Well, how do you know he won't fight more efficiently [quotation marks original]?'"[373]

---

[372] Gerassi, John. "Imperialism and Revolution in America," in The Dialectics of Liberation, ed. David Cooper. Hammondsmith, Middlesex, UK: Penguin Books, 1968 AA/AO, p. 90.

[373] Anonymous. "A Speech: Dialectics of Liberation," in *The Realist*, No. 81 (The Digger Papers), August 1968 [ep.tc/realist, hereinafter EPT], p. 6; Lee and Shlain, 1985, p. 157.

As for the man in the street, these tie-dyed people were inexplicable mutants, though possessed of considerable magnetism. And if they were actually numerous in absolute terms, they marched under the banner of a largely unpopular revolution: a technology oriented to emancipatory not manipulative goals, a demolition of institutional supports for an authoritarian mentality, individual liberty and dignity. These were (from Huxley onwards) the basic points of a revolutionary program clear in its goals and obscure in its methods, all of it too radical for the majority of the American public.

By 1970 the founder and director of the Free Medical Clinic in Haight-Ashbury (rebaptized as Psychedelphia by its inhabitants) indicated that it was suffering a wave of undesirable immigrants, attracted by the propaganda of the repressors. To begin with, these new refugees rarely took psychedelic drugs but only imitated superficially those who did, for the simple reason that they were neurotic, violent and alienated, and better satisfied with heroin, alcohol, barbiturates and amphetamines:

> A new population has moved into the district and taken over Haight Street like an occupying army. Transient and diverse ... alienated ... overtly psychotic ... psychopathic .... Some have grown long hair and assimilated the hip jargon in the process, but they resemble true hippies in no real way. ... Although they smoke marijuana incessantly and drop acid on occasion, they generally dismiss these chemicals as child's play and prefer to intoxicate themselves with opiates, barbiturates and amphetamines.[374]

Yet, whether through the years of travel and communal living, or simply from taking LSD and other hallucinogens, there remain today

---

374 Smith, David E., John Luce and Ernest A. Dernburg. "The Health of Haight-Ashbury," *trans action: Social Science and Modern Society*, Volume 7, No. 6, April 1970 AA, p. 36, col.2, p. 37, col. 1.

dispersed around the world millions of what were once known in the United States as acidheads. Although reabsorbed sooner or later by the System, their views of what *Grosse Politik* could be had been changed for ever.

Figure 492. Flower child.

BIBLIOGRAPHY

Aaronson, Bernard and Humphry Osmond, eds. Psychedelics: *The Uses and Implications of Hallucinogenic Drugs*. Garden City, NY: Doubleday & Company, Inc., 1970

Aasmundstad, Tor A., et al. "Biotransformation and pharmacokinetics of ethylmorphine after a single dose," *British Journal of Clinical Pharmacology*, Volume 39, 1995

"ABC: Hollywood Fights Back," broadcast 2 November 1947

Abramson, Harold A., editor. The Use of LSD in Psychotherapy: *Transactions of a Conference on d-Lysergic Acid Diethylamide (LSD) April 22, 23, and 24, 1959, Princeton, N.J.* NY: Josiah Macy, Jr. Foundation, 1960

"A Conversation on LSD, Featuring Myron Stolaroff, Sidney Cohen, Al Hubbard, Timothy Leary, Oscar Janiger, Humphry Osmond and Others," V1.1, 16 February 1979

Adams, Leonard P. "Appendix China: The Historical Setting of Asia's Profitable Plague, The Tarnished Crusades," in McCoy, 1973

Aguar, Octavio. *Drogas y farmacos de abuso*. Madrid: Consejo General de Colegios Oficiales de Farmaceuticos, 1982

Alles, Gordon A. "Some Relations between Chemical Structure and Physiological Action of Mescaline and Related Compounds," in Neuropharmacology: Transactions of the Fourth Conference September 25, 26, and 27, 1957, Princeton, N. J., ed. Harold A Abramson. NY: Josiah Macy, Jr. Foundation, 1959

--------------------- "Subjective Reactions to Phenethylamine Hallucinogens," A Pharmacologic Approach to the Study of Mind, Robert M. Featherstone, Alexander Simon, eds. Springfield, IL: Charles C Thomas Publisher, 1959

Amidror, Isaac. The Theory of the Moire Phenomenon, Volume I: Periodic Layers, Second Edition. London: Springer-Verlag, 2009

Andreas, Peter. Killer High: A History of War in Six Drugs. NY: Oxford University Press, 2020

Andrus, Burton C. I Was the Nuremberg Jailer. NY: Tower Publications, Inc., 1969

Aniszewski, Tadeusz. Alkaloids – Secrets of Life: Alkaloid Chemistry, Biological Significance, Applications and Ecological Role. Amsterdam, NL: Elsevier, 2007

Anonymous. "Report on T. D., 2 June 1943," The Antique Cannabis Book, Second Edition

--------------- "'Truth' Drugs in Interrogation," *Studies in Intelligence*, Volume 5, No. 2, Spring 1961

--------------- "Pop 'Pot,'" *The Lancet*, Volume 282 (orig. vol. 2), No. 7315, Saturday 9 November 1963

--------------- "Beatles Unwitting Agents of Red Subversion, Sez One Right-Wing Group," *Variety*, Volume 244, No. 3, Wednesday, 7 September 1966

--------------- "A Prophesy of A Declaration of Independence," *The San Francisco Oracle* #1 Love Pageant Rally, 20 September 1966 in Cohen, ed., 1991

--------------- "Ken Kesey and the Great Pumpkin," *The San Francisco Oracle*, Number 3, Ken Kesey's Graduation Party, November 1966 in Cohen, Allen, ed. The San Francisco Oracle Facsimile Edition: The Psychedelic Newspaper of the Haight-Ashbury 1966-1968. Berkeley, CA: Regent Press, 1991

--------------- "Governor Shafer Calls LSD Blindings a Hoax: Story of Six Students Who Stared at Sun is Laid to a Pennsylvania Official," *New York Times*, Volume 117, Issue 40,172, Friday 19 January 1968

--------------- "A Speech: Dialectics of Liberation," in *The Realist*, No. 81 (The Digger Papers), August 1968

BIBLIOGRAPHY

Anonymous. "Bad Trip for Learys," *The Crimson*, TCC, 17 March 1970

---------------- "Leary Sentenced on Coast in Second Marijuana Case," *New York Times*, 17 March 1970

---------------- "The New Public Enemy No. 1," *Time Magazine*, Volume 97, No. 26, 28 June 1971

---------------- "The Great Bus Race," The Last Whole Earth Catalog: Access to Tools, Stewart Brand, ed. Menlo Park, CA: Nowels Publications, 1971

---------------- "Special Report: G2 in Crumbland," *The Guardian*, Monday 7 Mar 2005

Artaud, Antonin. *Les Tarahumaras*. Décines, Isere, FR: L'Arbalète Marc Barbezat, 1955

--------------------- The Peyote Dance, tr. Helen Weaver. NY: Farrar, Straus and Giroux, 1976

Anthony, Gene. The Summer of Love: Haight-Ashbury at its Highest. San Francisco, CA: Last Gasp, 1995

Associated Press. "Ex-Soldier is Denied Damages for Army LSD Experiments in 1957," *New York Times*, 29 December 1981

---------------------- "$700,000 Awarded to Estate of Army Drug Test Victim," *Los Angeles Times*, 6 May 1987

Ball, John C. "Two Patterns of Narcotic Drug Addiction in the United States," *Journal of Criminal Law and Criminology*, Volume 56, Issue 2, June 1965

Ban, Thomas A. "Fifty years chlorpromazine: a historical perspective," *Neuropsychiatric Disease and Treatment*, Volume 3, No. 4, 2007

Baratta, Alessandro. "*Introducción a la Criminología de la Droga*," (tr. Mauricio Martinez), *Comunidad y droga*, 3, 1988

Barrett, Marvin. "Aldous Huxley, Merchant of Mescalin," *The Reporter*, Volume 10, Number 5, 2 March 1954

Barrettt v United States, 660 F. Supp. 1291, U.S. District Court S.D. New York, 5 May 1987

Barron, Frank, Murray E. Jarvik, and Sterling Bunnell, Jr. "The Hallucinogenic Drugs," *Scientific American*, Volume 210, No. 4, April 1964

Bateson, Gregory. Steps to an Ecology of Mind: Collected Essays in Anthropology, Psychiatry, Evolution, and Epistemology. Northvale, NJ: Jason Aronson Inc., 1972

Becker, Howard S. Outsiders: Studies in the Sociology of Deviance. NY: The Free Press, 1963

Bedford, Sybille. Aldous Huxley, A Biography, Volume Two, The Turning Points, 1939-1963. London: Quartet Books, 1979

Benavente (Motolinía), Fray Toribio de. *Historia de Los Indios de la Nueva España*. Madrid: Real Academia Española, 2014

Bender, Lauretta. "Children's Reactions to Psychotomimetic Drugs," in Efron, Daniel H., ed. Psychotomimetic Drugs. NY: Raven Press, 1970

Benjamin, Walter. "*Mylovice-Braunschweig [Hbf.]-Marseille. Die Geschichte eines Haschisch-Rausch*" *UHU*, Volume VII, No. 2, November 1930

--------------------- *Über Haschisch: Novellistisches, Berichte, Materialien*. Frankfurt am Main, DE: Suhrkamp Taschenbuch Verlag, 1972

--------------------- On Hashish, tr. Howard Eiland, et al. Cambridge, MA: The Belknap Press of Harvard University Press, 2006

Bergel, Franz and D. R. A. Davies. All about Drugs. London: Thomas Nelson and Sons Ltd, 1970

Berman, Steven M., et al. "Potential Adverse Effects of Amphetamine Treatment on Brain and Behavior: A Review," *Mol Psychiatry*, 14 (2), February 2009

Bewley, Thomas. "Recent changes in the pattern of drug abuse in the United Kingdom," *Bulletin on Narcotics*, 01/01/1966

Bisbee, Cynthia Carson, et al, eds. Psychedelic Prophets: The Letters of Aldous Huxley and Humphry Osmond. Montreal, Canada: McGill-Queen's University Press, 2018

Black, Perry ed. Drugs and the Brain: *Papers on the Action, Use, and Abuse of Psychotropic Agents*, Baltimore, MD: Johns Hopkins Press, 1969

Blackledge, Robert D. and Charlotte M. Taylor. "*Psychotria Viridis* - A Botanical Source of Dimethyltryptamine (DMT)," *Microgram Journal*, Volume 1, Numbers 1-2, January – June 2003

Blake, William. The Letters of William Blake, ed. Archibald G. B. Russell. London: Methuen & Co., 1906

------------------- The Marriage of Heaven and Hell. Boston, MA: John W. Luce and Company, 1906

Blewett, Duncan. "The Psychedelics and Group Therapy," in Aaronson and Osmond, 1970

Blofeld, John. "A High Yogic Experience Achieved with Mescaline," *Psychedelic Review*, No. 7, 1966

Bradbury, Ray. Fahrenheit 451. NY: Ballantine Books, 1979

Bramness, Jørgen G. et al. "Amphetamine-induced psychosis – a separate diagnostic entity or primary psychosis triggered in the vulnerable?" *BMC Psychiatry*, Issue 12, 2012

Brand, Stewart, ed. The Last Whole Earth Catalog: Access to Tools. Menlo Park, CA: Nowels Publications, 1971

Brauchitsch, Hans V. "*Endokrinologisehe Aspekte des Wirkungsmechanismus nenroplegiseher Medikamente*," *Psychopharmacologia*, Volume 2, 1961

Brecher, Edward M., et al. Licit and Illicit Drugs. Boston, MA: Little, Brown and Company, 1972

Brown, Norman O. Life Against Death: The Psychoanalytical Meaning of History, Second edition. Middleton, CT: Wesleyan University Press, 1985

Brown, Shauna. "Five times Hollywood films have influenced beer sales," *The Drinks Business*, 9 January 2023

Buckman, John. "Theoretical Aspects of LSD Therapy," in Abramson, Harold A., ed. The Use of LSD in Psychotherapy and Alcoholism. Indianapolis, IN: The Bobbs-Merrill Company, Inc., 1967

Burleigh, Nina. A Very Private Woman: The Life and Unsolved Murder of Presidential Mistress Mary Meyer. NY: Bantam Books, 1998

Burroughs, William S. "Letter from a Master Addict to Dangerous Drugs," *The British Journal of Addiction*, Volume 53, No. 2, 1956

---------------------------- "Points of Distinction Between Sedative and Consciousness-Expanding Drugs," in Solomon, ed., 1966

---------------------------- Junky. London: Penguin Books Ltd., 1977

---------------------------- Naked Lunch. London: Harper Collins *Publishers*, 1993

Busch, Anthony K. and Warren C. Johnson. "L. S. D. 25 As an Aid in Psycho- therapy (Preliminary Report of a New Drug)," *Diseases of the Nervous System*, Volume XI, No. 8, August 1950

Calcedo-Ordonez, A. "*Uso, abuso y dependencia de los psicoestimulantes*," *Rev. de Psiq. y Psicol. Med.* 516, 1970

Cameron, D. Ewen. "Psychic Driving," *The American Journal of Psychiatry*, Volume 112, No. 7, January 1956

Carey, Benedict. "Dr. Thomas Szasz, Psychiatrist Who Led Movement Against His Field, Dies at 92," *NY Times*, 11 Sep 2012

Carroll, Aaron E. "Alcohol or Marijuana? A Pediatrician Faces the Question," *The Incidental Economist* 18 March 2015

Castillo, Jose. "*La Funcion Social del Castigo: El Caso de la Prohibicion Legal del Consumo de «Droga»,*" *REIS*

Cedillo, Jaime. "*William S. Burroughs, el más sangriento de la generación 'beat,'*" *El Cultural*, 1 agosto 2022

Chang, Hsin-pao. Commissioner Lin and the Opium War. New York: W.W. Norton and Co., Inc., 1964

Charlesworth, Annemarie and Stanton A. Glantz. "Smoking in the Movies Increases Adolescent Smoking: A Review," *Pediatrics*, Volume 116, No. 6, December 2005

Charpentier, Paul et al. "*Recherches sur les diméthylaminopropyl-N phénothiazines substituées,*" Comptes Rendus Hebdomadaires des Séances de l'Académie des Sciences, Tome Deux-Cent-Trente-Cinquième, Juillet – Décembre 1952

Chawkins, Steve. "Joel Fort dies at 86; iconoclastic psychiatrist testified in Patty Hearst case," *Los Angeles Times*, 27 August 2015

Cheek, Francis E. and Carolyn M. Holstein. "Lysergic Acid Diethylamide Tartrate (LSD – 25) Dosage Levels, Group Differences, and Social Interaction," *Journal of Nervous and Mental Disease*, Volume 153, No. 2, 1971

Chen K. K. and Schmidt, Carl F. "The action and clinical use of ephedrine: an alkaloid isolated from the Chinese drug Ma Huang," *Journal of the American Medical Association*, Volume 87, No. 11, 11 September 1926

Chien, Isidor et al. The ROAD to H: Narcotics, Delinquency, and Social Policy. NY: Basic Books, *Inc. Publishers*, 1964

Cholden, Louis S., Albert Kurland, Charles Savage. "Clinical Reactions and Tolerance to LSD in Chronic Schizophrenia," *Journal of Nervous and Mental Disease*, Vol. 122, No. 3, September 1955

Chopra, M. D. G. S. and Chopra, M. D. Paramjeet Singh. "Studies on 300 Indian drug addicts with special reference to psychosociological aspects, etiology and treatment," *Bulletin on Narcotics*, 01/01/1965

Chow, Rachel T. S., et al. "An umbrella review of adverse effects associated with antipsychotic medications: the need for complementary study designs," *Neuroscience and Behavioral Reviews*, Volume 155, 2023

Clark, Matthew. "*Soma* and *Haoma*: Ayahuasca Analogues from the Late Bronze Age," *Journal of Psychedelic Studies*, Volume 3, Issue 2, 2019

Clark, Walter Houston. Chemical Ecstasy: Psychedelic Drugs and Religion. NY: Sheed & Ward, 1969

Cohen, Allen, ed. The San Francisco Oracle Facsimile Edition: The Psychedelic Newspaper of the Haight-Ashbury 1966-1968. Berkeley, CA: Regent Press, 1991

Cohen, Sidney. "Lysergic Acid Diethylamide: Side Effects and Complications," *Journal of Nervous and Mental Disease*, Volume 130, No. 1, January 1960

------------------ and Keith S. Ditman. "Complications Associated with Lysergic Acid Diethylamide (LSD-25)," *Journal of the American Medical Association*, Volume 181, No. 2, 14 July 1962

------------------ and Keith S. Ditman. "Prolonged Adverse Reactions to Lysergic Acid Diethylamide," *Archives of General Psychiatry*, Volume 8, Issue 5, May 1963

------------------ "Suicide Following Morning Glory Seed Ingestion," *American Journal of Psychiatry*, Volume 120, No. 10, April 1964

------------------ The Beyond Within: The LSD Story. NY: Atheneum, 1965

Comas Arnau, Domingo. "*La Medida de la Incidencia, Prevalencia y Problemas Causados por Drogas Ilegales*," REIS 1986

Comments on Narcotic Drugs: Interim Report of the Joint Committee of the American Bar Association and the American Medical Association on Narcotic Drugs by Advisory Committee to the Federal Bureau of Narcotics, US, Treasury Department, Bureau of Narcotics. Washington, DC: Government Printing Office, 1959.

Connell, P. H. "Amphetamine Dependence," *Proc. R. Soc. Med.* Volume 61, February 1968

Cooke, Rachel. "High Hitler: how Nazi drug abuse steered the course of history," *The Observer*, 25 Sep 2016

Cormack, Jack. "Dependence on Dextromoramide," *British Medical Journal*, 11 February 1967

Council on Drugs. "Evaluation of a Tranquilizing Agent Diazepam (Valium)," *Journal of the American Medical Association*, Volume 189, No. 5, 3 August 1964

Covner, Albert H. and Seymour L. Halpern. "Fatal Agranulocytosis Following Therapy with 'Presidon' (3,3-diethyl-2,4-dioxotetrahydropyridine), a New Sedative Hypnotic Agent," *The New England Journal of Medicine*, Volume 242, No. 2, 12 January 1950

Coyne, Christopher J. and Abigail R. Hall. "Four Decades and Counting: The Continued Failure of the War on Drugs," *Policy Analysis*, Number 811, 12 April 2017

Cozanitis, Dimitri A. "One hundred years of barbiturates and their saint," *Journal of the Royal Society of Medicine*, Volume 97, December 2004

Crewdson, John M. "Files Show Tests for Truth Drug Began in O.S.S.," *New York Times*, Monday, 5 September 1977

Curphey, Theodore J. "Statement by Theodore J. Curphey, M.D., Chief Medical Examiner-Coroner, County of Los Angeles, 17 August 1962," Marilyn Monroe Autopsy Report, 5 August 1962

Dalí, Salvador. The Secret Life of Salvador Dali, tr. Haakon M. Chevalier. NY: Dial Press, 1942

------------------ 50 Secrets of Magic Craftsmanship, tr. Haakon M. Chevalier. NY: Dove Publications, Inc., 1992

Dally, Peter. Chemotherapy of Psychiatric Disorders. London: Logos Press Limited, 1967

Daniel, Price. Illicit Narcotics Traffic, Hearings before the Subcommittee on Improvements in the Federal Criminal Code of the Committee of the Judiciary, United States Senate, Eighty-Fourth Congress, First Session, Part 7. Washington, DC: US Government Printing Office, 1956

Dass, Ram and Ralph Metzner. Birth of a Psychedelic Culture: Conversations about Leary, the Harvard Experiments, Millbrook and the Sixties. Santa Fe, NM: Synergetic Press, 2010

Davis, Charles A. and Robert D. Gruener. "Glutethimide – A New Nonbarbiturate Hypnotic," *California Medicine*, Volume 84, No. 4, April 1956

Defoe, Daniel. The Political History of the Devil, in one volume. Oxford, UK: Printed for D. A. Talboys, for Thomas Tegg, 1840

De la Vega, Garcilaſſo. *Primera Parte de los Commentarios Reales*. Lisboa: En la officina de Pedro Crasbeeck, 1609

-------------------------- The Royal Commentaries of Peru, in Two Parts, tr. Sir Paul Rycaut. London: Printed for *Miles Fleſher*, for *Jacob Tonſon*, 1688

Delay, J., et al. "*Premiers Essais de la Psilocybine en Psychiatrie* [First Trials of Psilocybin in Psychiatry]," Proceedings of the First International Congress of Neuropsychopharmacology, Rome, September 1958, ed. P. B. Bradley, et al. Amsterdam, NE: Elsevier, 1959

Delay, J., et al. "*Les effets somatiques de la psilocybine,*" in Abély, Paul, editor-in-chief. *Annales Médico-Psychologiques*, Tome Premier. Paris: Masson & Cie, Éditeurs, 1959

Devenyi, Paul and Mary Wilson. "Barbiturate abuse and addiction and their relationship to alcohol and alcoholism," *C. M. A. Journal*, Volume 104, 6 February 1971

Didion, Joan. "The Hippie Generation: Slouching Towards Bethlehem," *The Saturday Evening Post*, Volume 240, Issue 19, 23 September 1967

Dishotsky, Norman I. et al. "LSD and Genetic Damage: Is LSD chromosome damaging, carcinogenica, mutagenic, or teratogenic?" *Science*, Volume 172, Issue 3982, 30 April 1971

Doblin, Rick. "Pahnke's 'Good Friday Experiment:' A Long-Term Follow-Up and Methodological Critique," *The Journal of Transpersonal Psychology*, Volume 23, No. 1, 1991

----------------- "Dr. Leary's Concord Prison Experiment: A 34-Year Follow-Up Study," *Journal of Psychoactive Drugs*, Volume 30, Issue 4, Oct-Dec 1998

Dole, Vincent P. and Marie E. Nyswander. "Heroin Addiction – A Metabolic Disease," *Archives of Internal Medicine*, Volume 120, July 1967

Downing, Joseph. "Attitude and Behavior Change Through Psychedelic Drug Use," in Tart, Charles T., ed. Altered States of Consciousness. Garden City, NY: Doubleday & Company, Inc., 1969

Drewes, Asbjørn M., et al. "Differences Between Opioids: pharmacological, experimental, clinical and economical perspectives," *British Journal of Clinical Pharmacology*, Volume 75, Issue 1, 3 May 2012

Dumézil, Georges. *Le Festin d'Immortalité: Étude de Mythologie Comparée Indo-Européenne*, *Annales du Musée Guimet, Étude de Mythologie Comparée Indo-Européenne, Tome* 34. Paris: Librairie Orientaliste Paul Geuthner, 1924

Dunlap, Sir Derrick. "The Use and Abuse of Psychotropic Drugs," *Proceedings of the Royal Society of Medicine*, Volume 63, December 1970

Durkheim, Emile. *De la Division du Travail Social: Étude sur L'organisation des Sociétés Supérieures*. Paris: Ancienne Librarie Germer Baillière et Cie, 1893

---------------------- *Les Règles de la Méthode Sociologique*, Septiéme Édition. Paris: Librairie Félix Alcan, 1919

---------------------- The Division of Labor in Society, tr. George Simpson. Glencoe, IL: The Free Press, 1933

Dyck, Erica. "Psychedelic Research in 1950s Sasketchewan," The Canadian Encyclopedia, 2019

Editor. "Bigger Agricultural Subsidies ....," *The New York Times*, 1 February 1964

Editorial Board. "The Tobacco Subsidy," *The New York Times*, Section E, 15 March 1964

Editors. "Psychiatric Examination of Rudolph Hess," *Journal of the American Medical Association*, Volume 130, No. 12, 23 March 1946

Elder, Sean. "Revisiting the Violent, Sometimes Wacky World of America's 1970s Radical Underground," *Newsweek*, 20 April 2015

Elkes J. and Charmian Elkes. "Effect of Chlorpromazine on the Behaviour of Chronically Overactive Psychotic Patients," *British Medical Journal*, Volume 29, No. 4887, Saturday 4 September 1954

Ellis, Havelock. "Mescal: A New Artificial Paradise," in The Contemporary Review, Volume LXXIII, January – June. London: Isbister and Company Limited, 1898

Elton-Waters, Jack. "Tom Simpson 1937 – 1967: A Life in Pictures," *Cycling Weekly*, 31 July 2017

Essig, Carl F. and John D. Ainslie. "Addiction to Meprobamate (Miltown, Equanil)," *Journal of the American Medical Association*, 20 July 1957

Estrada, Alvaro. *La Vida de María Sabina, La Sabia de los Hongos*. Ciudad DF, MX: siglo vientiuno editores, sa, 1977

Eugster, C. H., G.F.R. Miiller & R. Good. "*Wirkstoffe aus Amanita muscaria: ibotensaeure und muscazon*," *Tetrahedron Letters* No. 23, 1965

Evans, Harold. "How men who blighted lives of thousands with thalidomide evaded justice," *The Globe and Mail*, 25 November 2014

Evans-Wentz, W. Y., tr. The Tibetan Book of the Dead. London: Oxford University Press, 1957

Eysenck, H. J. Crime and Personality. Great Britain: Routledge & Kegan Paul Ltd, 1964

Faggen, Robert. "The Art of Fiction CXXXVI: Ken Kesey," *The Paris Review*, Volume 36, No. 130, Spring 1994

Fahey, Todd. "The Original Captain Trips," *High Times Magazine*, November 1991

Fallon, Michael. "A New Paradise for Beatniks," *San Francisco Examiner*, 5 September 1965

------------------- "Bohemia's New Haven," *San Francisco Examiner*, 7 September 1965

Félice, Philippe de. *Poisons sacrés, Ivresses divines: Essai sur quelques formes inférieures de la mystique*. Paris: Albin Michel, 1936

Fiddle, Seymour. Portraits from a Shooting Gallery: Life Styles from the Drug Addict World. NY: Harper and Row, Publishers, 1967

Fifth International Tin Agreement (with annexes). Concluded at Geneva on 21 June 1975, Volume 1014, No. 14851. United Nations Treaty Series 1976

Fillingim, J. M. "Double-blind Evaluation of the Efficacy and Safety of Temazepam in Outpatients with Insomnia," *Br. J. clin. Pharmac.*, Volume 8, 1979

Finney, Nathaniel and Jay S. Siegel. "In Memoriam: Albert Hofmann (1906– 2008)," CHIMIA *International Journal for Chemistry*, Volume 62, No. 5, 2008

First International Coffee Agreement, 1962. United Nations Treaty Series, No. 6791, 1963

Flood, Richard. "Curzio Malaparte: Casa Malaparte, 1938," *Artforum Newsletters*, Volume 35, No. 10, Summer 1997

Fort, Joel. The Addicted Society: Pleasure-Seeking and Punishment Revisited. NY: Grove Press, Inc., 1981

Forte, Robert. "*The Harvard Crimson Story*: An Interview with Andrew Weil," in Timothy Leary: Outside Looking In, Robert Forte, ed. Rochester, VT: Park Street Press, 1999

----------------, ed. Timothy Leary: Outside Looking In. Rochester, VT: Park Street Press, 1999

Fotheringham, William. Put Me Back on My Bike: *In Search of Tom Simpson*. London: Yellow Jersey Press, 2002

Freedman, Daniel X. "On the use and abuse of LSD," *Archives of General Psychiatry,* Volume 18, No. 3, March 1968

Freud, Sigm. *Das Unbehagen in der Kultur*. Wien, AT: Internationaler Psychoanalytischer Verlag, 1930

---------------- Civilization and its Discontents, tr. Joan Riviere. London: Hogarth Press, 1930

Fuentes, Juan José, et al. "Therapeutic Use of LSD in Psychiatry: A Systematic Review of Randomized-Controlled Clinical Trials," *Frontiers in Psychiatry*, Volume 10, Article 943, 21 January 2020

Fulsom, Don. The Mafia's President: Nixon and the Mob. NY: St. Martin's Press, 2017

Gaines, Bob. "LSD: Hollywood's Status-Symbol Drug," *Cosmopolitan*, Volume 155, Issue 5, November 1963

Gaskin, Stephen. Haight Ashbury Flashbacks. Berkeley, CA: Ronin Publishing, 1990

Gawin, Frank H., et al. "Cocaine and other stimulants: Actions, Abuse and Treatment (Medical Progress)," *The New England Journal of Medicine*, Volume 318, No. 18, May 1988

Gerassi, John. "Imperialism and Revolution in America," in The Dialectics of Liberation, ed. David Cooper. Hammondsmith, Middlesex, UK: Penguin Books, 1968

Ghiabi, Maziyar. Drugs Politics: Managing Disorder in the Islamic Republic of Iran. Cambridge, UK: Cambridge University Press, 2019

Gilbert, Christopher L. "International Commodity Agreements: An Obituary," *World Development*, Volume 24, No. 1, 1996

Ginsberg, Allen. "First Manifesto to End the Bringdown," in Solomon, ed., 1966

Glatt, M. M. "The abuse of barbiturates in the United Kingdom," *Bulletin on Narcotics*, 01/01/1962

Goldberg, Peter B. and James V. DeLong. "Federal Expenditures on Drug-Abuse Control," in Wald, Hutt (1972)

Goldsmith, Margaret. The Trail of Opium: The Eleventh Plague. London: Robert Hale Limited, 1939

Goldstein, Kurt. The Organism: A Holistic Approach to Biology Derived from Pathological Data in Man. NY: American Book Company, 1939

Goode, Erich. "Marijuana and Sex," *Evergreen Review*, Volume 13, No. 66, May 1969

Grant, David N. W. "Benzedrine Alert," *The Air Surgeon's Bulletin*, Volume One, No. 2, February 1944

Graves, Robert. "The Poet's Paradise: Address to the Oxford University Humanist Group," in Oxford Addresses on Poetry. Garden City, NY: Doubleday & Co., Inc., 1962

-------------------- Difficult Questions, Easy Answers. NY: Doubleday & Company, Inc., 1964

Greene, Wade. "The Militants Who Play With Dynamite," *New York Times*, Volume CXX, No. 41,182, Sunday 25 October 1970

Greenfield, Robert. Timothy Leary: A Biography. NY: Harcourt, Inc., 2006

----------------------- Bear: The Life and Times of Augustus Owsley Stanley III. NY: St. Martin's Press, 2016

Griffiths, R. R. et al. "Psilocybin can occasion mystical-type experiences having substantial and sustained personal meaning and spiritual significance," *Psychopharmacology*, Volume 187, No. 3, Aug 2006

Grinker, Roy R. "*Editorials*: Lysergic Acid Diethylamide," *Archives of General Psychiatry*, Volume 8, Issue 5, May 1963

Grof, Stanislav. "Use of LSD 25 in Personality Diagnostics and Therapy of Psychogenic Disorders," in Aaronson and Osmond, 1970

------------------ and Joan Halifax. The Human Encounter with Death. NY: E. P. Dutton, 1977

Hagenbach, Dieter and Lucius Werthmüller. *Albert Hofmann und sein LSD*. Aarau, CH: AT Verlag, 2011

Harris, Titus H. "Methaminodiazepoxide," *Journal of the American Medical Association*, 12 March 1960

Heal, David J. et al. "Amphetamine, past and present – a pharmacological and clinical perspective," *Journal of Psychopharmacology*, 27(6) 2013

Heffter, A. "*Ueber Pellote*," *Archiv fur Experimentelle Pathologie und Pharmakologie*, Vol. 40, 1898

Heidegger, Martin. *Vorträge und Augsätze*. Pfullingen, DE: Verlag Gunther Neske, 1954

---------------------- The Question Concerning Technology and Other Essays, tr. William Lovitt. NY: Harper & Row, Publishers, 1977

---------------------- and Ernst Jünger. Correspondence 1949 – 1975, tr. Timothy Sean Quinn. London: Rowman & Littlefield, 2016

Heim, Roger and R. Gordon Wasson. *Archives du Muséum National d'Histoire Naturelle, Septième Série, Tome VI*: *Les Champignons Hallucinogènes du Mexique: Éudes ethnologiques, taxinomiques, biologiques, physiologiques et chimiques*. Paris: Éditions du muséum, 1958

Hernandez, Francisci. *Rerum Medicaum Novae Hispaniae Thesaurus seu Plantarum Animalium Mineralium Mexicanorum*, ed. Nardo Antonio Recchi. Roma: Ex typographeio Vitalis Mascardi, 1651

Hesse, Hermann. *Der Steppenwolf*. Frankfurt am Main, DE: Suhrkamp Verlag, 1961

-------------------- Steppenwolf, tr. Basil Creighton. NY: Bantam Books, 1963

Hoffer, Abram. "Treatment of alcoholism with psychedelic therapy," in Psychedelics: The Uses and Implications of Hallucinogenic Drugs, Bernard Aaronson and Humphry Osmond, eds. Cambridge, MA: Schenkman Publishing Company, 1971

------------------ and Osmond, H. The Hallucinogens. NY: Academic Press, 1967

Hofmann, Albert, Heim, R., Brack, A. and H. Kobel. "*Psilocybin, ein psychotroper Wirkstoff aus dem mexikanischen Rauschpilz Psilocybe mexicana Heim*," *Experientia*, Volume XIV, No. 3, 1958

--------------------- "The Active Principles of the Seeds of Rivea Corymbosa and Ipomoea Violacea," *Botanical Museum Leaflets, Harvard University*, Volume XX, No. 6, 22 November 1963

--------------------- LSD: My Problem Child, Reflections on Sacred Drugs, Mysticism, and Science, tr. Jonathan Ott. Los Angeles, CA: J. P. Tarcher, Inc., 1983

--------------------- *LSD - mein Sorgenkind: Die Entdeckung einer »Wunderdroge«*. München, DE: Deutscher Taschenbuch Verlag GmbH & Co. KG, 2001

Holden, Brad. Seattle Mystic Alfred M. Hubbard: Inventor, Bootlegger and Psychedelic Pioneer. Charleston, SC: The History Press, 2021

Hollingshead, Michael. The Man Who Turned On the World. NY: Bland & Briggs, Ltd., 1973

Hollister, Leo E., Francis P. Motzenbecker and Roger O. Degan. "Withdrawal reactions from chlordiazepoxide (Librium)," *Psychopharmacologia*, **2**: 63-68, 1961

Horowitz, Michael and Cynthia Palmer. Moksha: Aldous Huxley's Classic Writings on Psychedelics and the Visionary Experience. Rochester, VT: Park Street Press, 1977

---, eds. Moksha: Aldous Huxley's Classic Writings on Psychedelics and the Visionary Experience. Rochester, VT: Park Street Press, 1999

Huxley, Aldous. "Wanted, A New Pleasure," in Music at Night & Other Essays. London: Chatto & Windus, 1931

-------------------- The Art of Seeing. London: Chatto & Windus, 1943

-------------------- Time Must Have a Stop. London: Chatto & Windus, 1944

-------------------- The Perennial Philosophy. London: Chatto & Windus, 1947

-------------------- The Devils of Loůdun. London: Chatto & Windus, 1952

-------------------- "A Case for ESP, PK and PSI," *Life Magazine*, Volume 36, No. 2, 11 Jan 1954

-------------------- The Doors of Perception, Includes Heaven and Hell. NY: Harper & Row Publishers, 1954

-------------------- "Mescaline and the 'Other World,'" Proceedings of the Round Table on Lysergic Acid Diethylamide and Mescaline in Experimental Psychiatry held at the annual meeting of the American Psychiatric Association, Atlantic City, New Jersey, 12 May 1955, Louis Cholden, ed. NY: Grune & Stratton, 1956

-------------------- "Brave New World Revisited: Proleptic meditations on Mother's Day, euphoria and Pavlov's pooch," *Esquire, Magazine for Men*, Volume XLVI, No. 1, Whole No. 272, 1 July 1956

Huxley, Aldous. "History of Tension," *The Scientific Monthly*, Volume 85, July – December, 1957

------------------- "Drugs That Shape Men's Minds," *Saturday Evening Post*, Volume 231, Issue 16, 18 October 1958

------------------- Brave New World *and* Brave New World Revisited. NY: Harper & Brothers, Publishers, 1960

------------------- Collected Essays. NY: Harper & Row, Publishers, Inc., 1960

------------------- "Speaking Personally # 2 Aldous Huxley 1961," Interview with John Chandos 11 July 1961

------------------- Island. NY: Harper & Row, Publishers, 1962

------------------- "Has Man's Conquest of Space Increased or Diminished His Stature?" The Great Ideas Today 1963. Chicago, IL: Encyclopaedia Britannica, 1963

------------------- "a philosopher's visionary prediction," Playboy Magazine, Volume 10, No. 11, November 1963

Huxley, Julian, ed. Aldous Huxley 1894-1963: A Memorial Volume. NY: Harper & Row, 1965

------------------ Memories, Volume II. NY: Harper & Row, Publishers, 1973

Ibáñez, L. et al. "Agranulocytosis induced by pyrithyldione, a sedative hypnotic drug," *European Journal of Clinical Pharmacology*, Volume 55, February 2000

Illana, C. "*Robert Gordon Wasson: Un Pionero de la Etnamicologia*," *Boletín de la Sociedad Micológica de Madrid*, Volume 31, Octubre 2007

Ilnytzky, Ula. "What a trip: Timothy Leary's files go public in New York," 18 September 2013

International Cocoa Agreement, 1975, Volume 1023, No. 15033. United Nations Treaty Series 1976

International Narcotics Control Board. Narcotic Drugs: Estimated World Requirements for 2015, Statistics for 2013, Document E/INCB/2014/2. NY: United Nations, 2015

International Sugar Agreement of 1958, No. 5534. United Nations Treaty Series 1961

"Interview with Myles J. Ambrose," *Frontline*, WGBH

Irwin, Samuel and Jose Egozcue. "Technical Comment," on "Chromosome Damage Not Found in Leukocytes of Children Treated with LSD-25," *Science*, Volume 159, Issue 3816, 16 February 1968

Isbell, Harris, et al. "Tolerance and Addiction Liability of 6-dimethylamino-4-4-diphenyl-heptanone-3 (methadon)," *The Journal of the American Medical Association*, Volume 135, Number 14, 6 December 1947

------------------------ "Studies on Lysergic Acid Diethylamide (LSD – 25)," *A.M.A. Archives of Neurology and Psychiatry*, Volume 76, November 1956

Jackson, Robert H. Trials of War Criminals Before the Nuernberg Military Tribunals, Volume II. Nuernberg, DE: USGPO, October 1946 – April 1949

James, Clive. "Out of Sight," *The New Yorker*, Volume 79, Issue 4, 17 March 2003

James, William. The Varieties of Religious Experience, *A Study in Human Nature*. New York: The Modern Library, 1902

Janney, Peter. Mary's Mosaic: The CIA Conspiracy to Murder John F. Kennedy, Mary Pinchot Meyer, and Their Vision for World Peace. NY: Skyhorse Publishing, 2013

Janssen, Paul A. J. Synthetic Analgesics, Part I, Diphenylpropylamines. NY: Pergamon Press, 1960

Jefferson, Thomas. Notes on the State of Virginia. London: John Stockdale, 1788

Johnson, Donald McI. Indian Hemp: A Social Menace. London: Christopher Johnson, 1952

Johnson, Lyndon B. "Special Message to the Congress on the Food for Peace Program," The American Presidency Project, 31 March 1965

Jones, M. A. "Office Memorandum to Mr. Nichols, Subject: George H. White (Federal Bureau of Narcotics," United States Government, 28 February 1952

Jünger, Ernst. *Über die Linie*. Frankfurt am Main, DE: Vittorio Klostermann, 1950

----------------- *Besuch auf Godenholm* [Visit to Godenholm]. Frankfurt am Main, DE: Vittorio Klostermann, 1952

----------------- *Annäherungen: Drogen und Rausch*. Stuttgart, DE: Ernst Klett Verlag, 1970

----------------- Approaches: Drugs and Ecstatic Intoxication, unknown translator. Unknown place of publication: Unknown publisher, 1970

----------------- The Worker, tr. Bogdan Costea and Laurence P. Hemming. Stuttgart, DE: Klett-Cotta, 1981

----------------- *Der Arbeiter*. Stuttgart, DE: Klett-Cotta, 1981

Junkes, Larissa et al. "Leo Sternbach and the benzodiazepines 60 years on: A revolutionary treatment for anxiety disorders," *Pharmacological Research* **207**, 2024

Kast, Eric and Vincent J. Collins. "Study of Lysergic Acid Diethylamide as an Analgesic Agent," *Anesthesia and Analgesia,* Volume 43, No. 3, May-June 1964

Kast, Eric. "Pain and LSD-25: A Theory of Attenuation of Anticipation," in Solomon, David, ed. LSD: The Conscious - ness-Expanding Drug. NY: G. P. Putnam's Sons, 1966

-------------- "A Concept of Death," in Aaronson and Osmond, Psychedelics, 1970

Kelsey, Frances O. "Problems Raised for the FDA by the Occurrence of Thalidomide Embryopathy in Germany, 1960-1961," *American Journal of Public Health*, Volume 55, No. 5, May 1965

Kennedy, Edward. "Project MKULTRA, The CIA's Program of Research in Behavioral Modification," Joint Hearing before the Select Committee on Intelligence and the Subcommittee on Health and Scientific Research of the Committee on Human Resources, United States Senate, Ninety-Fifth Congress, First Session, 3 August 1977. Washington, DC: USGPO, 1977

----------------------- "First session on examination on the use and misuse of valium, librium, and other minor tranquilizers, September 10, 1979," Use and Misuse of Benzodiazepines: Hearing before the Subcommittee on Health and Scientific Research of the Committee on Labor and Human Resources, United States Senate, Ninety-Sixth Congress. Washington, DC: US Government Printing Office, 1980

Kennedy, John F. "Special Message to the Congress on Mental Illness and Mental Retardation," The American Presidency Project 5 February 1963

Kerouac, Jack. On the Road. NY: The Viking Press, Inc., 1957

Kesey, Ken. One Flew Over the Cuckoo's Nest. NY: Signet Books, 1962

-------------- Sometimes a Great Notion. NY: Bantam Books, 1972

-------------- *Intrepid Traveller and His Merry Band of Pranksters Look for a Cool Place: A Work in Progress by Ken Kesey, Episode One A Journey to the East*, 1999

Khadraoui, Norah. "Comparing the Anti-Drug Abuse Act of 1986 to the Boggs Act of 1951 and the Narcotic Control Act of 1956 in Levels of Severity," *The Young Researcher*, Volume 3, Issue 1, 2019

Kim, Leena. "Inside the Unsolved Murder of JFK's Mistress Mary Pinchot Meyer," *Town and Country*, 25 May 2020

King, Leslie A. The Misuse of Drugs Act: A Guide for Forensic Scientists. Cambridge, UK: The Royal Society of Chemistry, 2003

King, Rufus. Drug Addiction: Crime or Disease? Interim *and* Final Reports. Bloomington, IN: Indiana University Press, 1971

Kinzer, Stephen. Poisoner in Chief: Sidney Gottlieb and the CIA Search for Mind Control. NY: Henry Holt and Company, 2019

Kitrie, Nicholas N. The Right to Be Different: Deviance and Enforced Therapy. Baltimore, MD: The Johns Hopkins Press, 1971

Klee, Gerald D. and Walter Weintraub. "Paranoid Reactions Following Lysergic Acid Diethylamide (LSD-25)," in Bradley, P. B., et al., eds. Neuropsycho-pharmacology: Proceedings of the First International Congress of Neuropsycho-pharmacology, held in Rome, September, 1958. Amsterdam, NE: Elsevier, 1959

Knickerbocker, Conrad. "The Art of Fiction XXXVI, William Burroughs, An Interview," *The Paris Review*, Issue 35, Fall 1965

Koestler, Arthur. Drinkers of Infinity: Essays, 1955 – 1967. London: Hutchinson & Company, Ltd, 1968

Köhler, Wolfgang. The Task of Gestalt Psychology. Princeton, NJ: Princeton University Press, 1969

König, Daniel, et al. "Suicide risk after discharge from in-patient psychiatric care: A 15-year retrospective cohort study of individual patient data," *Journal of Affective Disorders*, Volume 354, 2024

Kwitny, Jonathan. The Crimes of Patriots: A True Tale of Dope, Dirty Money, and the CIA. NY: Simon and Schuster Inc., 1987

La Barre, Jean. "The pharmacological properties and therapeutic use of dextromoramide," *Bulletin on Narcotics*, Issue 4, 01/01/1959

Labin, Suzanne. *hippies, drogues et sexe*. Paris: La Table Ronde, 1970

-------------------- Hippies, Drugs and Promiscuity, tr. Stephanie Winston. New Rochelle, NY: Arlington House, 1972

Lamb, Charles. A Dissertation upon a Roast Pig. Boston, MA: D Lothrop Company, 1888

Lattin, Don. *The* Harvard Psychedelic Club: *How Timothy Leary, Ram Dass, Huston Smith, and Andrew Weil Killed the Fifties and Ushered in a New Age for America*. NY: HarperCollins Publishers, 2010

Laurie, Peter. Drugs: Medical, Psychological and Social Facts. Baltimore, MD: Penguin Books, 1967

Leary, Timothy. Interpersonal Diagnosis of Personality: A Functional Theory and Methodology for Personality Evaluation. NY: John Wiley & Sons, 1957

--------------------, George Litwin, Michael Hollingshead, Gunther Weil, and Richard Alpert. "The Politics of the Nervous System," in *Bulletin of the Atomic Scientists: The Magazine of Science and Public Affairs*, Volume 18, No. 5, May 1962

Leary, Timothy, Litwin, George H., and Ralph Metzner. "Reactions to Psilocybin Administered in a Supportive Environment," *Journal of Nervous and Mental Disease*, Volume 137, Issue 6, December 1963

------------------, Ralph Metzner, Richard Alpert. The Psychedelic Experience: A Manual Based on the Tibetan Book of the Dead. New Hyde Park, NY: University Books, 1964

------------------ "Statement of Timothy Leary, LSD Experimenter, Testifying on Behalf of the Castalia Foundation of Millbrook, N.Y.," The Narcotic Rehabilitation Act of 1966 Hearings before a Special Subcommittee of the Committee on the Judiciary United States Senate Eighty-Ninth Congress Second Session. Washington, DC: U.S. Government Printing Office, 1966 BGU, Friday, 13 May 1966

------------------ High Priest. Berkeley, CA: Ronin Publishing, 1968

------------------ "Memorandum of the Appellant Timothy Leary" Supreme Court of the United States, 1970

------------------ Flashbacks: A Personal and Cultural History of an Era: An Autobiography. NY: G. P. Putnam's Sons, 1990

------------------ The Politics of Ecstasy. Berkeley, CA: Ronin Publishing, 1998

Leary v United States, 395 U.S. 6 (1969)

Lee, Martin A. and Bruce Shlain. Acid Dreams: The Complete Social History of LSD: The CIA, The Sixties, and Beyond. New York: Grove Press, 1985

Leeds, Barry H. Ken Kesey. NY: Frederick Ungar Publishing Co., 1981

Lemere, Frederick. "Habit-forming Properties of Meprobamate (Miltown, Equanil)," *A. M. A. Archives of Neurology and Psychiatry*, **76**, August 1956

Lerner, Stephen D. "Leary Gets 30 Years on Marijuana Charge," *The Harvard Crimson*, 12 March 1966

Lerner, William, Chief. Statistical Abstract of the United States, 1971, 92nd Annual Edition. Washington, DC: US Bureau of the Census, 1971

Lertzman, Richard A. and William J. Birnes. Dr. Feelgood: The Shocking Story of the Doctor Who May Have Changed History By Treating and Drugging JFK, Marilyn, Elvis, and Other Prominent Figures. NY: MJF Books, 2013

Levine, Jerome. "LSD – A Critical Overview," in Black, ed., Drugs, 1969

Lewin, Kurt. A Dynamic Theory of Personality: *Selected Papers*, tr. Donald K. Adams and Karl E. Zener. NY: McGraw-Hill Book Company, Inc., 1935

Lewis, Clive Staples. "The Humanitarian Theory of Punishment," *Res Judicatae*, Volume 6, 1953

Lindesmith, Alfred R. The Addict and the Law. Bloomington, IN: Indiana University Press, 1965

Lintner, Bertil. Blood Brothers: The Criminal Underworld of Asia. NY: Palgrave MacMillan, 2003

Little, J. Crawford. "A Case of Primary Addiction to Meprobamate," *British Medical Journal*, 28 September 1963

Liu, Huan et al. "Ko Kuei Chen: a pioneer of modern pharmacological research in China," *Protein & Cell*, 14, 2023

Lock, Margaret M. East Asian Medicine in Urban Japan. Berkeley, CA: University of California Press, 1980

López-Muñoz, Francisco et al. "The history of barbiturates a century after their introduction," *Neuropsychiatric Disease and Treatment*, I (4), 2005

López-Muñoz, Francisco et al. "The discovery of chlordiazepoxide and the clinical introduction of the benzodiazepines: Half a century of anxiolytic drugs," *Journal of Anxiety Disorders*, **25,** 2011

Lorenz, Konrad. Studies in Human and Animal Behaviour, Volume I, tr. Robert Martin. Cambridge, MA: Harvard University Press, 1970

-------------------- *Der Kumpan in der Umwelt des Vogels: Der Artgenosse als auslösendes Moment sozialer Verhaltensweisen*. München, DE: Deutscher Taschenbuch Verlag, 1973

Ludwig, Arnold J. and Jerome Levine. "A Controlled Comparison of Five Brief Treatment Techniques Employing LSD, Hypnosis and Psychotherapy," *American Journal of Psychotherapy*, Volume 19, No. 3, July 1965

Lum, K. L., et al. "Signed, sealed and delivered: 'big tobacco' in Hollywood, 1927–1951," *Tobacco Control*, Volume 17, 2008

Maas, Peter. The Valachi Papers. NY: G. P. Putnam's Sons, 1968

MacLean, J. Ross, et al. "The Use of LSD-25 in the Treatment of Alcoholism and Other Psychiatric Problems," *The Quarterly Journal of Studies on Alcohol*, Volume 22, No. 1, 1961

Mailer, Norman. "The White Negro: Superficial Reflections on the Hipster," *Dissent*, Volume IV, Number 3, Summer 1957

Manvell, Roger and Heinrich Fraenkel. Hess: A Biography. London: MacGibbon & Kee, 1971

Marcuse, Herbert. Eros and Civilization: *A Philosophical Inquiry into Freud*. NY: Vintage Books, 1955

--------------------- One-Dimensional Man: Studies in the ideology of advanced industrial society. London: Routledge & Kegan Paul, 1964

Marcuse, Herbert. *Kultur und Gesellschaft 1*. Frankfurt am Main, DE: Suhrkamp Verlag, 1968

---------------------- An Essay on Liberation. Boston, MA: Beacon Press, 2000

Marks, John. The Search for the "Manchurian Candidate": The CIA and Mind Control. NY: Times Books, 1979

Martin, William R. and L. F. McNicholas. "Benzodiazepine Studies in Rodents," in Benzodiazepines: A Review of Research Results, 1980, eds. Szara, Stephen I. and Jacqueline P. Ludford. Rockville, MD: National Institute on Drug Abuse, 1980

Martindale, W. Harrison, rev. The Extra Pharmacopœia of Martindale and Westcott, Twentieth Edition, Vol. I. London: H. K. Lewis & Co., Ltd., 1932

Masters, Robert E. L. and Jean Houston. "Toward an Individual Psychedelic Psychotherapy," in Aaronson, Bernard and Humphry Osmond, eds. Psychedelics: *The Uses and Implications of Hallucinogenic Drugs*. Garden City, NY: Doubleday & Company, Inc., 1970

Mato Reboredo, Jose Maria. *Curso monográfico sobre drogas nocivas*. Madrid: Altamira Rotopress, 1969

----------------------------------- "*Droga y Criminalidad en España*," Conferencia Universidad Madrid, mayo, 1979

Matthiessen, Peter. The Snow Leopard. NY: Viking Press, 1978

Mattila, Taina et al. "Impact of DSM-5 Changes in the Diagnosis and Acute Treatment of Schizophrenia," *Schizophrenia Bulletin*, Vol. 41, No. 3, 2015

Matts, S. G. Flavell, et al. "Double Blind Trial of Dextromoramide, Methadone and Pethidine in the Treatment of Severe Pain," *Postgraduate Medical Journal*, Volume 40, February 1964

Mayhew, Henry. London Labour and the London Poor; Cyclopaedia of the Condition and Earnings of Those that *Will* Work, Those that *Cannot* Work, and Those that *Will Not* Work, Volume III. London: Griffin, Bohn, and Company, 1861

Mayor LaGuardia's Committee on Marihuana. The Marihuana Problem in the City of New York. Metuchen, NJ: Scarecrow Reprint Corporation, 1973

McCoy, Alfred W. The Politics of Heroin in Southeast Asia. NY: Harper & Row, Publishers, 1973

McNally, Dennis. A Long Strange Trip: The Inside History of the Grateful Dead. NY: Broadway Books, 2002

McWilliams, John C. The Protectors: Harry J. Anslinger and the Federal Bureau of Narcotics, 1930-1962. Newark, NJ: University of Delaware Press, 1990

Mendelson, Wallace B. "Benzodiazepines: The Accidental Tranquilizers," *Psychology Today*, 2 June 2020

Menninger, Karl. The Crime of Punishment. NY: The Viking Press, 1968

Merton, Robert K. Social Theory and Social Structure: Toward the Codification of Theory and Research. Glencoe, IL: The Free Press, 1949

Metzner, Ralph. "Reflections on the Concord Prison Project and the Follow-Up Study," *Journal of Psychoactive Drugs*, Volume 30, Issue 4, Oct-Dec 1998

Meuli, Karl. "Scythica," *Hermes*, Volume 70, Issue 2, 1935

Meyer, Kathryn and Terry Parssinen. Webs of Smoke: Smuggler, Warlords, Spies, and the History of the International Drug Trade. Lanham, MD: Rowman & Littlefield Publishers, Inc., 1998

Michaux, Henri. *Connaisance par les gouffres*. Paris: Librarie Gallimard, 1961

Michaux, Henri. Light Through Darkness, tr. Haakon Chevalier. NY: The Orion Press, 1963

-------------------- *Les grandes epreuves de l'esprit, et les innombrables petites*. Paris: Gallimard, 1966

-------------------- *Misérable Miracle (La Mescaline)*. Paris: Éditions Gallimard, 1972

-------------------- Miserable Miracle (*Mescaline*). San Francisco, CA: City Lights Books, 1972

Mill, John Stuart. On Liberty, Third Edition. London: Longman, Green, Longman, Roberts & Green, 1864

Miller, Norman. "Basel: The Birthplace of Hallucinogenic Science," 14 July 2020

Mills, C. Wright. White Collar: The American Middle Classes. London: Oxford University Press, 1969

Mitchell, S. Weir. "Remarks on the Effects of Anhelonium Lewinii (The Mescal Button)," *The British Medical Journal*, 5 December 1896

Mohsan Fání. The Dabistán, or School of Manners, tr. David Shea and Anthony Troyer, Volume I. Paris: Printed for the Oriental Translation Fund of Great Britain and Ireland, 1843

Morgan, Bill, ed. The Letters of Allen Ginsberg. Philadelphia, PA: Da Capo Press, 2008

Morgenstern, Matthis, et al. "Smoking in Movies and Adolescent Smoking Initiation: Longitudinal Study in Six European Countries," *American Journal of Preventive Medicine*, Volume 44, Issue 4, April 2013

Morimoto, Kiyoshi. "The Problem of the Abuse of Amphetamines in Japan," *Bulletin on Narcotics*, United Nations Office of Drugs and Crime, 1 January 1957

Munson, Sam. "The Outsiders' Insider," *NY Times*, 7 Sep 2008

Nadelmann, Ethan A., director. Stimulants: Cocaine and Amphetamine. NY: Open Society Institute, 1995

Nadkarni, K. M. Dr. K. M. Nadkarni's Indian Materia Medica, Volume One, third revised edition by A. K. Nadkarni. Bombay: Popular Prakashan Private Limited, 1976

Naughton, James M. "Agnew Assails Songs and Film That Promote a 'Drug Culture,'" *The New York Times*, Volume CXIX, No. 41,142, Tuesday 15 September 1970

NCPR News Reporters. "Why did black leaders support America's drug war for so long," NCPR, 19August 2013

Nelson, Elyda. "for the first time! the true life story of Marilyn Monroe," *Modern Screen*, Volume 46, No. 1, December 1952

Nichols, David E. and Mark A. Geyer. "Preface," The Heffter Review of Psychedelic Research, Volume 1, 1998

Nietzsche, Friedrich. *Jenseits von Gut und Böse. Vorspeil einer Philosophie der Zukunft*. Leipzig: Druck und Verlag von C. G. Naumann, 1886

------------------------- *Der Wille Zur Macht: Versuch Einer Umwertung Aller Werte*. Stuttgart, DE: Alfred Kröner Verlag, 1964

------------------------- The Will to Power, tr. Walter Kaufmann and R. J. Hollingdale. NY: *Vintage Books*, 1968

------------------------- Beyond Good and Evil: Prelude to a Philosophy of the Future, tr. Judith Norman. Cambridge, UK: Cambridge University Press, 2002

Nin, Anaïs. The Diary of Anaïs Nin, 1955-1966, Volume VI, Gunther Stuhlmann, ed. NY: Harcourt Brace Jovanovich, 1976

Nyswander, Marie. *The* Drug Addict *as a* Patient. NY: Grune & Stratton, 1956

Oberdorfer, Don. "JFK Had Affair With D.C. Artist, Smoked 'Grass,' Paper Alleges," *The Washington Post*, Issue 80, Monday 23 February 1976

Ohler, Norman. Blitzed: *Drugs in Nazi Germany*, tr. Shaun Whiteside. NY: Penguin Books, 2016

Olmo, Rosa del. *A Face Oculta da Droga*, tr. Teresa Ottoni. Rio de Janeiro, Brazil: Editora Revan, 1990

Onda, Masayuki, Fukushima, Hiroshi and Masuko Akagawa. "A Flycidal Constituent of Amanita pantherina (DC.) Fr.," *Chemical and Pharmaceutical Bulletin*, Volume 12, Issue 6, 1964

Osmond, Humphry and John Smythies. "Schizophrenia: A New Approach" in *The Journal of Mental Science*, Volume XCVIII, No. 411, April 1952

--- "The Present State of Psychological Medicine," *The Hibbert Journal: A Quarterly Review of Religion, Theology and Philosophy*, Volume LI, No. 2, January 1953

Ott, Jonathan. "Psycho-Mycological Studies of Amanita – From Ancient Sacrament to Modern Phobia," *Journal of Psychedelic Drugs*, Volume 8, No. 1, Jan-Mar 1976

Owens, David Cunningham and Eve C. Johnstone. "The development of antipsychotic drugs," *Brain and Neuroscience Advances*, Volume 2, 2018

Paddock, Alfred H. US Special Warfare, Its Origins, Psychological and Unconventional Warfare, 1941-1952. Washington, DC: National Defense University Press, Fort Lesley J. McNair, 1982

Pahnke, Walter. "Drugs and Mysticism: An Analysis of the Relationship between Psychedelic Drugs and the Mystical Consciousness," a thesis presented to the Committee on Higher Degrees in History and Philosophy of Religion, Harvard University, Cambridge, MA, June 1963

-------------------- "The Psychedelic Mystical Experience in the Human Encounter with Death," *Psychedelic Review*, Volume 11, Winter 1970/1971

Panko, Ben. "From Budweiser to Heineken, Alcohol Brands Are Rampant in Hollywood Films: Over the past two decades, even G-rated films have amped up the booze labels," *Smithsonian*, 9 May 2017

Pan Ling. <u>In Search of Old Shanghai</u>. Hongkong: Joint Publishing Co., 1983

Patocka, Jiri and Barbora Kocandrlova. "Pharmacologically and Toxicologically Relevant Components of *Amanita muscaria*," *Military Medical Science Letters*, Volume 86, Issue 3, 2017

Paz, Octavio. <u>Alternating Current</u>, tr. Helen Lane. NY: Arcade Publishing, 1990

Perera, W.M.D.S., et al. "Neuro-therapeutic effect of *Rauvolfia serpentina (Sarpagandha/Ekaweriya)*; A review," *Journal of Advances in Experimental Therapeutics and Neurotherapeutics*, Volume 1, Issue 2, June 2023

Perlman, David. "Joel Fort, psychiatrist who campaigned against orthodoxy, dies," *SF Gate*, 28 August 2015

Permanent Central Opium Board. <u>Report to the Economic and Social Council on the Work of the Board in 1958</u>, Document E/OB/14. Geneva, CH: United Nations Publications, November 1958

Perry, Helen Swick. <u>The Human Be-In</u>. NY: Basic Books, Inc., Publishers, 1970

Perry, Paul. On the Bus: The Complete Guide to the Legendary Trip of Ken Kesey and the Merry Pranksters and the Birth of the Counterculture. NY: Thunder's Mouth Press, 1990

Piel, Gerard. "Narcotics," *Life*, Volume 15, No. 3, 19 July 1943

--------------- "Narcotics: War has brought illicit traffic to all-time low but U.S. Treasury fears rising post-war addiction," *Life*, 1943

Ploscowe, Morris. "Appendix A: Some Basic Problems in Drug Addiction and Suggestions for Research," in Drug Addiction: Crime or Disease? Interim *and* Final Reports of the American Bar Association and the American Medical Association on Narcotic Drugs. Bloomington, IN: Indiana University Press, 1971

Preston, Andrew and Gerald Bennett. "The history of methadone and methadone prescribing," in Methadone Matters: Evolving Community Methadone Treatment of Opiate Addiction, eds. Gillian Tober and John Strang. Boca Raton, FL: CRC Press, 2003

Proceedings White House Conference on Narcotics and Drug Abuse. Washington, DC: U.S. Government Printing Office, 1962

Pross, Christian. "Breaking through the postwar coverup of Nazi doctors in Germany," *Journal of Medical Ethics*, Volume 17, Supplement, 1991

Quinn, William W. Dachau, US Army Report, IA, dachauOOunse. Unknown place: Printed by 649th Engr Topo Batallion, May 1945

Rasmussen, Nicolas. "America's First Amphetamine Epidemic 1929–1971: A Quantitative and Qualitative Retrospective With Implications for the Present," *American Journal of Public Health*, Vol 98, No. 6, June 2008

------------------------- "Medical Science and the Military: The Allies' Use of Amphetamine during WWII," *Journal of Interdisciplinary History*, XLII:2, Autumn 2011

Rasor, Robert W. and H. James Crecraft. "Addiction to Meperidine (Demerol) Hydrochloride," *The Journal of the American Medical Association*, Volume 157, No. 8, 19 February 1955

Rehman, Waqas, et al. "The rise, fall and subsequent triumph of thalidomide: lessons learned in drug development," *Therapeutic Advances in Hematology*, Volume 2, No. 5, 2011

Reinhold, Robert. "Biologist Doubts Man's Survival in a World Run by 'Idiots,'" *New York Times*, Volume CXIX, No. 40,935, Friday 20 February 1970

Reiser, P., et al. "The Use of Librium in General Practice," *Journal of the National Medical Association*, Volume 54, No. 2, March 1962

Reisman, David. The Lonely Crowd: A Study of the Changing American Character. New Haven, CT: Yale University Press, 1955

Rensberger, Boyce et al. "Amphetamines Used by a Physician to Lift Moods of Famous Patients," *The New York Times*, 4 December 1972

Report of the Permanent Central Opium Board. "Legal Trade in Narcotics," *Bulletin on Narcotics*, 01/01/1958

Reuter, Richard W., Director. The Twentieth Semiannual Report on Activities Carried on under Public Law 480, 83d Congress, as amended, Outlining Operations Under the Act During the Period January 1 through June 30, 1964. Washington, DC: Government Printing Office, 1964

Richer, Alanna Durkin. "'Acid is groovy; kill the pigs'; Man convicted of killing pregnant wife, daughters says drug-fuelled hippies were the real killers," *Toronto Sun*, 17 January 2017

Roberts, Andy. Albion Dreaming: A Popular History of LSD in Britain. London: Marshall Cavendish Publications, 2008

------------------ Divine Rascal: On the Trail of LSD's Cosmic Courier, Michael Hollingshead. London: Strange Attractor Press, 2019

Roberts, Michael James. Tell Tchaikovsky the News: Rock 'n' Roll, the Labor Question, and the Musicians' Union, 1942 – 1968. Durham, NC: Duke University Press, 2014

Robiquet, Pierre-Jean. "*NOUVELLES Observations sur les principaux Produits de l'Opium*," *Annales de chimie et de physique*, ed. Gay-Lussac and Arago, Tome LI. Paris: Chez Crochard, 1832

Rof Carballo, J. and A. Gonzalez Morado. "*Experiencia clínica con la dietilimida del ácido lisérgico (DAL)*," *Boletín del Instituto de Patología Médica*, Volume XIII, No. 10, Octubre 1958

Rosborough, Brian Alexander. "LSD: A Challenge to American Drug Law Philosophy," *Florida Law Review*, Volume 19, Issue 2, Article 5, 1966

Rosenbaum, Ron. "Back in the High Life: Timothy Leary, the acid sixties guru, is now tuned in to L.A.'s social circuit," *Vanity Fair*, Volume 51, No. 4, April 1988

Roszak, Theodore. The Making of a Counter Culture: *Reflections on the Technocratic Society and Its Youthful Opposition*. Garden City, NY: *Doubleday & Company, Inc.*, 1969

Rouhier, Alexandre. *Le Peyotl: La Plante Qui Fait Les Yeux Émervéilles*. Paris: Gaston Doin et Cie, 1927

Rowley, Hazel. Tête-à-Tête: *The Tumultuous Lives and Loves of* Simone de Beauvoir *and* Jean-Paul Sartre. NY: Harper Perennial, 2005

Rubington, Earl and Martin S. Weinberg. Deviance: The Interactionist Perspective; Text and Readings in the Sociology of Deviance. London: The Macmillan Company, 1968

Ruiz-Ogara, C., et al. "*Psicosis Lisérgica*," *Revista de Psiquiatria y Psicologia Médica de Europa y América Latinas*, Tomo II Anos 1955-1956, ed. L. Acevedo, et al. Barcelona, ES: Redacción y Administración, 1956

Rush, Benjamin. Letters of Benjamin Rush, Volume II: 1793 – 1813, ed. L. H. Butterfield. Princeton, NJ: Princeton University Press, 1951

Ruston, Alan R. The Hibbert Trust: A History. London: The Hibbert Trust, 1984

Sacquety, Troy J. "The Office of Strategic Services (OSS): A Primer on the Special Operations Branches and Detachments of the Office of Strategic Services," *Veritas: The Journal of Army Special Operations History*, PB 31-05-2, Volume 3, No. 4, 2007

"*Salvador Dalí reçoit à Portlligat*," Interview with François Barnole, montage de Benoít Grossin, August 1964

Sambhava, Padma. The Tibetan Book of the Dead, tr. Robert A. F. Thurman. NY: Bantam Books, 1994

Sandison, R. A., Spencer, A. M., and J. D. A. Whitelaw. "The Therapeutic Value of Lysergic Acid Diethylamide in Mental Illness," *The Journal of Mental Science*, Volume 100, No. 419, April 1954

Sanford, Nevitt. "Foreword" in Blum, Richard and Associates. Utopiates: The Use and Users of LSD 25. NY: Atherton Press, 1964

Sargent, William and J. M. Blackburn. "The Effect of Benzedrine on Intelligence Scores," *The Lancet* 12 December 1936

Sarro Burbano, Ramón. "*Farmacos y psiquiatria*," *Medicina Clínica*, Volume 26, No. 3, 1956

Savage, Charles, et al. "Therapeutic Applications of LSD," in Black, Perry, ed. Drugs and the Brain, 1969

-------------------- and O. Lee McCabe. "Residential Psychedelic (LSD) Therapy for the Narcotic Addict," *Archives of General Psychiatry*, Volume 28, June 1973

Schofield, Michael. The Strange Case of Pot. Harmondsworth, Middlesex, UK: Penguin Books Ltd., 1971

Scholem, Gershom, ed. The Correspondence of Walter Benjamin and Gershom Scholem, 1932 – 1940, trs. Gary Smith and Andre Lefevre. NY: Schocken Books, 1989

Schou, Nicolas. Orange Sunshine: The Brotherhood of Eternal Love and Its Quest to Spread Peace, Love, and Acid to the World. NY: St. Martin's Press, 2010

Schultes, R. E. "Peyote and Plants Used in the Peyote Ceremony," *Botanical Museum Leaflets, Harvard University*, Volume 4, No. 8, April 12, 1937

------------------- "Peyote (*Lophophora Williamsii*) and Plants Confused with It," *Botanical Museum Leaflets, Harvard University*, Volume 5, No. 5, November 19, 1937

------------------- "The Appeal of Peyote (*Lophophora williamsi*) as a medicine," *American Anthropologist*, Volume 40, 1938

------------------- "The Aboriginal Therapeutic Uses of Lophophora Williamsi," *Cactus and Succulent Journal*, Volume XII, No. 11, November 1940

------------------- A Contribution to Our Knowledge of Rivea Corymbosa: The Narcotic Ololiuqui of the Aztecs. Cambridge, MA: Botanical Museum of Harvard University, 1941

Schultes, R. E. "The Identity of the Malpighiaceous Narcotics of South America," *Botanical Museum Leaflets, Harvard University*, Volume 18, No. 1, 7 June 1957

Schur, Edwin M. Crimes Without Victims: Deviant Behavior and Public Policy; Abortion, Homosexuality, Drug Addiction. Englewood Cliffs, NJ: Prentice-Hall, Inc., 1965

Serra, Mauricio. *Malaparte: Vite e leggende*, tr. Alberto Folin. Venezia: Marsilio Editori, 2012

Severo, Richard. "Mainlining Amphetamines Rising Problem in Sweden," *The New York Times*, 10 April 1970

Seymour-Shove, R. "Dependence on Dextromoramide," *British Medical Journal*, 14 January 1967

Seymour-Smith, Martin. Robert Graves: His Life and Work. London: Bloomsbury Publishing Plc, 1995

Shafer, Raymond P., chairman. appendix marihuana: a signal of misunderstanding The Technical Papers of the First Report of the National Commission on Marihuana and Drug Abuse, Volume I. Washington, DC: U.S. Government Printing Office, 1972

-- drug use in america: problem in perspective, Second Report of the National Commission on Marihuana and Drug Abuse. Washington, DC: US Government Printing Office, 1973

Shane, Aubrey M. and Solomon Hirsch. "Three Cases of Meprobamate Poisoning," *The Canadian Medical Association Journal*, Volume 74, Number 11, 1 June 1956

Sidwells, Chris. Mr. Tom: The True Story of Tom Simpson. Norwich, UK: Mousehold Press, 2000

Sim, Van M. I. "Clinical Investigation of EA 1729," U.S. Army Chemical Research and Development Laboratories. Army Chemical Center, MD: Defense Technical Information Center, June 1961

Skett, Philippa. "The high life of the self-experimenters," *New Scientist*, 12 August 2004

Skolnick, Jerome H. "Coercion to Virtue: The Enforcement of Morals," *Southern California Law Review*, Volume 41, No. 3, 1968

Slack, Charles W. Timothy Leary, the Madness of the Sixties and Me. NY: Peter H. Wyden, 1974

Slater, J. "Suspected Dependence on Chlordiazepoxide Hydrochloride (Librium)," *Canadian Medical Association Journal*, Volume 95, 27 August 1966

Smart, Reginald G., et al. "A Controlled Study of Lysergide in the Treatment of Alcoholism," *Quarterly Journal of Studies on Alcohol*, Volume 27, Issue 3, September 1966

------------------------ and Karen Bateman. "The Chromosomal and Teratogenic Effects of Lysergic Acid Diethylamide: A Review of the Current Literature," *Canadian Medical Association Journal*, Volume 99, 26 October 1968

------------------------ and David Jackson. The Yorkville Subculture: A Study of the Lifestyles and Interactions of Hippies and Non-Hippies, prepared from the field notes of Gopala Alampur. Toronto, CA: Addiction Research Foundation, 1969

Smith, David E., John Luce and Ernest A. Dernburg. "The Health of Haight-Ashbury," *trans action: Social Science and Modern Society*, Volume 7, No. 6, April 1970

Smith, Grover, ed. Letters of Aldous Huxley. NY: Harper & Row, Publishers, 1969

Smith, Philip B. Chemical Glimpses of Paradise. Springfield, IL: Charles C Thomas Publishers, 1972

Smith, Robert E. "Psychologists Disagree on Psilocybin Research," *The Harvard Crimson*, 15 March 1962

Snyder, William U. "Psychotherapy," in Annual Review of Psychology, Volume 9, Farnsworth, Paul R. and Quinn McNemar, eds. Palo Alto, CA: Annual Reviews, 1958

Solomon, David, ed. LSD: The Consciousness-Expanding Drug. NY: G. P. Putnam's Sons, 1966

-------------------------- The Marihuana Papers. Indianapolis, IN: The New American Library, 1966

Somers, G. F. "Pharmacological Properties of Thalidomide (α-Phthalimido Glutarimide), A New Sedative Hypnotic Drug." *British Journal of Pharmacology*, Volume 15, 1960

Spencer, Herbert. The Man Versus The State, With Six Essays on Government, Society and Freedom. Indianapolis, IN: Liberty *Classics*, 1981

Spinks, G. Stevens. Psychology and Religion: An Introduction to Contemporary Views. Boston, MA: Beacon Press, 1963

Spinoza, Benedicti de. *Opera*, Vol. I. Lipsiae: Typis et Sumtibus Bernh. Tauchnitz Jun., 1843

---------------------------- Improvement of the Understanding, Ethics and Correspondence, tr. R. H. M. Elwes. London: L. Beling Tetens, 1901

Stafford, P. G. and B. H. Golightly. LSD: The Problem-Solving Psychedelic. NY: Award Books, 1967

Stanley, Theodore H. et al. "A Tribute to Dr. Paul A. J. Janssen: Entrepreneur Extraordinaire, Innovative Scientist, and Significant Contributor to Anesthesiology," *Anesthesia & Analgesia*, Volume 106, No. 2, February 2008

Stevens, Jay. Storming Heaven: LSD and the American Dream. NY: The Atlantic Monthly Press, 1987

Strawbridge, Rebecca et al. "The effects of reserpine on depression: A systematic review," *Journal of Psychopharmacology*, Volume 37, No. 3, 2023

Streatfeild, Dominic. Brainwash: The Secret History of Mind Control. NY: St. Martin's Press, 2007

Stroup, T. Scott and Neil Gray. "Management of common adverse effects of antipsychotic medications," *World Psychiatry*, Volume 17, Issue 3, October 2018

Strughold, Hubertus. Compendium of Aerospace Medicine, Volume 1. Brooks Air Force Base, TX: USAF School of Aerospace Medicine, 1977

Sullivan, Louis W. Seventh Special Report to the U.S. Congress on Alcohol and Health. Rockville, MD: Public Health Service, 1990

Swanberg, W. A. Luce and His Empire. NY: Charles Scribner's Sons, 1972

Szasz, Thomas. Ceremonial Chemistry: The Ritual Persecution of Drugs, Addicts, and Pushers. Garden City, NY: Anchor Press/Doubleday, 1974

------------------- The Theology of Medicine: The Political-Theological Foundations of Medical Ethics. NY: Harper & Row, Publishers, 1977

------------------- "The Protocols of the Learned Experts on Heroin," *The Libertarian Review*, Volume 10 No. 7, July 1981

Tanner, Stephen L. Ken Kesey. Boston, MA: Twayne Publishers, 1983

Tart, Charles T. On Being Stoned: A Psychological Study of Marijuana Intoxication. Palo Alto, CA: Science and Behavior Books, 1971

Taysom, Jay. "Why the BBC Banned 'A Day in the Life' by the Beatles," *Far Out Magazine*, Friday, 5 March 2021

Teff, Harvey and Colin R. Munro. Thalidomide: the legal aftermath. Westmead, Farnborough, Hants., UK: Saxon House, 1976

Teigen, Armfinn. "The Norwegian State Clinic for the Treatment of Addicts," *Bulletin on Narcotics*, 01/01/1964

Thompson, Brian A. M. "Addiction to Dextromoramide," *British Medical Jouanal*, 31 October 1964

Thompson, Hunter S. Hell's Angels: A Strange and Terrible Saga. NY: Random House, 1967

Tiedemann, Rolf and Hermann Schweppenhauser, et al, eds. Walter Benjamin, Gesammelte Schriften, IV – 1. Frankfurt am Main, DE: Suhrkamp Verlag, 1972

-- Walter Benjamin, Gesammelte Schriften, II · 1. Frankfurt am Main, DE: Suhrkamp Verlag, 1977

Trocchi, Alexander. Cain's Book. London: John Calder, 1992

Truman, Harry S. Executive Order 9835 – Prescribing Procedures for the Administration of an Employees Loyalty Program in the Executive Branch of the Government. The American Presidency Project, University of Santa Barbara, 21 March 1947

Turvey, S. E. C. "Meprobamate (Equanil) for Relief of Anxiety and Nervous Tension from Various Causes," *The Canadian Medical Association Journal*, Volume 74, Number 11, 1 June 1956

Unger, Sanford M. "LSD and Psychotherapy: A Bibliography of the English-Language Literature," *The Psychedelic Review*, Volume 1, No. 4, 1964

Ungerleider, J. Thomas, et al. "The Dangers of LSD: Analysis of Seven Months' Experience in a University Hospital's Psychiatric Service," *Journal of the American Medical Association*, Volume 197, No. 6, 8 August 1966

United Nations. Chapter VI. Narcotic Drugs and Psychotropic Substances. Title 15: Single Convention on Narcotic Drugs, 1961. New York: 30 March 1961

-------------------- Chapter VI. Narcotic Drugs and Psychotropic Substances. Title 6.16 Convention on Psychotropic Substances. Vienna, Austria: 21 February 1971

-------------------- The International Drug Control Conventions, Schedules of the Single Convention on Narcotic Drugs of 1961 as amended by the 1972 Protocol, as at 18 May 2016. New York: ST/CND/1/Add.1/Rev.2, 2016

-------------------- The International Drug Control Conventions, Schedules of the Convention on Psychotropic Substances of 1971, as at 13 November 2016. New York: ST/CND/1/Add.2/Rev.2, 2016

United Nations Conference for the Adoption of a Single Convention on Narcotic Drugs, Final Act, Volume I, Chapter VI. Narcotic Drugs and Psychotropic Substances, Title 15, 30 March 1961

United Nations Convention Against Illicit Traffic in Narcotic Drugs and Psychotropic Substances, 1988

United Press International reporter. "Control Law Set on LSD," *The Desert Sun*, Volume 39, No. 256, Tuesday, 31 May 1966

United States Statutes at Large containing the Laws and Concurrent Resolutions Enacted during the Eighty-Second Congress of the United States of America, 1951, Volume 65. Washington, DC: Government Printing Office, 1952

United States Statutes at Large, Volume 70. Washington, DC: Government Printing Office, 1956

Unknown author. "Development of Synthetic Narcotic Drugs," *Bulletin on Narcotics*, 01/01/1956

---------------------- "World Health Organization: Expert Committee on Drugs liable to Produce Addiction – Sixth Report," *Bulletin on Narcotics*, Volume VIII, No. 1, January-March 1956

Van Dyke, Craig and Robert Byck. "*Cocaína*," *Investigacion y Ciencia, Edición en español de Scientific American*, Número 68, Mayo 1982

Vargesson, Neil. "Review Thalidomide-Induced Teratogenesis: History and Mechanisms," *Birth Defects Research (Part C)*, Volume 105, 4 June 2015

Vogel, Friedrich. "Widukind Lenz – An Encomium," *American Journal of Medical Genetics*, Volume 37, Issue 3, November 1990

Vogel, Victor H. and Harris Isbell. "Medical Aspects of Addiction to Analgesic Drugs," *Bulletin on Narcotics*, Volume II, No. 4, October 1950

Villa Roiz, Carlos. "*¿Quien fue Fray Toribio de Benavente, 'Motolinía'?*" *Desde la Fe*, 2 August 2019

Wald, Patricia M. and Peter Barton Hutt. "The Drug Abuse Survey Project: Summary of Findings, Conclusions, and Recommendations," in Dealing with Drug Abuse: *A Report to the Ford Foundation*, chaired by Wald and Hutt. NY: Praeger Publishers, 1972

Waldron, Martin. "Friend Says Captain Discussed Tate Killing Before Family Died," *New York Times*, 20 February 1970

Walsh, Danielle. "What Every James Bond Drank, From Martinis to Heineken," *Bon Appétit*, 9 November 2012

Walsh, G., et al. "Meta-analysis of suicide rates among psychiatric in-patients," *Acta Psychiatrica Scandinavica*, December 2014

Walshe, Maurice O'C., tr., ed. The Complete Mystical Works of Meister Eckhart. NY: Crossroad Publishing Company, 2009

Wansell, Geoffrey. The Haunted Idol: The Story of the Real Cary Grant. NY: Quill, William Morrow, 1983

Wasson, R. Gordon. "Seeking the Magic Mushroom," *Life*, Volume 42, No. 19, 13 May 1957

------------------------- Soma: Divine Mushroom of Immortality. NY: Harcourt Brace Jovanovich, 1968

------------------------- "The Death of Claudius or Mushrooms for Murderers," *Botanical Museum Leaflets Harvard University*, Volume 23, No. 3, 7 April 1972

-------------------------, Albert Hofmann, Carl A. P. Ruck. The Road to Eleusis: Unveiling the Secret of the Mysteries. NY: Harcourt Brace Jovanovich, 1978

-------------------------, Stella Kramrisch, Jonathan Ott, and Carl A. P. Ruck. Persephone's Quest: Entheogens and the Origins of Religion. New Haven, CT: Yale University Press, 1986

Wasson, Valentina Pavlova and R. Gordon Wasson. Mushrooms, Russia and History, *Volume I*. NY: Pantheon Books, 1957

--- "The Hallucinogenic Mushrooms," *The Garden Journal of the New York Botanical Garden*, January-February, Volume 8, Issue 1, 1958

Watts, Alan. The Joyous Cosmology: Adventures in the Chemistry of Consciousness. NY: Vintage Books, 1962

--------------- In My Own Way: an autobiography, 1915 – 1965. Novato, CA: New World Library, 1972

--------------- This is IT and Other Essays on Zen and Spiritual Experience. NY: Vintage Books, 1973

Web Annex A. World Health Organization Model List of Essential Medicines – 23rd List, 2023. In: The selection and use of essential medicines 2023: Executive summary of the report of the 24th WHO Expert Committee on the Selection and Use of Essential Medicines, 24 – 28 April 2023. Geneva: World Health Organization, 2023

Weil, Gunther M., et al, eds. The Psychedelic Reader. NY: The Citadel Press, 1971

Weindling, Paul. Victims and Survivors of Nazi Human Experiments: Science and Suffering in the Holocaust. London: Bloomsbury, 2015

Wells, Brian. Psychedelic Drugs. NY: Jason Aronson, 1974

West, E. D. and A. Fernandes da Fonseca. "Controlled trial of meprobamate," *British Medical Journal*, 24 November 1956

Whyte, William H. The Organization Man. Harmondsworth, Middlesex, UK: Penguin Books, Ltd., 1963

Wickes, George and Ray Fraser, interviewers. "The Art of Fiction XXIV, Aldous Huxley," *The Paris Review*, Number Twenty-Three, Spring, 1960

Wilson, Andrew. "Mixing the Medicine: The Unintended Consequence of Amphetamine Control on the Northern Soul Scene," February 2009

Wimmelbücker, Ludger and Anita Kar. "A history of thalidomide in India," *Medical History*, Volume 67, No. 3, 2023

Winnick, Charles. "Narcotic Addiction and its Treatment," *Law and Contemporary Problems*, Volume 22, Winter 1957

Witte, Bernd. Walter Benjamin: An Intellectual Biography, tr. James Rolleston. Detroit, MI: Wayne State University Press, 1985

Wolfe, Tom. The Electric Kool-Aid Acid Test. NY: Bantam Books, 1969

INDEX

Abramson, Harold Alexander 2104
Agnew, Spiro Theodore 2367
Alles, Gordon A. 2063
Alpert, Richard 2178
Ambrose, Myles Joseph 1862
Anslinger, Harry Jacob 1832
Artaud, Antoine Marie Joseph Paul 2060

Bateson, Gregory 2104
Beauvoir, Simone de 1963
Becker, Howard S. 1916
Benavente, Toribio de 2327
Bender, Lauretta 2358
Benjamin, Walter Bendix Schonflies 2058
Berger, Frank M. 2013
Bispebjerg Intoxication Centre 1975
Black, Jack, ratcatcher 1830
Blake, William 2073
Blauer, Harold 2149
Bloch, Ernst Simon 2069
Bogg's Act 1852
Bradbury, Ray 1848
Brown, Norman Oliver 2177
Bureau of Narcotics and Dangerous Drugs 2041
Burroughs, William Seward 1842

C

Cameron, Donald Ewen 2146
Cassady, Neal Leon 2300
Castaneda, Carlos 2305

Castro, Fidel Alejandro 2146
Chiang Kai-shek 1863
Clarke, Arthur Charles 2304
Cleaver, Leroy Eldridge 2286
Cohen, Sidney 2206
Convention on Psychotropic Substances of 1971 1970
Cosa Nostra 1860
Cuban Missile Crisis 2182
Curcio, Renato 2324

Dalí, Salvador 2153
Daniel, Marion Price 1856
Daniel Subcommittee 1854
Defoe, Daniel 1827
Delay, Jean 2101
Donovan, William Joseph "Wild Bill" 2140
Douglas, William Orville 1895
Drugs (Prevention of Misuse) Act 1966
Dulles, Allen Welsh 2144
Dumézil, Georges Edmond Raoul 2113
Durkheim, David Émile 1907
Du Yuesheng 1874

Ellis, Havelock 2057
Ernst, Max 2180
Eysenck, Hans Jurgen 1960

Federal Bureau of Narcotics 1843
Félice, Philippe de 2113
Fernández-Savater Martin, Fernando 1830

Fifth International Tin Agreement 1937
First International Coffee Agreement 1935
Fort, Joel 2039
Fränkel, Fritz 2069

Gaskin, Stephen 2351
Genovese, Vito 1867
Gerassi, John 2368
Ginsberg, Irwin Allen 2105
Goethe, Johann Wolfgang von 2082
Gottlieb, Sidney 2144
Grant, Cary 2292
Grateful Dead 2306
Graves, Robert von Ranke 2067
Griggs, John Murl 2322
Grosse Politik 2055
Guercken, Valentina Pavlova 2094
Guerini, Antoine and Barthélemy 1880

Harlan, John Marshall 2283
Harrison Act 1852
Heffter, Arthur Carl Wilhelm 2057
Heim, Roger 2098
Heinlein, Robert Anson 2304
Herbert, Franklin Patrick 2304
Hernández, Francisco 2343
Hess, Rudolph Walter Richard 2147
Hesse, Hermann 2060
Hitchcock, Peggy Mellon 2241
Hitchcock, William Mellon 2324

Hodge, Harold Carpenter 2152
Hoffer, Abram 2210
Hofmann, Albert 2064
Hölderin, Johann Christian Friedrich 2082
Hollingshead, Michael 2240
Huang Jinrong 1872
Hubbard, Alfred Matthew 2090
Hussein, Gamal Abdel Nasser 2146
Huxley, Aldous Leonard 1839
Huxley, Julian Sorell 2157
Huxley, Laura Archera 2159
Huxley, Maria Louisa Nys 2157
Hyams, Joe 2292

I. G. Farbenindustrie 1987
International Cocoa Agreement 1938
International Narcotics Control Board 1931
International Sugar Agreement 1937

Jacobson, Max 1965
Janiger, Oscar 2105
Janssen, Paul Adrian Jan 1992
Joël, Ernst 2069
Johnson, Lyndon Baines 2043
Jünger, Ernst 2087

Kelsey, Frances Kathleen Oldham 2035
Kemp, Richard Hilary 2324
Kennedy, Edward Moore 2024
Kennedy, John Fitzgerald 1965

Kennedy, Robert Francis 2332
Kerouac, Jack 2246
Kesey, Kenneth Elton 2295
Khrushchev, Nikita Sergeyevich 1965
Koestler, Arthur 2131
Ko Kuei Chen 1940
Kosakiewicz, Wanda 1963

Laborit, Henri 2005
Lansky, Meyer 1845
Leary, Timothy Francis 2110
Lenz, Widukind 2034
Lewis, Clive Staples 1915
Lilly, John Cunningham 2158
Lindesmith, Alfred Ray 1883
Lorenz, Konrad Zacharias 2262
Long Yun 1870
Louis XIV 1830
Louria, Donald B. 2353
Lozano, Octavio Paz 2086
Luce, Claire Boothe 2290
Luce, Henry Robinson 2290
Luciano, Charles "Lucky" 1867

MacDonald, Jeffrey Robert 2351
Ma Huang (*Ephedra vulgaris*) 1940
Manco Capac 1946
Manson, Charles Miles 2350
Marks, John D. 2138
Mao Zedong 1871

Mailer, Norman Kingsley 1849
Meyer, Mary Eno Pinchot 2289
Mann, Paul Thomas 1851
Marcuse, Herbert 2177
McCarthy, Joseph Raymond 1845
McClelland, David Clarence 2222
McCoy, Alfred W. 1881
Menninger, Karl 1911
Merton, Robert King 1884
Merton, Thomas 2169
Metzner, Ralph 2178
Meuli, Karl 2114
Miceli, Vito 2325
Michaux, Henri 2086
Mill, John Stuart 1918
Mills, C. Wright 1848
Mitchell, Silas Weir 2057
MKULTRA 2144
Moniz, António Caetano de Abreu Egas 1908
Moore, George Edward 2241
Moore, John Alexander 2099
Moral Majority 1838
Mortenson, Norma Jeane 1978

Nagai Nagayoshi 1940
Nagyrápolt, Albert 2362
Narcotics Control Act 1857
Nin, Anaïs 2131
Nixon, Richard Milhouse 1845
Ngo Dinh Diem 1881
Ngo Dinh Nhu 1881

Office of Strategic Services 1879
Oglesby, Carl Preston 2270
Olson, Frank Rudolph Emmanuel 2150
Onassis, Jaqueline Lee Kennedy 1965
Osmond, Humphry Fortescue 2087
Overholser, Winifred 2141

Pahnke, Walter Norman 2235
Permanent Central Opium Board 1994
Pfeiffer, Carl Curt 2151
Phao Sriyanond 1881
Plötner, Kurt Friedrich 2140
Polakoff, Moses 1878

Reisman, David 1847
Ribicoff, Abraham Alexander 2360
Robiquet, Pierre-Jean 1997
Rockefeller, Nelson Aldrich 1965
Rosenberg, Julius and Ethel 1845
Roszak, Theodore 2177
Rush, Benjamin 1909

Sabina, María 2096
Sand, Nicholas 2320
Sartre, Jean-Paul 1962
Schicklgruber, Alois 1951
Scholem, Gershon 2069
Schultes, Richard Evans 2062
Schur, Edwin M. 1918
Scully, Robert Timothy 2320

Señora Juana 2224
Shafer, Raymond P. 2356
Shanghai Conference 1870
Shen Nung Pen Tshao Ching 1940
Simpson, Tom 1957
Single Convention on Narcotic Drugs, 1961 1924
Smythies, John Raymond 2087
Stanley, Augustus Owsley 2320
Sternbach, Leo Henryk 2016
Stoll, Arthur 2067
Stark, Ronald Hadley 2321
Strecker, Edward Adam 2141
Suckert, Kurt Erich 1992
Suzuki, Daisetzu Teitaro 2160
Szasz, Thomas 1911

Tang Jiyao 1870
Thomas, William Isaac 1885
Trafficante, Jr., Santo 1868
Trocchi, Alexander Whitelaw Robertson 1842
Truman, Harry S. 1851

Valachi, Joseph Michael 1860
Volstead Act 1867

Waldo, Edward Hamilton 2304
Wasson, Robert Gordon 2094
Watts, Alan Wilson 2131
Weil, Andrew Thomas 2255
White, George Hunter 2142

Whyte, William H. 1849
Wissing, Egon 2069
Wolfe, Thomas Kennerly 2296
World Health Organization 1956

Zwingli, Huldrych 2082